Small Business
FOR
DUMMIES®
4TH EDITION

by Eric Tyson and Jim Schell

WILEY

John Wiley & Sons, Inc.

Small Business For Dummies® 4th Edition

Published by
John Wiley & Sons, Inc.
111 River St.
Hoboken, NJ 07030-5774
www.wiley.com

Copyright © 2012 by Eric Tyson and Jim Schell

Published by John Wiley & Sons, Inc., Hoboken, New Jersey

Published simultaneously in Canada

For general information on our other products and services, please contact our Customer Care Department within the U.S. at 877-762-2974, outside the U.S. at 317-572-3993, or fax 317-572-4002.

For technical support, please visit www.wiley.com/techsupport.

Wiley publishes in a variety of print and electronic formats and by print-on-demand. Some material included with standard print versions of this book may not be included in e-books or in print-on-demand. If this book refers to media such as a CD or DVD that is not included in the version you purchased, you may download this material at http://booksupport.wiley.com. For more information about Wiley products, visit www.wiley.com.

Library of Congress Control Number is available from the Publisher.

ISBN 978-1-118-08372-7 (pbk); ISBN 978-1-118-21369-8 (ebk); ISBN 978-1-118-21371-1 (ebk); ISBN 978-1-118-21381-0 (ebk)

Manufactured in the United States of America

10 9 8 7 6 5 4 3 2

WILEY

About the Authors

Eric Tyson, MBA, has been a personal financial writer, lecturer, and counselor for the past 25 years. As his own boss, Eric has worked with and taught people from a myriad of income levels and backgrounds, so he knows the small-business ownership concerns and questions of real folks just like you.

After toiling away for too many years as a management consultant to behemoth financial-service firms, Eric decided to take his knowledge of the industry and commit himself to making personal financial management accessible to everyone. Despite being handicapped by a joint BS in Economics and Biology from Yale and an MBA from Stanford, Eric remains a master at "keeping it simple."

An accomplished freelance personal-finance writer, Eric is the author or coauthor of numerous other *For Dummies* national bestsellers on personal finance, investing, for seniors, and home buying and is a syndicated columnist. His *Personal Finance For Dummies* won the Benjamin Franklin Award for Best Business Book.

Eric's work has been critically acclaimed in hundreds of publications and programs, including *Newsweek, The Los Angeles Times, The Chicago Tribune, Kiplinger's Personal Finance Magazine, The Wall Street Journal, Bottom Line Personal,* as well as NBC's *Today* show, ABC, CNBC, PBS's *Nightly Business Report,* CNN, FOX-TV, CBS national radio, Bloomberg Business Radio, and Business Radio Network. His website is www.erictyson.com.

Jim Schell has not always been a grizzled veteran of the small-business wars, contrary to what some people may think. Raised in Des Moines, Iowa, and earning a BA in Economics at the University of Colorado, Jim served in the U.S. Air Force in Klamath Falls, Oregon. Jim's entrepreneurial genes eventually surfaced when he and three Minneapolis friends started The Kings Court, at the time the nation's first racquetball club. Two years later, Jim bought General Sports, Inc., a struggling sporting-goods retailer and wholesaler. After another two years, he started National Screenprint, and, finally, he partnered with an ex-employee in Fitness and Weight Training Corp. Each of the start-ups was bootstrapped, and each was privately held. For a period of exhausting years, Jim involved himself in the management of all four businesses at the same time. His third business, National Screenprint, ultimately grew to $25 million in sales and 200 employees.

Relocating to San Diego, Jim began a long-simmering writing career, authoring four books (*The Brass Tacks Entrepreneur, Small Business Management Guide, The Small Business Answer Book,* and *Understanding Your Financial Statements*) and numerous columns for business and trade magazines.

Citing culture shock, Jim and his wife, Mary — a sales trainer and longtime business partner — relocated to Bend, Oregon, where he continued his writing career. In 1996, he kicked off his fifth start-up, Opportunity Knocks (OK), a nonprofit that uses volunteers to organize, administrate, and facilitate the formation of small-business owners into teams that will serve as a member's board of advisors. In the last five years, Jim has also founded three additional nonprofits and participated in the turnaround of two more. Jim has three grown sons — Jim, Todd, and Mike — and five grandchildren.

Dedications

From Eric: To my wife, Judy; to my family, especially my parents, Charles and Paulina; to my friends; and to my counseling clients and students of my courses, for teaching me how to teach them about managing their finances.

From Jim: This book is dedicated to The Rocky Road, and to all those friends, employees, and customers who have traversed it with me. Most of all, it is dedicated to my wife, Mary, without whom The Rocky Road would have been The Dead End.

Authors' Acknowledgments

Many people contribute to the birth of a book, and this book is no exception. First, Eric would like to express his deep debt of gratitude to James Collins, who inspired him when he was a young and impressionable business school student. Jim encouraged Eric to try to improve some small part of the business world by being an entrepreneur and focusing solely on what customers needed rather than on what made the quickest buck.

The technical reviewer for this book, Lindsay Stevens, helped improve our book, and we are thankful for that.

Thanks to all the good people in the media and other fields who have taken the time to critique and praise our previous writing so that others may know that it exists and is worth reading. And to those who may not open the book because of its bright yellow color and low-brow title, "You can't judge a book by its cover!" Now that we've got your attention, flip through the pages and find out why readers everywhere know and trust books *For Dummies.*

And a final and heartfelt thanks to all the people on the front lines and behind the scenes who helped to make this book and Eric's others a success. A big round of applause, please, for Elizabeth Rea as project editor and Amanda Langferman as copy editor. Their attention to detail and ability to ask good questions helped make this book the best that it could be. Thanks also to the Composition, Graphics, Proofreading, and Indexing staffs for their great efforts in producing this book.

P.S. Thanks to you, dear reader, for buying this book.

More Bestselling For Dummies Titles by Eric Tyson

Investing For Dummies®

A *Wall Street Journal* bestseller, this book walks you through how to build wealth in stocks, real estate, and small business as well as other investments.

Personal Finance For Dummies®

The bestselling *Personal Finance For Dummies* has helped countless readers budget their funds successfully, rein in debt, and build a strong foundation for the future. Eric Tyson combines his time-tested financial advice along with new strategies that reflect changing market conditions, giving you an all-encompassing guide to taking an honest look at your current financial health and setting realistic goals for the future.

Personal Finance in Your 20s For Dummies®

This hands-on, friendly guide provides you with the targeted financial advice you need to establish firm financial footing in your 20s and to secure your finances for years to come. When it comes to protecting your financial future, starting sooner rather than later is the smartest thing you can do.

Home Buying For Dummies®

America's #1 real estate book includes coverage of online resources in addition to sound financial advice from Eric Tyson and frontline real estate insights from industry veteran Ray Brown. Also available from America's best-selling real estate team of Tyson and Brown — *House Selling For Dummies* and *Mortgages For Dummies*.

Real Estate Investing For Dummies®

Real estate is a proven wealth-building investment, but many people don't know how to go about making and managing rental property investments. Real estate and property management expert Robert Griswold and Eric Tyson cover the gamut of property investment options, strategies, and techniques.

Publisher's Acknowledgments

We're proud of this book; please send us your comments at http://dummies.custhelp.com. For other comments, please contact our Customer Care Department within the U.S. at 877-762-2974, outside the U.S. at 317-572-3993, or fax 317-572-4002.

Some of the people who helped bring this book to market include the following:

Acquisitions, Editorial, and Vertical Websites

Project Editor: Elizabeth Rea

(*Previous Edition: Alissa Schwipps*)

Acquisitions Editor: Erin Calligan Mooney

Copy Editor: Amanda M. Langferman

(*Previous Edition: Josh Dials, Kelly Ewing*)

Assistant Editor: David Lutton

Editorial Program Coordinator: Joe Niesen

Technical Editor: Lindsay Stevens

Editorial Manager: Michelle Hacker

Editorial Assistant: Alexa Koschier

Cover Photo: © iStockphoto.com/Ivan Kmit

Cartoons: Rich Tennant
(www.the5thwave.com)

Composition Services

Project Coordinator: Patrick Redmond

Layout and Graphics: Carl Byers, Julie Trippetti

Proofreader: Laura Bowman

Indexer: Palmer Publishing Services

Publishing and Editorial for Consumer Dummies

> **Kathleen Nebenhaus,** Vice President and Executive Publisher

> **Kristin Ferguson-Wagstaffe,** Product Development Director

> **Ensley Eikenburg,** Associate Publisher, Travel

> **Kelly Regan,** Editorial Director, Travel

Publishing for Technology Dummies

> **Andy Cummings,** Vice President and Publisher

Composition Services

> **Debbie Stailey,** Director of Composition Services

Contents at a Glance

Table of Contents

Introduction

• •

Small business is many things to those of us who have participated in it or have dreamed about participating in it. Without a doubt, the concept of "being your own boss" is an alluring one.

But not everyone can be his or her own boss — at least not a good or successful one. If you're currently someone's employee (not a boss), fantasizing about owning a business of your own is perfectly natural on those days when you're fed up with your current boss or job. Your fantasy is made even more attractive by the rags-to-riches stories you hear about entrepreneurs who've turned their visions into millions or even billions of dollars.

Please know, however, that small-business ownership has some not-so-appealing aspects as well. Most often, you have to spend many years working hard and making tough choices before the risks you take turn into rewards. Furthermore, a significant percentage of small businesses don't survive to enjoy the long-term rewards. And perhaps most difficult of all, the entrepreneurial career can be lonely at the top.

Of course, the thrill of being the ultimate decision-maker may be exactly what attracts you to small business in the first place. But you need to realize that this attraction also has its downsides, the most prominent of which is that it breeds trial and error, and trial and error begets mistakes. Mistakes are the most expensive (and most dangerous) way for the small-business owner to learn.

But wait! Before you plod back to your day job, we have some good news for you: The mistakes that you're likely to make have already been made by those who have gone before you — including us. If you can somehow avoid the trial and error that leads to mistakes (which is what we're here to help you do), your chances for success multiply many times over.

Despite the previously mentioned downsides, it's impossible to describe the sense of accomplishment you'll get from starting and running your own successful business. Like so many before you, you'll know the thrill of creation, you'll feel the pride of watching that creation grow, and you'll realize that your work and your vision have filled an identifiable void for your customers, for your employees, and, of course, for you and your family. And for those of you who rise to the top of the small-business pyramid, you'll enjoy the greatest upside of them all — *unlimited* upside. Ask Bill Gates about how this reward feels.

Although you can find plenty of small-business books out there, most of them aren't worthy of your time or dollars. *Forbes* magazine once said of the marketplace for small-business books, "Warning: Most how-to books on entrepreneurship aren't worth a dime." The marketplace apparently agrees — the vast majority of small-business books don't sell after their first year or two. We're proud to say that this updated and revised fourth edition launches the 14th year of this book's history! We're grateful for reviewers' kind words, such as the praise from Hattie Bryant, creator of the PBS series *Small Business School,* who said of our book, "No one should try to start a business without this book."

Michael Gerber, author of *The E-Myth* series of business books (HarperCollins), makes the point that "the one common denominator in every successful entrepreneur is an insatiable appetite to learn." If Michael is right, and we believe that he is, you've passed the first test of the successful entrepreneur: By purchasing this book, you've displayed a desire to learn. Keep it up — you're on the right track.

Small business isn't rocket science. You don't need to be a genius to start and run a successful small business. What you do need is help, which is exactly why we wrote this book. We're pleased that you chose us as your guides into the stimulating world of small business.

About This Book

The following backgrounds and philosophies serve as a guide to the advice we provide — advice from the field that makes our small-business book stand out from the rest:

- ✔ **We're small-business experienced, and we share the benefits of that experience with you.** Between us, we have six decades of experience in starting and running seven successful small businesses. In addition, we've worked with thousands of small-business owners. Jim has led numerous small-business peer-networking groups and has provided volunteer counseling services to small-business owners. Eric has conducted financial counseling for small-business owners, taught financial-management courses, and worked as a management consultant.

  Throughout this book, we share the experience we've gained, in the hopes that you'll use our advice to purge the trial and error from your inventory of management tools. We also share an ample collection of straight-from-the-horse's-mouth anecdotes, each one based on a true story.

✔ **We take an objective view of small-business ownership.** Although we firmly believe in the creative power of small business, we're not here to be its pitchmen.

Sadly, too many small-business books are written by folks with an agenda: a franchise to sell, a multilevel marketing scheme to promote, or a high-priced seminar to foist on the reader. Free of conflicts of interest, we're here to pass on the truth and let you decide. If you're the type of person who wants to get into this competitive career field, we'd like you to enter the race informed as well as inspired.

✔ **We take a holistic approach.** Because small business can at times be both demanding and intoxicating, running your own shop can threaten to consume your life. Although everyone knows that life is more than just business, striking a balance and staying in control can represent a colossal challenge. With that in mind, we take particular care to present the realities of running a small business within the larger (and more important) framework of maintaining a happy personal and financial life.

We're committed to updating this book so that you have the best and latest information and advice at your fingertips. Tax laws change, benefits change, technology changes, and so do many other facets of the small-business world. That's why we've remained on top of these changes and revised this book.

Conventions Used in This Book

Every book has its own conventions, and this one is no different. To make the most of the information we provide, keep your eye out for these conventions:

✔ *Italics* highlight new terms that we define.

✔ **Boldfaced** text indicates the keywords in explanatory bulleted lists and action steps in how-to numbered lists.

✔ `Monofont` sets web addresses apart.

What You're Not to Read

Of course, we'd love for you to read every word of this book, but we're realistic. We know you have important things to do. So if you're in a hurry (or if you're just not into reading the extra, nonessential information), you can safely skip text highlighted with the Technical Stuff icon or formatted in gray-shaded sidebars. This text provides plenty of helpful information, but the information isn't crucial to your understanding of the topic at hand.

Foolish Assumptions

Many small-business books assume that their readers are ready to make the leap into small business and are cognizant of the risks and pitfalls. We don't make that assumption here, and neither should you. That's why we include sections designed to help you decide whether small business is really for you. We spell out the terms of starting your own business, break down the tasks, and point out the dangers. We don't think that you're incapable of making the decision yourself; we just know that time is your most precious resource, and we think we can help you save it. You'll lose too many years of your career if you make the wrong choice.

Much of this book is targeted to running and managing your existing small business intelligently. Even if you have a great idea, operating a small business is much harder than it appears, so we show you the best ways to manage and grow your enterprise.

How This Book Is Organized

We've organized this book to satisfy different reading and personal styles. Some of you may read it from cover to cover, while others may refer to it to answer a specific question or address an immediate concern. For this reason, each chapter of the book is designed to stand on its own. We're flexible — read it as an all-in-one project or use it as a reference guide.

Much like every small-business owner, this book must wear a number of hats. We've organized those hats into five parts. Here's what each part covers.

Part 1: Becoming an Entrepreneur

Your first small-business decision may be to admit that you're not ready for this career — at least not yet. If you're straddling the fence, Chapter 1 is here to help you dismount onto one side or the other. We help you make the right choice by presenting you with an aptitude test that helps you determine whether this career works for you.

If you decide that small-business ownership is right for you, you're ready for the rest of this part. Make no mistake about it; no matter how creatively you and your lawyer attempt to structure the incorporation of your start-up, the business of small business involves risk. Therefore, before exposing yourself to such risk, we suggest that you get your personal finances in order. Enter Chapter 2, which covers personal money management.

As you move past your personal finances to the business you hope to start, take heart: The road in the early stages of a small business has so many detours and forks that you're bound to lose sight of the road itself. Chapters 3, 4, and 5 provide you with the map you need to reach your destination. In these chapters, we overturn all the stones of a typical small-business start-up, from choosing the right niche for you to writing a gangbuster business plan to creating the right legal framework to locating the financing that suits your needs.

Part II: Buying an Existing Business

So you say you're considering buying an existing business as opposed to starting one from scratch? That's all well and good, but you need to ask some finely tuned questions prior to making that decision. "What are the advantages of buying an existing business over starting a new one? What kind of business should I buy? How should I determine the price I can pay? What are the tax implications? What are the first things I should do after the sale is completed?" You find the answers to these questions (and many more) in Chapters 6 through 9.

Part III: Running a Successful Small Business

You'll soon discover that small-business ownership is really one never-ending exercise in problem solving. Lucky for you, we've designed Chapters 10 through 15 to help you solve small business's most compelling problems. Here's a partial list of those problems:

- **Sales creation:** No sales, no income, no business survival. Period.

- **Marketing:** Although such small-business functions as sales, accounting, and operations are primarily black-and-white issues, that isn't the case with marketing. Marketing is gray, fuzzy, and hard to define (go ahead, try defining the word *marketing* right now in one easy sentence). To make matters worse, it's one of those aspects of doing business that doesn't come naturally to most people.

- **Operational issues:** Operational issues are everything on that long list of day-to-day responsibilities, beginning with how you spend your day from the time you walk in the office or store in the morning until the time you go home at night. These issues include everything from collecting accounts receivable to understanding financial statements to taking good care of your customers. And don't forget the foremost operational issue: managing the lifeblood of your business — cash.

✔ **Long-range planning:** Small-business owners recognize that long-range planning is important, but unfortunately, they're often too busy dealing with day-to-day business minutiae to get around to it. They say they'll focus on planning tomorrow, but alas, tomorrow never comes.

✔ **Accounting and bookkeeping issues:** Double-entry accounting systems? Cash flow projections? Current ratios and inventory turns? You're probably saying, "Give me a break. What does all this have to do with my chocolate-chip cookie business?" You'll see!

✔ **Technology issues:** Today, new telecommunications and information-gathering tools are appearing faster than politicians promising to cut taxes and improve government services. Keeping up is sometimes challenging, but you must do it.

✔ **Financing issues:** Capital is the food that feeds every small business. If you lack money, you may not be able to get your business headed in the desired direction. No capital equals no fuel to make your business go.

✔ **Everything else:** This category includes but isn't limited to such issues as product development, pricing, budgeting, customer service, ownership issues, and lifestyle issues.

Part IV: Keeping Your Business in Business

After your company is underway, your focus shifts from getting started to staying in (and growing your) business. Here are just some of the issues we address in this part to help you delve deeper into the world of small-business ownership:

✔ **Employees:** Deciding when and whom to hire is a vital but difficult decision. Then, even when you've hired the right employees for the right jobs, you're faced with the never-ending task of motivating and retaining them — and sometimes replacing them.

✔ **Government regulations:** Because you'll likely have to deal with several layers of government regulators during the life of your small business, you need to know how to do so without breaking the bank or your sanity.

✔ **Taxes:** You have to understand the tax laws so that you can best position your small business to minimize your legally required taxes.

✔ **Growth:** All businesses want to grow, but you need to recognize the downsides and risks you'll encounter if you grow too rapidly or without proper controls in place.

Part V: The Part of Tens

There ought to be a rule that says every small-business owner should have his or her own mentor. Sadly, too few do. Meanwhile, the small-business owner's *Fortune* 500 cousins learned the mentorship lesson long ago, which is why every new management employee today has a mentor lurking somewhere nearby. Mentors typically are business veterans — people who've learned business's lessons the hard way. Mentors guide and teach, and that's exactly what certain chapters in this book are intended to do.

Chapters 21 and 22 act as the mentor you need to assist you in building your business. These chapters share a collection of suggestions, advice, and tips on subjects designed to make the difference between maintaining a stagnant or mediocre business and growing a healthy one. Included in these chapters are tips on such topics as how to succeed in your small business and how to avoid common small-business management mistakes.

Icons Used in This Book

To help you find the information you need to assist you on your entrepreneurial path, we've placed icons throughout the text to highlight important points.

This symbol indicates time-tested tips to make your small-business journey more profitable and easier. Often straight from the heart of experience, we clue you in on what works for us as we navigate the oft-troubled waters of small-business life.

We present tales from our own experiences to save you some trial and error. Enjoy the company of your fellow entrepreneurs and benefit from the lessons we've learned.

The path of small-business ownership can be fraught with peril. Some deals may be too good to be true, and some people may have their own interests at heart, not yours. This icon points out the dangers and helps you steer clear of them.

This icon points out stuff too good (and too important) to forget.

This icon asks you to do some thinking and checking before you take the plunge. You have a lot of important choices to make when running a small business, so don't rush in.

If you like to sweat the dull stuff, this icon points out the inner workings of the business world that you're likely to ignore as you get down to the real work.

Where to Go from Here

Where you go from here is up to you, but if you're just beginning to think about small business, we recommend that you read straight through, cover to cover, to maximize your small-business intelligence. But the A-to-Z approach isn't necessary. If you feel confident in your knowledge of certain areas, pick the topics that you're most interested in by skimming the table of contents or by relying on the well-crafted index at the back of the book.

Part I
Becoming an Entrepreneur

"So...how did our first-stage financing go today?"

In this part . . .

Do you have the right stuff to start and run your own business? In Part I, you can test your entrepreneurial aptitude, ensure that your personal finances can withstand the strain of starting a small business, figure out which business niche is right for you, and then start making your dream a reality with a well-designed business plan and a survey of financial and ownership options.

Chapter 1

Is Small Business for You?

In This Chapter

▶ Understanding the role of small business

▶ Determining whether you have what it takes to successfully run a small business

▶ Reviewing the reasons to own (and not to own) a small business

▶ Identifying alternatives to starting a business

An old friend of ours, who has been a small-business owner for more years than most of us have been alive, says, "Small business is a place where you can take your dog to the office whenever you choose." That's one way of looking at it, but we offer several other viewpoints as well.

Owning and running a small business can be rewarding — personally and financially — but only if you have what it takes to succeed. This chapter gives you all the know-how you need to be sure that you're making the right decision. In it, we pose a set of 20 questions to ask yourself about your skills, talents, and abilities. If you're honest with yourself — don't worry, there are no right or wrong answers — this test can give you the information you need to determine whether running a small business is the right move for you. If you find that running a small business isn't for you, we provide several alternatives, which may give you exactly what you're looking for.

Lots of important issues — from your financial situation to your desire to create a needed product or provide a needed service to your ability to be a jack-of-all-trades — should influence your decision to become an entrepreneur. This chapter helps you understand the realities of starting and running a small business so that you can figure out how and why it may or may not work for you.

Defining Small Business

The lingo of the business world — cash flow, profit and loss statements, accounts receivable, debt-to-equity ratio, and so on — makes small-business ownership appear far more complicated than it really is. Don't be fooled. You're probably more acquainted with the basic concepts of doing business than you think. If you've ever participated in a bake sale, been paid for a musical performance, or operated a baby-sitting, painting, or lawn-mowing service, you've been involved in a small business.

Being a small-business owner doesn't mean that you have to work 70 hours a week, make a six-figure income, or offer a unique product or service. We know many successful small-business owners who work at their craft 40 hours a week or less and some who work part-time at their business in addition to holding a regular job. The vast majority of small-business owners we know provide products or services quite similar to what's already in the marketplace and make reasonable but not extraordinary sums of money — and, thanks largely to the independence that small-business ownership offers, are perfectly happy doing so!

Small (and large) business basics

Imagine back to your childhood . . . it's a hot summer afternoon, and you're sweating it out under the shade of an elm tree in your front yard. "Boy, it's hot," you say to yourself, sighing. "I could sure go for a glass of lemonade." Eureka! With no lemonade stand in sight, you seize upon your business idea.

You start by asking some of your neighbors if they'd buy lemonade from you, and you quickly discover that the quality, service, and location of your proposed business may attract a fair number of customers. You've just conducted your first market research.

After you determine that your community has a need for your business, you also have to determine a potential location. Although you could set up in front of your house, you decide that your street doesn't get enough traffic. To maximize sales, you decide to set up your stand on the corner down the road. Luckily, Mrs. Ormsby gives you permission to set up in front of her house, provided that she gets a free glass of lemonade. You've just negotiated your first lease (and you've just had your first experience at bartering).

With a tiny bit of creativity and ego, you determine the name of your business: The World's Best Lemonade Stand. After some transactions with the grocery store, you have your lemonade stand (your store), your cash box, a table, a pitcher (your furniture and fixtures), and the lemonade (your inventory). The World's Best Lemonade Stand (your brand) is now ready for business!

From the moment you first realized that you weren't the only one who might be interested in buying some lemonade, you faced the same business challenges and issues that all small-business owners face. As a matter of fact, the business challenges and issues that a lemonade stand faces are the same that American Express, Boeing, Costco, Disney, and every other big company faces. The basics of doing business are the same, no matter what size the business is:

✔ **Sales:** Boeing manufactures and sells airplanes; you sell lemonade. A sale is a sale no matter what the product or service is or how large or small the ticket price is.

✔ **Cost of goods:** Boeing buys parts for its vendors and suppliers; you buy lemons, sugar, and paper cups from the grocery store.

✔ **Expenses:** Boeing has employee wages and pension plans (or employee benefits; see Chapter 17); you have sign-making costs and bubble-gum expenditures to keep your employees happy (also a form of employee benefits).

✔ **Profit:** Profit is what's left over after Boeing subtracts the cost of its goods and expenses from its sales; the same is true for your lemonade stand.

Financial basics: The same whether you're big or small

Not only are the concepts of Business 101 — sales, cost of goods, expenses, and profit — the same for all businesses, regardless of size or product offering, but many associated financial basics are the same, too. Here's what we mean:

✔ **Accounts payable:** Boeing owes money to its vendors who provide it with parts; you owe money to your local grocery store for supplies.

✔ **Accounts receivable:** Boeing has money due from its customers (major airlines and governments) that buy the company's airplanes. You have money due to you from Mrs. Huxtable, who wandered by thirsty without her purse.

✔ **Cash flow:** Boeing has money coming in and going out through various transactions with customers and vendors (sometimes cash flows positively, sometimes negatively), and so do you. (See Chapter 14 for much, much more on this important, but sometimes murky, concept.)

✔ **Assets:** Boeing has its manufacturing plants and equipment, inventory, office buildings, and the like; you have your lemonade stand and cash box.

✔ **Liabilities:** Boeing owes suppliers money; you owe money to your local grocery store.

✔ **Net worth:** Net worth is what's left over after Boeing subtracts what it owes (its *liabilities*) from what it owns (its *assets*). Ditto for your small-business enterprise.

This comparison between The World's Best Lemonade Stand and Boeing could go much deeper and longer. After all, the basics of the two businesses are the same; the differences are primarily due to size. In business, *size* is a synonym for *complexity.*

So you may be thinking, if business is so simple, why isn't everyone doing it — and succeeding at it? The reason is that even though the basics of business are simple, the details are not. Consider the various ways in which you grant your customers credit, collect the resulting accounts receivable, and, unfortunately, sometimes write them off when you're not paid. Consider the simple concept of sales: How do you pay the people who make those sales, where and how do you deploy them, and how do you organize, supervise, and motivate them? Think about all the money issues: How do you compile and make sense of your financial figures? How much should you pay your vendors for their products? And when you need money, should you consider taking in shareholders or should you borrow from the bank? And, lest we forget, how should you deal with the Internal Revenue Service (IRS), the Occupational Safety and Health Administration (OSHA), and your state's workers' compensation department? These are but a few of the complex details that muddy the waters of business.

Small business: Role model for big business

While working as CEO of General Electric, Jack Welch once said in a speech to his division managers, "Think small. What General Electric is trying relentlessly to do is to get that small-company soul . . . and small-company speed . . . inside our big-company body."

Think small? What's happening here? Why would the CEO of a gigantic company like GE want his employees to think small? Because Jack Welch knew that small can be beautiful and because success and survival in the business arena always favor the agile over the cumbersome, the small over the big. Thanks to this "small is beautiful" trend — and thanks to increasing technological advances — you no longer have to be big to appear big; you can be small and still compete in most of today's marketplaces.

Different people and businesses, similar issues

Okay, so you know what small business means and you can identify the people who create and run one, but what about your particular small business? After all, in your eyes anyway, the business you have in mind or the one you're already running is different from anyone else's. Different products, different services, different legal entity — the list goes on.

Small business by the numbers

The Small Business Administration defines *small business* as any business with fewer than 500 employees. To us, that seems a bit large. Consider this: Coauthor Jim's fourth small business had 200 employees. With 200 employees, you have, say, 400 dependents, maybe 1,000 customers, and 100 or so of the business's vendors all depending on you, trusting in you, and waiting for the mail to deliver their next check. That certainly isn't small by our standards — not if you measure size in terms of responsibility anyway.

For those of you who like to work with numbers, our definition of *small business* is any business with 100 employees or fewer, a category that includes more than 98 percent of all U.S. businesses.

The latest year's U.S. government figures show that the country is home to 27 million small businesses. Of those, approximately 21 million have no employees. Meanwhile, hundreds of thousands of new businesses open their doors each year. This kind of growth is an indicator of the appeal of owning a small business. (Or maybe it's an indicator of the lack of appeal of working for someone else.)

Not only do small businesses create opportunities for their owners, but they also create jobs. In fact, small firms create about three-quarters of the new jobs in the United States.

What all these numbers mean is that small business isn't really small — it's large, diverse, and growing. Not only is small business not small when speaking in terms of the sheer numbers of small businesses and their employees, it's also not small when talking about the tenacity and knowledge required to start and run a small business, which is where the remainder of this book comes in. You provide the tenacity part of the equation; we provide the knowledge.

The term *small business* covers a wide range of product and service offerings. A ten-person law practice is a small business. A doctor's office is a small business. Architects, surveyors, and dentists are also in the business of owning and operating small businesses. How about a Subway franchisee? You guessed it — small business. The same goes for freelance writers (hence, we, your humble authors, are both small-business owners), consultants, and the dry cleaner on the corner of Main and Elm Streets. Each one is a small business.

Small business also covers all legal business entities. So small businesses can be sole proprietorships, C Corporations, nonprofits, or limited liability corporations, as long as they have fewer than 100 employees. (We define these various business entities in Chapter 5.)

After all, each of the businesses and entities we list here has the same basic needs:

- ✔ Marketing to make its products or services known
- ✔ Sales to get its products or services in the hands of the customer

> ✔ Varying degrees of administration and financial accounting to satisfy a number of internal informational needs, as well as the needs of the IRS

Beyond the similarities in this list, each business is significantly different. Some need employees; some don't. Some require vast investments in real estate, equipment, and elaborate information systems; some can get by with a desk, computer, and phone. Some may need to borrow money to get the business up and running; many others get by with what's in the owner's savings account. These differences are what make owning a small business exciting because you should be able to find a good fit for your desires and resources.

Our definition of a small-business owner

A *small-business owner* (or entrepreneur), by our definition, is anyone who owns a business that has 100 or fewer employees, period. Everyone who hangs out a shingle qualifies for the title no matter whether the business is private, public, barely surviving, or soaring off the charts.

You're a small-business owner whether you've been in the saddle one day, one week, or one decade; whether you're male or female and have a college degree or not; whether you work out of your home or on a fishing boat somewhere off the coast of Alaska.

Everyone has his or her own definition of the small-business owner. We find these four of particular interest; pick one or combine them all:

> ✔ **Webster's Dictionary:** A person who organizes and manages a business undertaking, assuming the risk for sake of profit.

> ✔ **Peter Drucker:** Someone who gets something new done. (The late Peter Drucker is the Father of Modern Management. His books, primarily written for large companies, have virtually defined contemporary U.S. management theory.)

> ✔ **Jim Collins:** Best-selling author and business expert Jim Collins takes a broad view of the small-business owner. The traditional definition — someone who founds an entity designed to make money — is too narrow for him. He sees entrepreneurship as more of a life concept. Everyone makes choices about how to live life. You can take a paint-by-numbers approach, or you can start with a blank canvas. When you paint by numbers, the end result is guaranteed. You know what it's going to be, and though it might be good, it will never be a masterpiece. Starting with a blank canvas is the only way to get a masterpiece, but in doing so, you could also blow up. So are you going to pick the paint-by-numbers kit or the blank canvas? That's a life question, not a business question.

> ✔ **Us:** A person who is motivated by independence, creativity, and growth rather than by the security of an employer's paycheck.

All people have their own collection of unique characteristics that determine who they are, what makes them happy, and where they belong in this world. On those not-as-frequent-as-they-should-be occasions when our characteristics align snugly with the kind of work we're doing, we know how Cinderella felt when her foot slipped effortlessly into the glass slipper offered by the Prince.

In all fairness, we must warn those of you who are considering a future in small-business ownership that owning your own business can be addictive. We love it usually, hate it occasionally, and need it always, and we wouldn't trade professions with anybody — except for maybe a professional athlete.

Do You Have the Right Stuff?

To discover whether you have the right stuff to run your own small business, take the test we offer in this section. Don't close this book just because we said the word *test!* Tests don't have to be a pain in the posterior. In fact, they can be relatively painless (and useful) when you don't have to study for them, there are no right or wrong answers, and you're the only one who will find out the outcome.

Some words of caution here: This Small-Business Owner's Aptitude Test isn't scientific, but we think it's potentially useful because it's based on our combined six decades of experience working *as* entrepreneurs, as well as *alongside* them. The purpose of this test is to provide a guideline, not to cast in concrete your choice to start or buy a business. The results will be most meaningful when it comes time to make your decision if you're in the highest- or lowest-scoring groups. If you fall somewhere in the middle, we recommend more serious soul searching, consultation with friends and other small-business owners, and a large grain of salt.

Getting started with the instructions

Score each of the following 20 questions with a number from 1 (the entrepreneurially unfriendly response) to 5 (the entrepreneurially friendly response). Determine the appropriate numerical score for each question by assessing the relative difference between the two options presented and by how fervently you feel about the answer.

For example, one question asks, "Do you daydream about business opportunities while commuting to work, flying on an airplane, or waiting in the doctor's office, or during other quiet times?" Give yourself a 5 if you find yourself doing this a lot, a 1 if you never do this, or a 2, 3, or 4, depending on the degree of work-related daydreaming you do. A business, especially one that you own yourself, can be downright fun and all-consuming. For most successful entrepreneurs, their minds are rarely far away from their businesses;

they're often thinking of new products, new marketing plans, and new ways to find customers.

To make the test even more meaningful, have someone who doesn't have a vested interest in or a strong opinion about your decision — such as a good friend or coworker — also independently take the test with you as the subject. We seldom have unbiased opinions of ourselves, and having an unrelated third party take the test on your behalf can give you a more accurate view. Then compare the two scores — the score you arrived at when you took the test compared to the score your friend or peer compiled for you. Our guess is that your true entrepreneurial aptitude, at least according to our experience, lies somewhere between the two scores.

Answering the questions

After reading each question, write your response from 1 to 5 on a separate sheet of paper.

1. In the games that you play, do you play harder when you fall behind, or do you have a tendency to fold your cards and cut your losses? (5 if you play harder, 1 if you wilt under pressure)

2. When you go to a sports event or concert, do you try to figure out the promoter's or the owner's gross revenues? (5 if you often do, 1 if you never do)

3. When things take a serious turn for the worse, is your first impulse to look for someone to blame, or is it to look for alternatives and solutions? (5 if you look for alternatives and solutions, 1 if you look for someone to blame)

4. Using your friends and/or coworkers as a barometer, how would you rate your energy level? (5 if it is high, 1 if it is low)

5. Do you daydream about business opportunities while commuting to work, flying on an airplane, waiting in the doctor's office, or during other quiet times? (5 if you often do, 1 if you never do)

6. Look back on the significant changes you've made in your life — schools, jobs, relocations, relationships: Have you fretted and worried about those changes and not acted, or have you looked forward to them with excitement and been able to make those tough decisions after doing some research? (5 if you've looked forward to the decisions and tackled them after doing your homework, 1 if you've been overwhelmed with worry about the change and paralyzed from action for too long)

7. Is your first consideration of any opportunity always the upside or is it always the downside? (5 if you always see the upside and recognize the risks, 1 if you dwell on the downside to the exclusion of considering the benefits)

8. Are you happiest when you're busy or when you have nothing to do? (5 if you're always happiest when busy, 1 if you're always happiest when you have nothing to do)

9. As an older child or young adult, did you often have a job or a scheme or an idea to make money? (5 if always, 1 if never)

10. Did you work part-time or summer jobs as a youth, or did you not work and primarily recreate/enjoy a total break over the summer? (5 if you often worked, 1 if you never did)

11. Did your parents own a small business? (5 if they worked many years owning small businesses, 1 if they never did)

12. Have you worked for a small business for more than one year? (5 if you have, 1 if you haven't)

13. Do you like being in charge and in control? (5 if you really crave those two situations, 1 if you detest them)

14. How comfortable are you with borrowing money to finance an investment, such as buying a home or an automobile? (5 if owing money is not a problem, 1 if it's a huge problem)

15. How creative are you? (5 if extremely creative, 1 if not creative at all)

16. Do you have to balance your checkbook to the penny or is "close" good enough? (5 if "close" is good enough, 1 if to the penny)

17. When you fail at a project or task, does it scar you forever or does it inspire you to do it better the next time? (5 if it inspires you for the next time, 1 if it scars you forever)

18. When you truly believe in something, whether it's an idea, a product, or a service, are you able to sell it to someone? (5 if almost always, 1 if never)

19. In your current social and business environment, are you most often a follower or a leader? (5 if almost always a leader, 1 if always a follower)

20. How good are you at achieving/keeping your New Year's resolutions? (5 if you almost always achieve/keep them, 1 if you never do)

Scoring the test

Now total your score. Here's how to assess your total:

80 to 100: Go for it. If you read this book and continue to show a willingness to be a sponge, you should succeed!

60 to 79: You probably have what it takes to successfully run your own business, but take some time to look back over the questions you scored the lowest on and see whether you can discern any trends.

40 to 59: Too close to call. Review the questions on which you scored low and don't scrimp on learning more to tilt the scales in your favor.

20 to 39: We could be wrong, but you're probably better off working for someone else or pursuing one of the other alternatives to starting your own business (see the later section "Exploring Alternatives to Starting a Business" for details).

Analyzing your results

The truth about a subjective test such as this one is that it can serve as a helpful indicator, but it won't provide you with a definitive answer. We issue this disclaimer because the Small-Business Owner's Aptitude Test is, in effect, a measure of the way you have acted in the past and not necessarily how you will perform in the future.

Your future as a small-business owner will hold many surprises. (Don't panic! By the time you finish this book, you'll be prepared for many of them.) The skills and traits that you need to cope with those surprises will ultimately determine whether your choice to start or buy a small business is the right one. What exactly are those skills?

- ✔ **Numbers skills:** These skills include those related to borrowing money, accounting for it, and reporting on the financial performance of your company. (See Chapters 5, 10, and 14 for more information.)

- ✔ **Sales skills:** As a small-business owner, you're always trying to sell your products to someone — be it your customers, employees, or vendors. (See Chapter 11 for the skinny on sales.)

- ✔ **Marketing skills:** All small-business owners have to market their products or services — no one is exempt. (See Chapter 11 for details on marketing.)

- ✔ **Leadership skills:** The small-business owner is the Grand Poobah of his venture. Grand Poobahs are only as good as the manner in which the business's employees are led. (See Chapter 16 for everything you need to know about employer-employee relations.)

Does this mean that if you don't have these skills, you should remain on the receiving end of a paycheck? Thankfully, it does not.

Many successful entrepreneurs who have come before you made it without being able to personally perform all the skills necessary to run a business. What we're saying is that, over the course of your career, you'll have to either develop these skills or involve someone in the business who already has them (a partner, a key employee, or a hired advisor or consultant, for example).

Skills aside, successful entrepreneurs also need to have or adopt several required traits:

- ✔ **Confidence:** Small-business owners have to be able to coexist with risk and possibly debt. Capitalism offers its participants no guarantees; thus, the small business and consequently its owner are almost always at risk and sometimes in debt. Yet, the owner still has to sleep at night.

- ✔ **Intuition:** Call it intuition or call it gut instinct, the small-business owner has to call things right more often than wrong, or he'll soon be calling it quits.

- ✔ **Optimism:** Successful small-business owners often see good fortune, not misfortune; upsides, not downsides; and opportunities, not problems. The small-business owner can always hire a devil's advocate (that's what lawyers and accountants are for), but the enthusiasm and optimism necessary to drive the vision must come from the entrepreneur.

- ✔ **Drive:** Successful small-business owners are driven to create a product, service a customer, and build a successful business. Similar to the craving for chocolate, this drive doesn't go away.

- ✔ **Passion:** An entrepreneur's passion is infectious. Your employees, your vendors, and your customers — everyone you come in contact with — should feel your passion and feed off it.

If you don't have all five of these traits, should you resign yourself to always being an employee? In answering this question, you first need to recognize that being a good employee today also requires some of these traits, so owning a business isn't your only option. Then you need to come to terms with the fact that if you don't have most of these traits in healthy supply, you're probably better off as an employee rather than a small-business owner.

Identifying the Pros and Cons of Owning a Small Business

Even if you passed the test in the preceding section with flying colors and you think you qualify as a prospective small-business owner, the decision you're about to make isn't a simple, clear-cut one. After all, most of you can probably find as many compelling reasons why you shouldn't own a business as you can find reasons why you should. In the following sections, we present many of these reasons.

The reasons we present here aren't in any particular order. Everyone is different. The reasons why Bill Gates decided to start Microsoft may be vastly different from the reasons John Dough decided to buy his own pizza business. You won't find right or wrong reasons to start or buy a business; you'll only find right or wrong criteria that go into forming those reasons.

The reasons to own

We can think of many reasons to give your boss the heave-ho. In this section, though, we stick with the best reasons why people choose to own a business:

- ✓ **The satisfaction of creation:** Have you ever experienced the pride of building a chair, preparing a gourmet meal, or repairing a vacuum cleaner? Or how about providing a needed counseling service that helps people solve their vexing financial problems? The small-business owner gets to experience the thrill of creation on a daily basis, not to mention the satisfaction of solving a customer's problem.

- ✓ **Establishment of their own culture:** No more standing around the water cooler complaining about "the way things are around here." After you start your own business, the way things are around here is a direct function of the way you intend them to be.

- ✓ **Financial upside:** Consider Charles Schwab and Oprah Winfrey. It's no surprise that these one-time small-business owners are among the nation's wealthiest individuals. (A recent Small Business Administration study concluded definitively that although small-business ownership is risky, small-business owners had a significantly higher probability of being classified as high income and high wealth than their employed counterparts.)

- ✓ **Self-sufficiency:** For many people, working for someone else has proven to be a less-than-gratifying experience. As a result of such unfulfilling experiences, some people have discovered that if they want to provide for themselves and their families, they'd better create the opportunity themselves. It's either that or be willing to occasionally spend a long wait in the unemployment line.

- ✓ **Flexibility:** Perhaps you prefer to work in the evenings because that's when your spouse works or you want to spend more time with the kids during the day. Or you may prefer taking frequent three-day-weekend jaunts rather than a few full-week vacations every year. As a small-business owner, despite the long hours you work, you should have more control over your schedule. After all, you're the boss, and you can usually tailor your schedule to meet your personal needs, as well as those of your customers.

- ✓ **Special perks:** Small-business owners have several advantages over the typical employee. For example, small-business owners can sock away tens of thousands of dollars into their retirement accounts per year free of federal and state income taxes. And yes, similar to those corporate execs who wine and dine their clients and then write off the expenses, small-business owners also have the option of writing off such costs as long as they adhere to IRS rules. Chapter 19 explains what makes these rules tick and how they can work for you.

The reasons not to own

In light of the resounding potential benefits, why would any reasonable soul elect to continue receiving a paycheck? Why wouldn't everyone want to own a business? Let us count the nays:

- ✔ **Responsibility:** When you're a small-business owner, not only does your family depend on your business success, but so do your partners, your employees and their families, your customers, and sometimes your vendors. As much as we love our small businesses, every now and then even the most enthusiastic small-business owners wax nostalgic for the good old days when they would punch their time card and leisurely walk out the door — really, truly, done for the day.

  If you're the type of person who sometimes takes on more responsibility than you can handle and works too many hours, beware that another drawback of running your own business is that you may be prone to becoming a workaholic.

- ✔ **Competition:** Although some people thrive on competition, that same competition comes back to haunt you by threatening your security. You soon find out that a host of hungry competitors is pursuing your customers and threatening your livelihood, whether by cutting prices or offering a more complete package of unique services. Sure, competition is what makes capitalism go 'round, but you need to remember that in order to have a competition, someone's going to win and someone's going to lose. That someone could be you.

- ✔ **Change:** Products and services come, and products and services go. Nothing is sacred in the business of doing business, and the pace of change today is significantly faster than it was a generation ago — and it shows no signs of slowing down. If you don't enjoy change and the commotion it causes, then perhaps the stability that a larger, more bureaucratic organization provides is best for you.

- ✔ **Chance:** Interest rates, the economy, theft, fire, natural disasters, sickness, pestilence — the list goes on. Any of these random events can send your business reeling.

- ✔ **Red tape:** Taxes, health-care reform, bureaucracy, tariffs, duties, treaties, OSHA, FDA, NAFTA, glurg, glurg, glurg.

- ✔ **Business failure:** Finally, as if this list of a small business's enemies isn't long enough, the owner faces the specter of the ultimate downside: business failure in the form of bankruptcy. This is the stage where the owner stands back and watches the creditors swoop in like vultures to devour his remaining business — and sometimes personal — assets.

Now contrast the small-business owner's failure to the *Fortune* 500 employee who fails, collecting a tidy severance check as he packs up his calculator and waves goodbye on his way to register for unemployment compensation. No life's savings lost for this person, no second mortgages hanging over his or her home, no asterisks on the credit report. In our opinion, no other failure in the business world is as painful as the one facing the small-business owner. More than any other reason, this extreme cost of failure is the primary reason that owning a small business isn't for everyone.

Minimizing start-up risk with part-time ventures

Some people believe that starting a business is the riskiest of all small-business options. However, if you're starting a business that specifically uses your skills and expertise, the risk may not be nearly as great as you think. Besides, risk is relative: Those who are employed by someone else are taking a risk, too — a risk that their employer will continue to offer them the opportunity to remain employed. To our way of thinking, we'd rather control that risk ourselves than place it in the hands of someone else.

One way to minimize the risk of starting a full-time business is to ease into a part-time one. Suppose for a moment that you're a computer troubleshooter at a company and that you make $75,000 per year. You're considering establishing your own computer consulting service and would be happy making a comparable amount of money. If you find through your research that others performing the services you intend to provide are charging $75 per hour, you actually need to spend only about 20 hours a week consulting (assuming that you work 50 weeks per year). Because you can run your consulting business from your home (which can generate small tax breaks) and you can do it without purchasing costly new equipment,

your expenses should be minimal. (**Note:** We've ignored your employer's benefits here, which, of course, have value, too.)

Rather than leaving your day job and diving into your new business without the safety of a regular paycheck, you have the option of starting out by moonlighting as a consultant. Over the course of a year or two, if you can average ten hours a week of consulting, you're halfway to your goal. Then, after you leave your job and can focus all your energies on your business, getting to 20 hours per week of billable work won't be such a stretch.

Many businesses, by virtue of leveraging their owners' existing skills and expertise, can be started with low start-up costs. You can begin building the framework of your company by using *sweat equity* (the time and energy you invest in your business, as opposed to the capital) in the early, part-time years. As long as you know your competition and can offer your customers a valued service at a reasonable cost, the principal risk with your part-time business is that you won't do a good job marketing what you have to offer. After you've figured out how to market your skills, you're ready to make the break.

Exploring Alternatives to Starting a Business

More than a few small-business owners and entrepreneurial cheerleaders would have you believe that every employee would be happy and financially better off running his own small business. The reality is, of course, that the grass isn't always greener on the other side of the fence. Small business isn't the only game in town; in some cases, it isn't even the best option available.

If, after taking the Small-Business Owner's Aptitude Test earlier in this chapter, you feel that you don't fit the profile of the typical entrepreneur, don't despair. Some folks are happier working for a company, be it either for-profit or nonprofit. Here are several options for you to consider, in lieu of becoming an entrepreneur:

✔ **Become a better employee.** Companies of all sizes need good employees, and worthy companies are willing to go to a lot of trouble and expense to hire, retain, and pay them. (If you're not presently working for one of those good companies, you have plenty of choices to choose from.) So update your resume and keep improving your work ethic. Your willingness to put in the extra hours when needed and your accompanying willingness to accept more responsibility will bring a smile to the faces of employers. Keep learning. You don't need a PhD, a master's degree, or even an undergraduate college degree to succeed in business thanks to the knowledge you can pick up on your own through mentors, experience, and plenty of reading.

If you haven't completed your college or graduate degree and the industry you're in places particular value in those who have, investing the time and money it takes to finish your degree can pay big dividends. (More than a few of today's enlightened businesses will finance all or at least part of that education for you. Just ask.) Talk to others who have taken a similar mid-career educational path and see what they have to say.

✔ **Be an entrepreneur inside a larger company.** If you can find or create an entrepreneurial enterprise inside (or alongside) a larger company, in addition to receiving significant managerial and operational responsibility, in many cases you can negotiate sharing in the financial success that you help to create. Entrepreneurial opportunities can come from within businesses of all sizes, shapes, and forms. One large company — 3M, a *Fortune* 500 company — has long taken pride in a corporate culture that allows its employees to take an idea and build it into a separate company within 3M. Post-it Notes, those handy, sticky notes found everywhere in the offices of the world, is an example of a business started within a business by 3M employees.

Developing a business within a business can be a win-win situation for everyone. The employees involved can be compensated for the results of their newfound business, the companies, like 3M, add another terrific and profitable product to their empire, and a new business venture may be spun off to make more products and hire more employees, keeping the local economy humming.

✔ **Move from a large company to a small company.** Although we're not aware of any statistics measuring the movement of employees from large businesses to small businesses (or vice versa), we would guess the scale tilts significantly in favor of employees moving from large businesses to small businesses for several reasons: Employees get well-rounded experience working with small companies; small-business employees have opportunities for more responsibility; and employee decisions and actions have much more impact on a small business, and that impact is more visible than in a large business.

✔ **Buy an existing business.** In the likely event that you don't have a specific idea for a business you want to start but you have exhibited business-management skills, consider buying an established business. Although buying someone else's business can, in some cases, be riskier than starting your own, at least you know exactly what you're getting into right from the start. The good news is that you often don't have to waste time and energy creating an infrastructure — it's already in place, thereby allowing you, the buyer, to dive right into the business, without having to waste time on the peripherals.

Buying an existing business often requires that you shell out more money at the outset, in the form of a down payment to buy the business. Thus, if you don't have the ability to run the business and it performs poorly, you have a lot more to lose financially. Part II looks specifically at buying an existing business.

✔ **Invest in someone else's business.** If you find that managing the day-to-day headaches of a small business isn't for you, perhaps a viable alternative would be to consider investing in someone else's small business — assuming that you have the ability to identify potentially successful businesses. In our experience, however, few people have the knowledge and intuition to be investors in other people's small businesses. (For more information on this subject, see Chapter 5.)

Chapter 2

Laying Your Personal Financial Foundation

*W*hether you dream about owning your own business someday or you're currently living the reality of being your own boss, you know that money is important. Just as your car won't run without fuel, you can't sustain a roof over your head and provide food, clothing, and the rest of life's necessities if you can't pay for them.

Likewise, you can't start your own small business or continue buying what you want and need for your existing business without money. That's where getting your personal finances in tip-top shape comes into play, and that's what this chapter is all about.

Getting Your Financial Ducks in a Row

Having your personal finances in order is one of the most under-recognized keys to achieving success in your small business. Just one significant money oversight or mistake can derail your entrepreneurial dreams or venture. The following sections present several good reasons why your chances for success as a small-business owner are higher if your personal finances are in top shape.

Cutting the umbilical cord

One of the primary reasons why many aspiring entrepreneurs continue to work for someone else is the string of financial and accompanying psychological obstacles they face in leaving the security of a regular paycheck. The pressure and uncertainty of living paycheck to paycheck to meet monthly obligations serve as a huge wet blanket for most budding entrepreneurs' enthusiasm, and they don't do much to boost would-be entrepreneurs' resolve to leave behind the comfort of their paychecks and benefits.

Unless you prepare yourself fiscally and emotionally to leave your day job, you may never discover that you have the potential to run your own business. Money and mind issues cause many aspiring entrepreneurs to remain indentured servants to their employers and can cause those who do break their bondage to soon return to the relative comfort of being employees.

If you decide to start your own business, you'll quickly discover what every successful entrepreneur before you has discovered: You have a finite amount of time and energy. If your mind is preoccupied with personal financial problems, and resolving those problems requires too much of your thought and effort, something has to give. That something is likely to be either your family or your business — or perhaps both.

In the early years of your start-up business, you'll almost surely experience a reduction in your take-home income just as you'll also experience the feeling of a lack of security. You must plan accordingly so that you can stick with your plans and give them adequate time to work. The rest of this chapter tells you how to get started.

Improving your business survival odds

If you're successful in leaving your job and getting your business venture off the ground, you need to manage your money well to ensure continued success. (See the later section "Managing Your Personal Finances Post-Launch" for details on how to do so.) After all, money is a precious resource that, when squandered, is gone forever.

Of course, if you're wealthy to begin with, you can go on for quite some time before a lack of money forces you to give up your venture. But most people who start small businesses aren't super-affluent to begin with — after all, one of the attractions of achieving small-business success is building your own nest egg. Getting your financial house in order before you start your business can buy you critical time to make a success of your start-up.

Maintaining harmony on the home front

The financial and emotional stress that running a small business puts on many entrepreneurs not only affects them directly but also impacts their family members — especially spouses and children. Young children can pick up on the stress and feel the hurt of neglect from parents who forget their role as parents in their quest for success. Spouses can grow resentful of all the time and money their workaholic partners put into the fledgling business.

After years of hard work in the business and neglect of their partners and friends, successful and unsuccessful small-business owners alike can end up with a set of divorce papers and a lack of friends. (Of course, workaholic employees and company executives can end up in the same lonely boat.) Business success, if it comes as the result of ignoring your personal life, can be a lonely and unfulfilling reward.

Before you commit to launching your small business, consider this short but highly important list of things to accomplish on the home front:

✔ **Set aside time to talk about concerns.** Schedule time with your spouse and other family members to discuss their concerns and needs related to your starting a small business. Be sure to ask the following:

- How do they feel about the financial burden that's required?

- What do they think about leaving the corporate security?

- What concerns do they have about your working late hours?

- Do they see working from home (assuming that you're starting a home business) as a good thing or a bad thing?

- What role, if any, would they like to play in the new business?

Especially important is that you and your family come to an understanding as to what personal assets (savings, home equity, and so on) you agree can be used for the business. If you haven't yet discussed and assessed your personal financial situation, now is a good time to do so.

Allow your family members to speak their minds and get their concerns out on the table. Although it's easy to say and much harder to do, be sure that you don't get defensive or make them feel that they can't be heard. Your first job is to listen and really *hear* what they have to say.

✔ **Seek outside assistance for impasses.** Running your own business is demanding and stressful. You don't need the added pressure of problems on the home front. If your initial discussions with family members reveal problems that aren't easy to resolve, the time to get help is before your business is up and running. After your spouse has filed for divorce or your kids have become strangers to you, the damage too often is done. Marriage or family counseling with an experienced counselor can be an invaluable preventive investment. Finding a mentor or another entrepreneur who has built a business of his or her own can give you the additional insight of experience. You may also try reading some quality self-help/family-relationship books.

Creating Your Money To-Do List

We hope you agree that getting your personal finances in order before you set up shop makes a lot of sense. But you have so much to do and so little time! Where to begin and what to do? This section provides a short list of the important financial tasks you need to undertake.

Assess your financial position and goals

Where do you stand in terms of retirement planning? How much do you want to have saved to pay for your children's educational costs? What kind of a home do you want to buy?

These and other important questions can help shape your personal financial plans. Sound financial planning isn't about faithfully balancing your checkbook or investing in stocks based on a friend's tip. Rather, smart financial management is about taking a hard look at where you are, figuring out where you want to go, and making sure that you're prepared for occasional adverse conditions along the way — a process, incidentally, that isn't unlike what you'll be doing when you run your own business.

Measuring your net worth

The first step in assessing your financial position is giving yourself a financial physical. Start with measuring your *net worth,* a term that defines the difference between your financial assets and your financial liabilities.

Begin by totaling up your financial assets (all your various bank accounts, stocks, mutual funds, and so on) and subtracting from that the sum total of all your liabilities (credit-card debt, auto loans, student loans, and so on). *Note:* Because most people don't view their home as a retirement asset, we've left your home's value and mortgage out of your net worth calculations. (Personal property — furniture, cars, and so on — doesn't count as a financial asset.) However, you may include your home if you want, especially if you're willing to tap your home's equity to accomplish goals such as retiring.

Now, don't jump to conclusions based on the size of the resulting number. If you're young and still breaking into your working years, your net worth is bound to be relatively low — perhaps even negative. Relax. Sure, you have work to do, but you have plenty of time ahead of you.

Ideally, as you approach the age of 40, your net worth should be greater than a year's worth of gross income; if your net worth equals more than a few years of income, you're well on the road toward meeting larger financial goals, such as retirement.

Of course, the key to increasing your net worth is making sure that more money comes in than goes out. To achieve typical financial goals such as retirement, you need to save about 10 percent of your gross (pretax) income. If you have big dreams or you're behind in the game, you may need to save 15 percent or more.

If you know you're already saving enough, or if you know it won't be that hard to start saving enough, then don't bother tracking your spending. On the other hand, if you have no idea how you'll start saving that much, you need to determine where you're spending your money. (See the later section "Shrink your spending" for insight on how to start saving.)

Telling good debt from bad debt

After you calculate your net worth, categorize your liabilities as either good debt or bad debt:

- ✔ *Good debt* refers to money borrowed for a long-term investment that appreciates over time, such as a home, an education, or a small business.
- ✔ *Bad debt* (also called *consumer debt*) is money borrowed for a consumer purchase, such as a car, a designer suit, or a vacation to Cancun.

Why is bad debt bad? Because it's costly to carry, and if you carry too much, it becomes like a financial cancer. If the outstanding balance of all your credit cards and auto loans divided by your annual gross income exceeds 25 percent of your income, you've entered a danger zone, where your debt can start to snowball out of control.

Don't even consider starting a small business until you've paid off all your consumer debt. Not only are the interest rates on consumer debt relatively high, but the things you buy with consumer debt also lose their value over time. A financially healthy amount of bad debt — like a healthy amount of cigarette smoking — is none.

Reducing debt

If you have outstanding consumer debt, pay it off sooner rather than later. If you must tap into savings to pay down your consumer debts, then do it. Many people resist digging into savings, feeling as if they're losing hard-earned money. Remember that your net worth — the difference between your assets and liabilities — determines the growth of your money. Paying off an outstanding credit-card balance with an interest rate of 14 percent is like finding an investment with a guaranteed return of 14 percent — tax-free. (*Note:* We recognize that some small-business owners finance their small businesses via credit cards, and in some cases, because this debt would be investment debt and investment debt is "good debt," we feel this situation may be acceptable. We discuss business financing options in Chapter 5.)

If you don't have any available savings with which to pay off your high-interest-rate debts, you'll have to climb out of debt one month at a time. The fact that you're in hock and without savings is a sign that you've been living beyond your means. Devote 10 to 15 percent of your income toward paying down your consumer loans. If you have no idea where you'll get this money, detail your spending by expense category, such as rent, eating out, clothing, and so on. You'll probably find that your spending doesn't reflect what's important to you, and you'll see fat to trim. (This process is similar to budgeting and expense management in business; not being able to manage your personal expenses may be a telltale sign of your inability to manage a business.)

While paying down your debt, always look for ways to lower your interest rate. Apply for low-interest-rate cards to which you can transfer balances from your highest-interest-rate cards. Haggling with your current credit-card company for a lower interest rate sometimes works. Also, think about borrowing against the equity in your home, against your employer-sponsored retirement account, or from family — all options that should lower your interest rate significantly.

If you're having a hard time kicking the credit-card habit, get out your scissors and cut up your cards. You can still enjoy the convenience of purchasing with plastic by using a Visa or MasterCard debit card, which is linked directly to your checking account. The major benefit of using a debit card rather than a credit card is that you can't spend beyond your means. Merchants who take Visa or MasterCard credit cards also accept these companies' debit cards.

Buying insurance

Before you address your longer-term financial goals, you need to make sure that you're properly covered by insurance. Without proper insurance coverage, an illness or an accident could quickly turn into a devastating financial storm.

Buy long-term disability insurance if you lack it. This most-overlooked form of insurance protects against a disability that curtails your greatest income-generating asset: your ability to earn money. If anyone depends on your employment income, buy term life insurance, which, in the event of your death, leaves money to those financially dependent on you. Make sure that your health insurance policy is a comprehensive one. Ideally, your lifetime benefits should be unlimited; if the policy has a maximum, it should be at least a few million dollars. (We provide more details on these important coverages later in this chapter in the section "Assessing and Replacing Benefits.")

Also check your auto and home policies' liability coverage, which protects you in the event of a lawsuit; you should have at least enough to cover twice your assets.

For all your insurance policies, take the highest deductible you can afford to pay out of pocket should you have a claim. Of course, if you have a claim, you'll have to pay more of the initial expense out of your own pocket, but you'll save significantly on premiums. Buy insurance to cover the potentially catastrophic losses, not the small stuff.

Planning for the long term

In coauthor Eric's experience as a financial counselor, he has seen many examples prove that earning a high income doesn't guarantee a high rate of savings. The best savers he knows tend to be goal oriented; in other words, they earmark their savings for specific purposes.

If you know that you're an undisciplined saver, you may consider adopting the technique of designating certain savings or investment accounts toward specific goals. After all, if you're feeling tempted to buy a luxury car, it's a lot harder to take money out of an account earmarked for Timmy's college education than from a general savings account.

Perhaps because it's the farthest away, retirement is the most difficult long-term goal to bring into focus. Retirement is also much tougher to plan for than most goals because of all the difficult-to-make assumptions — inflation, life expectancy, Social Security benefits, taxes, rate of return, and so on — that go into the calculations.

Use a good retirement planning workbook or program. Check out the resources online from T. Rowe Price (www.troweprice.com) or Vanguard (www.vanguard.com). These retirement planners can help you transform a fuzzy dream into a concrete action plan, forcing you to get specific about retirement issues you may not have thought about and opening your eyes to the power of compounding interest and the importance of saving now.

Goal-specific saving is challenging for most people given their many competing goals. Even a respectable 10 to 15 percent of your income may not be enough to accomplish such goals as saving for retirement, accumulating a down payment for a home, saving for children's college expenses, and tucking away some money for starting a small business.

So you have to make some tough choices and prioritize your goals. Only you know what's important to you, which means that you're the most qualified person to make these decisions. But we want to stress the importance of contributing to retirement accounts, whether you use a 401(k), SEP-IRA, Keogh, or IRA. Not only do retirement accounts shelter your investment earnings from taxation, but contributions to these accounts are also generally tax deductible.

As for the money you're socking away, be sure to invest it wisely. Doing so isn't as difficult as most financial advisors and investment publications make it out to be. (Some make it sound complicated in order to gain your confidence, business, and fees.)

What's your reward for whipping your finances into shape and staying the course? Although it's true that money can't buy happiness, managing your personal finances efficiently can open up your future life options, such as switching into a lower-paying but more fulfilling career, starting your own business, or perhaps working part-time at a home-based business when your kids are young so that you can be an involved parent. Work at achieving financial success and then be sure to make the most of it.

Shrink your spending

Do all you can to reduce your expenses and lifestyle to a level that fits with the entrepreneurial life you want to lead. Now is the time to make your budget lean and entrepreneurially friendly.

Determine what you spend each month on rent, mortgage, groceries, eating out, insurance, and so on. Your checkbook register, your credit-card statement, and your memory of cash purchases should help you piece together what you spend on various things in a typical month. The best way to track your expenses is to pay either by credit card, debit card, or check. Cash doesn't provide you a paper trail to reconcile your expenses at the end of the month.

Beyond the bare essentials of food, shelter, health care, and clothing, most of what you spend money on is discretionary — in other words, luxuries. Even the dollars you spend on the so-called necessities, such as food and shelter, are usually only part necessity, with the balance being luxury.

If you refuse to question your current spending or if you view all your current spending as necessary, you'll probably have no option but to continue your career as an employee. You'll never be able to pursue your dream! Overspending won't make you happy; you'll be miserable over the years if your excess spending makes you feel chained to a job you don't like. Life is too short to work at a full-time job that doesn't make you happy.

Build up your cash reserves

Shrinking your spending is a means to an end — that end being the ability to save for a rainy day. In the embryonic years of your business, you're going to see your fair share of rainy days; you may even experience years predominated by rain.

Your wherewithal to stick with an entrepreneurial endeavor depends, in part, on your current war chest of cash. At a minimum, you should have three to six months of living expenses invested in an accessible account, such as a money market fund with low operating expenses. If you have consumer debt, after you finish paying off your debt, your top financial priority should be building this account. The bigger the war chest, the better; if you can accumulate a year's worth of living expenses, great!

Stabilize income with part-time work

One way to pursue your entrepreneurial dreams — and not starve while doing so — is to continue working part-time in a regular job at the same time you're working part-time in your own business. If you have a job that allows you to work part-time, seize the opportunity. Some employers even allow you to maintain your benefits.

When coauthor Eric was planning to start his financial counseling business, he was able to cut back his full-time job to half-time for four months, using his time away from his regular job to start his financial counseling business. Similarly, in the first year of coauthor Jim's initial entrepreneurial venture, he continued his full-time job working for a wood-products business.

In addition to the monetary security you get from a regular job, splitting your time allows you to adjust gradually to a completely new way of making a living. Some people have a difficult time if they quit their job cold turkey and start working full-time as an entrepreneur.

If you're not interested in keeping your current job, you can completely leave that job and line up a different form of work that will provide a decent income for at least some of your weekly work hours. Consulting for your former employer is a time-tested first "entrepreneurial" option with low risk — just one of many reasons why you should endeavor to leave your current job without burning bridges in the process.

Another option to working part-time is to depend on your spouse's income while you work on beefing up your own. Obviously, this option involves sacrifice from the love of your life, so be sure to talk things through with your partner to minimize misunderstandings and resentments. Perhaps someday you'll be in a position to return the favor — that's what Eric did. His wife, Judy, was working in education when Eric started an entrepreneurial venture after business school. They lived a Spartan lifestyle on her income. Several years later, when Eric's business was on solid footing, Judy left her job to start her own business.

Assessing and Replacing Benefits

For some aspiring entrepreneurs, the thought of losing their employee benefits is even scarier than cutting off their paychecks. Insurance coverages in particular — especially health insurance — seem daunting to replicate outside of the friendly umbrella of a corporation or nonprofit institution.

Some people are so intimidated by the thought of giving up their benefits that they jettison their dreams of becoming small-business owners. One working father said to coauthor Eric, "I can't go into business for myself because health insurance is too costly." That situation is unfortunate: Neither health insurance nor any other benefit should stand in the way of your small-business dreams.

You may be surprised at how quickly and inexpensively you can replicate your employer's benefits in your own business. And, as you can see in this section and in even more detail in Chapter 17, as a small-business owner, you may have access to some valuable benefits that your employer doesn't or can't offer you. So if you're dreaming of starting your own business, don't view your employer's benefits package as a ball and chain tying you to your current job.

Retirement savings plans and pensions

If your employer offers retirement savings programs, such as a 401(k) plan or a pension plan, don't despair about not having these benefits in the future if you should start your own business. Of course, what you've already earned and accumulated (or *vested*) as an employee is yours.

Some of the best benefits of self-employment are the available retirement savings plans — SEP-IRAs (Simplified Employee Pension Individual Retirement Accounts) and Keoghs. SEP-IRAs and Keoghs allow you to shelter far more money than most corporate retirement plans do. With SEP-IRA and Keogh plans, you can plow away up to 20 percent of your net income on a tax-deductible basis.

Retirement plans are a terrific way for you, as a business owner, and your employees to tax-shelter a healthy portion of earnings. Especially if you don't have employees, making regular contributions to one of these plans is usually a no-brainer. If you do have employees, the decision is a bit more complicated but still often a great idea. We explain all these plans in Chapter 17.

Health insurance

If you're in good health and you've decided to start your own business, start investigating what will happen to your health insurance coverage when you leave your job. The first option to explore is whether you can convert your existing coverage through your employer's group plan into individual coverage. If you can, great; just don't act on this option until you've explored other health plans, which may offer similar benefits at a lower cost. Also get proposals for individual coverage from major health plans in your area. Be sure to select a high deductible, if available, to keep costs down.

Health savings accounts (HSAs) have become far more attractive and increasingly available. Like the best retirement accounts, HSAs offer an upfront tax deduction on contributions as well as tax-free compounding of investment earnings over time. HSAs also offer tax-free withdrawals so long as the money is used for eligible expenses. So, unlike any retirement account, HSAs are so-called triple-tax-free accounts. For all the details on these terrific tax-saving vehicles for small-business owners and their employees, turn to Chapter 17.

Disability insurance

Well in advance of leaving your job, be sure that you secure long-term disability insurance. *Long-term disability insurance* protects your income in the event of a disability. If you're like most people, your greatest financial asset is your ability to earn employment income. If you suffer a disability and are unable to work, how will you and your family manage financially? Most people, of course, couldn't come close to maintaining their current lifestyle if their employment income disappeared.

Don't wait until you leave your job to shop for disability coverage. After you quit your job and no longer have steady employment income, you won't be able to qualify for a long-term disability policy. Most insurers will then want to see at least six months of self-employment income before they're willing to write a policy for you. The risk is that, if you become disabled during this time, you'll be completely without insurance.

Several proven sources for securing long-term disability insurance include

- ✔ **Professional associations:** Thanks to the purchasing power of the group, associations that you may be a member of — or could become a member of — often offer less costly disability coverage than what you could buy on your own.
- ✔ **Insurance agents:** Consider shopping for an individual disability policy through agents who specialize in such coverage.

Life insurance

If you have life-insurance coverage through your employer, odds are you can replicate it on your own. If you have dependents (children, a spouse, or others) who rely on your income, you need life insurance.

The amount of life insurance you carry depends on how much annual income you're trying to protect and over how many years. For example, to replace your income over the next decade, multiply your annual after-tax income by 8.5. So if you annually make $30,000 after taxes, you should buy about $250,000 of life insurance. You only need to replace your after-tax income because the death benefits on a life-insurance policy are free of income tax.

Term life insurance, which is pure life-insurance protection, offers the best way to buy needed coverage at the lowest cost. Other policies, such as universal, whole, and variable life, which are collectively referred to as *cash-value policies,* combine life-insurance coverage with an investment account. For an equivalent amount of coverage, a cash-value policy typically costs about eight times what a term policy costs. Furthermore, in the early years of a cash-value policy, the bulk of that cost difference builds little in the way of cash value and instead goes mostly to pay insurance agent commissions and administrative costs.

In the long run, you would do best to separate your life insurance from your investments. Buy term insurance and invest your savings through your employer's retirement savings plan. Contributions to 401(k) plans and the like typically offer an upfront tax deduction at the federal and state levels. Money put into a cash-value life-insurance plan offers no such deduction.

The good news is that if you need life insurance, you can probably purchase an individual life-insurance policy at a lower cost than you could purchase such coverage through your employer.

Insurance agency quotation services send you a handful of relatively user-friendly proposals from the highest-rated, lowest-cost companies available. Like other agencies, the services receive a commission if you buy a policy from them, which you're under no obligation to do. They'll ask you for your date of birth, whether you smoke, and how much coverage you'd like. Reputable firms in this line of work include SelectQuote (`www.select quote.com`) and Term4Sale (`www.term4sale.com`).

Dental, vision, and other insurance

You may have other insurance programs besides the traditional health, life, and disability. Some employers offer insurance plans for dental and vision care, and occasionally some other unusual benefits, such as prepaid legal plans.

As an aspiring or new entrepreneur, you can't afford to waste money. Insurance programs that cover small potential out-of-pocket losses aren't worth purchasing. Don't waste your money buying such policies. Remember that insurance companies are in business to make money. On average, insurers pay out no more than about 60 cents in claims per dollar paid to them in policyholder premiums. The other 40-plus percent goes to administration and profits.

Social Security taxes

Another "benefit" of working for an employer is that the employer pays for half (7.65 percent of your income) of your Social Security and Medicare taxes. Don't despair of the extra cost of having to pay both halves of this tax when operating your own business. Although you do have to pay the entire tax (15.3 percent of your income up to a certain threshold amount) when you're self-employed, the IRS allows you to take half of this amount as a tax deduction on your Form 1040. The value of your deduction depends on your marginal tax rate; if you're in, say, the 28 percent federal income tax bracket, then the actual cost of your self-employment tax is 5.51 percent: $7.65 - (7.65 \times 0.28) = 5.51$. Thus, the tax isn't as painful as you think. (State tax deductions decrease the effective costs of self-employment taxes even further.)

When pricing your products or services, you can build the cost of this tax, as well as other benefits you'll pay for out of pocket, into your calculations. (After all, this is what your current employer does.) We explain pricing strategies in Chapter 11.

Time off

All work and no play make Mary and John dull and probably overstressed entrepreneurs. When you work for a company, we trust that it provides you with certain holidays and at least a couple of weeks of vacation each year. You may never have considered that your paycheck covers the cost of these normal workdays when you're allowed time off.

Again, when you price your products and services, you need to factor in that, given holidays and two to three weeks of annual vacation, you probably won't be working about 5 weeks out of the 52 weeks in a year. Although some new entrepreneurs don't take much vacation time or many holidays off, we certainly don't want you to plan for that; if you do, you'll burn yourself out and not be much fun to be around!

Managing Your Personal Finances Post-Launch

It continues to amaze us: We see savvy small-business owners who are successful when it comes to managing their companies. However, when you glance at their personal finances, they may look like personal financial misfits — underinsured, overextended on credit, undiversified in investments, behind on retirement planning, and so on.

Dismissing this trait as a mere foible, in much the same way that you may chuckle at a genius with a messy desk, is easy to do. However, such sloppiness with personal financial management is an unfortunate tendency because it downplays the seriousness of the problem: Poorly managed personal finances can destroy a business, no matter how successful and well run it is. Also, we've noticed that poor personal financial management often leads to more of the same on a business level. Old habits aren't easy to change.

This chapter focuses on getting your finances in order before you start your business. However, keeping your personal finances on track (living within your means, planning how much you need to save for various goals, selecting sound investments, and maintaining catastrophic and cost-effective insurance coverage) post-launch is vital to your financial future as well as to the viability of your business. If you don't know how to do these things well, pick up a copy of the latest edition of Eric's book *Personal Finance For Dummies* (Wiley).

As a small-business owner, you need to be especially careful to stay on top of your required tax payments for both yourself and your employees. (We cover small-business tax issues in Chapter 19.) You also need to protect your personal finances from business-related lawsuits — an important topic that we cover in Chapters 5 and 18.

Chapter 3

Finding Your Niche

*A*lthough your business niche and the idea behind your business are important, neither makes the primary difference when it comes to the survival of your business. Rather, the primary difference maker is *you!* The niche and the idea are only small parts of the puzzle that is success. In this chapter, we discuss a few of the most important puzzle pieces, including the cornerstone piece (that being you), and we explain why you need to put them all together to ensure your business's success.

Why You Don't Need a New Idea to Be Successful

Most small-business owners dive into their niches because they love the product or service they provide. The history of small business is filled with tales of founders who cared so deeply about their product or service that they subsequently decided to make it their life's work so that they could enjoy getting up in the morning again.

Examples of businesses that have grown and prospered as a result of an entrepreneur's passion for a particular activity include these and many others:

✔ Jim Gentes was a passionate biker who had ideas about bike helmets that led him to found Giro.

✔ L.L. Bean developed a line of outdoor gear that he couldn't find elsewhere.

✔ John Bogle founded the Vanguard Group of mutual funds to deliver low-cost funds that served investors' best interests.

Of course, many small-business owners (the vast majority, in fact) don't break new ground. Plenty of tax preparers, dry cleaners, and restaurant owners happily make a comfortable living by doing what many others before them have already done.

Unfortunately, having a groundbreaking idea, extensive product knowledge, or unbridled enthusiasm has little real influence on your long-term business success. Even if you make the best chocolate chip cookies this side of Mrs. Fields, your business could still crash and burn. Maybe you don't sell enough cookies, or you have a hard time accounting for the ones you do sell. Maybe you sell ocean tankers filled with cookies but your prices are too low to make a profit, or your customers won't pay their bills.

Having a good product and knowing the product well are only the beginning of building a successful business; you must also perform a long list of sometimes arduous day-to-day chores to be a successful small-business owner. Those chores may include the following:

- ✔ Find good customers and convince them to buy (see Chapter 13).

- ✔ Deal with difficult, hard-to-please customers.

- ✔ Provide cost-effective customer service that retains customer loyalty (see Chapter 13).

- ✔ Understand financial statements, including balance sheets, profit and loss statements, and cash flow statements (see Chapter 14).

- ✔ Grant credit to customers and know how (and to whom) to grant it.

- ✔ Collect *receivables* (the money you're owed).

- ✔ Juggle and prioritize the payment of *payables* (the money you owe to others).

- ✔ Understand the mystifying concept of cash flow and then figure out how to manage it (see Chapter 14).

- ✔ Compute inventory turn, days-in-receivables, current ratios, and return on sales (we cover all these items in Chapter 14).

- ✔ Use such management tools as organization charts, job descriptions, and performance reviews (see Chapter 16).

- ✔ Purchase the right computer and software and then figure out how to use it (see Chapter 12).

- ✔ Collect and disburse sales tax, income tax, and Federal Insurance Contributions Act (FICA) tax, and perform all those other services the government requires of small businesses (we explain government requirements in Chapter 18 and taxes in Chapter 19).

- ✔ Protect yourself from lawsuits — both from your employees and your customers — including sexual harassment suits and product liability suits.

> ✔ Avoid (and deal with when you can't) such headaches as Occupational Safety and Health Administration (OSHA), workers' compensation, and unemployment problems.
>
> ✔ Deal with drug- and alcohol-related problems, pacify smokers and nonsmokers, and recognize and deal with malingerers, embezzlers, and shoplifters.
>
> ✔ Know how and when to use small claims court.
>
> ✔ Know how to hire, fire, train, motivate, and hold employees accountable; control expenses; manage crises; balance cultures; deal with bankers; budget; forecast — the list goes on and on.

Of course, not all businesses have to deal with all the items in the preceding list. If your business doesn't have inventory, for example, you won't have to deal with the myriad issues relating to it.

Our point here is that the niche or idea won't ultimately make or break your business; the day-to-day running of the business itself is what ultimately determines success — or failure. Or stated another way, you show us a crackerjack business person, and we'll show you someone who can get rich in the cookie business whether or not he or she personally has the foggiest idea about how to bake the darned things.

Inventing Something New

Benjamin Franklin, Thomas Edison, Henry Ford, Wilbur and Orville Wright — American history is filled with folks who created something new that changed an industry or even the average person's way of life. Most people know the "famous" inventors, but many unknown folks have invented things that later became business successes, too.

Coauthor Jim had a marine biologist friend who invented a device to count and sort fish eggs. The inventor added a small manufacturing facility to the back of his garage and sold or leased his device to fish and conservation departments all over the world. For ten years, he, his wife, and his oldest son manufactured fish egg sorters and built a strong business with real value before selling it to a younger buyer interested in growing the business.

In this section, we highlight some helpful places to turn to (and harmful ones to run from) if you aspire to be an inventor.

Say yes to useful invention resources

In 1999, Congress signed into law the American Inventor's Protection Act to better protect American entrepreneurs who create something that could be patented or otherwise protected, including new products, services, or processes.

One reason Congress passed the Act was to protect would-be inventors from hyped invention promotion firms, which take your money and provide you little (if anything) in return (see the next section for details).

Fortunately, would-be inventors can find several truly helpful resources out there. The following resources are among the best and most interesting:

- ✔ **Nolo Press books on patents and inventions:** Nolo Press, publisher of hundreds of legal books and software programs, has numerous helpful books on patents and inventions. Go to www.nolo.com for details.

- ✔ **Peer networking groups:** Most large communities have peer networking groups of inventors. Check with your local Chamber of Commerce or Economic Development Department.

- ✔ **United Inventors Association (UIA):** This nonprofit was founded by Roberta Toole in 1990. Its website (www.uiausa.org) is a treasure trove of resources for inventors worldwide. Membership is required to access most of their resources and costs $99 a year.

- ✔ **U.S. Patent and Trademark Office (USPTO):** For a government operation, the USPTO website (www.uspto.gov) has a lot to offer would-be inventors. Click the Inventors tab to find an array of resources. One of the most useful is the Scam Prevention section (located on the left-hand side of the page), which provides a public forum for the publication of complaints concerning invention promoters/promotion firms (which we discuss in the next section); the USPTO also publishes responses to the complaints from the invention promoters/promotion firms.

Run away from invention promotion firms

Hundreds of invention promotion firms siphon hundreds of millions of dollars from naive wannabe entrepreneurs each year. The good news is that government regulators are finally taking some action. To find out more about these scam firms, review the following helpful summary by the Federal Trade Commission (FTC) on invention promotion firms:

". . . many inventors pay thousands of dollars to firms that promise to evaluate, develop, patent, and market inventions. Unfortunately, many of these firms do little or nothing for their fee.

The Federal Trade Commission (FTC) has found that many invention promotion firms claim — falsely — that they can turn almost any idea into cash. But, the agency says, smart inventors can learn to spot the sweet-sounding promises of a fraudulent promotion firm. Here's how to follow up if you hear the following lines:

We think your idea has great market potential. *Few ideas — however good — become commercially successful. If a company fails to disclose that investing in your idea is a high-risk venture, and that most ideas never make any money, beware.*

Our company has licensed a lot of invention ideas successfully. *If a company tells you it has a good track record, ask for a list of its successful clients. Confirm that these clients have had commercial success. If the company refuses to give you a list of their successful clients, it probably means they don't have any.*

You need to hurry and patent your idea before someone else does. *Be wary of high-pressure sales tactics. Although some patents are valuable, simply patenting your idea does NOT mean you will ever make any money from it.*

Congratulations! We've done a patent search on your idea, and we have some great news. There's nothing like it out there. *Many invention promotion firms claim to perform patent searches on ideas. Patent searches by fraudulent invention promotion firms usually are incomplete, conducted in the wrong category, or unaccompanied by a legal opinion on the results of the search from a patent attorney. Because unscrupulous firms promote virtually any idea or invention without regard to its patentability, they may market an idea for which someone already has a valid, unexpired patent. In that case, you may be the subject of a patent infringement lawsuit — even if the promotional efforts on your invention are successful.*

Our research department, engineers, and patent attorneys have evaluated your idea. We definitely want to move forward. *This is a standard sales pitch. Many questionable firms do not perform any evaluation at all. In fact, many don't have the "professional" staff they claim.*

Our company has evaluated your idea and now wants to prepare a more in-depth research report. It'll be several hundred dollars. *If the company's initial evaluation is 'positive,' ask why the company isn't willing to cover the cost of researching your idea further.*

Our company makes most of its money from the royalties it gets from licensing its clients' ideas. Of course, we need some money from you before we get started. *If a firm tells you this but asks you to pay a large fee upfront — or to agree to make credit payments — ask why they're not willing to help you on a contingency basis. Unscrupulous firms make almost all their money from advance fees.*

The American Inventors Protection Act of 1999 gives you certain rights when dealing with invention promoters. Before an invention promoter can enter into a contract with you, it must disclose the following information about its business practices during the past five years:

- ✔ *How many inventions it has evaluated*
- ✔ *How many of those inventions got positive or negative evaluations*

> *✔ Its total number of customers*
>
> *✔ How many of those customers received a net profit from the promoter's services*
>
> *✔ How many of those customers have licensed their inventions due to the promoter's services*

This information can help you determine how selective the promoter has been in deciding which inventions it promotes and the degree of success he has enjoyed. Invention promoters also must give you the names and addresses of all invention promotion companies they have been affiliated with over the past 10 years. Use this information to determine whether the company you're considering doing business with has been subject to complaints or legal action. Call the U.S. Patent and Trademark Office (USPTO) at 1-866-767-3848 and the Better Business Bureau, the consumer protection agency, and the Attorney General in your state or city and in the state or city where the company is headquartered.

If a promoter causes you financial injury by failing to make the required disclosures, by making any false or fraudulent statements or representations, or by omitting any fact, you have the right to sue the promoter and recover the amount of your injury plus costs and attorneys' fees."

Choosing Your Business

Finding the right business to buy or start can be a bit stressful, but don't worry. We offer plenty of help in the following sections. We assist you in matching your skills, interests, and job history with a suitable business, and we help you select the niche that works best for you, given who you are, what you like to do, and what you're capable of doing.

Consider your category

Before you decide which business venture would be best for you, you need to understand the four major business categories that you can consider: retailing, service, manufacturing, and wholesaling. Here are some important characteristics you need to know about these four categories:

- ✔ **Retailing:** Retailing is the general category that most people are familiar with because the typical American deals with at least one retailer every day. Since most people are familiar with the retail business, the learning curve is usually much easier in retailing than in the other three categories (although this benefit is true for your retailing competitors as well). Also, because most retail businesses deal primarily with cash or near-cash equivalents (credit cards), funding requirements for accounts receivable are relatively low compared with some of the other business categories, which means, in turn, that the capital requirements for entry can be comparatively low, depending on how much inventory is required. (See Chapter 5 to determine your initial cash needs.)

E-commerce (retailing over the Internet) is changing the parameters of the retailing category. The barrier to entry in retail-oriented entrepreneurial endeavors is becoming smaller as some successful retailing entrepreneurs choose web pages over storefronts. However, success online isn't as easy or as lucrative as some would have you believe.

✔ **Service:** The service industry is the fastest growing of the four categories, in part due to the low cost of entry (that is, you typically need no significant inventory outlays and minimal equipment). Additionally, if you're among the increasing number of service providers who choose to work out of their homes, occupancy expenses are relatively low and tax advantages are a potential perk.

✔ **Manufacturing:** Save up your hard-earned cash if you're thinking of becoming a manufacturer; this category is a veritable cash-guzzling machine. Inventory, accounts receivable, equipment, physical plant, employees — you name the cash-draining asset, and most manufacturers have gotta have it.

Although manufacturing is typically the most expensive of the four categories in terms of entry-level capital requirements, it offers great potential for rewards. Look at the high-tech industry for examples of wealth being created (not just for the founders but for key employees as well) in short periods of time; companies such as Microsoft, Intel, and Apple were start-up manufacturers not that long ago.

✔ **Wholesaling:** The middleman in capitalism's distribution channel, *wholesalers* act as intermediaries between manufacturers and retailers or consumers. The wholesaler's role is to buy large quantities of products at discounted prices (discounted from retail prices that is) from manufacturers, break them down into smaller quantities, and sell them at a markup to retailers or consumers. Like manufacturers, wholesalers require significant cash outlays for inventory, receivables, physical plant, and employees; thus, the start-up capital requirements for wholesalers are correspondingly high.

Take advantage of accidental opportunities

Many small-business owners are "accidental" entrepreneurs — that is, they stumble on a good business to start or buy. Maybe a favorite retail store suddenly comes up for sale (this is exactly what jump-started coauthor Jim's entrepreneurial career), or a friend informs them of a can't-miss opportunity, or a customer of the business they're working for now invites them to do some freelance consulting — an invitation that turns into a business opportunity. In these cases, the lucky entrepreneur doesn't set out to own a business. Instead, he or she stumbles on the right opportunity. As with so many other directions people take in life, the time and the place just happen to be right.

When considering your accidental opportunity, if you don't enjoy what you're about to do, your chances for success will decrease. Make sure that your accidental opportunity is in a niche that you like.

Inventory your skills, interests, and job history

Most people aren't lucky or fortunate enough to stumble upon the right business. And the kinds of people who discover the right business are often those who are willing to go to a lot of trouble to find good opportunities.

If the perfect business opportunity doesn't just fall into your lap (and, actually, even if it does), you need to do some introspection to determine what type of business is right for you. The following questions can help you take an inventory of your business expertise and interests. (You can get a piece of paper and treat these questions like a quiz if you want to.) The answers you get will help you select the best possible business opportunity for you.

- ✔ **What top-three business skills have you displayed over your business career?** Examples include sales, accounting, marketing, administration, writing, communications, quantitative analysis, hiring, training, employee motivation, product development, customer service, focus, delegation, accountability, attention to detail, and so on.

- ✔ **In which business skills are you the weakest?** Refer to the examples in the preceding bullet for ideas.

- ✔ **Over your working history (including part-time and full-time jobs), what three jobs have you enjoyed the most and why?** After listing three jobs, consider (and list) the reasons why you liked those particular jobs.

- ✔ **During your working history, what three jobs have you enjoyed the least and why?** Similar to the preceding question, consider and then list the reasons why you disliked those particular jobs.

- ✔ **What are your top-three overall personal skills?** Examples include leadership, communication, intelligence, creativity, vision, cheerleading, invention and/or innovation, listening, problem solving, counseling, and so on.

✔ **If this were a perfect world and you could select the industry in which you'd like to spend the rest of your life, what would be your top-three choices?** Examples include sports, music, movies, art, finance, education, telecommunications, electronics, computers, medicine, architecture, agriculture, transportation, insurance, real estate, financial services, food and beverage services, apparel design and manufacture, furniture and home products, outdoor products, printing, photography, chemistry, plastics, and so on.

✔ **What three favorite hobbies or special interests of yours might be conducive to creating a business?** Many people turn a hobby or special interest (such as photography, golf, or coin collecting) into a business.

✔ **Given what you know about the retailing, service, manufacturing, and wholesale career choices, rank these four in order of desirability.** Refer to the earlier section "Consider your category" for details on each of these categories.

When you can't think of an answer to one or more of these questions, ask your spouse or a couple of good friends for advice. Oftentimes, they know you best.

Don't expect to answer these questions and determine that — eureka! — you should immediately open a retail clothing store, start a financial consulting business, or import rare ostrich eggs. Instead, use these questions to help you inventory your skills, interests, and job history. The results should help stimulate the thought processes that will assist you in developing a list of businesses that may work for you.

If, for example, your strengths (and interests) are in sales, you may want to consider a business where sales is the primary function of the business (manufacturer's representative, for instance). If you indicate that you have weaknesses in such areas as attention to detail, delegation, and administration, you may want to consider operating a business solo as opposed to one that requires employees. If you determine that over your job history, you didn't like those jobs where you dealt directly with customers, the retail business would probably not work for you.

These questions are intended to help you take an introspective look at yourself and lead you to where you would logically fit in the broad spectrum of business opportunities. That's why we say you'll find no quick answers here, but rather an opportunity to jump-start the narrowing-down process. Come back to these questions several times over a period of weeks; few people arrive at a solution the first time through.

"How hard can it be to run a card shop?"

Our hero (we'll call him Aaron) decides that it's time to make a lifestyle change. He and his family relocate to Bend, Oregon, where, he figures, the world rotates at half the speed it does in the San Francisco Bay Area.

Aaron, a marketing consultant for a high-powered firm, decides to become a Hallmark franchisee, so he and his wife purchase an existing store in a Bend mall. Because Aaron had been consulting with Hallmark for several years on how to resolve its marketing issues, he figures he knows the industry inside and out.

"Hey," he tells his friends in a statement he will regret for years, "how hard can it be to run a card shop?"

Aaron found out exactly how hard it can be to run a card shop. Suddenly, instead of having to know everything there is to know about Fortune 500–style marketing, he had to know a smattering of everything there is to know about accounting and bookkeeping procedures; hiring, training, motivating, and firing employees; payroll; government regulations; cash flow; budgeting; inventory; dealing with bankers, lawyers, and accountants; and . . . well, you get the point.

"When I was consulting and would work with Hallmark management in problems relating to its franchisees," he says today, "my marketing firm's management and I would go nuts. We'd say things like 'Those little guys just don't get it,' and we'd want to tear out our hair in frustration."

"Well, I'm one of those 'little guys' today, and it's me who's tearing out what's left of my hair in frustration. We small-business owners see the world through a different set of sunglasses than the corporate consultants."

Would Aaron do it all over again?

"Well, yes. The change in scenery has been worth it. But I can tell you this much," he says, returning an out-of-place Charlie Brown birthday card to its rightful slot. "There are two kinds of businesses in this world. The first is where you have to be a jack of only one trade. The second is where you have to be a jack of all trades, where you're the person who's responsible for ensuring that everything else is taken care of. I went from the first to the second, and now I know that the two aren't even in the same universe."

Narrow your choices

When considering a business opportunity, you need to answer the following questions to assure yourself that the business you're considering is the right one for you:

✔ **Is it a business that suits your personality?**

- Consider a retail business if you like dealing directly with people, don't mind keeping regular hours, and can handle being tied to one spot for long periods of time. The converse, of course, also applies. If you don't like dealing directly with people, keeping regular hours, or being tied to one spot for long periods of time, don't consider the retail business.

- Consider the service business if you like dealing with people, solving problems, and working in spurts and flurries.

- Consider a wholesaling business if you're a detail-oriented person, if you enjoy supervising employees, and if you don't mind risking the significant amount of capital that carrying and distributing inventory requires.

- Consider the manufacturing business if you're a quality-conscious and detail-oriented person who enjoys searching for solutions to such engineering-oriented issues as process and flow and quality control. You should also enjoy supervising employees.

Within each of the four major business categories, you can get more specific and narrow down your choices to specific industries. For example:

- Consider the financial services or accounting/tax-preparation business if you like working with numbers.

- Consider the restaurant or entertainment business if you don't mind working unusual hours.

- Consider a banking, telephone sales, or consulting business if you don't mind spending long periods of time sitting at a desk.

✔ **Is it a business or product in which you have experience?** Experience is the world's best teacher. If you don't have it, your competitors who do have it are bound to have a sizable competitive edge over you. Sixty percent of successful business owners have gravitated to products or services in industries with which they were previously familiar.

✔ **Is it a business you can afford?** A service business is usually the least expensive of the four business categories to start, followed by retailing, wholesaling, and, finally, manufacturing. For more information on how to compute the cash requirements of your business, see Chapter 5. (Yes, you should take into consideration the amount of money you can borrow, or find investors for, when answering this question.)

✔ **Is it a business with too much risk?** Can you live with the risk inherent in this business? Generally, the bigger the capital requirement, the larger the risk. Are you sure you're prepared to live with the risk of starting a manufacturing company? If not, consider becoming a service provider instead — it's more suited to the average pocketbook. (If you have an idea for a new widget but don't have the resources to manufacture it, you can always outsource the manufacturing of it and then sell, service, and maintain it yourself.)

✔ **Is it a business in which you have a competitive advantage?** Can you make, service, or sell your product better? If not, you need to ask yourself what will motivate your customers to work with you. (If your answer is price, you're in trouble already, unless you've figured out a clear and high-quality way to create and deliver a product or service cheaper and better than the industry leaders.)

✔ **Is it a business in which you can become a specialist?** There's power in being a specialist, and there's danger in being a generalist. Today's movers and shakers have learned a valuable lesson from past experience: Focus on doing those things you can do better than anyone else. (Consider all those takeovers of a few years ago, with steel companies buying insurance companies and filmmakers buying bookstores. Many of those odd companions are companions no more. Many were spun off to other businesses more knowledgeable about that industry and better able to provide a quality product at a competitive price.)

Go in search of fast growth

Every year *Inc.* magazine publishes its list of "The 500 Fastest Growing Companies in America" (*Inc.* also publishes the top 5,000; the top 500 are just the top companies from that list). This list includes tomorrow's potential goliaths of the business world. Such companies as Microsoft, Timberland, Oracle, and Cablevision have graced and then graduated from the list since its inception.

As you take a look at the most recent *Inc.* list, pay attention to the niches that are currently enjoying the fastest growth. A number of past *Inc.* 500 fastest-growing companies are no longer in business. Risk and growth are common bedfellows, and one entrepreneur's riches may lead to another entrepreneur's rags. Thankfully for most people, other, less glamorous industries offer plenty of room for success. Because the industry you choose can greatly affect your success, consider the following industry-specific questions:

✔ **Do you believe in the industry you plan to do business in?** Industries such as the tobacco industry, firearms industry, or debt-collection industry aren't for everyone. Be sure to select an industry that will allow you to sleep at night and feel good about what you're doing.

✔ **Is it an industry that isn't overcrowded or dominated by a few well-marketed companies?** You say you're thinking about a coffee house or a bagel shop? Good luck. You'd better know something or be prepared to offer a different product or service than Starbucks, Bruegger's, or Noah's Bagels. Every industry has a saturation point; you want to make sure that your chosen industry isn't one of them. (You can usually determine the saturation point by observing how successful the existing businesses are. You can usually measure such success by observation — the condition of the business's premises, the quality and professionalism of the employees, and the prices charged; for example, is there room in the prices to make a profit?)

✔ **Is your potential business in an industry that's moving at a pace that you could be comfortable with?** Some industries move faster than others; for example, the biotech industry moves faster than the gift-shop industry. Make sure that you have a comfort level with the pace of your chosen industry. Some industries will leave you breathless (and moneyless) if you can't keep up with the pace. The gift-shop industry will leave you bleary eyed and passionless if you thrive on the rush you get from constant activity and change.

✔ **Is it an industry that you can get passionate about?** Can you love the product and the customers? Passion helps sell products to customers and vision to employees.

Timing your start-up

When is the best time to start your new business? Should you begin your new enterprise when the economy is strong or when the economy is in a recession? Does the economy even matter? What economic forces should drive your decision?

Forget the economy, folks. We won't come right out and say that the economy doesn't matter, because depending on your niche, it can. But by and large, generally speaking, the economy doesn't matter. For instance, the best time to start a business could be when the economy is booming, because people are in a strong buying mode. But there are downsides to starting a business in booming economies, including the fact that unemployment is usually low (which means good employees are hard to find).

Economic recessions can also cut both ways. The bad news about recessions is that consumers are wary buyers in recessions, and wary buyers mean low margins, and low margins usually mean low profits. But the good news is that recessions serve as sort-out time (that is, they sort out the weak businesses from the strong ones and allow the strong ones to survive and grow). As the weak businesses disappear, they leave in their place an opportunity for newer, stronger competitors to surface.

The bottom line: The best time to start a business is when the timing is right for you and your niche. If you're prepared in terms of finances and experience (see Chapters 1 and 2), if the niche is right and available (as discussed throughout this chapter), and if you're passionate about what you do, the best time is right now. If you and the niche aren't prepared, the time is wrong. No economic indicators can tell you this. You have to listen to your gut.

Take advantage of government resources

Everyone likes to poke fun at the government (hey, what are governments for, anyway?). But now and then, when you least expect it, your government surprises you and does something useful. The small-business arena is one of those areas where the government has made strides in doing something helpful. We cite the following examples:

✔ **The Small Business Administration (SBA):** The SBA offers a wide variety of educational materials and seminars for both current and aspiring small-business owners. They also provide financial assistance through loans and loan-guarantee programs. In recent years, these programs have become significantly more user-friendly, and today the SBA is, in most cities anyway, an excellent resource for the capital-seeking small-business owner who has trouble finding funding through the conventional private-sector sources. For more information on SBA loans, see Chapter 5; for more information on how the SBA can be of assistance locally, go to www.sba.gov to find the field office near you.

✔ **Service Corps of Retired Executives (SCORE):** Federally funded, SCORE consists of more than 10,000 volunteers in hundreds of cities across the United States who provide free counseling and advice to prospective or existing small businesses.

SCORE, an excellent concept to be sure, can be a tad on the hit-or-miss side due to the fact that the majority of SCORE's volunteers are former employees of large companies. Thus, not all of them have known what it's like to watch their own small business take off. If you happen to be assigned to the right volunteer, however, SCORE can be the best deal in town — occasionally even providing you with a much-needed mentor. SCORE is definitely a service worth trying, especially given its cost to you, which is absolutely nothing — it's free! Visit its website at www.score.org to pose online questions to counselors or to contact the office nearest you (or call 800-634-0245).

✔ **Small Business Development Centers (SBDCs):** There are hundreds of SBDCs in the United States, most of which are located on college and university campuses. The SBDC program is sponsored by the SBA in partnership with state and local governments and the educational community. Its mission is to provide business counseling, training, and various other educational resources to help both start-ups and existing small businesses.

Unlike SCORE, SBDC services are provided on a fee basis, and SBDC employees are usually educators (rather than volunteers like SCORE). Most have not owned a small business of their own. As a result, similar to SCORE, the services they offer can be hit or miss. Call 703-271-8700 for the SBDC center nearest you or visit www.sba.gov/sbdc.

✔ **The SBA Answer Desk:** This free service of the SBA allows you to call 800-827-5722 to speak with a living, breathing SBA employee who will provide you with a thorough list of governmental resources and referrals, along with a smattering of advice. Your questions can be specific or general; ultimately, you'll be referred to a website, a SCORE or SBDC chapter, or an SBA publication.

✔ **Your state's Department of Commerce and/or Economic Development Department:** Most Commerce or Economic Development Departments have small-business assistance centers, most of which are replicated on the web. These centers contain information on licensing and permit regulations and provide information packets on starting and running a business. Check your state government pages, use an Internet search engine, or call your state's Department of Commerce or Economic Development Department. (Some states include commerce under the Office of the Secretary of State.)

Recognizing Your Number One Asset — You

Turn back the clock to the middle of the 20th century. Imagine you're a small-town banker somewhere in the state of Arkansas. In the course of a day's business, you look up from your desk to see a man in his 30s stride into your office and plop down a business proposal. It seems this fellow intends to buy a soft ice cream machine to put on the sidewalk outside of his Ben Franklin dime store, and he wants you to help him finance it.

"Oh, brother," you think to yourself. "This guy must be one pickle short of a barrel. If he can't scrape up $1,800 from the profits on his little dime store, what makes him think I should finance this new venture? $1,800 is a lot of ice cream cones."

Then you pause in the midst of your thoughts and take a deeper look into the man's eyes as he passionately describes his vision for peddling ice cream cones on the sidewalk. And lo and behold, you see a fire burning inside as he explains his ideas for selling ice cream and attracting customers to shop in his store while they enjoy the ice cream cone. And the more the man talks, the more you come to understand that this fellow is driven by a dream, a dream that goes far beyond peddling ice cream. After listening for longer than you had intended, you make an uncharacteristic decision to cough up the dough — not because of the uniqueness of the entrepreneur's idea but because of the uniqueness of the entrepreneur himself. Despite the humdrum notion of selling ice cream on the sidewalk, you fork over the check. Then you sit back and watch as two years later he pays off the five-year note and goes on to eventually create and build Wal-Mart, the mightiest retailer in the land.

Yes, you, the banker, made your decision based on the man, Sam Walton, and not his ice cream machine. Given his passion and degree of commitment, it was only natural that the success of his business would follow.

Avowedly, most of us are not Sam Walton. We don't have his sense of detail, his drive, his leadership abilities, or his vision for his niche. But the world has plenty of room for folks who don't build Wal-Marts. Visit any community in the United States, and even the smallest will have a number of Sam Waltons, those small-business owners who have made their furniture store the best in the three-county area, those small-business owners who build the best fly rods in the great Northwest, and those small-business owners who sell more ice cream cones than anyone north of Boston. You don't have to be the largest retailer in the world to be a smashing success. Plenty of mini Sam Waltons are hanging around.

And so it will be for you if you choose to follow in Sam Walton's footsteps — you alone will either make or break your company. Sure, the niche will be important, but you will select it. And certainly your employees will be important, but you will choose the people you hire (and the people you fire). And, of course, your products (or services) will be important, but you will have the final word in defining them. Everything that happens within your business will have your own personal stamp on it. Nothing will be outside of your grasp.

Today's venture capitalists have for many years understood the same lesson that Sam Walton's banker learned in the course of that long-ago meeting. The small-business owner is the number one determinant of his or her company's success or failure.

Chapter 4

First Things First: Crafting Your Business Plan

After you've made the commitment to start your own business, you need to embark on your first meaningful hands-on task: developing and writing your business plan. But before you get started, you need to write a mission statement to set the stage for that plan. Over the life of your business, you'll use that mission statement in many ways, from creating a vision for your business's future (that is, the big-picture overview) to developing a year-to-year strategy to setting annual goals for you and your employees.

Your Mission: Impossible If You Fail to Define It

A good *mission statement* is a written, easy-to-remember sentence, a short list of bullet points, or a paragraph illustrating your business's goals and purpose in life. Or, as coauthor Jim believes, it's what makes your company special. Mission statements come in many sizes, shapes, and forms, but they all have one common purpose: to guide you and your employees in making the critical decisions that affect your company's direction. Additionally, your mission statement should identify your company to outsiders — your customers, your vendors, the media, and others.

To give you an idea of how well-developed mission statements identify the businesses behind them, try to match the following companies with their mission statements (well, if these aren't their official mission statements, we think they ought to be):

Company	Mission Statement
1. Disney	A. "To give unlimited opportunity to women."
2. Boeing	B. "To solve unsolved problems innovatively."
3. 3M	C. "To make people away from home feel that they're among friends and really wanted."
4. Mary Kay	D. "To make people happy."
5. Marriott	E. "To push the leading edge of aviation, taking on huge challenges and doing what others cannot do."

Our guess? You didn't have much trouble coming up with the following matches:

- ✔ **Disney:** "To make people happy." (This one clearly meets the requirement of easy to remember.)

- ✔ **Boeing:** "To push the leading edge of aviation, taking on huge challenges and doing what others cannot do." (A tad fluffy perhaps, but certainly challenging.)

- ✔ **3M:** "To solve unsolved problems innovatively." (No restrictions to the range of niches here. No wonder its products range from fishing line to sealing tape to Post-it Notes to Thinsulate Insulation.)

- ✔ **Mary Kay:** "To give unlimited opportunity to women." (And Mary Kay has done exactly that — for women and for men. Countless new businesses over the years have emulated their networking approach to sales.)

- ✔ **Marriott:** "To make people away from home feel that they're among friends and really wanted." (This mission statement says what the company is trying to do; at the same time, it provides guidelines to its employees for how to deal with customers.)

In the following sections, we help you write your own mission statement.

Writing your mission statement

Every successful company these days is in the business of providing solutions to customers' needs, desires, or problems. Thus, the question you should answer when creating your mission statement is, "What solution do I provide, and what must I do to make sure that the solution I provide is consistently delivered?"

So how should your mission statement read? Here are a few examples to get you thinking:

✔ If you were going to open a new bookstore, would your mission statement state "to sell books" or "to increase the educational and enjoyment levels of customers"?

✔ If you were going to start a contracting business, would your mission statement read "to build houses" or "to provide affordable building solutions for customers"?

✔ If you were writing a how-to book for small-business owners, would your mission statement be "to write a 400-page business book" or "to provide readers with solutions to their business problems and suggestions for taking advantage of their business opportunities"?

We're guessing you'd choose the second option for each example. Notice the common inference in all three of these mission statements to the key word *solutions.*

Give yourself plenty of room to grow within your niche when you develop your business's mission statement. For instance, when a bookstore owner defines the mission behind her business as "education and enjoyment," she leaves open the option to sell DVDs rather than just books. When a contractor defines his purpose to provide "building solutions," he has the option to build garages, barns, and outbuildings, in addition to homes. Finally, when the writer makes "providing readers with solutions" the central part of her mission, she retains the option to develop DVDs, not to mention to serve as a consultant or hold seminars.

The power of a mission statement

Coauthor Jim facilitated a "strategic meeting" for the Central Oregon Regional Housing Authority (CORHA), a Redmond, Oregon–based organization that offers affordable housing to the citizens within its designated geographical boundaries. The agenda of the strategic meeting included a review of CORHA's existing mission statement, which, at the time, read "to provide affordable housing opportunities to Central Oregon residents."

Following an hour of discussion with the key staff and board members who were in attendance, the group ultimately crafted and agreed upon a new mission statement. That new, shorter mission statement read "to foster dignity through affordable housing."

Suddenly, instead of being an organization that was in the business of "providing affordable housing," CORHA became an organization in the business of "fostering dignity." Affordable housing was simply the tool by which the organization would foster that dignity. You can imagine the impact such a change in mission had on CORHA's employees — and the manner in which they treated customers.

Such is the power of a well-worded, well-thought-out mission statement. This mission statement made the CORHA organization "special," and at the same time it defined the manner in which it should treat its customers — a huge dividend for such a small investment.

Mission statements aren't forever. Mission statements, like people and environments, can change. Your business may morph into something entirely different as time passes. That's certainly acceptable, as long as you recognize the change and make sure that your mission statement keeps pace with the direction of your business.

Keeping your mission in people's minds

For your mission statement to be effective, it should be readily accessible to your customers, employees, and all those who come into contact with your business. So after your company is up and running, be sure to display your mission statement in the following places:

- **On the walls and bulletin boards in the most visible places in your business:** Posting your mission statement in such visible places serves as a constant reminder to you, your employees, and your customers of what your business is all about.

- **In the executive summary section of your business plan:** Investors and other important outsiders are often busy and appreciate reading the highlights of your plan first and then selectively delving into the details as they feel necessary. (The rest of this chapter discusses the business plan and explains how to write it.)

- **On the first page of your employee manual, if your business is large enough to warrant a manual:** This prominent placement demonstrates to employees what their number one concern should be when they come to work each day. (We discuss employee manuals in Chapter 16.)

- **On every document your company generates, including but not limited to stationery, faxes, newsletters, and e-mails:** This may seem like overkill, but it helps everyone to internalize the company's purpose.

Your Business Plan: Don't Start Up without It

You say you don't need a plan?

Sure, and neither did Wrong Way Corrigan, Alice in Wonderland, or Dr. Livingstone (who presumed to know where he was going as he disappeared into the African bush), as well as tens of thousands of other folks who got lost along their way. If you prepare a well-defined plan and if you update your plan as you proceed, point A will lead to point B rather than to point Q or to no point at all. And so it is with your business.

If ensuring that you're traveling in the right direction isn't enough of a reason to prepare a plan, talk to some of the people in the business of loaning or investing money (see Chapter 5). These folks won't even think about doling out their cash unless you present a quality business plan. And it had better be a humdinger of a plan, at that.

A business plan serves two distinct purposes: to serve as your business's road map and to attract capital through loans or investments. The first reason points out why you should have a plan even if you don't intend to solicit outside funding.

Using your business plan as a road map

Bankers, venture capitalists, and other folks who see a lot of business proposals have discovered that viable ideas are a dime a dozen — the idea itself won't make or break a business; the person behind the idea and the idea's execution holds the key to business success. (Or as someone once said, "Anyone who can take a shower can have a good idea. What matters is what happens *after* you towel off.") So how do you show the average business plan reader what kind of person is behind the idea? And where does the execution of that idea begin?

Execution begins with the business plan. Sure, the content of the business plan begins its steady march to obsolescence the day the ink is dry — after all, things happen fast in small business. But even more important than the business plan itself is the process you go through when you're writing your plan and the knowledge you gain. A well-thought-out business-plan-writing process asks the right questions, forcing you to research and think through the solutions at the outset instead of waiting to crisis-manage them all later. As a result, you minimize your chances of falling prey to major problems down the road.

An example of this foresight is the Risks section of the business plan. Most entrepreneurs don't envision the risks inherent in starting a business, as optimism and a half-full glass rule the day. Having to write the Risks section, however, forces you not only to itemize the risks but, when possible, to explain how you intend to manage them. (See the later section "Part 5: Risks" for more on this part of the business plan.)

If you value time, money, and a pleasant experience, you wouldn't take a trip to a new destination without first consulting a map, would you? Why should running your business be any different?

Finding financing with your business plan

Lenders and professional investors read a business plan as much to find out about the preparer as to understand the business. They look for thoroughness, professionalism, and attention to detail in the plan, in addition to the presentation of a credible scenario for running a successful business. After all, thoroughness, professionalism, and attention to detail are the same traits they want to see in the person responsible for managing the money they invest in or lend to the business. What better early indication of these characteristics than the business plan?

The sophisticated investor has learned from experience — horses don't win races; jockeys do. The jockey is you, the business owner, and the business plan is the first official indication of the kind of race your horse is going to run.

Business plans take a lot of time and focus to prepare well and are not to be confused with an afternoon jaunt at the beach. Similar to successfully locating the right financing and finding the right mentor, developing a successful business plan separates the potential doers from the dreamers.

By and large, only the truly committed take the trouble to prepare a business plan. You find some exceptions, of course; some potential small-business owners have enough acumen and experience to carry a good business plan in their head. And, yes, some of those business owners have gone on to achieve great success. But you'd have a hard time convincing us that these same business owners couldn't have accomplished even greater success and avoided some early mistakes if they had taken the time to record and refine their ideas in a tangible business plan. The depth of your early commitment to writing a business plan directly correlates to your chance for success. And a well-thought-out business plan demonstrates the depth of commitment necessary for you to end up at the helm of a successful small business.

Writing Your Business Plan

How detailed should you make your business plan? A simple, more short-term-focused plan (ten pages or so) is adequate if, say, yours is a home-office business and the plan is for your benefit alone. However, if you intend to expand your business, hire employees, or open multiple locations, then your plan should cover the long-term issues more extensively and, thus, be lengthier (say, 20 to 50 pages). Finally, no matter what size or direction you contemplate for your business, if you intend to use the plan as a tool to look for outside investors or professional lenders, you need to write an even more complete business plan.

Not all business plans need to contain all the parts we describe in the following sections. If you plan to give your business plan to outsiders, such as bankers, from whom you're seeking money or some other commitment, you should cover all the following bases. If your business plan is solely for your own use, at a minimum you should cover the marketing and financial management sections.

However long you decide to make your business plan, keep in mind that you can always add to and/or upgrade it to meet your needs. Later on, after you've completed the plan and your business takes off, you'll have plenty of opportunities to rewrite and update your plan (see the section "Keeping Your Plan Current" for details).

As you write your business plan, keep in mind these additional pointers:

- ✔ **Always double-space.** Double-spacing allows for easier reading and provides room for making handwritten notes or comments.

- ✔ **Begin each part (business description, management, marketing plan, and so on) on a new page.** Within each part, the text can be continuous, but be sure to make significant space breaks between each subsection.

- ✔ **Feel free to change the wording or add titles to our recommended sections.** No two businesses are exactly the same.

   Note: Although you should maintain the order of the parts, you can always vary the order of the sections within those parts.

- ✔ **Prepare and present the business plan so that it's tailored to the end user.** If you're giving it to a professional, such as a banker, because you're seeking funding, make the plan look professional. In other words, it should be professionally bound.

In the following sections, we give you a suggested format for your business plan. Whether you use this particular format or adapt one of your own choosing, your business plan should address the issues listed here.

Part 1: Business description

The purpose of this part is to provide the reader with an overview of the business. After reviewing this part, the reader should understand exactly what business you're in, what its legal entity is, and how your business intends to differentiate itself from its competitors. Don't take this challenge lightly; the reader's decision to peruse the plan in more depth will depend on his initial reaction to this description.

A. Mission statement

Write your mission statement as we describe earlier in the section "Your Mission: Impossible If You Fail to Define It."

B. Summary of the business

This section answers the basic question, "What business am I in?" Begin this summary with a one-sentence definition of exactly what your business will do or does. This sentence should be the same to-the-point definition you'll ultimately use as your one-minute pitch when explaining your business to everyone from bankers to customers to cocktail party acquaintances.

If you can't define your business in one sentence, something is probably wrong with your vision and focus of what your business should be.

The concept of your business doesn't have to be unique or extraordinary. Electricians, tax preparers, and computer consultants will always be in demand. More businesses succeed by being managed efficiently and wisely than by providing a new and unique product or service. (See Chapter 3 for details on how to find the right business niche for you.)

If you want your business to really be different, you can put a new twist on a concept that has been around for a while. Suppose, for example, that you're a veterinarian who recognizes that more than a few people in your area are too busy to bring their pets to your office for treatment. Thus, you may create a new business — say, Vet on Wheels. (After all, Domino's Pizza decided it could vastly expand its customer base by delivering pizzas rather than waiting for customers to walk in the door.) You also have the option to run your veterinarian business the traditional way (that is, by offering quality services at a competitive price to walk-in customers). Plenty of room in the pet-care industry exists for both.

C. Legal description

Is your business a sole proprietorship, partnership, C Corporation, S Corporation, or limited liability corporation? (See Chapter 5 for complete details on these options.)

D. Competitive edge

Answer the following questions to clearly communicate how you intend to differentiate your company from your competitors:

✔ **Who are your competitors, and what (in your opinion) is currently their competitive edge?** Here you want to identify your competitors' strengths so that you can, in the early stages of your business anyway, avoid competing directly against them.

- ✔ **What are your competitors' weaknesses?** By identifying their weaknesses, you open the opportunity to hit 'em where they're the most vulnerable.

- ✔ **What will distinguish your products or services from those of your competitors?** This distinction doesn't have to be something new and unique. Simply doing something better often suffices. If you're operating a lawn-care business, for customers who use your services throughout the grass-cutting season, you could trim their bushes at no charge as a customer loyalty bonus.

- ✔ **Service, quality, or price — which of the three do you intend to emphasize?** Remember, you can't be all things to all people. Where do you intend to position your product in the marketplace? Do you intend to be the top service and quality provider within your niche, or do you plan to concentrate on the low end of the niche by focusing mainly on price? (You can generally find a number of positions in every marketplace, so there should be plenty of room for you if you do what you do better than your competitors.)

It's extremely difficult, if not impossible, for most small businesses to be the "low-cost player" in a niche. In most cases, small businesses should focus on service and quality and leave the low pricing to someone else.

Part 2: Management

The management section is the most important part of your business plan if you intend to use your plan as a vehicle to raise money. Intelligent investors recognize that the success or failure of a business hinges on the quality of the management team. Hence, the management section is one of the first places investors look when they pick up your plan. If they aren't impressed with the management team, you can rest assured that they won't go any further.

Begin your management section with biographies of the principal members of your business: the president, vice president, sales and marketing managers, board members, and so on. Be accurate in outlining their backgrounds and remember that the prudent investor checks references. In each descriptive biography, include the following information:

- ✔ Education
- ✔ Prior positions
- ✔ Noteworthy achievements

As you write the management section, remember that you're selling your management team to the reader; include what makes them special. Pay the most attention to the bio pertaining to the person who makes the most difference to the business — you!

If you use the business plan only as a road map and not as an inducement for investment, the management summary is less important. However, putting the qualifications and employment histories of the major players on paper may help you better think through whether the players fit well together and will make a synergetic and complementary team.

Part 3: Marketing plan

The marketing part of your business plan provides the reader with an overview of the industry in which your business competes, a description of your business's potential customers, and an explanation of how you intend to sell, distribute, and promote your product or service.

This part of the plan is often the most difficult — and the most important — for companies to complete. Many competing products and services will fall within your niche. The difficulty, of course, is in differentiating and highlighting your products and services to prospective customers and then convincing them to buy them. The marketing part of your plan will make or break your success in this aspect of the business. Read on to find out how to write it.

A. The industry at large

In this section, you provide an overview of the industry (within the geographical area you expect your business to cover) by answering the following questions:

- ✔ How competitive is the industry?
- ✔ What are the growth opportunities?
- ✔ Who are the industry leaders?
- ✔ Where are the niches in addition to yours?

You can usually obtain answers to these questions by reviewing websites, talking to customers, and speaking with people at your industry's trade associations. You can also consult those who are already in specified niches within the industry, such as wholesalers or manufacturers' reps.

B. Potential customers

If your business sells to consumers rather than to other businesses, consider gender, age, income, geographic location, marital status, number of children, education, housing situation (rent or own), and the reasons why they may want your product or service. Which of these demographics represent your desired customers?

Create a profile of how your target market behaves as customers. Consider what motivates them to buy and how they buy, including

INVESTIGATE

Research model companies

If your business provides products or services similar to those offered by others, identify one, two, or three of your successful competitors that seem most similar to what you'd like your company to be like. Which of these companies do you want to emulate? In what areas can you improve or differentiate your offerings to create a unique niche and to attract customers to your business over competing alternatives?

Even if you have an innovative and unique concept, identify those companies in related, and even dissimilar, fields to find a few that you want to mimic. Never underestimate the value of mimicry; many successful entrepreneurs are inveterate copycats.

For each model company you examine, answer the following questions:

✔ Why did they choose their location?

✔ How do they promote their services and products?

✔ What types of customers do they attract?

✔ What are their revenues, expenses, and profitability?

✔ How have they grown and expanded over time?

✔ What are their plans for the future?

How can you determine the answers to these questions? Ask the model company's customers or become a customer yourself (before you open your own doors, of course). Or if the model company is a publicly held company, buy a few shares of their stock or obtain their filed financial statements and documents. Or better yet, talk to the vendors that are common to your two businesses. Most vendors, in an attempt to be a "friend" to their customers, will spill more beans than they should about their customers.

✔ Whether they rely on recommendations from others

✔ What their product usage-rate tendencies are

✔ When they make their purchases

✔ Whether they buy online, on credit, or on impulse

This target customer profile information will come in handy when you're ready to select the right media advertising vehicle to use.

If you sell to businesses (B2B), you need to understand similar demographic issues that relate to them. What types of businesses will buy your products and services? Who within those businesses will be the ultimate decision-makers, and how can you reach them? What problems of the ultimate decision-makers will you solve with your products or services?

C. The benefits of your product or service

Too many businesses know exactly how to describe the *features* of their products or services but don't know how to point out the *benefits*. Today's consumers, particularly the more sophisticated ones, are more interested in hearing about the benefits of your gizmo than in hearing about its features.

You're manufacturing a new computer? Don't tell me about its dimensions and its horsepower; tell me about what it will do for me that the others won't. You're selling a promotional product? Don't tell me about where it's manufactured or how much it weighs; tell me about how it can benefit the growth of my business.

D. Geography

Identify your primary geographic focus — that is, where do you expect your customers to come from? Will your customer focus be within local markets? Statewide? Nationwide? International? Clearly, your advertising and other promotions will be quite different if you're marketing overseas rather than simply in your hometown.

E. Distribution

Explain how you intend to get your products or services to the marketplace. Describe your role in the industry and your distribution plan. Are you a manufacturer? Service provider? Wholesaler? Retailer? Will you utilize a direct sales force? Manufacturers' reps? Catalogs? Telemarketing? Direct mail? An e-commerce website? (See Chapter 11 for the information you need to answer these questions.)

F. Advertising

Identify how you can best reach your potential customers. Will you do so via newspaper, radio, television, magazines, direct mail, phone, or the Internet? Which advertising methods are the most economically feasible within your budget? Which ones do your desired customers most heavily utilize? What internal programs or external agencies can you use? (See Chapter 11 for more about advertising.)

Don't forget to include your social media plan in this section. Do you intend to maintain a Facebook presence? What about Twitter? Linked In? Groupon? (Turn to Chapter 12 for more on these and other technology opportunities.)

G. Public relations

Public relations is the art of keeping your name in the public in a positive way other than through paid advertising. Public relations involves such activities as employee, community, industry, and government relations; customer and prospective customer relations; and — the best-known aspect of public relations — publicity.

Publicity resources are usually free; the trick is to get the attention of the writer or reporter who can do you the most good when your competitors and, indeed, just about everyone else in the business world are trying to do the same thing. A good public relations plan can help you build a positive image in the minds of those in your target audience and guide your efforts as you seek to generate publicity that can expand awareness of your product or service.

This section of your business plan should answer the following questions:

- What public relations techniques will you use?
- What is your business's publicity hook, and why will it interest editors, reporters, and those in your target audience?
- How will you build relationships with those in your target market, as well as with select editorial contacts?
- How can you tap into your network of friends and business associates to build a positive image of your business and to gain editorial introductions?

For example, in the restaurant business, one of the best public relations hits is a favorable review in the local newspaper. Within your community and in other media outlets, you can find many similar and effective public relations resources. Consider participating in career day at a local school, sponsoring a runner in a charity marathon, or designating a portion of a road or highway to be maintained by your business. And don't forget the simple press release, alerting the media and community to worthwhile achievements of your company and its people. (See Chapter 11 for more about public relations.)

H. Pricing

Explain your short-term and long-term pricing. Include information on costs and profit expectations, along with a thorough review of your competitors' pricing and your perceived price-point position within the industry. Do you intend to be the low-cost provider or the high-end producer? How do you intend to position your product?

When pricing your products, always consider the current competitive climate first. Research the pricing of similar services or products in the marketplace and then price your product accordingly. Don't make the mistake early on of pricing your products based on some predetermined profit margin that you or your accountant would like to achieve. Instead, price your products based on what your competitive research (primarily talking to customers) determines the market will bear.

Don't be afraid to sell your services or products at healthy margins when the opportunity presents itself. Rest assured, the opportunity won't last forever. (For more on pricing, see Chapter 11.)

1. Sales terms and credit policies

A sale is never complete until you deposit the proceeds safely in your business account. With this in mind, you need to spell out the terms of the sale and the conditions governing the granting of credit and the acceptance of payment before you make your first sale. For more on sales, see Chapter 11.

Part 4: Operations

This part outlines the nuts and bolts of the operational issues involved in managing your company. The scope of your operations or management plan covers a wide range of functions, from dealing with employees to purchasing from vendors to maintaining your company's accounting records.

A. Employees

Many small businesses are one-person operations. If you fall into this category, you don't have to suffer any of the headaches of hiring, motivating, training, and firing employees. The only person you have to worry about is you, which, if you're anything like your humble authors, should be no small project in itself.

However, if you do plan to have employees, you need to answer the following questions in this section of the business plan:

- How will you assemble your team — by leasing your employees or by hiring them outright?
- Where will you find the employees you intend to hire yourself?
- What benefits will you offer?
- What motivational incentives will you use?
- Will you assemble an employee manual?
- Will you offer a retirement plan?
- Will there be down-the-road opportunities for ownership for key employees?
- How will you train your employees?

See Chapters 16 and 17 for a discussion of these employee issues.

B. Compensation

Too many small businesses hire their first employees without first devising an overall compensation plan. Such an oversight inevitably leads to a lack of uniformity in compensation. When employees perceive that you're not compensating them fairly relative to other employees and that you haven't communicated an objective reason for this discrepancy, a line may begin to form outside your office.

For purposes of the business plan, you need to objectively define the basics of your compensation plan for hourly, salaried, and commissioned employees. Don't forget to include bonus plans and perks. (For more on compensation plans, see Chapter 16; for more on benefits, see Chapter 17.)

C. Vendors and outside resources

What vendors and outside resources do you intend to use? How do you plan to kick off your relationship with key vendors? Vendor accessibility is an important issue in many industries. Frequently, the best vendors don't make their line of products available to every customer, especially the new kid on the block with no history, no prior connections in the industry, and an anemic balance sheet. You need to have answers to their qualifying questions before you make your first call. Completing this section will provide you with the material you'll need to respond to their queries.

D. Accounting and/or bookkeeping

Describe who will take care of your accounting and bookkeeping duties. Answer these questions:

- ✔ Will you hire an experienced bookkeeper, CPA, controller, or chief financial officer?
- ✔ Do you intend to computerize your accounting system?
- ✔ What accounting software package will you use?
- ✔ Do you plan to outsource your bookkeeping or accounting? What outside resource will you use?

This section is particularly important for those businesses that intend to use the business plan as a tool to invite a loan or an investment. The smart lender or investor wants to be sure that the financial responsibilities of running the business are in good hands. This is especially true when the entrepreneur isn't particularly strong on the financial side of business. (See Chapter 10 for details on setting up an accounting system for your business.)

Part 5: Risks

You, as well as potential lenders and investors in your business, should care about the potential risks in your business. The better you understand them, the better able you'll be to anticipate them, minimize them, and keep your business in business.

Risks are inherent in every business, and yours will be no exception. Identify those risks in your business plan and be candid and thorough in describing them. Investors and lenders know that every business faces risks, so they'll be looking for honesty and awareness here, not ambivalence or avoidance. They know how to recognize the difference.

Risk: You have to see it to beat it

You must recognize risk before you can face it. Mary, an experienced small-business veteran, was asked to serve on the board of a local nonprofit agency that was having serious financial problems. Its recently fired executive director had, over a period of years, spent hundreds of thousands of the agency's dollars on personal cars, vacations, and even a second home. The agency faced serious financial problems. Not only had it lost money to the crooked director, but due to the resulting adverse publicity, many of the nonprofit's sources for donations began drying up.

Before agreeing to accept the position, Mary asked the board chairperson for a current business plan (that is, a plan on how the nonprofit expected to turn around its financial problems). To the nonprofit's credit, it had prepared one.

Following an interview with the executive director and the chairman, she turned down the board position. Here's why: "The business plan read like an ad-agency marketing brochure," she later explained. "All it talked about was the wonderful opportunity for the agency to make a difference, the terrific future of the nonprofit's cause, and the need for such an organization in the local community. It was as if their cash flow problems, their public image, and their publicity problems didn't exist."

"My interview with the executive director and the board chairman was more of the same," Mary continued. "A good break here, a random

event there, and everything was bound to come up roses. Try as I did to change the subject and discuss the immediate risks that faced the agency and their need to confront them, neither the director nor the chairperson would face up to the risks that currently faced the agency. Failure was right around the corner, yet they refused to acknowledge it, much less do anything about it."

"You know," Mary laughed, "one of the things I love about small-business owners is their unbridled optimism. Their glasses are always half-full; there is nothing they can't do, given a little time and a lot of hard work. That's the good news! The bad news is that there has to be the voice of the devil's advocate somewhere in the back of a successful business owner's head that recognizes and helps formulate sensible actions to minimize that risk."

"The experiences of this nonprofit are a perfect example," Mary concluded. "If you refuse to recognize the risk in the beginning, you're eventually going to be blindsided by it."

When asked what she looked for in the nonprofit's turnaround plan, she replied, "A good turnaround plan is not that different from a good business plan. I would look first to the people issue — that is, what is the nonprofit going to do to replace the departing executive director, and how do they intend to motivate and upgrade their current staff? After that, I would want to know what they intend to do to solve their image problems."

Part 6: Financial management plan

Your good idea is likely to turn into your worst nightmare if you ignore or are unrealistic about the financial aspect of your business. If you're one of those creative types or a mover and a shaker who hates to work with numbers, you may decide to blow off the financial part of the business plan. Doing so, we're sorry to tell you, could cost you at minimum the dollars you need to grow your business and at maximum the very existence of the business itself.

Along with marketing, financial management is the most-often neglected part of every small-business venture. Don't let it be yours!

Before you launch your business, do the research to come up with the financial projections we describe in the following sections. But before you do any of your financial projections, consider the following:

✔ Ask your tax advisor (if you're working with one) to show you examples of similar financial projections from other business plans to use as a guideline.

✔ Don't bother projecting more than three years out; the assumptions you make will be too vague. (Exception: Some outside investors may require five-year projections.)

✔ Thoroughly identify the assumptions you make. The garbage-in, garbage-out theory is alive and well when it comes to projecting financial results. The conclusions you reach will be no better than the quality of your assumptions. Prominently itemize these assumptions in your business plan to allow the reader to know exactly what they are and how they were made.

✔ In the likely event that you don't know how to produce the pro forma profit and loss statement, balance sheet, and cash flow projections (all of which we explain in the following sections), you can

- Hire a tax advisor.

- Hire a business-plan consultant.

- Purchase a business-plan-software package.

- Learn to use spreadsheet software and do the projections yourself. We recommend that you use a program such as Microsoft Excel for your projections. If you don't know how to use a spreadsheet, either find out how (from computer-training companies in your community or good books on the topic) or have someone else set one up for you.

If you don't understand the difference between a profit and loss statement and a balance sheet, turn to Chapter 14. Spreadsheets and financial statements are tools that every successful small-business owner needs to understand. You can find out how to use them now or later — but sooner is better!

A. Pro forma profit and loss statement

A *pro forma profit and loss statement* is a projected income and expense plan that summarizes your estimated revenue and expenses over a specified period of time. The accuracy of your pro forma profit and loss statement depends on the quality of the assumptions you make. If you make good assumptions going in, then you can expect meaningful results. Preparing a pro forma profit and loss statement forces you to think through the questions you need to answer to arrive at the assumptions you make.

Estimating your expenses for your pro forma profit and loss statement is relatively easy. The most difficult assumptions you have to make are your sales and other income (revenues) and your gross margin (gross profit). Many small-business owners generate two or even three separate pro formas — for example, a best-case scenario, a middle-case scenario, and a worst-case scenario.

Prepare your profit and loss projections for the first three years of your business (unless you're seeking venture capital funding, in which case the first five years may be required). Anything longer requires too many far-out, hard-to-make assumptions. Compute the first year's pro forma on a monthly basis and the second and third years' on a quarterly basis.

If you don't know how to read financial documents, much less prepare them, we suggest that you pick up a copy of the latest edition of coauthor Eric's best-selling book *Investing For Dummies* (Wiley) and/or take a good class in how to read financial statements at a local college. Also, you can take advantage of business plan software (such as Business Plan Pro), most of which include financial projection templates.

B. Balance sheet

A *balance sheet* measures your business's resources (assets) and obligations (liabilities) at a particular time. The balance sheet is important to understand and, incidentally, is just as relevant to your personal financial situation as it is to your business one. As a matter of fact, if you apply for a loan at a financial institution, you'll almost certainly have to submit a personal balance sheet. (If you aren't currently keeping one to track your family's assets, you should be.)

Although we recommend that every business include a balance sheet in its business plan, it's especially relevant for those businesses that have significant noncash assets tied up in such categories as inventory and accounts receivable.

As with the profit and loss statement, prepare a projected balance sheet for the first three years of business; project the first year on a monthly basis and the second and third years on a quarterly basis.

C. Cash flow projections

Cash flow is the amount of cash that moves through your business in the form of receipts (representing an increase in cash) and expenses and capital expenditures (representing a decrease in cash). Cash flow is the practical side of the accounting equation, representing the cash required to keep your business operating on a day-to-day basis.

Don't confuse cash flow with *profitability,* an accounting term that measures the results of the entire operation of the business (of which cash is only one important part) over a given period of time. While profitability provides the benchmarks for measuring the effectiveness of your operations, cash flow is what pays the bills.

As a prospective business owner, you need to project your business's cash needs before going into business so that you know how much money you need to raise. As with profit and loss and balance sheet projections, project your cash flow needs for the first three years of the business. For more information on cash flow (and profitability), see Chapter 14.

Keeping Your Plan Current

Guarantees are dangerous in small business, but we can make two without hesitation:

- The immediate progress of your business will deviate from your original plan.
- Your business will change dramatically from what you've envisioned even in the first year.

Deviation and change are constants in this sometimes roller-coaster endeavor, but deviation and change are why many small-business owners select this career path in the first place.

To make the necessary adjustments in response to the deviation and change you're sure to experience, you must keep your business plan current. Take a day away from the office every 6 to 12 months to dissect the important parts of your business plan — particularly those involving staffing, marketing, distribution, and product development — and answer the following questions:

✔ Has the business developed according to plan within each of these areas (staffing, marketing, distribution, and product development)? If not, why?

✔ In areas where the business hasn't developed according to plan, do you want to get back on track? What adjustments will you make in each area to get back on track?

✔ Given the passage of time, where do you want your business to be a year from now, and what changes should you make to support that new direction?

Then work at making your changes to the plan, remembering that, if those changes have a financial impact on your business (most important changes do), you must also apply the changes to the pro forma profit and loss statement and to your balance sheet and cash flow projections.

A significant change in bottom-line income will obviously impact key balance sheet numbers, which in turn will affect such key measures as the debt-to-equity ratio and the current ratio (see Chapter 14 for an explanation of these terms). Extreme variations in these ratios influence your credit lines, your relationships with lenders and vendors, and your long-range plans for capital expenditures and new hires.

Creating a business plan is a one-time experience, but keeping it up to date is an ongoing task — which, when you think about it, is not unlike the relationship between starting a business and actually running and maintaining one.

Chapter 5

Making Financing, Ownership, and Organizational Decisions

In This Chapter

▶ Figuring out how much money you need to launch your business

▶ Deciding how and where to finance your business

▶ Considering your ownership options

▶ Selecting the legal entity that works best for you

*A*fter you discover where you want to go with your small business and commit to the journey, you need to begin making some important decisions about how you're going to reach your goals. In this chapter, we help you estimate how much cash you need to get started, where you can expect to obtain that money, whether you want to set out on your own or with others, and what kind of business entity you need to get you where you want to go.

Determining Your Start-Up Cash Needs

Before you determine where you're going to get your start-up funds, you need to understand that your business's initial cash requirements include not only one-time start-up costs but also working capital and a reserve. Here's what these requirements mean:

✔ **One-time start-up costs:** *Start-up costs* include such one-time expenses as legal fees, licenses and permits, utility and lease deposits, furniture and fixtures, inventory, leasehold improvements (such as remodels or additions to the store or office space you rent or lease), signage, and everything you need to initially open for business. Consult another business's profit and loss statement (P&L) or a pro forma P&L sample on a business plan template for a listing of the typical day-to-day ongoing expenses you're going to incur (or see Chapter 14).

✓ **Working capital:** *Working capital* is the cash you need to stay open for business. It includes such ongoing, everyday expenditures as inventory and raw materials, accounts receivable, hiring of employees, and the general day-to-day operation of your business until you become consistently profitable and can fund the cost of operations out of internally generated cash flow. Don't forget to include debt payments — both interest and principal — when arriving at this figure. (Although principal payments aren't an expense, they do reduce available capital.)

✓ **Reserve:** The *reserve* is the amount of capital you need to overcome forecasting mistakes and/or make up for variances from your budget. If you end up having neither forecasting mistakes nor budget variances, we suggest you give Guinness World Records a call!

So where's all this money going to come from? You can use two basic methods to finance your start-up:

✓ **Bootstrapping:** The internal generation of initial financing, using primarily your own personal resources, and sometimes complemented by various forms of equity investments or loans from family and friends

✓ **Outsourcing:** The external generation of financing for both start-up expenses and ongoing business needs, using outside resources, such as banks, angel investors, and venture capitalists (which we cover later in this chapter)

For most start-ups, bootstrapping is a much more likely source of funds than outsourcing. Besides, providers of outsourced funds aren't likely to give you the money you need unless they see that you've done your bootstrapping first. (For more on bootstrapping, see the section "Using Your Own Money: Bootstrapping.")

Whether you bootstrap the financing of your business or finance it by using money from outsiders, you must first estimate your cash needs. Why? If you plan to go the bootstrapping route, you need to estimate your cash needs to minimize the chances of running out of money, a situation that can lead to the failure of your business and the loss of all the invested capital. If you plan to outsource your capital, you need to estimate your cash needs to ensure potential lenders that you have solid projections for your future cash needs.

Just as remodeling work on a home almost always takes longer and costs more than expected, many entrepreneurs find that their start-up requires more cash than they originally expected. That's why you must allow yourself sufficient time to investigate, reflect on, and estimate the costs associated with starting your chosen business.

If you end up obtaining outside capital, nothing shouts inexperience like having to go back to your source at a later date and ask for more money. Looking for a surefire way to raise a red flag in front of your banker or investor? Tell him or her that you made a mistake in forecasting and you need

more capital than you had originally asked for. Whether you get more capital the second time around is up for grabs, but one thing is certain: You'll get increased scrutiny. Bankers and investors don't like oversights and mistakes, especially when those mistakes have to do with their money.

The following worksheet is designed to help you estimate your business's capital requirements. If you've completed your profit and loss statement, balance sheet, and cash flow projections, this exercise should be simple. If you haven't, this exercise will be a headache, so do yourself a favor and take a look at Chapters 4 and 14 before you start filling out this worksheet.

Estimated Capital Requirement Worksheet

1. Add all one-time, pre-opening costs, such as legal fees; licenses and permits; utility and lease deposits; furniture and fixtures; inventory; leasehold improvements; logo, stationery, and signage; insurance; and so on (your one-time start-up costs). _____

2. Add your projected early-month con- secutive losses from your profit and loss statement. Be sure to include debt pay- ments, both interest and principal (the first part of your working capital). _____

3. Add the anticipated purchase of assets from your balance sheet for the first year: equipment, inventory, furniture, and fixtures (the second part of your working capital). _____

4. Add the amounts from Steps 1, 2, and 3. _____

5. Multiply the amount from Step 4 by 0.25 to get your reserve. (Note: The percent- age required by this reserve figure will vary depending on the experience of the person or persons starting and running the business. The more experienced you are, the lower the reserve has to be; the less experienced you are, the higher it has to be. A reserve of 25 percent repre- sents our best guess as an average.) _____

6. Add the amount from Step 4 to the amount from Step 5 to get your total capital requirements. _____

This figure represents the amount of capital your business will require from all sources before start-up. After you determine how much capital you need, the real hard work begins — finding it.

Using Your Own Money: Bootstrapping

If your small-business start-up is like most others, you probably won't utilize outside capital, so bootstrapping will have to do. But don't worry; you're in good company.

Inc. magazine annually publishes the *Inc.* 5000, a list of fast-growing private companies in the United States. A recent survey illustrated the sources of original financing from those *Inc.* 5000 companies. Table 5-1 lists the results of that survey.

Table 5-1	Where Inc. 5000 Companies Got Their Original Financing
Resource	*Percentage of CEOs Who Tapped the Resource*
Self-financed	82%
Loans from friends, family, or business associates	22%
Bank loans	18%
Lines of credit	18%
Venture capital	8%
SBA or other government funds	4%

Note: The total exceeds 100% because some CEOs tapped more than one resource.

As you can see from the table, bootstrapping sources emerge as the clear winner in the start-up financing competition, even for this exclusive list of fast-track, rapid-growth companies. When you think about it, the fact that bootstrapping is so pervasive and works so well makes sense. First, what better way to instill discipline and make things work efficiently than to have a limited supply of funds? Second, because you care deeply about risking your own money or that of family and friends, you have a powerful incentive to work hard and smart at making your business succeed.

So take heart if you think that you need vast sums of cash to start a small business or if you've been turned down (perhaps more than once) by outside sources of funding. As you can see in Table 5-1, the entrepreneurial traits of hard work, perseverance, and, yes, good old-fashioned scrounging can help you locate the money you need to start your business.

Profiling bootstrappers

Bootstrappers come in all sizes, shapes, and forms. Some prefer to conduct their growing businesses alone, some jump from start-up to start-up, and some — those who are capable of adopting a range of managerial skills — make the transition from small business to large business.

Here are a few profiles of typical bootstrappers:

- ✔ **Eric:** Before coauthor Eric set out to start his financial counseling business, he kept his expenses low enough to save about half of his employment earnings each year over several years, which provided a nice nest egg to finance his business start-up. While living in Boston and still single, Eric shared apartments with two to four roommates at a time to keep his rental expenses low. As he made the transition into his entrepreneurial endeavor, Eric worked half-time for four months so that his salaried income didn't completely disappear.

- ✔ **Jim:** Coauthor Jim's fourth business (all four were bootstrapped) was started to provide a needed service to his sporting-goods business. He purchased a screen-printing company from its owner for $10,000, moved the business out of the owner's basement, and funded its growth from the revenues of the sporting-goods business until the screen-printing company was profitable and could stand on its own. Eighteen years later, he sold the business when its revenues reached $25 million.

- ✔ **Ted Waitt:** Ted quit college to take a job selling PCs, and then, as so many bootstrappers do, he quit that job to start his own company. Using a portion of his grandmother's nest egg as collateral, he borrowed $10,000 to start a business in his father's South Dakota barn. That business later became Gateway 2000, a leading computer manufacturer.

These examples point out the typical pattern of bootstrapping. The founder and/or family and friends provide the start-up capital. Then profits from the business, money from outside resources (banks, shareholders, and so on), or a combination of both funds future growth.

Tapping into bootstrapping sources

Bootstrapping, as the examples in the preceding section point out, begins at home. If you're like us and the majority of entrepreneurs, you can locate the funds you need to finance your start-up by following these steps:

1. **Take stock of your personal assets and liabilities.**

   As we discuss in Chapter 2, you should get your personal finances in order and determine where you stand in terms of common important goals such as retirement planning. Only then can you begin to determine what portion of your assets you feel comfortable using in your business.

2. **Assuming that your parents and other family members are financially able to help, gingerly approach them.**

The family resource is appropriately known as *relationship investing* or *relationship lending.* Although relationship investing is a widely used resource for raising money, it's also the most potentially dangerous. Telling the bank you can't meet repayment obligations is one thing; telling a close relative that you've lost his money is quite another. The good news is that you'll work that much harder to succeed when family or friends are involved; the bad news is that losing the investment could damage existing relationships. Proceed with great care and be clear with family and friends about the risks, including the risk that they could lose their entire investment if your business gets into trouble!

3. **Ask friends, especially those friends who can bring expertise along with money to the table, to contribute to your business's start-up.**

Be aware, however, that the risks involved when borrowing money from friends are similar to the risks involved when borrowing from family. The downsides can be just as painful.

4. **If Steps 1, 2, and 3 still aren't enough, start looking for a, gulp, partner (or partners).**

We talk more about the role of partners in the section "Exploring Ownership Options" later in this chapter. Suffice it to say that partners are a roll of the dice — make a good roll, and your business will prosper beyond what it could with you alone; make a bad roll, and your problems could multiply.

5. **When all else fails, look to outside resources, even though they're historically unlikely to fund start-ups.**

Look for angel investors before heading for the banks, the Small Business Administration, and Small Business Investment Companies (we explain all these resources in the next section). If your idea or concept is compelling enough and if *you* are compelling enough, you may even consider approaching venture capitalists.

After you've tapped your own resources but before you begin probing family and friends, remember to tape the Golden Rule of Bootstrapping to the middle of your forehead and then take a long look in the mirror. In the event that you haven't come across it yet, the Golden Rule of Bootstrapping is as follows:

Do not do unto others until you've done unto yourself.

Or, stated in words that apply specifically to your search for capital:

If you aren't willing to risk your own money, why should other people, especially family and friends, risk theirs?

The purpose of the Golden Rule of Bootstrapping is to make sure that you, the bootstrapper, don't even *think* about asking your family and friends for money before you've contributed yourself. The first question family and friends will ask is, "How much of your own money are you investing?"

These then are some of the most common places to find bootstrapping capital:

- ✔ **Savings, investments, and salable assets:** This is always the first place to look. Theoretically, all you're doing here is transferring your assets from one investment (your savings account) to another (your new business). Okay, so you're increasing your risk by a quantum leap, but you're also increasing your opportunity for reward.

- ✔ **The family and friends network:** Be sure to make your relationship loans as official as possible; always create a promissory note complete with a fixed interest rate (at least 1 percent over prime to avoid IRS scrutiny) and include cast-in-stone payback terms. Consult a lawyer when larger loans (in excess of $10,000) are required.

- ✔ **Life insurance:** If you own life insurance policies with a cash value, consider cashing in such policies and putting that money to far better use — your business. Besides, term life insurance is a far better deal (see Chapter 2). Remember, however, that you may owe some income tax on accumulated interest (in excess of the premiums you paid) from your life insurance policy.

  Ask yourself whether you really need life insurance at all. If you have no financial dependents, you won't need it to replace your income if you pass away. If you do need life insurance, however, secure good term life coverage before you cancel or cash in your current policy. Otherwise, your dependents will be in trouble if you pass away after you've canceled your current policy but before you've secured new coverage.

- ✔ **Credit cards:** Credit cards provide expensive money, perhaps, but easy money as well. No personal guarantees and no bankers looking over your shoulder; just sign your name and get on with the business at hand. Given the highly competitive credit-card market, be sure to shop around instead of simply accumulating a balance on whatever platinum-hued card you currently have in your wallet or heard about in an ad. When you carry a balance from month to month, always make your credit-card payments on time unless you enjoy paying even higher interest rates — upwards of 20 percent in many cases.

- ✔ **Home equity:** Proceed with extreme care when borrowing against home equity. A misstep could cost you the roof over your family's head. Remember that home prices can go down and you may find yourself in a situation where you're unable to refinance and are stuck with a larger, riskier mortgage. Don't even consider this option until you've thoroughly reviewed your overall personal financial situation (see Chapter 2 for details on how to do so).

Outsourcing for Your Capital Needs

As you can see in Table 5-1 earlier in the chapter, outsourcing institutions — banks, the Small Business Administration (SBA), Small Business Investment Companies (SBICs), angel investors, and venture capitalists — are *not* primary resources for start-up capital. Why not? Because most of these outsourcers are looking for either significant collateral and operating history (as is the case with banks and the SBA) or a business in an industry with uncommon opportunities for return on investment (as is the case with venture capitalists). Angel investors are the most versatile of the outsourcing resources, but they're also the most difficult to find.

Outsourcing resources fall into two general categories: banks and, er, nonbanks. Some outsourcers loan you money (banks, SBA, and others); others invest their money (venture capitalists, some angel investors, and the like). Stated another way, some outsourcers are creditors; others are part owners. We talk about each of these resources in this section.

Outsourcers, with the possible exception of SBICs, have a well-deserved role in the financing world; that role just doesn't happen to be at the start-up stage, especially for first-time business owners. After your business has matured and has a track record, and after you have matured and have a track record, outsourcers may become a part of the financing game for your business.

Banking on banks

Contrary to the popular opinion that bankers enjoy turning down prospective borrowers, bankers are in business to lend money. Effects of the Great Recession may have impacted this perception, but banks are still lending, albeit with a bit tighter credit standards, and actively looking for small-business deals to make.

Every time bankers sit down in front of a prospective borrower, they should hope that what they're about to see is a deal that will work. After all, no loans mean no lending income for the bank, and no lending income means no marble columns — and without marble columns, what would hold up their gold-inlaid ceilings? Make no mistake about it, banks are in business to lend money and make profits, which banks do by *playing the spread* — charging you more to use their money than they're paying somebody else (namely, depositors) to get it.

Most banks don't make start-up loans to small-business owners unless an owner's collateral covers 100 percent of the loan. Examples of such collateral include real estate (including home equity), savings accounts, and stocks and bonds.

A bank's primary role in the small-business lending arena is funding growth — for example, financing the expansion of a small business that has a track record. Most banks can offer a wide variety of creative loan packages designed to help finance existing small businesses. These loans include the following financing possibilities:

- **Asset-based financing:** The situation whereby a lender accepts the assets of a company as collateral in exchange for a loan. Most asset-based loans are collateralized against either *accounts receivable* (money owed by customers for products or services sold but not yet paid for), inventory, or equipment. Accounts receivable are the favorite of the three because they can be converted into cash more quickly (theoretically within 30 days, if you're offering these terms). Banks advance funds only on a percentage of receivables or inventory, the typical percentages being 75 percent of receivables and 50 percent, or less, of inventory.

  For example, using these percentages, if your business has $30,000 in receivables due from customers and $50,000 in inventory, the bank may loan you 75 percent of $30,000 (which equals $22,500) and 50 percent of $50,000 (which equals $25,000). The total of the two ($47,500) would then be available for you to use as working capital. These percentages vary based on the industry and the quality of the receivables and inventory.

  The form of asset-based lending in which the borrower's inventory is used as collateral for the loan is called *floor planning.* Car dealerships and RV dealers often use floor planning as their primary financing tool.

- **Line of credit:** The situation whereby the bank sets aside designated funds for the business to draw against the ebb and flow of cash as needs dictate. As line-of-credit funds are used, the credit line is reduced; conversely, when payments are made, the line is replenished.

  An advantage of line-of-credit financing is that no interest is accrued unless the funds are actually used. Surprisingly enough, the best time to arrange for your business's line of credit is when your business is doing well and you need the money the least. Why? Because that's when getting approval from the banker for the line of credit is easiest and you can qualify for the best loan terms.

  Don't make the mistake of overlooking a line of credit just because you don't presently need money. (Remember, a line of credit doesn't cost you if you don't draw against it.) Establish your credit line when things are going well. Sooner or later, if you're like most small businesses, you'll need the cash. (Ironically, the growth of a business, as opposed to its decline, is the situation that most often requires using a line of credit.)

- **Letter of credit:** A guarantee from the bank that a specific obligation of the business will be honored. Letters of credit are most often used to buy products sight unseen from overseas vendors. The bank generates its income in these situations by charging fees for making the guarantee.

Getting money from nonbanks

Banks don't have a lock on the small-business lending market. Investment brokerage firms and major business conglomerates can be important players in the small-business lending market, too.

Most nonbank lenders find their niche by specializing in a specific category of loan, such as leasing or asset-based financing. As a matter of fact, leasing companies (where you can lease your business's equipment or furniture and fixtures) are the most common nonbank financing resource; 25 percent of small businesses have some sort of leasing financing. *Leasing,* in case you've never done it, is basically the same as renting; you pay a monthly fee for the use of an item, and at the end of the lease term, you return the item to the company that leased it to you.

We explain some other important nonbank resources that small businesses can utilize in the following sections.

The Small Business Administration (SBA)

An *SBA loan* is a loan made by a local lender (bank or nonbank) that is, in turn, guaranteed by the SBA. The SBA provides its backup guarantee as an inducement for banks to make loans that otherwise may be too risky from a banker's perspective. Only in rare cases does the SBA actually provide the money itself.

SBA loans usually provide longer repayment terms and lower down-payment requirements than conventional bank loans. They're available to most for-profit small businesses that don't exceed the SBA's parameters on size (which can vary depending on the industry). SBA loans can be used for a number of reasons, including (in rare cases) start-up monies if, as with all SBA loans, you have sufficient collateral in long-term, tangible assets, such as real estate, machinery, and equipment.

Getting an SBA loan isn't a sure thing; on the contrary, the agency is extremely selective about whom it approves. Take a look at the primary criteria the SBA looks for when considering guaranteeing a loan:

- ✔ The owner must have invested at least 30 percent of the required capital and be willing to guarantee the balance of the loan.
- ✔ The owner must be active in the management of the business.
- ✔ All principals must have a clean credit history.
- ✔ The business must project adequate cash flow to pay off the loan, and the debt/net-worth ratio must fall within the SBA's approved guidelines.

To find a local bank or nonbank institution that works with the SBA, look in the Yellow Pages for SBA Approved Lending Sources (ALS) or call the SBA at 800-827-5722. On the web, go to www.sba.gov for more information about SBA loans that may work for you.

For an inventory of the three kinds of loans that the SBA makes, go to www.sba.gov/loans-and-grants, where you find a handy tool called the Loans and Grants Search tool. (Don't ask us why the link to that page includes the word *grants* when the SBA doesn't give any.)

Small Business Investment Companies (SBICs)

Small Business Investment Companies (SBICs) are privately owned, quasi-venture capital firms organized under the auspices of the SBA. SBICs either lend money to or invest money in small businesses primarily within their local area. Categorized as *Federal Licensees* (meaning that the federal government has given them its stamp of approval), SBICs either fund start-ups or provide operating funds to existing businesses that want to expand. Through their relationship with the SBA, SBICs are also able to offer particularly favorable terms and conditions to *disadvantaged businesses* (businesses owned by women and minorities).

Hundreds of SBICs operate around the country. To find out more about them, go to www.sba.gov/content/sbic-program-0, call the SBA at 800-827-5722, or contact a nearby Small Business Development Center (SBDC; see Chapter 3 for the lowdown on SBDCs).

Certified Development Companies (CDCs)

Another program of the SBA, the *Certified Development Company (CDC) program* (also known as the *504 Loan Program*), provides long-term (10- and 20-year), fixed-rate loans for small businesses. This program focuses on financing fixed assets, such as real estate (land and buildings). CDCs work with a local lender; typical financing may include 50 percent from the local lender, 40 percent from the CDC, and 10 percent down from the small business being helped. The asset being purchased serves as the collateral.

Several hundred CDCs exist nationwide. To find the CDC nearest you, go to www.sba.gov/content/cdc504-loan-program, call the SBA at 800-827-5722, or search the web for the 504 Loan Program.

Your state's Economic Development Department

Many states have an Economic Development Department (sometimes a stand-alone governmental agency; oftentimes housed within the state's Department of Commerce) that offers a variety of loan programs to statewide businesses. The programs offered are usually modeled after SBA loans but can often offer better terms and conditions than the SBA, especially for those businesses that employ many local employees. Such state departments also generally offer *microloan programs* that are designed to assist small-business start-ups by giving super-small businesses the opportunity to borrow money (less than $25,000) to get started. Since banks don't fund start-ups and don't like such small loans, these microloan programs are often the only available resource. Visit your state's Economic Development Department website for more information.

Angels: Investors with heart

Angel investors (often called *angels,* for short) are individuals — usually ex-entrepreneurs who are experienced enough to understand and live with the financial risks they take — with money available to lend or invest. The angels' motives may vary: Most seek to increase their net worth, some want to help aspiring entrepreneurs, and some simply crave being a part of the action.

Angels come in many forms: Some fly in flocks (that is, belong to angel organizations or investment groups), some work solo, some look for a piece of the company's ownership (equity), and others prefer lending (debt). Almost all angels demand personal involvement in your business, however, and in many cases, the know-how an angel can bring to the table is worth more than the capital itself.

Angels are like the highway patrol: When you need them the most, they're the most difficult to find. Fortunately, movements are afoot to make the identity of angels more accessible. For example, most large cities now have angel associations, which you can find through your favorite search engine. You can also ask your local bankers, accountants, financial advisors, or lawyers for their input on how to find a local angel-matching program. Or you can call your local Chamber of Commerce or your state's Department of Commerce.

Venture capital

Venture capital firms and organizations offer cash in exchange for equity in start-up companies, so they are, in effect, an organized version of angel investing. As opposed to more conservative sources of capital, which look closely at a business's past performance and its collateral before handing out cash, venture capital firms focus primarily on future prospects when looking at a business plan. Thus, venture capital is useful for a few sophisticated businesses in higher-risk, higher-reward industries. Venture capital firms look for the possibility of hefty annual returns (30 percent or more) on their investments in order to offset the losses that are sure to occur within their high-risk portfolios.

One angel's investing criteria

Angels do their investing for a number of reasons, ranging from greed to boredom to altruism. The best angels we know, however, are those who invest not because they're looking to make money, but because they enjoy the thrill of the start-up and like working with aspiring entrepreneurs. One such fellow is Norm Brodsky, who writes a column for *Inc.* magazine.

Brodsky, who views himself as much as a mentor as he does an angel, lists four basic rules for any angel investor:

Rule 1: Invest in people who want your help, not your money. Brodsky is looking for people who will listen. If they aren't ready to listen and are unwilling to take an old pro's advice, Brodsky sees no compelling reason to get involved.

The lesson for you: Angels are usually ex-entrepreneurs with deeply ingrained ideas on how to create and build a business. Be willing to use their ideas and suggestions, or you'll probably lose the angels. The flip side, of course, is to be sure that an angel's view of the world and your own business mission match. No investment is worth compromising your principles and vision.

Rule 2: When possible, go it alone. Independence is, and always will be, one of the entrepreneur's primary traits, in Brodsky's mind anyway. Entrepreneurs need to have things done their way, not someone else's way.

The lesson for you: One angel is preferable to a team of angels. In general, Brodsky believes that the "too-many-cooks-spoil-the-broth" principle is at work here. In some situations, however, more than one angel may be preferable — for example, when one angel doesn't have enough cash to meet your business's growth needs or where one angel may add flavors to the broth that the other angel doesn't.

Rule 3: Take a majority stake (become a partner) until your investment has been paid. Preservation of capital is of the utmost importance to sophisticated angels. They know that if they don't preserve it, they won't have it to invest again.

The lesson for you: Expect your angel to be demanding on the issue of ownership; he wants a voice in the direction of the business. He needs to have control, at least until it's obvious that the business is going to be successful and that the investment goals will be achieved.

In the end, of course, if you don't have enough money to go it alone and the angel is the one who makes the difference in whether your business gets off the ground, he will have great influence over the ultimate terms. We suggest, however, that you not give up the controlling equity in your company (51 percent) unless doing so is absolutely, positively your last course of action in obtaining financing. The amount of equity to be ceded is always negotiable; try to hold out for at least 51 percent for yourself.

Rule 4: Retain the right to force a payout (payback including interest) of the loan or investment. A business's profitability doesn't necessarily foretell a payout, unless it's specified in the agreement. Although the profitability of the business is important to the angel, the payout of the loan or investment is even more important. Success without a return isn't success; it's only grounds for disagreement.

The lesson for you: Expect your angel to demand in writing a payout that would come from future earnings, even though you'd prefer to spend or invest the cash elsewhere.

Few small-business start-ups are in a position to take advantage of venture capital financing. The typical venture capital firm funds only 2 percent of the deals it sees, and that 2 percent has to meet a wide range of investment criteria, such as highly attractive niches, sophisticated management, and potential for high return — criteria that the typical small-business start-up can't begin to meet. Don't be disappointed at not qualifying for venture capital funding. As this chapter details, many other, more appropriate financing resources with more attractive terms exist for you, the small-business owner.

Minority funding resources

The resources for low-income and minority funding (which in many cases includes women-owned businesses) are many. Look to the following for starters:

- ✔ The National Bankers Association (NBA) in Washington, D.C., represents minority-owned banks that target loans to minority-owned businesses. For the nearest member bank in your area, visit www.nationalbankers.org or call 202-588-5432.

- ✔ Most states have an agency that provides one-stop assistance on financial services for small businesses. Check your local library or phone book for such an agency in your state and then ask about state-operated minority funding resources.

- ✔ On the federal level, the SBA can help direct you to local organizations that can, in turn, help locate low-income and minority funding opportunities. Check out the SBA website at www.sba.gov or call 800-827-5722 to find the resource nearest you.

- ✔ The U.S. Department of Commerce's Minority Business Development Agency funds Business Development Centers nationwide; one of their functions is to help minority-owned start-up businesses. Go to www.mbda.gov or call 888-324-1551 for more information.

Exploring Ownership Options

In theory, all businesses have three ownership options:

- ✔ Privately held, with the founder being the only shareholder
- ✔ Privately held, with the founder sharing ownership with partners or other shareholders
- ✔ Publicly held, with the founder sharing ownership with the general public via one of the public stock markets

In reality, of course, most businesses have only the first two options — going it alone or having partners or minority shareholders. Few businesses have the management, resources, and appeal needed to go public, either at the start-up stage or in the course of the business's growth.

There's no right or wrong answer as to which of the three options you should use, but there is a right or wrong way to determine which one works best for you. At the heart of making that decision is . . . you guessed it . . . you! You're the primary ingredient that will determine which of the three options is best for your business. The criteria you need to use in making this decision include the kind of person you are, the way you communicate, the way you delegate, and the manner in which you work with people.

The role of business incubators

A *business incubator* is, quite simply, a building that's divided into units of space, which are then leased to early-stage small businesses. The result is a collection of offices and small warehouses filled with businesses (most likely in the light manufacturing, service, or technology sectors) that have one thing in common: They're businesses in the early stages of development. Each of the businesses has problems and needs that are similar, and each is in need of a variety of help, ranging from technical assistance to shared business opportunities to a simple pat on the back. Attesting to the benefits that incubators offer is the fact that the National Business Incubation Association now has more than 1,900 members in 60 nations.

Business incubators aren't intended to provide permanent homes to their client businesses but rather to provide them with a temporary nurturing environment until they're financially healthy. Upon reaching more predictable profitability, the incubated businesses are then expected to "graduate" and move on to typical offices or warehouse buildings.

The advantages of working in a business incubator environment are many; here are some of the most important ones:

✔ **Financing:** Most incubators offer some kind of access to capital. Because business incubators carefully screen all incubator companies, a business that has been accepted into an incubator offers somewhat of a stamp of approval in the eyes of potential lenders and investors. Also, angels tend to hover around business incubators, so acceptance into one is usually a surefire way to get in touch with the local angel community.

✔ **Shared opportunities:** Sales leads, new business opportunities, strategic alliances — all are part of an incubator's offerings.

✔ **Shared business services:** You find a number of important business services inside an incubator, including but not limited to personalized telephone answering, bookkeeping services, access to fax and copy machines, and a wide variety of services and equipment that would otherwise require outlays by the start-up business.

✔ **Affordable rents and flexible real estate:** Rental costs are often a bit below market, and the sizes of the offices and warehouses vary widely, thereby affording clients more flexibility.

✔ **Networking with peers:** Imagine a collection of small-business owners, people like you, in every workspace in your building. Being a small-business owner doesn't have to be lonely.

We recommend that you consider a business incubator unless yours is a business that depends on a geographic location that the incubator can't provide. To find the small-business incubator nearest you, visit the National Business Incubation Association's website at www. nbia.org or call 740-593-4331.

The kind of business you intend to start can also be a factor. If, for example, you intend to start a high-tech manufacturing business, you may find that the key employees you want to hire will demand some ownership (such as stock options) as part of their compensation packages (see Chapter 16 for details on how to find and keep superstar employees). On the other hand, if you intend to go into the consulting business, sole ownership is the likely ticket for you.

The following sections offer a brief discussion of the pros and cons of each of the three ownership options.

You as the sole owner

Sole ownership is always the least conflictive and most popular of the three options for starting a company, assuming that you have access to the necessary funds to launch your business, industry knowledge, and energy to make a go of the business by yourself. Sure, the leverage and financial benefits that partners and shareholders bring to the table can be worthwhile, but decision making in shared-ownership situations requires consensus, and consensus can take a lot of time. Besides, consensus doesn't always represent your personal best interests, and when your name is on your loan's personal guarantee's dotted line, your personal best interests should be at or near the top of the reasons for making decisions.

Being the only owner has the following advantages:

- ✔ **It's generally easier, quicker, and less expensive.** You don't need any lawyers to write up a Partnership Agreement or assist in determining answers to all the questions that a Partnership Agreement requires.

- ✔ **The profits belong solely to you.** You don't have to share the fruits of your hard work.

- ✔ **You have no need for consensus.** Your way is the only way.

- ✔ **You don't waste time catering to the often-aggravating demands of shareholders, minority or otherwise.** There's no possibility of shareholder lawsuits.

On the other hand, being the only owner has the following disadvantages:

- ✔ **You have no one to share the risk with.** This is the downside of the "profits belong solely to you" advantage that we describe in the preceding list.

- ✔ **Your limited skills have to carry your business until you can hire someone with complementary skills.** The small-business owner has to wear many hats; unfortunately, many of those hats simply don't fit. The day you can begin hiring employees who are capable in areas where you're not will be one of the highlights of your small-business career.

> ✔ **Single ownership can be lonely.** Many times, you'll wish you had some-
> one with whom to share the problems and stress. If you're lucky, you
> may be able to do this with trusted, senior employees. Of course, if you
> have good friends and/or a strong marriage partner, these people can
> also be a source of much-needed support.

Sharing ownership with partners or minority shareholders

Partners make sense when they can bring needed capital, along with complementary management skills, to the business. Unfortunately, partners also
present the opportunity for turmoil, and especially in the early stages of a
business's growth, turmoil takes time, burns energy, and costs money — all
of which most small-business founders lack.

If you're one of those rare individuals who is fortunate enough to have found
the right partner, go for it; work out a deal. We've seen this proven many
times over: A partnership in the right hands can outperform a sole proprietorship in the right hands.

Having *minority shareholders* (any and all shareholders who collectively own
less than 50 percent) can also make sense, especially after the business is
out of the blocks and has accumulated value. The most common methods of
putting stock in the hands of employees include stock-option plans, bonuses,
and Employee Stock Ownership Plans (ESOPs). See Chapter 17 for details.

Here's a warning based on our personal experience: Minority shareholders
can be a pain; they have legal rights that often run counter to the wishes of the
majority. Because majority shareholders are ceded the right to make the final
decisions, courts have determined that minority shareholders must have an
avenue of appeal. Thus, minority shareholders, particularly in today's litigious
society, sometimes look to the courts whenever they feel their rights of ownership are being violated.

As a result of the potentially tenuous relationship that can exist between majority and minority shareholders, you should always — we repeat, *always!* —
involve an attorney when inviting minority shareholders to the party, and you
should always include a buy-sell agreement in the deal. In the event that the
relationship doesn't turn out to be what all parties expected, buy-sell agreements establish procedures for issuing, valuing, and selling shares of the company, including how to determine the value of shares when one or more of the
owners want to cash out.

Occasionally, especially where venture capital financing is involved, the founder of the business may find herself working for majority shareholders. Fortunately, this situation rarely occurs because the typical small-business founder has already proven that taking orders from others is not exactly one of her inherent strengths. We've found that, on the infrequent occasions when this situation does occur, more often than not the founder of the company is the first one to get the boot when the going gets tough, as the chief financiers step in to protect their investment. That's why we strongly recommend that you find a way to retain majority control.

Deciding between sole and shared ownership

Still confused as to whether you want to go it alone or share ownership? Answer the following questions to help you make the decision:

- ✔ **Do you believe that you need a partner?** Do you absolutely, positively need a partner? To provide cash? Knowledge? If you do, that settles the issue; if you don't, continue with the following questions.

  Providing cash and additional knowledge are correct reasons for choosing a partner. Incorrect reasons include picking a partner because he or she is your friend or picking a partner because you're afraid of running a business by yourself.

- ✔ **Are you capable of working with partners or shareholders?** Will you have a problem sharing the decisions and the profits as well as the risks?

- ✔ **Does your business fit the multiple-ownership profile?** In other words, does your business have room for two partners, and is it a business that has the growth potential to support two partners? Will a partner have an important role in the organization? Would your partner's complementary skills enhance the business's chance for success?

- ✔ **What are the legal requirements of multiple ownership?** Can you live within these legal parameters? (Read through this chapter and then consult with an attorney if you still have questions.)

- ✔ **What do you have in common with other business owners who have opted for multiple ownership? Where do you see conflicts?** Ask your banker, accountant, or attorney for the names of other business owners who have opted for multiple ownership. Interview those owners and get their feedback on the list of pluses and minuses.

- ✔ **What's the likelihood of finding a partner with complementary skills and a personality compatible with yours?** This depends on how wired into the business community you are and what line of work you're going into. If you have a lot of business contacts and know exactly what you want, finding a partner may be easy. More typically, it isn't.

After you answer these questions, you should have enough information to make the decision, but take your time. Make a list of pros and cons and try to answer this question: Will your business have a better chance of success with just you at the helm, or are other skills immediately needed?

If you opt for multiple or shared ownership, you have to live with the decision for a long, long time. If you elect sole ownership at the start, however, you can always seek partners later if you feel that you need them to achieve the business success that you desire.

Going public: Cashing in

No question about it, the lure of liquidity and the possibility of interest-free capital can be overpowering to the small-business owner, especially after years of personally guaranteeing debt, scraping for money, and living on a reduced (or no) salary. Many small-business owners at one time or another fantasize about going public, yet few businesses ever make it. The biggest reason why few small businesses go public is that the stock markets are selective; they function for businesses that have outstanding track records and that meet particular hurdles. (Although we realize that this statement may be a bit hard to swallow if you've personally lost money investing in newly issued stock that went belly up, it still generally holds true.)

Here's what it takes to get your stock listed on the major U.S. stock exchanges:

- **National Association of Securities Dealers Automated Quotation system (NASDAQ):** NASDAQ has companies ranging from small emerging firms to large firms like Microsoft. Listing requirements include either a market value of at least $8 million and pretax income from continuing operations of at least $1 million or a market value of at least $18 million, 400 or more shareholders, and an operating history of at least two years. Tens of thousands of other companies are part of the over-the-counter market (NASDAQ allows brokers to trade "over the counter" from their offices all over the country), but these companies are so low priced and/or infrequently traded that they aren't listed on NASDAQ.

- **American Stock Exchange (AMEX):** AMEX is the second-largest stock exchange in the United States and typically lists mid-size firms. Listing requirements include a pretax annual income of at least $750,000 or a market value of at least $15 million.

- **New York Stock Exchange (NYSE):** NYSE is the largest stock exchange in the world in terms of total volume and value of shares traded. It lists more than 2,000 companies, which tend to be among the oldest, largest, and best-known American corporations. To be listed on the NYSE, a company must annually earn at least $2.5 million before taxes and must have a market value of at least $100 million, among other criteria.

In truth, going public has downsides that are easily overlooked. Although the capital raised may be interest-free, it is by no means hassle-free. The army of outside shareholders that comes with going public, in concert with the Securities and Exchange Commission (SEC), requires an avalanche of public filings. Yes, a public business is liquid, but at what cost to management's time? You also have to pay hefty fees to investment bankers to issue stock and to the stock exchange to initiate your listing and to maintain it over time. And in public companies, every shareholder, customer, media person, and competitor can peer into your financial records and ask you those questions that you may not have the time or the desire to answer.

Going public only works for a sophisticated chosen few, so don't waste a lot of time fantasizing about being the CEO of a public company. Given the entrepreneurial characteristics of the vast majority of people who typically decide to start businesses, combining public companies and small-business owners is like squeezing a size-12 foot into a size-9 shoe.

Deciding Whether to Incorporate

The legal entity options we describe in the upcoming sections are intended to serve only as guidelines. Although the entity decision you make won't necessarily be forever (your legal framework can and may change as your business changes), the choice you make now is bound to have significant short-term financial and legal implications — implications that will far exceed the cost of any upfront legal fees.

Before we discuss the variety of legal entities available to you, we must first pass on one piece of overriding advice. Today's high cost of legal consultations notwithstanding, making the entity decision is one of those half dozen or so times when consulting a good lawyer usually makes sense. On a related issue, at the time you're making the entity decision, a good attorney may ask you what your exit strategy is for your business. If you reply that your exit strategy may be to eventually sell the business, for example, your attorney will recommend certain options to you. Too often, we've seen business owners who suddenly decide they want to sell their businesses find out that, as a result of bad entity decisions made early on, they'll be taxed twice at the time of the sale. (*Note:* If your business is currently a C Corporation, make sure that this entity really, truly fits your needs. We'll bet there are better options.)

The first decision that you must make in the process of determining which legal entity to adopt is whether or not you want to incorporate. If your decision is to incorporate, your choices are then to become a C Corporation, a Subchapter S Corporation, or a limited liability corporation (LLC). In the following sections, we discuss the factors involved in your decision to incorporate or remain unincorporated, as well as your options within each category. Be sure to research all aspects of this issue, because you need to consider a host of tax, liability, and administrative issues before you decide.

If you prefer to do most of the incorporating work yourself without involving an attorney, refer to the book *Incorporating Your Business For Dummies* by The Company Corporation (Wiley). You can also visit the website www. corporate.com for more information and assistance on the subject.

Weighing unincorporated options

The preponderance of small-business entities — at least those whose owners aren't interested in significant growth but rather are looking to their business to provide a living — are unincorporated for any number of valid reasons (such as the cost and complexity of the incorporating process, which we talk about in the later section "Considering incorporated business entities"). If you decide to remain unincorporated, your business will automatically become either a sole proprietorship or, if you have a partner or partners, a partnership.

Sole proprietorships

If you're a typical small-business owner, especially one of the home-office variety, your first entity consideration should be the *sole proprietorship,* which is generally the simplest and least costly way to structure a business. Simply open your door, hang out your shingle, and zap, zap, you're a sole proprietorship. Little muss, little fuss, and little paperwork.

So why doesn't everyone become a sole proprietor if it's so simple? The primary reason is the personal liability issue: A sole proprietor is personally liable for the business and puts her nonbusiness assets at risk. If you've selected an industry in which the chances for liability are high (consulting, for example), you should at least consider the option of incorporating.

Most people decide to open sole proprietorships by using their own names as the principal owners because doing so is the best, and simplest, choice. If you decide to use a fictitious name or a trade name, however, you need to file a Certificate of Conducting Business Under an Assumed Name with your state or local town/city/county clerk. You can obtain the forms from good self-help law books; the filing fee is minimal.

Other important things you need to know about the sole proprietorship include the following:

- ✔ Ownership must be limited to a single owner or a married couple.
- ✔ Taxable income is subject to both income and self-employment tax (see Chapter 19).
- ✔ Business losses may offset income from other personal sources subject to certain limitations.

✔ Some states allow protection of personal assets from business risks if you own them jointly with your spouse or if you transfer them to your spouse or children. (Check with an attorney or your state's attorney general's office for details.)

✔ Insurance is available to cover some of the risks of a sole proprietorship. (Check with associations that are appropriate for your profession; also check with local insurance agents who specialize in working with small-business owners.)

✔ Legal termination of the business is easy for the sole proprietorship, especially compared to all the legal ramifications required when terminating something like a C Corporation. When putting an end to a sole proprietorship, simply close the doors and (assuming that you have no outstanding creditors) walk away.

Partnerships

Similar to a sole proprietorship, a *general partnership* (also known as a *standard partnership*) can be started simply by opening the doors. A partnership may include two or more partners and is similar to the sole proprietorship in that little paperwork is required in the formation stage. The individual partners are taxed on their percentage of the partnership income; therefore, the partnership itself, like the sole proprietorship, doesn't pay taxes.

In a partnership, all partners are personally liable for their obligations to the partnership. Because of this liability issue, partnerships can be particularly sticky relationships unless the partners are capable of resolving disagreements amicably.

In addition to the general partnership, you can create a business entity known as a *limited partnership* — a combination of at least one general partner and one or more limited partners. The limited partners are liable only to the extent of the cash and/or property they've contributed to the partnership; the general partners are liable for everything else. The general partners are the managing partners; the limited partners are only passive investors.

When you make the decision to involve a partner or partners in your small business, we strongly recommend that you (and an attorney) prepare a Partnership Agreement. Although this agreement isn't legally required for a partnership to conduct its business, we recommend that you prepare one in order to outline what happens should various and inevitable problems or issues arise, such as one partner wanting out of the business or the need for the infusion of new capital in unequal contributions by the partners.

In the absence of a Partnership Agreement, the division of ownership, profits, and liabilities among partners is legally assumed to be equal, regardless of whether some partners have contributed more assets or time than others to the business.

A good Partnership Agreement includes the following specifics:

- ✔ **The duration of the partnership:** Generally, a Partnership Agreement's duration is *in perpetuity* (or for an indefinite period of time). However, you may have reasons why one partner or another may specify that the agreement will lapse, such as when a business reaches a certain size or when profits are available to repay one partner's initial investment.

- ✔ **The time or money each partner will contribute:** The time and money contributed will rarely be the same throughout the duration of a partnership. When an unplanned difference between the two exists (for example, one partner works longer hours than the other or one partner contributes new money to the company while the other does not), a good Partnership Agreement spells out a way to equate the disparity.

- ✔ **The methods for making business decisions:** Generally speaking, someone has to have the final word in the likely event that the partners have disagreements.

- ✔ **The sharing of profits and losses:** Normally, profit sharing (as well as loss sharing) is in concert with the percentage of ownership; however, you may have occasions when one partner will receive more than the other. These occasions, which should be spelled out in the Partnership Agreement, may include new responsibilities, new investments, or new workloads.

- ✔ **The determination of when to distribute profits:** Partners' wishes on this issue aren't always consistent; one partner may want to take money out of the partnership, while the other may want to leave the money in to help the company grow.

- ✔ **The dissolution or restructuring of the partnership in the event of death or disability of a partner:** Sooner or later, death and/or disability is going to happen, and when it does, you must have a way to determine the valuation of the partnership for estate or cash-out purposes and for redefining the ongoing business.

Considering incorporated business entities

A *corporation* is a legal entity of its own; thus, its owners (shareholders or stockholders) aren't personally liable for the business's liabilities, losses, and risks. Shareholders can come and go, but, unlike a sole proprietorship or a partnership, the business will continue to exist in spite of any change in the corporation's ownership.

Husband-and-wife partnerships: A union not always made in heaven

Daryl and Helen's business started out the way many husband-and-wife partnerships do, evolving from the skills of the husband. Daryl was an Earthmover extraordinaire and had been driving those monstrous yellow machines you see rumbling around highway construction projects since he graduated from high school. He could turn a rolling hill into a parking lot quicker than you could utter the word *excavate.* After ten years of moving dirt for someone else, Daryl decided he was ready to start moving it for himself, whereupon he started Whitney and Sons Excavations. Who better to take care of the bookkeeping and office chores than his wife Helen?

The company grew in the early years, both in revenues and in profits. At the beginning, Daryl was an enthusiastic hands-on manager, directing every job himself. Several years passed, and the company had 20 employees and bank borrowings to finance hundreds of thousands of dollars in heavy equipment. Daryl's workdays were long and emotionally draining. Instead of driving the Earthmovers, he was "baby-sitting" other people who drove them. Meanwhile, Daryl and Helen's personal problems had escalated — they were learning the lesson so many husband-and-wife partnerships have learned over the years: Just because the husband is a talented craftsman doesn't necessarily mean he can manage a business with a group of employees (including his wife).

The company's bottom line turned to red, employee unrest multiplied, and cash disappeared. Helen's job became harder and harder. She was the one who had to manage the bank loans and vendor payables, and she was the one who had to scrounge to find the cash to make the payrolls. She hated her job — not the bookkeeping part, but the cash-managing part — keeping unhappy bankers and vendors and employees at bay as she juggled the company's waning assets. Daryl and Helen's communications, never great even at the beginning of their partnership, worsened, and they soon had to seek marriage counseling.

Finally, Daryl and Helen could take it no more. They swallowed their pride and declared bankruptcy. Helen took a job as an accountant for Brown County while Daryl, you guessed it, hired on as a Cat driver for a large company in a neighboring county. The marriage sputtered for another year or so before both Daryl and Helen decided too much damage had been done. Sadly, that partnership ended, too.

The moral of this story? No matter what the legal entity is, a husband-and-wife business is a partnership, in the true sense of the word. Just because you can manufacture a widget together, don't assume that you can manage a company. Partnerships are risky arrangements. The good ones prosper; the bad ones can ruin friendships and marriages. If a husband and wife don't communicate well *before* they go into business, they shouldn't expect to begin communicating well *after* they go into business together.

Yes, many wonderful companies have evolved thanks to fruitful and binding partnerships between spouses. Sadly, however, too many more have failed. Tread carefully as you ponder the decision to enter into another partnership.

Generally speaking, the decision to incorporate is usually made either as a result of the business's growth and the issues that accompany that growth or when the personal tax considerations of one or more of the owners warrant incorporation. The desired benefits of making the incorporation decision usually include the following:

- ✔ **Shielding the company's principals from personal liability:** Consider whether the type of business you're getting into or are already in has high potential for lawsuits.

- ✔ **Providing an opportunity to raise capital by selling stock:** The alternative to raising capital by selling stock is accumulating debt, and too often lenders aren't interested in under-capitalized businesses.

- ✔ **Enabling the business owners to more quickly and easily transfer ownership from one shareholder to another:** Each share of stock has a value and, thus, can be bought and sold at whatever price that value represents.

- ✔ **Allowing for the adoption of a variety of employee benefits (such as the corporation's ability to fully deduct employee health and disability insurance premiums paid) not available to other types of unincorporated entities:** See Chapter 17 for a discussion of benefits.

Every corporation with multiple owners needs to execute a buy-sell agreement, which always involves the assistance of an attorney competent in this area. Among other things, the buy-sell agreement dictates how a person's shares of stock will be handled if that person retires from the business, becomes disabled, or dies. This exit-strategy issue is one of the most overlooked potential problems among entrepreneurs.

Given the benefits of incorporating, you may assume that you'll find significant disadvantages to incorporating; otherwise, everyone would do it. Correct-amundo! The primary disadvantages of incorporating are

- ✔ **The cost and hassle of going through the incorporation procedure and complying with the public agencies (federal and state) that oversee corporations:** The act of incorporation can be expensive, especially from the perspective of a budding entrepreneur with limited cash and few or no customers. The cost depends on the state in which you incorporate, but it can range from about $100 to approximately $1,000 for incorporation fees. Plus, the corporation must pay an annual tax that varies by state. These costs don't include attorney's fees or any other fees that may crop up. (Yes, you can incorporate online, but we don't recommend it. For matters like incorporating, you need a more personal experience — a name and a face to help you through the process.)

Filings can take from a few days to several weeks, again depending on which state you're in and who's handling the process within that state. In some states, filings can take up to two months because the secretary of state and county officials must review them.

- **The hassle and potential liability from shareholder lawsuits involved in dealing with shareholders:** Shareholders have legal rights and often those rights aren't in tandem with the wishes of the owner.

- **The "double taxation" that occurs in a C Corporation when dividends are paid:** When corporations earn profits, those profits are taxed at the corporate level. If some of those profits are then paid in dividends to company shareholders, company shareholders also must pay income tax on the dividends, hence the term *double taxation*.

If you decide to incorporate, you have three kinds of corporations to consider: the C Corporation, the Subchapter S Corporation, and the limited liability corporation. We discuss each one in the sections that follow.

C Corporations

Most big businesses and some small corporations elect *C,* or *regular, Corporation* status, primarily because of their need for the liability protection that C Corporations offer. Because of their size and the public nature of their business, these large corporations don't qualify for either Subchapter S or limited liability company status.

A C Corporation is taxed as an entity separate from any of the individuals comprising it, and all the profits of the business are taxed at the corporate level. If some of those profits are paid in dividends to the corporation's shareholders, the shareholders have to pay ordinary income tax on those dividends, too. The result is the so-called double-taxation status of corporations.

As with the other types of corporations, C Corporations are expensive and time-consuming to create. The process includes getting the owners of the business (the shareholders and stockholders) to agree on the following:

- The name of the business
- The number of stock shares the company can sell, the class of stock, and its value
- The number of shares the owners will buy
- The amount of money (or other assets) the owners will contribute to buy shares of stock
- The directors and officers who will manage the corporation

Subchapter S Corporations

Named after the Internal Revenue Code section that allows them, *Subchapter S Corporations* are the "little folks" — smaller companies that need the liability protection afforded but don't have the issue of multiple shareholders to worry about. Subchapter S status is reserved for businesses with no more than 75 shareholders. Both new and existing businesses may elect to adopt Subchapter S status.

When does becoming an S Corporation make sense? As with a C Corporation, an S Corporation provides the liability protection, but unlike a C Corporation, it avoids the double-taxation status by allowing the income of the corporation to pass through to its owners/shareholders. So the major difference between an S Corporation and a C Corporation is that the S Corporation income is subject to only one tax — the personal income tax.

S Corporation status is the usual choice of small-business owners who make the decision to incorporate for liability purposes. This is especially true for start-up businesses because early-stage losses can be offset against your personal income.

Before deciding to create a Subchapter S Corporation, consider the profitability expectations of your business. In the start-up years, if you're like most small businesses, you can expect your business to lose money. In this case, opting for Subchapter S status is advisable, because you can offset your business losses against your personal income. In later years, as your business becomes profitable, paying taxes at the corporate rate rather than the personal rate may become more advantageous, so you'd be wise to switch to C Corporation status.

The election of Subchapter S status has many other varied ramifications. We strongly recommend that you have an attorney or qualified tax advisor help you make this decision.

Limited liability companies: A hybrid invention

The *limited liability company* (LLC) is the newer kid on the corporate block. The IRS officially awarded the LLC favorable tax status in 1988; today, all 50 states and the District of Columbia allow this unique entity. An LLC is a hybrid entity. It combines the benefits of a corporation with those of a partnership:

- ✔ As in a corporation, investors in an LLC don't face personal liability for the debts or obligations of the LLC.

- ✔ Like a partnership, the LLC is afforded favorable tax treatment because the income and losses of the business flow through to the individual investors, who are called *members,* and are reported only once on each investor's personal income tax return.

Another advantage of an LLC is its flexibility. Unlike an S Corporation, an LLC can be structured to allocate the profits of the business differently among the various members, while at the same time preserving the flow-through tax treatment. An LLC has the added advantage over a partnership of providing the members with limited liability. The relationship of the members in an LLC is controlled by an operating agreement, a document not unlike the Partnership Agreement we describe in the earlier section "Partnerships." As you may imagine, the operating agreement can be quite complex.

LLCs are relatively new, so we recommend that you consult an attorney with significant experience in establishing LLCs for small businesses like yours to help you decide whether an LLC can work for your business and to help draft the operating agreement. Find an attorney who really understands the ins and outs of LLCs and ask for attorney referrals from other business owners who've incorporated.

Part II
Buying an Existing Business

The 5th Wave   By Rich Tennant

BUSINESS
FOR SALE

In this part . . .

Some small-business owners are better suited to buying an existing small business than to starting one from scratch. This part explores the advantages and disadvantages of buying an existing business and helps you determine what kind of business to buy and what you should pay for it. In this part, we also cover the tax implications and potential employee issues involved with buying an existing business, and we provide you with a process for moving forward after you make your purchase.

Chapter 6

Exploring Buying a Business

· ·

· ·

*A*fter a business has been created, it can have a life of its own. The umbilical cord to its creator can be cut, and the business can pass onto various owners. In some cases, a great small business can outlive its original owners — assuming, of course, that subsequent owners have the necessary entrepreneurial and management skills.

In this chapter, we tell you the reasons why you should buy a business, but we also steer you clear when your personality and resources don't make purchasing a good match.

Understanding Why to Buy a Business

Every year, hundreds of thousands of small businesses change hands. Why? For the same reasons that many people purchase an already-built home instead of building one from scratch — because building a home or business takes a lot of time and work and has lots of potential for problems.

We don't mean for you to take this building analogy too far. After all, you can start most small businesses without drawing on your carpentry skills. However, as with buying an existing home, you may find that the advantages of buying an existing business outweigh the advantages of building one yourself.

As if the issue of saving time and energy in the building process isn't enough, another reason for buying a business is that, historically, the failure rate is twice as high for starting a business as compared to buying one. So why doesn't everyone buy a business rather than start one? Because not that many good businesses make it to the auction block. Many of the good ones never hit the market; instead, they're passed on within the family or are sold in private transactions without ever being listed for sale.

Dissatisfaction: A catalyst for change

As sometimes happens in life, people who end up buying a business often end up doing so as a result of some outside force or circumstance that propels them in that direction.

Consider the case of David, a veterinarian who worked for an owner who agreed to offer David 10 percent of the practice after David had worked there for a number of years. Over time, however, the owner engaged in various legal maneuverings that allowed him to wiggle out of the offer. David became dejected and upset; he'd been a loyal and highly competent employee over the years. His customers enjoyed working with him and requested his services when scheduling future appointments. David couldn't understand how the owner could treat him so poorly despite his years of excellent

service to the business. David couldn't see that the owner was greedy and unethical, because David was neither.

The silver lining to this story is that this horrible experience was the catalyst David needed to go into business for himself. Instead of building a practice from scratch, however, David bought an existing practice — and he's glad that he did. David hit the ground running with the established practice and used his energies and talents to make the practice bigger and better. After many years of building the business and enjoying the challenges, David sold it and is enjoying his semiretirement as a highly financially secure multimillionaire.

In the following sections, we discuss reasons why you may want to buy an existing business rather than build one from scratch. (In Chapter 7, we discuss how to find the best businesses to buy.)

To reduce start-up hassles and headaches

Running a business is always a juggling act, but you often have more balls in the air during those start-up years than at any other time in the life of the business. Beyond formulating a business plan, you have to develop a marketing plan, find customers, hire employees, locate space, and possibly incorporate. Although you still need a game plan when buying an existing business, many of these start-up tasks have already been done.

Consider the learning curve for the type of business you're thinking of purchasing. Buying an existing business makes sense if the business is complicated. For example, purchasing a business that manufactures an intricate product makes more sense than purchasing a house-painting business, which doesn't require much more than the necessary tools and equipment and painting know-how. Also, unless you have already built the product the company manufactures and you understand the intricacies of the production process, starting such a complicated business from scratch is quite risky and perhaps even foolhardy.

To lessen your risk

In situations where a business has an operating history and offers a product or service with a demonstrated market, you remove some of the risk when you buy the company (compared with starting from scratch). Although no investment is a sure thing, the risk involved in an already-established business should be significantly lower than the risk involved in a start-up. Because an existing business has an operating history, you can use past financial statements (see Chapter 14) to help you make more accurate financial forecasts than you can with a start-up venture that has no history.

As we explain in Chapter 8, before you buy a business, you must do your homework, which means carefully inspecting the business you're considering buying and its financial statements (this careful inspection is known as *due diligence*). You can't take at face value how the business appears on paper or in site visits, because more than a few business sellers have been known to dress up the books and the business to hide problems and flaws.

To increase profits by adding value

Some business owners who decide to sell their company don't see the potential for growth or don't want to grow their business. They may be burned out, content with their current earnings, lacking in needed business-management skills, or simply ready to retire. Finding a business that has the potential to improve operating efficiency and expand into new markets is difficult but not impossible — if you have the time and patience to wait for the right one to come along. In fact, finding small companies that are undervalued relative to the potential they have to offer is probably easier to do than finding undervalued stocks or real estate when investing in those markets.

Just because you think you see the potential to improve a business, never, ever pay a high acquisition price based on your expectations of being able to add that value. Even if you're correct about the potential, why should you pay the current owner for the hard work and ingenuity you plan to bring to the business? If you're wrong, you could grossly overpay for the business. If you're right, you could miss out on some really big profits. On the other hand, if you always offer a fair price based on the value of the business at the time you purchase it, you can realize the rewards of your improvements after you make them. (We explain how to arrive at this fair price figure in Chapter 9.)

A smart seller will try to convince you that he has underachieved with the business and that all it needs is your energy, enthusiasm, and fantastic business acumen. Don't fall for the compliments; remember that sellers sell the future while buyers buy the past. What this saying means is that the person who's buying the business shouldn't listen to the seller talk about the grandiose things that can be done with the business but should instead focus on what the business has already done (recognizing, of course, that the business may actually be worsening in the short-term and may not even be capable of generating what it did in the recent past). In other words, the buyer isn't buying the seller's vision; he's buying what's in place today.

To establish cash flow

One of the biggest unknowns involved in starting a business from scratch is estimating the new business's cash flow. (We discuss cash flow in detail in Chapter 14.) Will the business generate cash quickly, or will it take a long time? How long will collecting monies due from customers (receivables) take? How long will selling inventory take? How much will you have to invest in fixed assets? How quickly will your sales be established?

With start-up businesses, estimating these figures is fraught with the potential for wide margins of error. Fortunately, that's not the case when you buy an existing business. The track record of the previous owners has already answered most of these questions. Assuming that you don't walk in and make immediate, glaring changes to the business's products or operations, the cash flow pattern should continue somewhat as it has done in the past. Take it from us: As a small-business owner, you'll feel reassured by having a reasonably predictable cash flow. You and your family, your banker, and other investors will deeply appreciate it. Conversely, unpredictable cash flow is troublesome at best and will keep you from sleeping at night. (Just remember that your cash flow needs may be higher than the current owner's because you may have to repay the loan you used to buy the business.)

As a bonus, borrowing money from banks and raising money from investors is often easier to do when you buy a business instead of doing a traditional start-up. Lenders and investors rightfully see more risk with a start-up than with an established enterprise with a good track record. Plus, they have the business's existing assets with which to collateralize their loans. For the amount they invest, investors usually demand a smaller percentage of ownership in an existing business than in a new business.

To capitalize on someone else's good idea

We've said it before: You don't need an original idea to go into business for yourself. Plenty of successful small-business people enjoy running a business; whether they sell tires or trim trees doesn't matter.

If you know you want to own a business but you lack an idea for a product or service to sell, chalk up another good reason to buy an existing business. Just make sure that you have some passion for the industry you're thinking about joining.

To open locked doors

In certain businesses, you can enter geographic territories only as a result of buying an existing business. For example, suppose that you want to own a Lexus dealership within an hour of where you currently live. If Lexus isn't granting any more new dealerships, your only ticket into the automobile industry may be to buy an existing Lexus dealership in your area.

To inherit an established customer base

If you're not good at selling (maybe because you dislike it), buying a business may be the best way for you to enter the world of business ownership. After all, buying an existing business gives you a ready-built stable of customers, which means you don't have to recruit them yourself. Then, if you can provide quality products or services and meet customers' needs, you can see your business grow through word-of-mouth referrals.

In the long term, your lack of sales ability could wreck even an established business. All businesses, even those that don't want to grow, need to add new customers if only to replace those who inevitably leave. If you can't sell (or figure out how to sell) to new customers, your business eventually may flounder. Be sure your new business has employees on staff with sales skills or be ready to hire people with the necessary selling skills. (See Chapter 16 for details on hiring good employees and check out Chapter 13 for more on retaining loyal customers.)

Knowing When You Shouldn't Buy

Of course, you can find more than a few downsides to buying an existing business. Similar to the advantages, the relative weight of these disadvantages depends largely on your personality and available resources.

You dislike inherited baggage

When you buy an existing business, you get the bad along with the good. All businesses have their share of the bad. A business may have problem employees, for example, or it may have a less-than-stellar reputation in the marketplace. Even if the employees are competent, they and the culture of the company may not mesh with your direction for the company in the future.

Do you have the disposition and desire to motivate your employees to change or to fire employees who don't want to change? Do you have the patience to work at improving the company's products and reputation? Do you have the cash to upgrade the technology or remodel the dated offices? All these issues are barriers to running and adding value to a company. Some people enjoy and thrive on such challenges; others toss and turn in their sleep with such pressures. Think back on your other work experiences for clues about what challenges you've tackled and how you felt about them. (If you haven't done so, take the quiz in Chapter 1 to help you assess your workplace likes and dislikes.)

You're going to skimp on inspections

If you think buying a company is easy, think again. Before you sign on the dotted line, you must know exactly what you're buying, so you need to do a comprehensive inspection of the company (see Chapter 8 for details on how to do so). For example, you (or a competent financial/tax person) need to analyze the existing business's financial statements to ascertain whether the company really is as profitable as it appears and to determine its current financial health.

After you close the deal and transfer the money or duly record the IOUs, you can't turn back. Unless a seller commits fraud or lies (which is difficult and costly for a buyer to prove in a court of law), it's "buyer beware" with the quality of the business you're buying. In Chapter 8, we cover all the homework you should do before you decide to buy.

You lack capital

Why do a lot of people start a business instead of buying one? Because they simply don't have enough cash — or credit potential — to buy one. Existing businesses have value over and above the value of their hard assets, which is why you generally need more upfront money and credit to buy a business than to start one. Although you may feel like you're more the business-buying type than the business-starting type, if you don't have the necessary dough, and if you can't find investors or lenders to provide it, then your avenue to business ownership may be decided for you, regardless of the avenue you'd prefer.

The wrong reasons for buying a business

Jeff was a successful electronics wholesaler. As Jeff approached the age of 50, he and his wife began to think more and more about where they might spend their retirement. As is typical of many Midwesterners fed up with long and dreary winters, Florida jumped to mind.

During a winter vacation in Naples, Florida, Jeff was idly perusing the classified ads when he noticed a business for sale in the wholesale electronics industry. His curiosity got the better of him, so he visited the company and talked at length with the owner. Before you could mutter the words *spring break,* Jeff had purchased the company with one-third of the purchase price in cash and the balance borrowed as a long-term loan.

Jeff's primary reason for buying the business? To give himself and his family a chance to travel to Naples on the company expense account, mixing golf with business during those cold Midwestern winters. "A great way to ease into retirement," he told his friends.

Fast-forward two years. The Naples business was floundering badly. Apparently, many of the company's customers had been *relationship customers* (people who mainly did business with the company because of their friendship/relationship with the owner), and now that the previous owner was gone, so were they.

(It didn't help that Jeff was only around three months out of the year, and the company's efficiency suffered accordingly.) Additionally, Jeff discovered that managing his new Deep South employees had little in common with managing his old Midwest employees. Meanwhile, the business was hemorrhaging money.

Six months later, Jeff reluctantly closed the company's doors by transferring the remaining inventory to Minneapolis, taking a $250,000 hit to his bottom line in the process. A hefty price to pay, he admitted, for a few rounds of wintertime golf and some tax deductions.

In the end, Jeff's business failed because he purchased it for the wrong reasons. He purchased the business to get away from Minnesota winters and to earn some meager tax deductions, which, Jeff can tell you in retrospect, weren't nearly enough. He didn't purchase it because he had a passion for his customers, or because he had an urge to make a difference for his employees, or because he had a driving need to create something meaningful, or for any other strategic business reason.

The lesson here? You should have compelling reasons to buy a business. As Jeff learned the hard way, golf in Florida and tax deductions just aren't enough.

You think you'll miss out on the satisfaction of creating a business

Whether it nourishes their souls or simply gratifies their egos, entrepreneurs who build their own businesses get a different rush than those who buy existing companies. Certainly you can make your mark on a business you buy, but doing so takes a number of years. Even then, the business is never completely your own creation.

Recognizing Prepurchase Prerequisites

Not everyone is cut out to buy an existing business, and we're not just refer-ring to those who don't have enough cash or credit. In fact, you can purchase a good small business with little or, in rare cases, no money down.

The process of buying a business requires a lot of work. However, success-fully running the business day in and day out is much harder for most people than finding and buying it. Some succeed wildly at running the business they buy; others fail miserably. So what, then, are the traits common to people who successfully buy and operate an existing small business? We cover them in the following sections.

Above all else, being persistent, patient, and willing to spend time on things that don't lead to immediate results pays off. You need to be willing to sort through the rubbish to find the keepers. If you're a person who needs immedi-ate gratification in terms of completing a deal, you may become miserable as you search, or you may end up rushing into a bad deal. Try breaking the pro-cess into steps to provide more success points and give yourself time for clear thinking.

Business experience and training

You need to have the necessary business experience and background if you want to buy a business. If you were an economics or business major in col-lege and you took accounting and other quantitatively oriented courses, you're off to a good start.

If you've worked on business-management issues within a variety of indus-tries (as consultants who work as generalists do), you also may have the proper background. However, one danger in having done only consulting is that you're usually not on the front lines where you confront most of the seri-ous day-to-day operational issues. We've seen plenty of sophisticated con-sultants who didn't have the foggiest idea how to meet payroll or ship a UPS order or read an accounts receivable aging report.

If neither of these backgrounds applies to you, you won't necessarily fail if you decide to buy a business, but the odds are against you. If you don't have a business background and work experience, you may still succeed. However, you'll probably simply survive (and just surviving probably isn't what you're after). Plus, your prospects for outright failure are relatively high, as com-pared to your experienced competitors.

We strongly encourage you to get some hands-on, small-business management experience, which is more valuable than any degree or credential you earn through course work. You'll find no substitute for real-life experiences in marketing to and interacting with customers, grappling with financial statements, dealing with competitive threats, and doing the business of everyday business.

If you want to own a computer repair service, go work in a good one. If you want to run a jet-ski rental business, go work in a successful one. Try to wear as many hats in the business as the boss allows. Consider the experience as paid, on-the-job training for running your own business. You're getting your unofficial MBA, and someone is even paying you for it!

We're not saying that you should avoid academia. You may, in fact, have to get a certain credential to do the work that you want to do. If you don't need a specific credential, taking selected courses, as well as reading relevant business books, can boost your knowledge.

For those of you with a large company or government background, be advised that there's a huge difference between working for IBM or the U.S. government and owning a small business. Most skills required simply aren't transferable, plus you must wear a plethora of business hats (sales, marketing, shipping and receiving, customer service, and so on) when you own a small business. Too many corporate or government employees have bit the proverbial dust when buying a small business because they made the erroneous assumption that running a small business requires the same skills as working in a large organization.

Down-payment money

When purchasing a business, as in purchasing real estate, you generally must make a significant down payment on the negotiated purchase price. In most cases, you need to put down at least 25 to 30 percent of the total purchase price. Bankers and business sellers who make loans to business buyers normally require down payments to protect their loans. They've learned from past experience that small-business buyers who make small down payments are more likely to walk away from a loan obligation if the business gets into financial trouble.

For example, consider what happened with coauthor Jim's fourth business, which he sold for 33 percent of the sales price in cash and the balance (67 percent) in a ten-year loan. Two years after the sale, the buyers declared bankruptcy, leaving Jim holding the bag on the remainder of the loan, which was still more than 60 percent of the purchase price. Had Jim not required a down payment, he would have received no cash from the deal, only a long-term note that he would eventually eat; on the other hand, had he required 50 percent down, he would've received another 17 percent of the purchase price in cash, thereby reducing the amount of the note he would eventually write off.

If you lack a sufficient down payment, try asking family or friends to invest or lend you the cash. (See Chapter 5 for more on bootstrapping options.) You can also set your sights on a less-expensive business or seek out business sellers willing to accept a smaller down payment.

If you find a business for sale in which the owner wants less than 20 percent down, you may be on to something good. Be careful, though; owners willing to accept such small down payments may be having a difficult time selling because of problems inherent in the business or simply because they've overpriced the business. Smart sellers want to maximize the amount of the down payment. Your intent as a buyer should be to keep the down payment to a minimum (subject, of course, to obtaining favorable loan terms), thereby retaining as much cash as possible to use in operating the business.

Beware of the all-cash deal, even if you can afford it. If the business turns out to be something less than what was presented, you, the buyer, will lose all your leverage to negotiate. He who has the cash has the power — and you don't if you've paid 100 percent cash for the business purchase.

You can purchase many existing small businesses with a loan from the seller. Also, check with banks that specialize in small-business loans. For more financing options, see Chapter 5.

Chapter 7

Finding the Right Business to Buy

- -

In This Chapter

▶ Developing your business-shopping criteria

▶ Discovering the best resources for generating leads

▶ Surveying franchises and multilevel marketing companies

▶ Evaluating the legitimacy of work-from-home opportunities

- -

*A*fter you make the decision to purchase a business, be realistic as you start your search for a worthy business to buy. Give yourself plenty of time to research potential candidates. After all, haste makes for lost money if you purchase a business without thinking through what you want and taking the proper steps to buy a quality business for a fair price.

Finding a good business can easily take a year or two. Even if you can afford to search full time, you can still expect to spend several months on the prowl. This chapter offers our suggestions for uncovering the best business to buy.

Defining Your Business-Buying Appetite

Many businesses are for sale (in other words, everything has its price). To conduct an efficient search, you need to set some preliminary criteria. Although you don't have to define every detail of the business you want to purchase, setting a few well-chosen parameters can help focus your search and keep you from spinning your wheels.

Although everyone has a different set of business-shopping criteria, you probably want to specify the following general issues:

✔ **Type of business:** Businesses to buy come in four major categories:

- Retail (includes restaurants)
- Manufacturing
- Service
- Wholesale

Usually a good manufacturing business is the hardest to find, followed by service and wholesale. Most communities have an adequate quantity of retail and restaurant businesses available to buy.

✔ **Industry:** We highly recommend that you focus on specific niches in industries that interest you or that you know something about. Focusing helps you conduct a more thorough search and find high-quality companies. In addition to the industry knowledge you bring to the table, the knowledge you accumulate in your search can pay big dividends during your years of ownership.

If you have a hard time brainstorming about specific industries, here's a suggestion to jump-start your cerebral synapses. Take a walk through your local Yellow Pages. Listed alphabetically are all the businesses known to exist in your area. Remember that a separate Yellow Pages directory exists for businesses that sell mainly to consumers, while a "business-to-business" phone directory lists businesses whose customers are primarily other businesses. Look at either or both, depending on the types of businesses in which you're interested.

You also may want to buy a business in a sector that's experiencing fast growth so that you, too, can ride the wave. Check out *Inc.* magazine's annual *Inc.* 500 list of the fastest growing smaller companies in America and their *Inc.* 5000 list of fast-growing private companies.

✔ **Lifestyle:** The type of lifestyle you want your small business to provide can narrow your search significantly. If you're going into small business because you'd like to work from home, for example, then you obviously don't want to buy a business that depends on a nonresidential, bricks-and-mortar location. Also, consider how large an income you hope to generate, how many employees you want to manage, and whether or not you want to travel.

✔ **Size/purchase price:** Unless you can cleverly craft a deal with a low down payment, the money you have to invest in a business constrains the size of business you can afford. As a rule, figure that you can afford to pay a purchase price of about three times the down payment amount you have earmarked for the business. For example, if you have $30,000 saved for the down payment, you should look at buying a business for $100,000 or less. Because many business sellers overprice their businesses, you can probably look at businesses listed at a price above $100,000 — perhaps even as high as $150,000 — because you can probably negotiate to buy such businesses for less.

Don't invest all your money in the purchase — you'll need some money to finance the day-to-day operations of the business until it becomes profitable.

✔ **Location:** If you're rooted to a location already and don't want to move or have a long commute, the business's location further narrows the field. Although you may be willing to consider broader territory — maybe even nationally if you're willing to relocate — evaluating businesses long distance is difficult and expensive. Unless you're in the market for a highly specialized type of company, try to keep your search local.

✔ **Opportunity to add value:** For most people, managing an ongoing business is enough of a challenge. As with real estate, most people are happier leaving the fixer-uppers to the contractors with experience in rehab, otherwise known as turnaround experts in the business world. However, some buyers want to purchase a business with problems that need fixing or with untapped opportunities. In fact, some businesses with correctable problems (weak or unproductive employees, inadequate systems and controls, or a shortage of cash, for instance) offer significant untapped potential and usually can be purchased at bargain prices.

After you define your shopping criteria, you're ready to go to the marketplace of businesses for sale. We recommend that you type your criteria on a single page so that you can hand it to others who can put you in touch with businesses for sale. (For ideas on whom to give it to, see the next section.)

Generating Leads

Break out your Sherlock Holmes cap and magnifying glass because finding a good business to buy is a lot more like doing detective work than shopping at the mall. Be prepared to turn over a lot of stones and follow a lot of tracks, many of which will lead to dead ends. But perseverance pays off, and the following sections cover some proven resources for generating leads in your search for the right business to buy.

Perusing publications

If you focus on specific industry sectors, you may be surprised to discover how many specialty newsletters and magazines are out there. Just think of the fun you can have reading publications like *Marine Store Merchandising, Piano Technicians Journal,* and *Diaper Delivery Service Business Guide!* Specialty publications get you into the thick of an industry and also contain ads for businesses for sale or business brokers who work in the industry.

A useful reference publication that you can find in public libraries is the *Small Business Sourcebook* (Gale). This enormous reference (which retails for $681) contains listings of publications, trade associations, and other information sources by industry. Also peruse the classified ads in leading business publications, such as *The Wall Street Journal,* where owners wanting to sell small businesses can buy ads in the full-run or regional editions of the newspaper.

Conducting literature searches of general-interest business publications helps you identify articles that can keep you up-to-date on your industry of interest. You can use online computer searches to find the most useful articles. Check out Chapter 12 for tips on how to get the most out of the web and other technological resources.

Networking with advisors

Speak with accountants, attorneys, bankers, financial advisors, Chamber of Commerce employees, and business consultants who specialize in working with small businesses. These advisors sometimes are the first to find out about a small-business owner's desire to sell. Advisors can also suggest good businesses that aren't for sale but whose owners may consider selling in the future.

Knocking on doors

If you were a homeowner and someone came to your door and said she was interested in buying your home, you'd probably say that you're not interested in selling. If the interested buyer said she really liked the type of property you had and was willing to pay what you consider to be a good price, the person may get a little more of your attention, but you'd still likely turn her away. But if you, as the homeowner, were considering selling anyway, you'd be all ears — especially if you think you can sell directly and save paying a broker's selling commission.

Some business owners who haven't listed their businesses for sale are right now thinking about selling. So if you approach enough businesses that interest you, you may find some of these not-yet-on-the-market businesses. (Who knows, the business owner you approach may not be interested but may know another business owner who is.) The reason to go to this trouble is that you increase the possibility of finding the right business. You may also get a good deal on such a business. You can negotiate with the seller from the beneficial position of not having to compete with other potential buyers.

Instead of calling on the phone or knocking on the business's door, start by sending a concise letter of introduction that explains what kind of business you're seeking and what buyer qualifications you possess. This step demonstrates that you're investing some time in the endeavor. Follow up by phone a week or so after you send the letter.

Enlisting business brokers

Some sellers list their businesses for sale with business brokers (or *intermediaries*). Just as a real estate agent makes a living by selling real estate, a business broker earns his livelihood by selling businesses. Business brokers provide a number of services:

- ✔ Establish a confidential selling process
- ✔ Maintain an inventory of businesses for sale
- ✔ Assist in determining a fair market value of a business
- ✔ Work with potential buyers
- ✔ Help clients negotiate and structure their offers
- ✔ Assist through the close of the transaction

You'd hire a business broker for similar reasons that you'd hire a real estate broker:

- ✔ **Technical expertise:** Business brokers understand the process. They also understand the pros and cons of most businesses because they've seen a number of similar businesses throughout their career. The trick here is to find a broker you can trust. When you've done that, the broker can take a lot of mystery out of the process and a lot of risk out of the purchase.

- ✔ **Emotional noninvolvement:** The broker serves as a middleman between the buyer and seller. As everyone who has ever bought or sold a business knows, the process can get quite emotional.

- ✔ **An ability to see the deal from both sides:** You can bet you and the seller will have two points of view!

Of course, working with business brokers isn't problem-free. Here are some of the main issues you may face if you decide to go the broker route:

✔ **Commission conflicts:** Brokers aren't business advisors; they're commissioned salespeople. That fact doesn't make them corrupt or dishonest, but it does mean that their interests aren't always in line with yours. Their incentive is to do a deal and do the deal soon — and the more you pay, the more they make. Business brokers typically get paid 8 to 10 percent of the sales price of the business. Technically, the seller pays this fee, but as with real estate brokers, the buyer effectively pays, too, because the seller builds the commission into the price.

If a broker isn't involved, the seller can sell for a lower price and still clear more money, which makes the buyer better off, too.

✔ **Undesirable businesses:** Problem and marginal businesses are everywhere, but a fair number of them end up with brokers. The reason: The owners had trouble selling them on their own.

✔ **Deceiving packaging:** This problem relates to the previous two potential pitfalls. Brokers help not-so-hot businesses look better than they really are. This typically involves stretching the truth — that is, omitting the negatives and hyping the positives. (Yes, owners selling their business themselves may do these things as well, but not as "effectively.")

You (and your advisors) need to exercise due diligence on the business you're thinking of buying. Never, ever trust or use the selling package a broker (or an owner) prepares for a business as your sole source of information. Unscrupulous brokers, as well as unscrupulous sellers, can stretch the truth, lie, and commit fraud. (See Chapter 8 for more on how to evaluate a business.)

✔ **Access to limited inventory:** Unlike a real estate broker who typically has access, through a shared listing service, to almost all the homes currently for sale in a particular area, a business broker can generally tell you only about his office's listings. Confidentiality is an issue, because a shared listing service increases the number of people who can find out that a business is for sale and the particulars of the sale, which may hurt future business or cause a key employee exodus.

If you plan to work with a business broker, use more than one. Working with a larger business brokerage firm or one that specializes in listing the type of businesses you're looking for can maximize the number of possible prospects you see. In some areas, brokerages pool listings to allow access.

✔ **Few licensing requirements:** Unlike real estate agents in most states, the federal government doesn't regulate the business brokerage field or require any official licensing. The majority of states don't have any requirements, either, so anyone can hang out a shingle and work as a business broker. Some states require real estate licenses of business brokers who operate in their states. After all, real estate transactions or leases are part of many business deals. Some states allow those with securities brokerage licenses to operate as business brokers.

Business brokers generally sell smaller small businesses — those with less than $1 million in sales annually. These businesses tend to be family owned or sole proprietorships and include restaurants, dry cleaners, other retailers, service firms, and small manufacturers and wholesalers. Approximately half of such small businesses are sold through brokers.

Most business brokerage firms sell different types of businesses. Some firms, however, specialize in only one industry or a few industries. If you don't have your heart set on buying a particular type of business — a computer repair business, for example — one advantage of working with brokers is that they can expose you to other businesses you may not have considered. Brokers can also share their knowledge about some of your ideas — like the fact that, if you buy a computer repair business, you'll need to work on the weekends to fix your best customers' computers so that they're ready for Monday. Still want to buy one?

So how do you find potential business brokers? Ask tax, legal, and business consultants for good brokers they know. Also check out ads for businesses for sale; they may lead you to a broker. If you've found a broker you think you'd like to work with, check that the broker works full time at his profession and has solid experience. Some business brokers only dabble in the broker business part time and make their living other ways. These brokers may lack focus and experience.

When evaluating a potential broker, ask for the names of several buyers that the broker has worked with in the past six months. Ask for buyers of businesses in your field of interest so that the broker can't simply refer you to the three best deals of his career. Then contact those buyers to see what they thought of the broker. Also, check with the local Better Business Bureau and any state regulatory department (for example, real estate, attorney general, or department of corporations) that oversees business brokers to see whether any complaints have been filed against the broker in question.

Considering a Franchise

Among the types of businesses that you can purchase are franchise operations. Some companies increase the number of their locations by selling replicas, or *franchises,* of their business. When you purchase a franchise, you buy the local rights within a specified geographic area to sell the company's products or services under the company's name and to use the company's system of operation. In addition to an upfront franchisee fee, franchisers typically charge an ongoing *royalty* (percentage of sales).

As a consumer, you've likely done business with franchises. Franchising is a huge part of the business world. Companies that franchise — such as McDonald's, H&R Block, Subway, and FootLocker — account for about $2 trillion in sales annually. Purchasing a good franchise can be more expensive in upfront dollars but can also be a relatively safer ticket into the world of small-business ownership. In the next sections, we cover the pros and cons of buying a franchise.

Franchise advantages

Unlike when you buy other businesses, you don't buy an existing enterprise when you purchase a franchise. Although the parent company should have a track record and multiple locations with customers, you start from scratch when you purchase a new franchise (unless you purchase an existing franchise directly from its owners). As the proud owner of a new franchise, you don't have customers. Just as you'd have to do with any new business, you must recruit your customers.

So why would you want to pay a chunk of money to buy a business without getting any customers in the deal? Actually, you should consider purchasing a good franchise for the same reasons that you'd purchase any other solid, established business. A company that has been in business for a number of years and has successful franchisees proves that there's a demand for the company's products and services and that its system for providing those products and services works. The company has worked out the bugs, developed marketing programs that work, established a brand, and (you hope) solved common problems. As a franchise owner, you benefit from and share in the experience that the parent company has gained over the years.

Franchises offer two additional advantages that most other small businesses don't:

- **A larger and successful franchise company has brand-name recognition.** In other words, consumers recognize the company name and may be more inclined to purchase its products and services. Or stated another way, the franchiser has already done the marketing and public relations. When you purchase the franchise, you're buying into the fruits of those efforts.

- **A franchise offers centralized purchasing advantages.** As you'd hope and expect from a corporation made up of so many locations, the franchisor can buy supplies and accessories at low prices. Such volume-purchasing generally leads to bigger discounts to customers and bigger profit margins to franchise holders. In addition to possibly saving franchisees money on supplies, the parent company can take the hassle out of figuring out where and how to purchase supplies.

Franchise disadvantages

Franchises aren't for everyone. As with purchasing any other small business, pitfalls abound in buying franchises. Some common problems that you need to watch for include the following:

- **You may not be the franchise type.** When you buy a franchise, you buy into a system that the franchiser has created for you. People who like structure and established rules and systems more easily adapt to the franchise life. But if you're the creative and free-wheeling sort (that is, the typical entrepreneur) who likes to experiment and change things to keep life interesting, you'd probably be an unhappy franchisee.

   Unlike starting your own business in which you may get into the game without investing a lot of time and money, buying a franchise business that ends up not being what you want can be a more expensive learning experience. For example, you may discover that you don't like being on the phone and dealing with the public after shelling out significant money to purchase a travel-agency franchise.

- **You're required to buy overpriced supplies.** Centralized, bulk purchasing through the corporate headquarters is supposed to save franchisees time and money on supplies and other expenditures. Some franchisers, however, attempt to make big profit margins by putting large markups on the proprietary items that they contractually obligate franchisees to buy from them.

- **The franchise may be unproven.** One of the problems with buying a franchise is that you may not be buying an ongoing, established business complete with customers. If the concept has not stood the test of time and survived the experiences of other franchisees, you don't want to be a guinea pig as an early franchisee. Plus, some franchisers are more interested in simply selling franchises to collect the upfront franchise money. Reputable franchisers want to help their franchisees succeed so that they can collect an ongoing royalty from the franchisees' sales.

- **The franchise may be a pyramid scheme.** Unscrupulous, short-term-focused business owners sometimes attempt to franchise their business and sell as many franchises as quickly as possible. Some even have their franchisees sell franchises and share the loot with them. Everything becomes focused on selling franchises rather than operating a business that sells a product or service intended to satisfy customers. In rare cases, franchisers engage in fraud and sell next to nothing, except the false hope of getting rich quick. (See the next section for more on these schemes.)

Evaluating Multilevel Marketing (MLM) Firms

A twist, and in many cases a bad one, to the franchising idea (see the preceding section) is a *multilevel marketing* (MLM) company. Multilevel marketing is designed to replace the retail store as a conduit for selling certain products. Advocates of the MLM business model maintain that, when given identical products, the one sold face to face (without the cost of maintaining a storefront and hiring employees and paying insurance) is less expensive than the same product sold in a store. Additionally, MLM advocates believe that buying a product from someone you know and trust makes more sense than buying from a clerk behind a retail counter.

Sometimes known as *network companies,* MLM companies can be thought of as a poor person's franchise. For those weary of traditional jobs, the appeal is obvious: Work part time from home, with no employees and no experience necessary, and make big bucks. We've heard claims that you can make tens of thousands of dollars per month for just a few hours per week.

As a representative for an MLM company, you're treated as an independent contractor, and your job is to solicit new customers as well as to recruit new representatives. These new reps are known in the industry as your *down line.* The big selling point is that you make money not only off your own customers but also off the business that your down-line recruits bring in.

Being wary of pyramid schemes

The number one trait of MLM that leads to its all-too-frequent excesses is that everyone can get in for little money upfront; thus, everyone does get in. And we do mean everyone — hence, MLM's often shaky reputation.

The problem is that the worst of the MLM companies are the equivalent of *pyramid schemes.* They offer no legitimate or proven service or product and exist solely to "sign up" as many reps as they can before someone realizes that the castle has been built on a cloud — at which point they take the money and run.

MLMs have been known to offer the pitch that you can make tens of thousands of dollars monthly while sitting on your duff and letting someone else do the work. All you have to do is sign up a few friends and relatives to sell the company's widgets. Then, before you can shout the words *easy money,* the big bucks come rolling in. We know many people who have been taken for thousands of dollars in MLM schemes; all they found was a quick way to lose money and to alienate friends and relatives.

Anyone considering becoming an MLM investor needs to keep in mind that any network marketing arrangement is really just another form of a job. No company, MLM or otherwise, can offer to pay you money while you're busy watching the soaps. As with any other worthwhile venture, time — three to five years, in most cases — and a lot of hard work are required to create a business that will provide you with a decent living. If the MLM business were as simple as some in the business lead you to believe, everyone would dive in and get rich.

For sure, some legitimate, successful companies are MLMs — Mary Kay and Tupperware, for example. However, they're the exception rather than the rule, particularly among the types of MLMs that you're likely to have aggressively pitched to you by others.

Finding the better MLMs

Quality MLM companies make sense for people who really believe in and want to sell a particular product or service and don't want to or can't tie up a lot of money by buying a franchise or other business. Just remember to check out the MLM company and realize that you won't get rich in a hurry, or possibly ever. Capitalism has taught us over the years that whatever looks too good to be true usually is. Be sure to check the references of the MLM company that you're considering.

Remember that due diligence requires digging for facts and talking to people who don't have a bias or reason to sell to you. Do the same homework that we recommend in Chapter 8 when you're thinking about buying into an MLM firm. Assume that an MLM company isn't worth pursuing until your due diligence proves otherwise.

Legitimate MLMs put as much emphasis, if not more, on the products or services they offer as they do on recruiting new reps, and they don't claim that you'll make a killing without working hard to find new customers. Although not shy about advertising the big earnings its successful salespeople make, Mary Kay doesn't hype the income potential. Local sales directors typically earn $50,000 to $100,000 per year, but this income comes after years, not weeks or months, of hard work. Mary Kay rewards its top sellers with gifts, such as the coveted pink Cadillac.

The ingredients for Mary Kay's success include competitive pricing, personal attention, and social interaction, which many stores don't or can't offer their customers. "We make shopping and life fun . . . we make people look and feel good," says one of Mary Kay's sales directors. Mary Kay encourages prospective reps to try the products first and host a group before they sign up and spend approximately $100 to purchase a showcase of items to sell. To maximize sales, Mary Kay representatives are encouraged to keep a ready inventory because customers tend to buy more when products are immediately available. If reps want out of the business, they can sell the inventory back to the company at 90 cents on the dollar originally paid, a good sign that the company stands behind its product.

If you do decide to buy into an MLM company that seems reputable, think twice before signing up relatives, friends, and coworkers in your MLM venture — at least until you're satisfied that the concept is a viable one. The particular danger in doing business with people you care about, and who care about you, is that, in addition to your reputation and integrity, your friendships and family relations are on the line.

Checking Out Work-from-Home Opportunities

Ads that promote ways to make piles of cash while working out of your home are easy to find these days, especially in the magazines that cater to small-business owners and wannabes and through e-mail spam solicitations. They read something like this:

> "Earn $10,000 monthly! We'll even help you hire agents to do the work for you . . . FREE! Thirty days is all it takes!"

> "FIRE YOUR BOSS AND DOUBLE YOUR INCOME! Earn $2,000 to $5,000 weekly — starting within 3 to 6 weeks. Own your own business. Control your destiny! Work from home! No overhead; no employees; no commute! 55 to 70 percent + profit margins."

> "Work out of your home. Company needs help. Earn $500 to $900 per week. Anyone can do this — will train. Full time or part time. Only for the serious — please!"

And so the refrain goes. In many cases, these ads are just another form of overhyped multilevel marketing scams and should be avoided. In these and other similar ads, no legitimate company may exist, but rather, you'll find a person or two with a post office or e-mail box somewhere who wants to sell you a package of "confidential information" explaining the business opportunity du jour. This package of confidential information may cost you several hundred dollars or more. More often than not, this information ends up being worthless marketing propaganda and is rarely useful.

Our advice? Read this book and tap the other helpful resources we list in it to understand more about legitimate small-business opportunities. You'll find more and better information, and the price will be far lower.

Remember one more thing about such money-making, can't-miss "opportunities": Never buy into one that's pitched over the telephone or that requires a nonrefundable cash outlay — unless, that is, you want to lighten your pocketbook and feel like a doofus.

Myriad opportunities are available in today's fast-paced entrepreneurial economy. The best ones come from your studies into the local economic environment, from your discovery of a niche within your current job, or from your exhaustive research of the business community as a whole. Beware of those "opportunities" that promise overnight success. And beware of those "opportunities" that promise you something for nothing.

Chapter 8

Evaluating a Business to Buy

In This Chapter

▶ Conducting a comprehensive pre-offer evaluation of the company, its owners, and its employees

▶ Analyzing the company's financial statements and investigating the lease contract terms

▶ Considering the unique issues in franchises

*I*n the American legal system, a person is presumed innocent until proven guilty beyond a reasonable doubt. When you're purchasing a business, however, you should assume that the selling business owner is guilty of making the business appear better than it really is until you prove otherwise.

We don't want to sound cynical, but more than a few owners have tried to make their businesses look more profitable, more financially healthy, and more desirable than they really are. The reason is quite simple: Business sellers generally seek to maximize the price their businesses will command.

Buying a business can be tricky because the business brokerage market rarely favors the buyer. The following list presents some of the obstacles you're likely to encounter when buying a business:

- ✔ **The necessary confidentiality of transactions:** You can't publicly investigate a lot of the background information.

- ✔ **Few listings:** A lack of businesses for sale means that the seller is in control. Good businesses that are fairly priced usually have numerous potential buyers.

- ✔ **Unpublished prices of previous sales:** You often don't have any benchmarks or templates to follow.

- ✔ **Emotional circumstances surrounding the sale:** People can get more emotional about selling their business than they do about selling real estate. Blood, sweat, retirement, and yes, egos, are all involved. Emotions run high on both sides of the deal.

Buying a business is a long, detail-ridden, and usually stressful procedure. Don't rush it; be sure to cover your bases. We hit all the key points of consideration in this chapter.

Kicking the Tires: Doing Your Due Diligence

Before you make an offer to buy a small business, you need to do some digging into the company to minimize your chances of mistakenly buying a problematic business or overpaying for a good business. This investigative process is known as *due diligence,* and it's every bit as important as hiring an attorney or signing the purchase agreement.

Smart buyers build plenty of contingencies into a purchase offer for a small business, just as they do when buying a home or other real estate. If your financing doesn't come through or you find some dirty laundry in the business (and you're not buying a laundromat), contingencies allow you to legally back out of the deal. However, knowing that all your purchase offers will include plenty of contingencies shouldn't encourage you to make any purchase offer casually.

Making an offer and doing the necessary research are costly, in both time and money, but you'll be glad you did both after the deal is done and you can rest easy, knowing that you've purchased a good business. So before making an offer for any business, make sure that you investigate all the important issues that we discuss in the upcoming sections.

Buyer beware

Katie made a gut-level decision when she decided to buy a restaurant from a silver-haired, distinguished-looking gentleman named Max. Well-dressed, well-educated, well-traveled, and well-versed in his wines, Max charmed Katie, flattering her about how successfully she could run his restaurant. (His French accent didn't hurt either.)

Max's "fact sheet" on the business was also impressive. It showed, over a period of several years, steadily increasing revenue and even more rapidly increasing profits for the restaurant. In the 12 months before the negotiations, the restaurant grossed more than $500,000 and had pretax profits of about $150,000.

A wine collector and food connoisseur, Katie had always dreamed of running her own restaurant. But she wanted no part of the grunt work of a start-up: developing a complete menu from scratch, negotiating a lease on a good location, advertising for and interviewing prospective employees, and so on. However, with a recently received inheritance, Katie could now afford to bypass the start-up stage and purchase an established restaurant, such as the one Max offered for sale.

After just a couple of offers and counteroffers, Katie paid cash for the business. Max turned over the restaurant, hailed a cab for the airport, and headed for a retirement cottage in the south of France.

The first few months, business seemed a little slower than Katie had anticipated, but, overall, things seemed to be going okay. However, by the end of the first year, Katie found that she had serious problems.

First, expenses were higher and revenues lower than Max's historic financial statements had indicated they would be. For the first full year under Katie's ownership, the restaurant grossed about $300,000, which, after expenses, was just barely enough to break even.

Second, Katie ended up with lease problems. In her tenth month of ownership, the owner of the building that housed Katie's restaurant politely informed her that the restaurant's lease was about to expire; when it did, he was going to triple the rent! Katie couldn't believe it. Max had never mentioned that the lease was about to expire or that he had negotiated a rate well below market value a long time ago and that it was bound to jump up when it did expire.

In the ensuing months and years, Katie's restaurant eventually dragged her into personal bankruptcy. As it turns out, when Max was preparing the financial statements for Katie, he exercised quite a bit of creative license — also known as *Enroning* your financials.

Katie was never able to track Max down in France. If she had found him, she could have sued him for misrepresenting the business's profitability. Of course, that's probably why Max did such a good job covering his tracks.

Although somewhat extreme, problems of the magnitude left hidden in Katie's restaurant aren't that unusual among businesses for sale. Don't expect the business seller to point out the cracks in the foundation; you have to hunt for them yourself. (In Katie's case, Max's financial shenanigans would've been easy to discover with the proper amount of due diligence.)

Until you prove to yourself beyond a reasonable doubt that negative surprises don't exist, don't go through with a business purchase.

Examining owners' and key employees' backgrounds

A business is usually only as good or bad as the owners and key employees who run it. Ethical, business-savvy owners and key employees generally operate successful businesses worthy of buying. Unscrupulous, marginally competent, or incompetent business owners and key employees are indicative of businesses that you should avoid.

Just as you wouldn't (we hope) hire employees without reviewing their resumes, interviewing them, and checking employment references, you shouldn't make an offer to buy a business until you do similar homework on the owners and key employees of the business for sale. Here's a short list of what to look for and how to find it:

✔ **Business background:** Request and review the owners' and key employees' resumes. Are the backgrounds impressive and filled with relevant business experience? Just as you should do when hiring an employee, check resumes to make sure that the information they provide is accurate. Glaring omissions or inaccuracies send a strong negative message as to the kind of people you're dealing with.

✔ **Personal reputations in the business community:** The geographic and professional communities to which most business owners and employees belong are quite small. Any business that has been up and running for a number of years has had interactions with many people and other companies.

Take the time to talk to others who may have had experience dealing with the business for sale (including vendors, the Chamber of Commerce, the Better Business Bureau, and so on) and ask them their thoughts on the company's owners and key employees. Of course, we shouldn't need to remind you that you can't always accept the statements of others at face value. You have to consider the merits, or lack thereof, of the source.

✔ **Credit history:** If you were a banker, you certainly wouldn't lend money to people without first assessing their credit risk. At a minimum, you would review their credit history to see how successful they've been at paying off their loans on time. Even though you won't be lending money to the business seller you're dealing with, we recommend that you check his credit records. A problematic credit record may help you uncover business problems that the owner has had that he may be less than forthcoming in revealing. The major agencies that compile and sell personal credit histories and small-business information are Experian (www.experian.com), Equifax (www.equifax.com), TransUnion (www.transunion.com), and Dun & Bradstreet (www.dnb.com).

✔ **Key customers:** In most cases, the people who can give you the best indication of the value of a business for sale are its current customers. Through your own research on the business or from the current owner, get a list of the company's top five to ten customers and ask them the following questions:

- In general, how is the company perceived by its customers?

- Does it deliver on time?

- How do its products or services compare to its competitors' offerings?

- Does it have a culture of integrity?

- What does the company do best?

- What does it need to improve?

✔ **Key employees:** If the employees of the business for sale are aware of the prospects of the impending sale, be sure to interview them and get their insider's take on the condition of the business. Also try to find out whether they intend to remain as employees under the new ownership. (If Katie, in the earlier "Buyer beware" sidebar, had interviewed the restaurant's employees, she surely would've found out about Max's character and credibility shortcomings and maybe even gained insight into the false revenue figures he presented.)

Finding out why the owner is selling

As part of your due diligence of a potentially attractive business, you need to try to discover why the owner is selling. Small-business owners may be selling for reasons that shouldn't matter to you (such as they've reached the age and financial status where they simply want to retire), or they may be selling for reasons that you need to think twice about (such as the business is a never-ending headache to run, it isn't very profitable, or competition is changing the competitive landscape).

Just because an owner wants to sell for some negative reason doesn't necessarily mean you shouldn't buy the business. If the business has a low level of profitability, it isn't necessarily a lemon; quite possibly the current owner hasn't taken the proper steps (such as cost management, effective marketing, and so on) to boost its profitability. You may well be able to overcome hurdles that the current owner can't. But before you make a purchase offer and then follow through on that offer, you absolutely, positively must investigate many aspects of the business, including, first and foremost, why the current owner wants out.

Here's how to discover why the current owner is selling (where appropriate, get the current owner's permission to speak to certain people):

✔ **Chat with the owner.** Okay, so this isn't a terribly creative, Sherlock Holmes–type method, and, yes, we know that many sellers aren't going to be completely candid about why they're selling, but you never know. Besides, you can verify the answer you get from the owner against what other sources (like the business's listing broker) tell you about the owner's motivations to sell.

✔ **Talk to the business owner's advisors.** As we explain throughout this chapter, in the course of evaluating the worth of a business, you should speak to various advisors, including those you hire yourself. Don't overlook, however, the wealth of information and background that the current owner's advisors have. These advisors may include lawyers, accountants, bankers, and/or the business's own board of advisors or directors. Sure, they may not be completely candid, but your job is to read between the lines of what they have to say.

- ✔ **Confer with industry sources.** Most industries are closely knit groups of companies, each one knowing, in general, what's going on with the other businesses in the same industry. Most importantly, the vendor salespeople or manufacturers' representatives who sell products or services to the industry can be a useful source for information. Just remember to take what anyone says with a grain or two of salt.

- ✔ **Seek out customers.** The business's current customers usually have a good idea of why a business is for sale. They can provide you with the information you need to determine whether the current owner is selling from strength or from weakness.

- ✔ **Discuss with employees.** Some employees probably know the real answer as to why the business is for sale. Your job: Find out what they know.

In your discussions with and investigations about the current owner, also reflect upon these final, critical questions: How important is the current owner to the success of the business? What will happen when he or she is no longer around? Will the business under new management lose key employees, key customers, and so on?

Knowing how to tell whether a seller is motivated

Imagine that you're in the market to buy a home. In the course of touring houses for sale in a neighborhood you'd like to live in, you discover two houses — one on Elm Street and the other on Oak Street — that meet your wish list of criteria. Both houses have the right amount of space and good-sized yards and are located on quiet streets. In all other respects, the two houses are similar, and your analysis of comparable house sales in the neighborhood indicates that each house is worth about $240,000.

The Elm Street house is priced at $299,000, and the Oak Street house is priced at $249,000. The owner of the Oak Street house has already had the house inspected, has provided a copy of the inspection report, and has offered to correct the problematic items in the report at his cost. You also notice that the Oak Street house has been cleaned up both inside and out and looks ready to move into.

Now, assuming that you like both houses equally well, which house would you be more interested

in making an offer on? It should be no contest. Clearly, the Oak Street house owner is more motivated and serious about selling. You can tell this not only from the more realistic asking price but also from all the time, effort, and money the owner has put into getting the house ready to sell.

So when you're shopping for a small business to buy, look for similar ways to identify a motivated seller. Just as with real estate, a significant portion of small-business sellers aren't serious or motivated about selling. And just as with some house sellers who don't need to sell, some small-business owners stick a high price on their business and are willing to sell only if some salivating pushover comes along and is willing to (over)pay.

Other small-business owners aren't really emotionally ready to part with their "babies." If you follow our advice in this chapter and in Chapter 9, you won't be anyone's fool because you'll know how to value a business for sale and how to identify whether the owner is motivated to sell.

Surveying the company culture

Buying a small business is similar to adopting someone else's child. Depending on the strength of its already-formed personality and the degree to which it meshes with yours, you may or may not be successful in molding that business into your image.

Thus, another important element of your due diligence is to find out what kind of culture the business has. How, for example, are employees viewed and treated in the company? In meetings, are subordinates allowed (or even encouraged) to challenge the thinking of their supervisors?

Larry was an MBA from one of the nation's top business schools. He thought he could make a bundle of money by buying a small manufacturing company and running it better than its current owners. Given his blue-chip credentials, he thought running the company would be a snap. So Larry purchased the company with a 35 percent down payment of the purchase price, with the seller carrying a note for the balance.

Larry's first task was to clean house of the "deadwood," firing key employees so that he could replace them with people who would better measure up to his high standards. Larry made his downsizing decisions after just a couple of weeks on the job. He didn't seem to know (or perhaps didn't care) that the company had a history and culture of respect for its employees. Even during slow economic times, previous management hadn't let people go but instead had scaled back hours of operation.

Not surprisingly, after nearly 20 percent of the staff was gone, Larry had earned himself the reputation as the "grim reaper" because many of Larry's new hires couldn't do the jobs as well as the previous job holders who had been fired. The original staff that remained, not surprisingly, feared for their jobs; thought Larry was callous, incompetent, and uncaring; and worried about the future of the company. Many of the best remaining employees had updated their resumes and were actively seeking employment elsewhere in an attempt to escape the negative culture that Larry had brought with him. Gradually, most of the good employees who had survived Larry's initial bloodlettings quit as the company went into a financial tailspin. Eventually, Larry himself had to move on.

What's the point of this story? What should Larry have done differently?

> ✔ **Before buying the company, Larry should've taken the time to understand the company's culture.** Changing employees may not be impossible in the company you buy, but attempting to change the culture, especially in such a short period of time, is a too-often-fatal endeavor. Cultures are a sensitive business asset and should be treated accordingly. Larry should've spent more time assessing and considering the company's culture both before he bought the business and after he made the purchase.

✔ **Larry should've known that preconceived notions rarely withstand the scrutiny of day-to-day operations.** Buying and running a company isn't as easy as people like Larry may think. An MBA from a top business school and specific work experience don't come close to guaranteeing success when buying and managing a business. Larry should have maintained the company as it had been run until he studied and learned its real strengths and weaknesses, knew the business well enough to recognize the skills of the employees, and could formulate an informed plan to move the company forward.

Inspecting the financial statements

Reviewing the financial statements — including the balance sheet and the profit and loss statement — of the business for sale is an important part of your due diligence. The following sections explain what to look for and what to watch out for in the profit and loss statement and balance sheet. If you're unfamiliar with those statements, you're at a huge disadvantage in evaluating businesses for sale; turn to Chapter 14 for the ins and outs of financial statements.

Interpreting the profit and loss statement

A company's *profit and loss statement,* or P&L (also known as the *income statement*), details its profits, which are simply revenues minus expenses. Revenues are the money that the company receives from its customers as payment for its products or services. Expenses are the company's costs of doing business. Just as much of your personal income or revenue goes toward income taxes, housing, food, and clothing, company expenses exhaust much and sometimes all of a company's revenue.

When considering buying a business, take the time to examine the following issues on the company's profit and loss statement:

✔ **The owner's salary and bonuses:** Of utmost importance when computing the profitability of any business is the determination of how much money the current owner is (or has been) taking out of it. The profitability of the business may look large at first glance, but the owner may be paying himself little in order to fatten the bottom line. Or the owner may be taking out excessive salary and bonuses, minimizing the business's profitability in the process. (In most cases, the owner will be quick to tell you about his penchant to take excessive salary and bonuses and reluctant to reveal that he has been underpaying himself.)

✔ **Change in revenues over time:** Examine at least the last three years of profit and loss statements. Do you see a steady or increasing rate of growth in a company's revenues? If a company's revenues are growing slowly or shrinking, you have to ask the important question, "Why?" Is it because of poor service or product performance, better competitor offerings, ineffective marketing, or an owner who is financially set and unmotivated to grow the business? Before you buy is the time to find out the answer to this question.

✔ **Revenues by product line:** For companies with multiple divisions or product lines, ask for the revenue details of each product line. Find out what's spurring, or holding back, the company's overall growth. One red flag is if the business has acquired other businesses that don't really fit with the company's other business units. Some larger small companies that are struggling to build revenues sometimes try to "enter" new businesses through acquisition but then don't manage them well because they don't understand the keys to success in those businesses.

✔ **Revenues by individual stores:** With retail stores, such as a picture-framing enterprise that has multiple locations, examine the revenues on a store-by-store basis. If the business has been opening new sites, also determine the change in revenues from opening new locations versus the change at existing locations. A company can show overall revenue growth by simply adding new stores while the existing locations may actually be experiencing declining revenues.

✔ **Expense details:** To help you identify which expense categories are growing and which ones are shrinking over time, take a look at the expense categories for the past three years and calculate what percentage of the company's revenue each category makes up. As a well-managed and financially healthy company grows, expenses as a percentage of revenues should decrease. Not all expense categories necessarily decrease. Research and development, for example, may be expanding in a company awash in revenues and seeking to create and offer new products and services.

✔ **The bottom line:** The net result of revenues that increase faster than expenses is a fatter *bottom line* (the last line of the profit and loss statement that indicates net profits or losses after taxes). When you examine how a company's profits change relative to total revenue received, focus on *operating income,* which is the net income from operations before one-time write-ups or write-downs. (Sometimes companies experience one-time, revenue-enhancing or revenue-reducing events that can change profits temporarily.)

Even healthy, growing businesses can get into trouble if their expenses balloon faster than their revenues. Well-managed companies stay on top of their expenses during good and bad times. Don't be fooled into thinking that all is well financially just because a company's revenues have been increasing. It's easier for companies to get sloppy during good times.

✔ **Other expenses:** Thoroughly examine other expense items — such as automobile expenses and travel and entertainment — for insight as to how the business has spent its money in the past. You may unearth some excessive, unnecessary expenses that, if you're successful in cutting, could immediately improve your bottom line.

Audited and unaudited financial statements

In your initial evaluation of a potential business to purchase, you'll receive (at your request) the company's financial statements. Some business owners will be reluctant to release too much financial data, usually due to concerns about confidentiality or because they may not be convinced that you're a serious buyer.

You may be asked to sign what's called a *non-disclosure agreement* (NDA), which legally binds you to keep confidential any information that the company shares. NDAs are fine as long as signing one doesn't tie your hands from evaluating similar businesses for sale, including those that compete with the one under consideration. Don't sign an NDA without your attorney's consent.

If the financial statements you receive haven't been independently audited by a reputable accounting firm, be extremely cautious in assuming accuracy and honesty in the statements. In the "Buyer beware" sidebar earlier

in this chapter, had Katie demanded that Max's financial statements be audited by a reputable accounting firm, either she wouldn't have bought the company or she wouldn't have paid the high price that she did. On the other hand, don't take financial statements at face value simply because they've been audited. The accountant who did the audit could be incompetent or unethical (too friendly with the seller).

An excellent way to uncover inflated profitability as reported on the financial statements that the current business owner shares with you is to ask the seller for a copy of the business's income tax returns. Owners are more likely to try to minimize reported revenue and maximize expenses on their tax return to keep from paying more tax. (*Warning:* If you discover that the business owner has overtly tried to cheat the government, chances are he may try the same thing on you.)

A term you may come across when you're dealing with attorneys, accountants, business brokers, or sophisticated buyers is *EBITDA*. EBITDA is an acronym that stands for Earnings Before Interest, Taxes, Depreciation, and Amortization. Many business sales are made on the basis of EBITDA earnings rather than net income. Be aware of which of the two methods you'll be using in determining the value of the business.

Reviewing the balance sheet

A *balance sheet* is a snapshot-in-time summary of a company's assets and liabilities. This financial report is typically prepared as of the last day of the company's fiscal year-end, which for most companies is December 31. (Some companies have a fiscal year that ends at a different time of the year.)

The *assets* section of the balance sheet summarizes what the company holds or owns that is of significant value. The *liabilities* section details what the company owes to others. Here are several key line items to look for when reviewing a company's balance sheet:

✔ **Accounts receivable:** Also known as *receivables,* this line item is money that's owed to a company for products or services already sold but not yet paid for. As companies grow, so, too, do their receivables (unless the business deals only in cash, in which case the business shouldn't have any receivables at all). Be on the lookout, however, for accounts receivable that are growing at a faster rate than the company's revenues (in other words, receivables that are becoming a larger portion or percentage of the company's revenues). Bloated receivables may indicate that the company is having problems with the quality of its product or pricing. Dissatisfied customers pay more slowly and/or haggle for bigger discounts. Out-of-proportion receivables may also indicate that the company's customers are having financial problems of their own. Be sure to ask for the business's *accounts receivable aging* — a listing of the monies owed to the company accompanied by the length of time the bills have gone uncollected.

Throw a red flag if the business doesn't maintain an aging — unless all its customers are paid to date.

✔ **Property and equipment:** All companies require equipment, such as office furniture, computers, and so on, otherwise known as *fixed assets.* Manufacturing companies also own machinery for making their products. Equipment becomes less valuable as it becomes more obsolete over time. This depreciation of fixed assets is charged against profits by the company as a cost of doing business each year. Thus, even if a company ceases buying new equipment, its balance sheet will continue to show fixed asset charges — not for purchases but for depreciation of the value of property and equipment. As depreciation is subtracted from the value of the equipment, the amount shown for fixed assets on the balance sheet will gradually decrease.

If a company hasn't been periodically upgrading its equipment, you could get stuck buying a company that needs a lot of costly new equipment. When a company's balance sheet indicates a continual decline in the bookkeeping value of the company's equipment, beware that the company may simply be deferring new equipment purchases. Inspect the company's equipment and talk with others who are familiar with the type of business so that you can understand how outdated the equipment really is and how much you're likely to have to expend on replacement equipment if you buy the business.

✔ **Inventory:** The balance sheets of manufacturing and retail companies should detail *inventory,* which is simply the cost of the products that have not yet been sold. As a business expands over time, inventory should follow suit. However, beware if you see inventory increasing faster than revenues because it may signal several problems, including customers who are scaling back on purchases, poor management, or an obsolete or inferior collection of goods. Inventory is the most dangerous asset of all because a swollen inventory often represents cash that can't be redeemed.

✔ **Accounts payable:** When companies purchase supplies, equipment, or products for resale for their business, they generally have a period of time (typically 30 days) to pay the bills. Similar to inventory and accounts receivable, *accounts payable* (which appear on the liability side of a company's balance sheet) usually increase in tune with a company's increasing revenues. Accounts payable that are growing faster than revenues may or may not indicate financial trouble. The increase may simply be good financial management (the slower a company is with paying bills, the longer the funds can be drawing interest in corporate accounts). On the other hand, if the company is struggling to make ends meet, an accumulation of accounts payable can occur and can be an early warning sign of financial trouble.

✔ **Debt:** *Debt,* both short term and long term, is money that the company has borrowed and must someday pay back. Footnotes to the financial statements (assuming they're audited) generally detail the terms of the debt, such as when the debt is to be paid back. In Chapter 14, we explain important ratios and calculations you can use to help you size up the amount and type of debt a company is carrying. If the financials you're working with haven't been audited, be sure to either ask for a thorough explanation of the debt or, better yet, leave the debt out of the purchase.

✔ **Other assets:** This catchall category is for the other assets of the company and can include stuff that will make your eyes glaze over. For example, companies keep a different set of books for tax purposes (yes, doing so is legal). Not surprisingly, companies do this because the IRS allows, in some cases, more deductions than what the company is required to show from an accounting standpoint on its financial statements. (If you were a company, wouldn't you want your shareholders, but not the IRS, to see gobs of profits?) The benefit of deferring taxes is treated as an asset until the IRS gets more of its share down the road.

Even if you're competent in reading financial statements, never purchase a business without involving a good tax advisor to help you evaluate the value of the business and the financial terms of the transaction. Buying a business isn't the time to rely on your own trial and error; be sure to involve someone in the buying process who can bring her financial/tax expertise to the table.

What are the "off-balance-sheet" assets worth?

The value of a company's assets includes not only tangible items, such as inventory, accounts receivable, furniture, fixtures, and equipment, but also soft assets, such as the firm's name and reputation with customers and suppliers, customer lists, patents, and so on. These soft assets are also known, in accounting jargon, as *goodwill.* In many cases, the value of this goodwill is greater than the value of the hard assets.

If you're seriously interested in making an offer to buy a particular business, take time to investigate the worth of the company's goodwill. As part of your investigation, be sure to assess whether the current customers of the business will continue buying from the business after you take it over and to evaluate the quality of the key employees. And don't forget to look into the business's relationships with suppliers — are they good or bad? In addition, check out the competition — does it seem formidable?

Ask key employees these questions:

✔ What do you like the most about your company? What do you like the least?

✔ How do you see the future of the company?

✔ Can the products or services be improved?

✔ What would be the first improvement you'd make if you owned the business?

Ask suppliers these questions:

✔ Does the company pay its bills on time?

✔ Do you get an inordinate amount of returns from them?

✔ Compared to other companies in the industry, how does the company treat its suppliers — as partners or as a necessary evil?

✔ If you could change one thing about the company, what would it be?

Some final points about goodwill: Companies work hard to attract and retain customers through advertising, product development, and service. Companies can't put an exact value on the goodwill they've generated, but when they purchase (acquire) another firm, some of the purchase price is considered goodwill. Specifically, if a company is acquired for $100 million yet has a net worth (assets minus liabilities) of just $50 million, the extra $50 million is considered to be goodwill. This goodwill then becomes an asset on the balance sheet, which, similar to equipment, is amortized (depreciated) over the years ahead. (Goodwill is amortized over 15 years, while equipment is usually depreciated over 4 years.)

Uncovering lease contract terms

A soon-to-expire lease at a low rate can ruin a business's profit margins. With a retail location, the ability to maintain a good location is critical as well.

Check comparables — that is, what similar locations lease for — to see whether the current lease rate is fair and talk to the building owner to discover his plans. Ask for and review (possibly with the help of a legal advisor) the current owner's lease contract. Pay extra-careful attention to the provisions of lease contracts that discuss what happens if the business is sold or its ownership changes.

Evaluating Special Franchise Issues

As we discuss in Chapter 7, buying a reputable franchise can be the right ticket into the small-business world. However, no matter what type of franchise you're buying, you need to do plenty of homework before you agree to buy. The following sections describe the unique steps you need to take when evaluating a franchise.

You may be tempted to cut corners when reviewing a franchise from a long-established company. Don't. You may not be a good fit for the specific franchise, or perhaps the "successful" company has been good at keeping its franchisee problems under wraps.

Thoroughly review regulatory filings

The Federal Trade Commission (FTC) requires all franchisers to issue what's called the *Uniform Franchise Offering Circular* (UFOC) at least ten days before a prospective franchise buyer writes a check or signs a document to purchase. We recommend that you ask for this valuable document well before that deadline if you're seriously interested in a particular franchise.

Don't be put off by the size of the UFOC. It contains the following valuable information, so be sure to read it cover to cover:

✔ The names and addresses of the ten geographically closest franchises to the one you may buy, as well as a list of franchises that were terminated, not renewed, or bought back by the company.

Speaking with franchisees for whom things didn't work out may help you uncover aspects of the business that are turnoffs for you. Now isn't the time to stick your head in the sand about possible problems or drawbacks of a given franchise. After all, finding out about those downsides now is better than finding out about them after you've plunked down a chunk of your money, borrowed even more, and gone through a lot of work to buy a franchise.

✔ Disclosure of pending or settled litigation, as well as a detailing of potential or actual troubles between franchisers and franchisees.

✔ The employment background of the senior management of the franchiser.

✔ The costs to the franchisee of purchasing a franchise, as well as required inventory, leases, and other costs.

Evaluate the franchiser's motives

A good franchising company will want to check you out as much as you should want to check it out. Successful franchisers don't want to sell a franchise to someone who is likely to crash and burn and tarnish the reputation they've worked so hard to build. These companies know that their interests are aligned with yours — they make more money from ongoing royalties if they sell franchises to solid franchisees who are determined to be successful. At the outset of your investigation, ask yourself whether the franchisers are looking for a long-term business partner or simply the fast sale of another franchise.

Closely observe how the franchising company interacts with you. Be wary if the franchiser seems more interested in selling franchises than in finding and helping the most qualified franchisees succeed. Obviously, franchising representatives will be generally enthusiastic about their company. But a fine line exists between enthusiasm and a hard sell.

Run in the opposite direction if a franchiser tells tales of great riches from just a small investment of your time and money. Run extra fast if the franchiser is pressuring you into making a quick decision to buy and is evasive about providing detailed information about the business. And if the franchiser doesn't want to give you the UFOC (see the preceding section), sprint!

Interview plenty of franchisees

Interview as many of the company's franchisees as is practical — both current owners as well as those who quit or were terminated. Skip the list of references that the franchise company eagerly provided and go to the lists of franchisees provided in the UFOC (see the earlier section "Thoroughly review regulatory filings"). Ask the franchisees what their experiences, both good and bad, have been with the parent company. Those franchisees for whom things didn't work out are generally more forthcoming about the warts of the system, but don't take everything they say at face value. Try to identify whether some of these people were poor fits.

Conversely, active franchisees are more likely to see things through rose-colored glasses, perhaps for no other reason than to reassure themselves about their decision to buy the franchise. If active franchisees are dissatisfied, steer clear. Observe which franchisees are happiest and most successful and see whether you share their business perspectives and traits.

Understand what you're buying and examine comparables

Most reputable franchises require you to plop down a chunk of cash to get started. Home-office-based service businesses may charge a $25,000 upfront franchise fee, compared to the several hundred thousand to one million dollars required for the bricks-and-mortar locations of established franchisers, such as McDonald's. Additionally, ongoing franchise royalties can range from 3 to 10 percent of gross revenue. The UFOC should detail all the upfront costs (see the earlier section "Thoroughly review regulatory filings" for details on the UFOC).

As you evaluate the costs involved in buying a franchise, ask yourself the following questions: What are you receiving for these payments? Are the system and brand name really worth this fee? What kind of training will you receive? What kind of assistance does corporate management provide? What programs are in place to foster communications with other franchisees?

Few franchises are unique. Compare the cost of what a franchise is offering to the cost of purchasing franchises from different companies in the same business. For example, if you're considering the purchase of a franchise from Wendy's, compare the terms and offerings to those of McDonald's and Burger King.

If you look at the "best" franchises in a particular industry and think, "Hey, I can do this as well or better and at less cost on my own," remember that you don't *have* to buy a franchise. Consider the start-up alternative. Be realistic, though, because many hidden costs — both out-of-pocket financial costs and costs in the form of time and energy — are involved in starting a business from scratch (see Part I). And the franchise has a head start in name recognition and customer base.

Check with federal and state regulators

Franchises are generally regulated at both the federal and state levels. The FTC regulates nationally (www.ftc.gov/bcp/menus/consumer/invest/business.shtm; 877-382-4357), and the state-level regulatory agency is usually called something like the Department of Corporations or the Attorney General's Office. Check with these regulators to see whether complaints about a franchiser are on file.

The UFOC should detail pending litigation against the franchising company by disgruntled franchisees (see the section "Thoroughly review regulatory filings" for details on the UFOC). For lesser-known franchises, you may also want to check with the Better Business Bureau in the city where the franchising company is headquartered to discover whether anything negative is on file.

Investigate the company's credit history

Just as you have a personal credit report on file, every business has a credit report that shows how the company has dealt with payments and debts owed to suppliers and creditors. The franchiser's credit report is a good indicator of how well it maintains its business relationships and how financially stable it is. Where the franchiser is publicly owned, obtain a copy of the company's annual report and Form 10-K. Examine the company's stock price over recent years.

Analyze and negotiate the franchise contract

If your digging has made you feel more, rather than less, comfortable with the franchise purchase, you need to get down to the nitty-gritty of the contract in order to move forward. Franchise contracts are usually long, tedious, and filled with legalese. Read the contract completely to get a sense of what you're getting yourself into. Also be sure to have an attorney who's experienced with franchising agreements review the contract.

In addition to the financial terms, the franchise contract should specify how disputes are to be handled, what rights you have to sell the franchise in the future, and under what conditions the parent company can terminate the franchise. Make sure that you can live with and be happy with the nonfinancial, as well as the financial, terms in the contract.

Almost everything is negotiable, especially when you're dealing with a lesser-known franchiser that's in the early stages of its business growth. Although some of the more successful franchisers offer their best deal upfront and refuse to engage in haggling, others don't initially put their best terms and conditions on the table, hoping that you'll simply sign and accept the inferior terms and conditions.

Every business buyer or seller should remember this saying: "You name the price, I'll name the terms." What this saying means is that the terms can be more important than the price in making the deal work. What if, for example, you buy a business that's somewhat overpriced, but you have to pay only 10 percent down, the interest rate on the balance is 2 percent, and you don't have to pay off the note for 30 years? In this example, the terms are much more important to the deal than the price.

Chapter 9

Negotiating Terms and Sealing the Deal

Ask yourself this important and (we hope) revealing question: "How many businesses have I purchased in my lifetime?" If you're like most people we know, the answer is a big, fat zero.

Now, you're an intelligent and discerning person, as evidenced by the fact that you bought this book. And we, as your humble authors, have high hopes that you'll gain a wealth of practical insights and knowledge by reading our book. However — and this is a most important however — we firmly believe that, when buying a business, you'll benefit from retaining the services of experts with extensive small-business deal-making experience. (Chapter 10 tells you how to get the most out of your relationships with experts.)

Negotiating is a skill that improves with experience. Experienced advisors can help you inspect the business you're buying and look for red flags in the company's financial statements. Advisors can also help structure the purchase to protect what you're buying and to gain maximum tax benefits. To get the best deal, you need to do a number of things well, the first of which is to put a realistic and accurate value on the business you intend to buy. This chapter starts there and then moves on to cover how to decide on the purchase price, how to do your due diligence, and how to start off strong after you become the owner.

Valuing the Business

When you begin exploring businesses for sale, you don't know exactly what a given business is worth and you risk overpaying for that business if you jump into a deal too soon. However, with time and the right resources, combined with a little investigative work, you can get a good handle on a particular business's worth, which may or may not be close to the owner's asking price. (For more on the search process, see Chapter 7.)

You can start by taking a cue from smart home buyers and real estate investors: To find out how much a property is really worth, consider *comparable sales* — that is, the amounts that similar properties have sold for. Compared to business buyers, however, home buyers have it relatively easy. Real estate transactions are a matter of public record; small-business sales aren't. So you have to do some extra sleuthing to find the specific price and terms of comparable businesses that have sold.

In the end, however, after you've done the math and developed a dollar value for the business, remember one thing: Similar to buying a house, the real worth of a business is what you, or someone else, will pay for it. A business isn't a car with a factory sticker price; it's a multidimensional, complicated organization of people, assets, and systems. Its true value is in the eyes of the beholder, and the beholder is you.

The following sections walk you through the process of valuing a business. You won't have to go through every step (especially if you hire a business broker to manage the process for you), but each one is a viable option to consider.

Exploring valuing methods: Multiple of earnings and book value

Many methods exist for valuing a business. Some are unnecessarily complicated; others won't provide you with sensible answers. For example, some advisors and business brokers advocate using a multiple of revenue to determine the value of a business — that is, if a business has $300,000 in revenues, it may be valued at $450,000 (a multiple of 1.5 times revenue). However, revenue is a poor proxy for profitability. Two businesses in the same field can have identical revenue yet quite different profitability due to the efficiency of their operations, the pricing of their products and services, and the types of customers they attract. Also, the multiple of revenue that a business may be worth varies depending on what industry the business is in. For example, the multiple for a manufacturing business is higher than the multiple for a retail establishment or a restaurant.

Other measures are more exact. Here are our preferred valuation measures for small businesses:

- **Multiple of earnings:** When you compare the sales data for comparable companies to the sales data for the one you're interested in buying, determine what multiple of earnings these businesses sold for. Divide the price the business sold for by its annual pre-tax earnings (profits) to arrive at the *multiple of earnings* (also known as the *price-earnings ratio*) of that transaction.

  When the multiple is low, say 3 to 1 (for example, if the business had earnings of $50,000 and a selling price of $150,000), the buyer and seller don't have great expectations for the business's future earnings. However, when the multiple is high, say 12 to 1 (if the business had earnings of $50,000 and a selling price of $600,000), the buyer's and seller's expectations of future earnings are correspondingly high.

  Future earnings are what will provide the return on the buyer's investment; therefore, the higher the buyer expects those potential earnings to be, the more he or she is willing to pay for the business. (In general, a business should be able to pay for itself in three to five years. If the time period is any longer than that, you're probably paying too much for the company.)

  Small, privately held businesses typically sell for lower multiples of earnings than larger companies in the same line of business. The reason: Small companies are less established and are riskier from an investing standpoint. Plus, your investment in their stock will be *illiquid* (that is, even in good times, the stock generally can't be converted into cash within a reasonable period of time).

- **Book value:** In addition to looking at the sales price of other businesses relative to earnings, you can consider the value of a company's assets. The *book value* of a company is the company's assets minus its liabilities, which is the same as the net worth of the business as stated on its balance sheet. (We're assuming here that the values for the assets and liabilities on the balance sheet are accurate; see Chapter 14 for more on balance sheets.) The figures that go into determining book value should be checked carefully to ensure that the underlying asset values and liability accounts are correct.

Of these two approaches, each of which has advantages as well as imperfections, the multiple-of-earnings approach is generally considered to be far superior to the book-value method. After all, what you're purchasing when you buy a business isn't primarily its assets but rather its ability to generate profits (earnings), using those assets. Some businesses, such as consulting firms, have little in the way of tangible assets — the personnel may be the firm's greatest asset, and valuing that is difficult. Because the determination of a price-earnings multiple figure is based on an income-generating formula, it's generally a better indicator than the book-value approach, which simply measures the difference between assets and liabilities.

Keep in mind that the figure you come up with when using the multiple-of-earnings approach represents the goodwill portion of the business only and doesn't include the value of the business's assets. (*Goodwill* is, in essence, the value of the business's reputation and existing customer list.) Thus, you have to add the value of the assets to the goodwill number. The assets involved in a typical small-business purchase include accounts receivable (make sure that they're all collectable), inventory (make sure that what you're buying is merchantable), and equipment, furniture, and fixtures (the fair market value thereof).

Getting a professional appraisal

Business appraisers make a living out of estimating the value of businesses. If you want to buy a business and your initial investigation suggests that the seller is committed and serious about selling the business, consider hiring an appraiser. Although the fees professional appraisers charge vary depending on the size and complexity of the prospective business, you can usually expect to pay somewhere north of $5,000 for the typical small business.

Tax advisors, lawyers, and business consultants who specialize in working with small businesses may be able to refer you to a good business appraiser if they can't do the appraisal themselves. The Institute of Business Appraisers (www.instbusapp.org; 954-584-1144) can provide you with a list of association members in your area. Also, check the business-to-business Yellow Pages in your area under "Appraisers — Business."

Tracking businesses you've explored that have sold

If your search for a business to buy lasts months or perhaps years, keep track of similar businesses you've considered that eventually sell. These sales provide valuable comparables because you've seen the businesses up close and have obtained details about their financial position that give you perspective in assessing the sales.

Obtaining the final selling price of a small business can be challenging. You can try asking the ex-owner, or you can speak with advisors or business brokers who are involved in such deals. For details on working with advisors, see the next section; for details on brokers, see the later section "Enlisting the services of a business broker."

Tapping the knowledge of advisors who work with similar companies

Business consultants, attorneys, and tax advisors you work with can assist you with pinning down sales data for companies comparable to the one you're considering buying. The key is to find advisors who have knowledge of, and experience with, both small businesses in general and businesses similar to the one you're thinking of buying.

If you end up buying a small business, you'll benefit from having competent advisors on your team who have worked on comparable deals. But before you hire an advisor for tax, legal, or business advice, be sure to check references. Also ask the advisor for a comprehensive list of business deals (including the purchase or sale price and the industry) that he has been involved in over the past year.

Don't be deterred by the cost of such advisors, especially tax advisors and attorneys. The terms you agree to in the purchase of a business will be with you for a long, long time.

Consulting research firms and publications

Finding the details on similar companies that have sold can be difficult. Wouldn't it be helpful if a service compiled such information for you? Well, you'll be happy to know that some companies do publish comparable sales information or conduct company searches for a fee.

One such company, BIZCOMPS, releases an annual publication that provides sales price, revenue, and other financial details for businesses sold. This compendium of sales information is available for different major regions and industries in the United States (Western, Eastern, Industrial, and Food Service). Visit www.bizcomps.com or call 702-454-0072 for a sample of this publication. Each directory sells for $165. The company also offers online access to business sales data through an annual membership fee (which varies).

Turning to trade publications

Trade publications can help you find out more about a particular industry, as well as how to value companies within that industry. Most publications are willing to send you past articles on a topic, typically for a small fee. Or you may be able to access articles from the publication's website.

Enlisting the services of a business broker

If you're already working with a *business broker* (a salesperson who lists small businesses for sale and who works with buyers as well) or looking at a business listed for sale through a business broker, the broker should be able to provide a comparable market analysis of similar businesses that the broker's office has sold.

Don't put too much weight on a business broker's analysis. Unfortunately, a broker's "analysis" may be less analytic and more sales oriented than you want. After all, business brokers earn commissions based on a percentage of the selling price of the business that you may buy through them. (The commissions generally range from 6 to 10 percent, depending on the size and complexity of the deal.) Also, understand that business brokers generally have access to sales data only on the small number of similar businesses that their particular office has sold. Unlike real estate agents, business brokers who work for different brokerage firms in a given community don't share their sales data with one another.

Before enlisting the services of a broker, be sure to check her references carefully — especially given the fact that business brokers are in a virtually unregulated industry that requires no specific credentials or educational training to enter. Be sure to involve your own attorney when the closing comes around. Having your own attorney takes the broker's bias out of the equation and helps ensure that what you get is best for you. You can generally depend on your attorney to represent your best interests; the same cannot be said about your business broker.

Developing Purchase Offer Contingencies

When you make an offer to buy a home, you generally make your purchase offer contingent upon (dependent on) obtaining mortgage loan approval, satisfactory inspections, and proof that the property seller holds a clear title to the home. When you make an offer to buy a business, you need to make your purchase contingent upon similar issues, including the following:

- ✓ **Inspections and due diligence:** Your purchase offer for a business should be contingent upon a thorough review of the company's financial statements and interviews of key employees, customers, and suppliers (this overall evaluation is called *due diligence*). You should be allowed to employ whomever you like to help you with your evaluation. The typical period of time allowed for due diligence is 30 to 60 days, more if the business is large. (For how-to advice, see the later section "Doing Due Diligence" or turn to Chapter 8.)

✓ **Financing:** Unless you're paying cash for the full purchase price of the business (which would be unusual), another condition of your purchase offer may be an acceptable seller-provided loan. Sellers can be a great financing source, and many are willing to lend you money to purchase their business. Seller financing is quite common in small-business purchases; in fact, about 90 percent of all small-business sales include seller financing. Yes, occasionally partial financing for a business purchase can come from traditional lending sources (banks, relatives, friends, angel investors, and so on), but the seller is always your number one opportunity. Think about it: If your seller still has "skin in the game," he's that much more motivated for you to succeed, which means he'll be that much more likely to help you through the transition period.

Be sure to compare the terms that the seller is offering to those of some local banks that specialize in small-business loans. (See Chapter 5 for your best financing sources.) In the purchase offer, specify the acceptable loan terms, including the duration of the loan and the maximum interest rate. If interest rates jump before your loan is finalized, you don't want to be forced to complete your deal at too high of an interest rate.

✓ **Noncompete clause:** You don't want to buy a business only to have the former owner set up an identical one down the block and steal his previous customers from you. To avoid this unpleasant possibility, be sure that your purchase offer includes a *noncompete clause* that states that the seller can't establish a similar business within a certain nearby geographic area for a minimum number of years — or something like that.

You may consider asking the owner, as part of the purchase deal, to make himself available to consult with you, at a specified hourly rate, for 6 to 12 months to make sure that you tap all his valuable experience, as well as to transition relationships with key employees, vendors, and customers. To further align the selling owner's interests with yours, consider having a portion of the total purchase price dependent on the future success of the company.

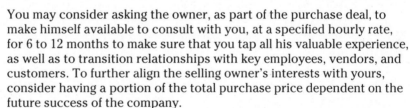

If the transaction includes seller financing, most sophisticated sellers want to continue to work with you for a period following the sale to help you get off on the right foot. Beware of those who don't want to hang around. (Restaurant owner Max from a story in Chapter 8 illustrates this concern; he couldn't get out of Dodge fast enough when his deal was done. The reason: too much dirty laundry in his hamper.)

✓ **Limited potential liabilities:** When you buy a business, you buy that business's assets and usually (but not always) its liabilities. Some potential liabilities don't show up on a company's balance sheet and could become a thorn in your side. Make sure that the seller is liable for environmental cleanup and other undisclosed existing liabilities (debts). Conduct legal searches for liens, litigation, and tax problems. (Your attorney should conduct these searches for you as a part of the closing process.)

Allocating the Purchase Price

When you pay $300,000 for a business, you're not simply paying $300,000 for the business. You're paying, for example, $60,000 for the inventory, $40,000 for the accounts receivable, $50,000 for the company equipment, $100,000 for goodwill, and so on.

No matter how you determine the purchase price, you must always break down that price, or *allocate* it, among the assets of the business and other categories. This requirement applies whether you set the price of the business by determining the value of its assets (such as through the multiple-of-earnings method that we describe earlier in this chapter) or by using some other method. Although allocating assets may cause your eyes to glaze over, snap to attention when the subject comes up, because how you structure the purchase can save you tens of thousands of dollars in taxes.

Experienced tax advisors will tell you that you generally want to allocate much of the purchase price to specific assets of the business. Some assets are what their numbers make them out to be (such as accounts receivable), while others can be negotiable (such as equipment and goodwill). The reason for the negotiation is that different assets can be written off (or *depreciated*) over different periods of time. For instance, equipment can be depreciated over as little as 4 years, while goodwill takes 15 years to depreciate.

You must report the purchase of the business and the allocation of the purchase price among business assets on IRS Form 8594 (Asset Acquisition Statement). Make sure that you do so, because if you don't, the penalty is stiff — up to 10 percent of the amount not reported.

Doing Due Diligence

After spending months searching for the right business to buy and finding one that fits your fancy, you may well spend weeks negotiating an acceptable deal. Just as you're about to stumble across what you think is the finish line, you realize you have plenty more work left to go.

After all, now is the time to get out the microscope and really nitpick. Before you go through with the deal and fork over the dough, you have one last chance to discover any hidden problems that exist within the business you hope to buy. Of course, all businesses have their warts, but better for you to uncover them now so that the purchase price and terms reflect those warts.

The process of thoroughly investigating your prospective business is called *due diligence*. During due diligence, you need to answer important questions like these:

- ✔ Is the business as profitable as the financial statements indicate?
- ✔ Will the business's customers remain after a change in ownership?
- ✔ What lease, debt, or other obligations will you be assuming when you buy the business?

Due diligence typically lasts for 30 to 60 days, depending on the complexity of the company you're hoping to purchase.

The same experts you're working with to put together a good deal for your small-business purchase will form your due-diligence team. For details on how to work successfully with your experts, see Chapter 10.

In addition to the evaluation tips we give you in Chapter 8, we recommend that you take some additional due-diligence steps before making an offer. We go over these steps in the following sections.

Think about income statement issues

The profitability of the business is probably the single most important aspect you need to consider during due diligence. To help you deal with income statement concerns, we suggest that you take the following steps:

- ✔ **Have an experienced small-business tax advisor review the company's financial statements.** She'll know what to look out for. Just be sure to agree on a budget for the cost of the advisor's services (and, therefore, the time she will spend) upfront.

- ✔ **Adjust for one-time events.** If necessary, factor out one-time impactful events from the profit analysis. For example, if the business got an unusually large order last year that is unlikely to be repeated, subtract the amount of that order from the profitability analysis.

- ✔ **Check the owner's compensation.** Examine the owner's salary to see whether it's too high or low for the industry the business is in. Owners can pump up the profitability of their company in the years before they sell by reducing or keeping their salary to a minimum or by paying family members in the business less than fair-market salaries.

- ✔ **Consider how the building expense will change.** Consider whether the rent or mortgage expense will be different after you buy the business. Any large change in that cost will clearly affect the profitability of the business.

- ✔ **Factor in financing expenses.** Be sure to calculate what will happen to profits when you factor in the financing costs from borrowing money to buy the business.

- ✔ **Pay attention to trends.** How are the sales and the profits trending? If this year's profits were, say, $80,000 and last year's were $100,000, the trend is unfavorable. On the other hand, if this year's profits were $70,000 and last year's were $50,000, you're looking at a good trend. Knowledgable buyers are generally willing to pay a higher multiple for favorable trends.

Consider legal and tax concerns

Before you make a deal, follow these steps to research any legal or tax issues the business may have:

- ✔ **Look for liens.** Check to make sure that no liens are filed against assets of the business and, if you're buying real estate, that the property title is clear. A competent attorney can help with this tedious and important legal task.

- ✔ **Get proof that all taxes are paid.** Get the seller to provide proof, certifying that federal and state employment, sales, and use taxes are all paid up.

Moving Into Your Business

If you've made it through the searching, researching, negotiating, and closing phases, you're now a bona fide small-business owner. Congratulations and welcome to your new business! You've completed a lot of challenging and important work and should feel proud of yourself.

After your deal is closed, be sure to take care of the following tasks as soon as possible:

- ✔ **Disclose ownership transfer.** Notify creditors of the transfer of ownership. In the counties where the company does business, publish a transfer-of-ownership notice in a general circulation newspaper. If you omit this step, you risk having unsecured creditors come after your business for outstanding debts that the previous owner had.

✔ **Write a business plan and mission statement or refine your plan if you've already started it.** If you researched the industry and evaluated in detail the business you bought, you should be able to generate a good business plan, including an applicable mission statement, without too much hassle. Although completing your business plan will take some time and thinking, doing so early on in the process will benefit you and your business in increased sales, reduced costs, and happier employees. If you ever intend to seek outside capital from a banker or investor, you'll need a good business plan. We explain how to write your business plan and mission statement in Chapter 4. *Note:* An ideal time to begin work on this business plan is during the due-diligence phase.

✔ **Plan the company's finances.** Going forward, you need to have a firm handle on the revenue, expenses, and cash flow of your business. For example, you need to set up a budget for your business and forecast future needs for capital, both of which should be included in the business plan. See Chapters 4 and 14 for details.

✔ **Consider the entity/legal form of organization.** Just because the business you bought was structured as a sole proprietorship or corporation doesn't mean that legal entity makes the most sense for you. We provide the framework for you to think through this important decision in Chapter 5. Your attorney and tax advisor should be part of this decision.

✔ **Spend time understanding your customers.** Get to know your best customers as soon as the ink is dry on the sales agreement. Without good customers who buy profitable products and services and who pay their bills on time, you don't have a viable long-term business. Even the best business is bound to lose customers for a variety of reasons beyond the business owner's control. So don't skimp on understanding your customers' needs, particularly what makes them buy your company's wares and what their ongoing customer service needs are. Completing your business plan can help you clarify many of these vital issues (see Chapter 4). Plus, you can get a feel for how to market your products and services to customers and how to keep your customers loyal in Chapters 11 and 13.

✔ **Get to know your employees.** Employees who liked the previous owner(s) will take time to warm up to you. Some employees may fear for their jobs or worry that a change in ownership will lead to reduced job satisfaction. Err on the side of doing more listening to your employees rather than always being the one jabbering about all your grand plans. The employees contain a wealth of knowledge about the business from which you can learn, and the better you listen, the more the employees will grow to respect and like you.

Be sure to evaluate the employee benefits package and compensation structure (see Chapters 16 and 17). Don't make rash changes in this area, especially if you're thinking about reducing benefits and/or compensation. Early, negative changes can have ugly long-term consequences.

✔ **Walk; don't run.** Don't make huge changes your first day, week, or even month at the helm. Take your time to discover the culture of the business, the needs of its customers, and the idiosyncrasies of its vendors before you attempt to make major changes. Employees, customers, and vendors don't like quick change, especially when the person behind the change is new and relatively unknown.

✔ **Consult the prior owner.** Don't expect to know everything there is to know about running your new business. No matter how much better a business manager you may think you are than your predecessor, he or she has certain knowledge and skills that you don't have. Don't let your ego stand in the way of asking the previous owner for advice.

✔ **Work with a good tax advisor.** You don't want to fall behind in filing your taxes or filling out the right tax forms, or you'll have a nasty surprise in the form of an unexpectedly large tax bill. The tax advisor who helped you with evaluating your business purchase may be able to recommend a tax advisor you can work with at least during your first year of business ownership. You also need to make sure you come out of the starting gates with well-organized and accurate financial statements. See Chapter 19 for more details.

Much like a first-time home buyer's excitement at moving into a newly purchased home, your euphoria at owning your business may quietly slip into anxiety when you realize that your work is just beginning. Relax, take deep breaths, and use the time-tested method of breaking a big task into many smaller manageable ones. Also, rest assured that if you take the advice we offer throughout Part II and you do your homework before buying your business, you should end up purchasing a company that doesn't have major problems and that you have the skills to run well.

Part III
Running a Successful Small Business

The 5th Wave   By Rich Tennant

MR. FRANK

"Aside from that, what makes you think you qualify for a small-business loan?"

In this part . . .

Small-business ownership is a never-ending exercise in problem solving. This part is designed to help you resolve a small business's most compelling challenges, including "the care and feeding" of customers, improving sales and increasing profitability, using advertising and publicity, developing strategies for pricing and distribution, keeping tabs on the all-important profit and loss statement, and harnessing the power of technology.

Often, the best way to solve the problems that accompany many small businesses is by asking someone who's already been there, done that, which is why we dedicate a whole chapter to learning from others' experiences.

Chapter 10

The Owner's Responsibilities in the Start-Up and Beyond

. . . .

In This Chapter

▶ Handling the details of a start-up

▶ Determining which tasks you want to outsource

▶ Establishing a bookkeeping system that works for you

▶ Managing your expenses

▶ Maintaining relationships with vendors and other people outside your business

. . . .

*I*n the beginning, you as the owner will perform all your start-up's chores, or at least you will personally see to it that they get done. Well, you'll personally take care of all the *important* tasks at least — those responsibilities that will, down the road, either make or break your enterprise if they aren't done correctly.

More often than not, however, many of those early-stage duties fall under the category of grunt work — the not-so-exciting-to-entrepreneurs stuff that doesn't involve dealing with customers, creating new products, or generating much-needed cash. Instead, the duties are often yawn-inducing things like appeasing the government, developing a bookkeeping system, and covering your behind in the event of adversity — you know, the kind of stuff that, if it doesn't get done, will come back to haunt you.

In this chapter, we walk you through the many hats you must wear as you navigate these sometimes mundane details.

Dotting Your i's and Crossing Your t's: Start-Up Details

When we talk about taking care of the early-stage chores of starting a business, we're assuming that you've already completed the big-picture tasks of the start-up (such as writing a business plan, finding a mentor, determining the legal entity that works best for you, locating financing, and developing the product or service), many of which we discuss in Part I of this book. Now you have to dive into the nitty-gritty details.

Buying insurance

One of the first things you need to do when you start a business is to purchase insurance. We're talking about liability insurance — auto, fire, theft, business interruption, and so on — as well as workers' compensation insurance.

Unfortunately, insurance is an expense that never goes away and generally increases every year. Making things worse is the fact that, if you're like most entrepreneurs, after you sign the original policies, you'll file them away and won't consider shopping around to get a better price for long periods of time because you're so busy running your business. In other words, unless you're the exception, the expenses related to insurance policies will be etched on your profit and loss statement as a fixed cost even though the expenses should be a variable cost — meaning that they should be reviewed every year.

Don't even think about entrusting the creation and negotiation of your initial insurance package (and the creation of the costs related to it) to anyone else. You need to take care of this important task.

Liability insurance

In most cases, insurance is a necessary expense, not unlike a host of other necessary expenses, such as rent, telephone, and salaries. In some cases, the justification for insurance is the owner's logic; in other cases, insurance is required by an outsider — a bank or a property-leasing company.

Following are the four main categories of liability insurance every small-business owner needs to consider. One of them — aptly called *liability insurance* — is a must; if you don't have liability insurance, a dissatisfied customer or even an on-premise passerby could shut your business down for good. Generally speaking, you can add the other three as your business (and its profitability) grows to the point where you can afford them.

- ✔ **Liability insurance:** No telling what may happen on your business premises in these litigious times. *Our recommendation:* Buy enough liability insurance to protect at least twice your combined personal and business net worth.

- ✔ **Theft insurance:** Sooner or later, someone is going to steal something of value from you. (Statistics show that this someone is likely to be an employee.) *Our recommendation:* If you're in the high-ticket retail or wholesale business (automobiles, appliances, and the like), you should purchase theft insurance. (You don't need to purchase enough theft insurance to cover all your inventory; just buy enough to cover what one person could reasonably steal.) Otherwise, take your chances until you're profitable, especially in the early stages of your business.

- ✔ **Property damage insurance:** In addition to the physical property you own, rent, or lease, property damage insurance covers your inventory. Similar to homeowner's insurance, property damage insurance is often required by the terms of a lease or bank loan. *Our recommendation:* If you're in a service business with little expensive equipment and you're leasing or renting in an office building, take your chances if your lease will allow you to do so (until you're profitable). Otherwise, buy enough property damage insurance to cover the cost of replacement.

- ✔ **Business interruption insurance:** This insurance covers the possibility of your business being halted by any number of random events, most of them being natural disasters. Business interruption insurance reimburses you for the profits you don't make during your downtime. *Our recommendation:* In your business's early stages, you probably won't have much business to interrupt. Spend your scarce money elsewhere. However, this situation (we hope) will change. When it does, business interruption insurance is a must-buy. Your insurance agent can help you determine how much to buy. Some businesses, especially capital-intensive ones, will take a long time to open the doors after an accident or act of God. Other businesses, usually those that sell services, can get back on their feet relatively quickly.

Workers' compensation insurance

Workers' compensation is payment for insurance that provides benefits — in the form of medical expense reimbursement and replacement of lost wages — to employees injured on the job. Workers' compensation is a state-mandated, no-fault insurance system, and, when you have employees, it appears as a hefty expense on your profit and loss statement.

Shop around for a trustworthy insurance agent (use referrals from satisfied small-business customers), set up a meeting with him or her along with a representative of the state (your prospective insurance agent can tell you how to locate that person), and find out what you need to do to keep your experience modification factor to a minimum. The *experience modification factor* is a numerical expression of a company's accident and injury record compared with the average for the firm's industry. The higher your experience modification factor, the higher the cost for workers' compensation insurance.

In addition to the experience modification factor, job classification plays an important role in determining the cost of your workers' compensation insurance. The state assigns each job (or employee) in your small business a particular rating — and subsequently a particular premium — based on the estimated level of risk involved in the performance of that job. (The higher the job classification, the higher the cost for you. Because the classification criteria are often fuzzy, argue for the lower classification when possible.)

Don't take the job classification process lightly. You can choose from myriad job categories, and a lot of overlap exists among various job categories. You and your business will waste a bunch of insurance money if you don't make the effort to properly classify your employees.

Because workers' compensation insurance is a state-run program, ask your insurance agent for the telephone number and address of the applicable state agency if you have questions about the program. Or go to the National Association of Insurance Commissioners (NAIC) website (www.naic.org), click on the States & Jurisdiction Map tab, and click on your state for more details.

Paying federal, state, and local taxes

Federal taxes (income, Social Security, unemployment, and excise) come in a mind-boggling array, as do state and local taxes (income, real estate, sales, and assorted other special levies, depending on your industry).

When you're short on cash (don't kid yourself; sooner or later, it's bound to happen), make sure that you pay any taxes you owe the government first, even if you have to put off paying your private vendors. Governments, especially the federal government, have an enormous array of collection tools at their disposal, and they have the right to extract a dear price (in the form of onerous penalties and interest rates) from those who don't follow the letter of the law. So be sure to pay your taxes on time (we hope we're not the first people to tell you this). For more on the taxes that affect your small business, see Chapter 19.

Negotiating leases

When you're leasing space for a start-up, aim for a two-year lease, or three years as an absolute maximum. If you think you may want the space for a longer term, consider negotiating and adding to your lease agreement an escalation clause that stipulates upfront how much the rental rate will increase should you choose to extend the lease for a subsequent year or multiyear period.

Unfortunately, reading, understanding, and creating a lease are tasks for lawyers, not laypeople. Pay the legal fees and don't get locked into any long-term leases with the lure of free rent or equipment use.

Long-term leases are a no-win situation for the small-business owner: If your business grows, it will outgrow the long-term lease and you'll pay a higher price for its cancellation; if your business doesn't grow, you'll pay an even greater price to get out of the lease. What do we mean by *long-term?* Any lease for more than two years. Many landlords offer long-term leases (three to five years) with all sorts of exotic discounts; don't be lured into taking them unless you can afford to pick up the final years out of your own pocket should the business no longer want, need, or be able to pay for the space.

Maintaining employee records

The day you hire your first employee is the same day you must create and begin maintaining your first employee-personnel folder. Be sure to maintain a written record for every employee, covering such issues as employment agreements (including salary history), performance reviews, business goals, commendations, and, of course, reprimands.

These records come in handy as you manage and motivate your employees. Such key managerial and motivational tools as goal-setting and performance reviews require that you keep detailed employee records for them to work. (For more information on these two subjects, see Chapter 16.)

Also, assuming that you employ living, breathing human beings, you can count on the fact that, sooner or later, you'll have a conflict with one or more of those living, breathing human beings — a conflict that in the worst case is likely to end up in court. When a legal battle occurs, the party who can back up his or her claims with the most information usually prevails. Don't be the one who's handicapped by poor record-keeping and documentation.

Some states are *at-will* employment states, which simply means the employer has the right to terminate employees "at will." In effect, you don't have to clarify the reason for termination; all you have to tell the terminated employee is that "things just aren't working out." Other states aren't so lenient or understanding. Find out where your state stands on the issue by calling your state's Employment Department; it will have a long list of rules that will determine the employee records you need to maintain.

Getting licenses and permits

Almost all businesses require filing certain licenses and obtaining particular permits. We tell you what you need to know (and do) about permits in Chapter 18.

Signing the checks

As we're sure you already know, checks represent cash; from the day you hang out your shingle until the day you close your doors, cash will be the lifeblood of your business. The annals of small business are filled with stories of $12-an-hour bookkeepers who helped themselves to a hardworking entrepreneur's cash.

If your spouse is your bookkeeper, you can (we hope) rest easy. But what do you do when your bookkeeper isn't your spouse? You guard your cash like it's your life, because it is (well, it's your business life, anyway). Following is a list of tips on how to do exactly that:

- ✔ Schedule an audit at the end of every year. It doesn't have to be a full-fledged, expensive, cover-every-detail audit. Simply ask your certified public accountant (CPA) to spend half a day reviewing your books. Your CPA knows the sensitive areas to focus on.

- ✔ Make sure your bookkeeper takes a vacation every year. Most bookkeepers who are siphoning off their employers' cash don't want anyone else probing their books, even for short periods of time.

- ✔ Review and approve every invoice yourself.

- ✔ Balance the bank statement yourself.

- ✔ Require two signatures on every check (or require one signature — yours).

Outsourcing: Focus on What You Do Best

We define *outsourcing* as delegating services you don't want to do, or don't have time to do, to someone outside your company (not an employee), who can usually do them better and faster. The term *outsourcing* is a buzzword that has surfaced more in the past decade, but the concept itself isn't new. Businesses have been outsourcing, in one form or another, for many years. We outline the basics in the sections that follow.

Surveying the most commonly outsourced tasks

The following list tells you which small-business functions are most frequently outsourced. See the next section to determine which outsourcing options make the most sense for you.

- ✔ **Accounting and bookkeeping:** *Accounting* (the beginning-to-end process of collecting financial data, generating financial statements, and preparing tax forms) and *bookkeeping* (the collecting-of-financial-data function only) provide the gamut of outsourcing opportunities. You can, for example, hire someone to do all your accounting and bookkeeping, or you can hire someone to do only your payroll, only your financial statements, or only your tax returns. Because the typical entrepreneur usually isn't well versed in accounting and bookkeeping skills, we suggest that these functions be among the first you consider for outsourcing.

- ✔ **Human resources:** As your company grows, the various functions of human resources should be next in line for outsourcing consideration. Human resources includes a wide variety of nonproduct-, noncustomer-, and nonsales-related issues, such as

  - New-employee hiring procedures

  - Policies and procedure manuals for employees

  - Payroll and related information-gathering systems

  - Employee training on human resource issues

  - Employee training on a wide variety of sensitive issues, such as ethics and sexual harassment

- ✔ **Manufacturing:** The manufacturing process for most products is expensive, time-consuming, and extremely detail oriented. For many entrepreneurs, especially the creative and/or sales types who typically gravitate to this career, outsourcing the manufacturing function makes a lot of sense.

  Even if your core business is manufacturing, some elements of your product may lend themselves to outsourcing their manufacture to subcontractors. Even behemoth manufacturers such as General Motors and Apple subcontract a good deal of their work.

✔ **Sales:** Outsourcing sales is certainly the most potentially dangerous of the outsourcing options, but some businesses, including those that employ manufacturers' reps, do use it. We say "potentially dangerous" because it's difficult to impart to outside sales people the enthusiasm and knowledge necessary to effectively sell your business's product or service. Sales is definitely the last of the responsibilities to consider outsourcing, although doing so works well for some small businesses. (For more on manufacturers' reps and sales, see Chapter 11.)

Figuring out what to outsource

Here's the $64,000 question: How do you determine which services to outsource and which ones to retain in-house? Each business and owner is different, of course, but answering the following questions can help you make the best decision for your situation:

✔ **Can I better manage my available cash if I outsource?** The answer here primarily depends on how much cash you have. For example, by outsourcing the manufacturing process, you avoid the costs associated with maintaining an inventory of raw materials and hiring manufacturing employees. By outsourcing your sales functions, you avoid the costs associated with maintaining a sales force.

✔ **What do I do best?** Because your time is finite, why spend a lot of time doing the things you don't do well (such as bookkeeping) when you can farm out those duties, thereby leaving you with more time to do the things you do well? If you're sales oriented or product oriented, for example, doing your business's bookkeeping yourself simply doesn't make sense.

✔ **Will the cost of the outsourcing tasks include a product (or service) whose quality is better than what I can produce at that same cost?** The answer to this question is often yes, given the fact that the best outsourcing sources are almost always specialists in their areas of expertise. Of course, you shouldn't outsource until you find a competent specialist.

✔ **What do I enjoy doing the most?** We can guarantee you this: If you choose to keep your bookkeeping or human resource functions in-house, you will, over the years, end up spending no small amount of time dealing with issues related to these functions. Is this the way you want to spend your time?

In the final analysis, the decision whether to outsource should be based primarily on what you enjoy spending your time doing and where your personal skill sets lie.

Simplifying Your Accounting

If this were a perfect world, you wouldn't need an accounting system — you'd simply let your business checkbook do the talking. You'd pay your bills and deposit your receipts, and whatever was left over at the end of the year would represent your profit. How simple (and inexpensive) such a procedure would be.

Alas, this isn't a perfect world, and your checkbook does the talking only when measuring one of your assets (cash). Furthermore, your checkbook only measures today's cash; it doesn't give you the foggiest idea of what tomorrow's or next month's cash balance will be. Will you have enough cash in the bank to pay the month's bills, to meet next Friday's payroll, or to pay the quarterly tax payments that will be due in 30 days? Who knows? The checkbook isn't talking.

The problem is that your business's checkbook can't do any of the following things:

- ✔ Keep score (of anything but cash)

- ✔ Give you the information you need to pay your income taxes

- ✔ Provide you with the percentages and ratios you need to help you manage your business

- ✔ Provide you with the trends you need to determine the direction of your business

- ✔ Present you with the information you need to value your business

Like it or not, accounting is one of the most important functions of running your business. Whether you intend to eventually outsource your accounting or do all the work yourself, at the start-up stage, accounting demands your undivided attention. One of the most common mistakes we see entrepreneurs make in the start-up stage is to not learn how basic accounting works or how it applies to their business. Take it from us: Learn the basics early, or you'll never take the time.

Introducing some common systems

You have three options to consider when determining which accounting system to employ:

- ✔ An outside accounting service

- ✔ An in-house manual bookkeeping system

- ✔ An in-house computer-based accounting system

If you decide to go the outsourcing route (using an outside accounting service), you need to make that decision before you open your business's doors. If you decide to use an in-house accounting system, read on to find out more about the manual and computer-based options. (In Chapter 19, we provide advice on how to hire good tax and bookkeeping assistance.)

Manual bookkeeping systems

Maintaining a manual bookkeeping system is certainly the quickest and easiest of the two in-house options. All you have to do is visit your local office-supply store, purchase one of the many manual bookkeeping ledger and journal systems available (the entire package should cost $25 or less), and — voilà! — before you can mutter the words *green eyeshades,* you're a bookkeeper. You won't need to buy an expensive computer or the software to go with it; the only accessories required are a #2 pencil or a pen and, depending on the complexity of your business, no small amount of your (or someone else's) time.

In addition to the low cost of a manual bookkeeping system, another advantage of using such a system is that you learn the basics of the standard double-entry accounting system from the ground up — a skill that will hold you in good stead as your business grows. (See the sidebar "A collection of accounting definitions" if you need more information about double-entry accounting.)

The downside of the manual-entry system, especially when your business has a lot of activity, is that it can be extremely time-consuming, and time is money in the small-business world. Also, the information that you collect manually won't always provide you with the depth of financial data you need for making important business decisions. Finally, manual bookkeeping is more prone to human error (intentional or unintentional) than computer-based systems are.

After you purchase your manual system, follow the step-by-step directions inside the ledgers and journals to perform a relatively uncomplicated, connect-the-dots bookkeeping process. During the course of your fiscal year, make your entries in the general journal pages (*journals* are where you make the entries; *ledgers* are where you total the journal entries). The manual system you buy will include definitions of each of the following categories, along with examples:

- Your disbursements, according to their expense and/or capital account category
- The receipts (income) of your business
- Various period-ending adjusting entries designed to record such items as depreciation, accrued taxes, and accrued payroll

Simple accounting can work!

A Greek restaurant owner in Cleveland had his own bookkeeping system. He kept his accounts payable in a cigar box on the left-hand side of the cash register, his daily cash returns in the cash register, and his receipts for paid invoices in another cigar box on the right. When his youngest son graduated from Harvard with his MBA, the young man was appalled by his father's primitive accounting methods. "I don't know how you can run your business that way," the son scolded. "How do you know what your profits are?"

"Well, son," the father replied, "when I got off the boat from Greece I owned nothing but the pants I was wearing. Today your brother is a doctor, you have an MBA, your sister is an investment banker, and your mother and I have two nice cars, a city house, and a country home. We have a fine business, and everything is paid for. Add that together, subtract the pants, and there's my profit."

At the end of the year, complete your journal entries to summarize the year's activity. Then, if you prefer, you can turn over your journals to a tax advisor or CPA, wait a few weeks, and be rewarded with a professionally prepared profit and loss statement, a balance sheet, and the balance due for your year-end tax payment. (See Chapter 14 for details on the different financial statements and Chapter 19 for details on small-business taxes.)

If, on the other hand, you're that special entrepreneur who actually enjoys the bookkeeping process, you can expand the manual bookkeeping process to include the year-end preparation of your profit and loss statement, as well as the balance sheet, leaving only your taxes to be computed by a tax practitioner.

Finally, in those cases where your business is a relatively uncomplicated sole proprietorship or partnership (see Chapter 5), you may decide to carry the manual process through the preparation of Schedule C of IRS Form 1040 and on into the preparation of your personal income tax return.

When it comes to how much of your own bookkeeping and taxes you perform yourself, the only limits are your time, skills, and patience. The primary issue to consider when determining how much, or how little, of your accounting you should do is how best to utilize your finite time.

In addition to the general ledger and journal functions previously described, most manual bookkeeping ledger and journal systems also include the forms you need to maintain such subsidiary records as monthly payrolls, schedule of accounts receivable, schedule of accounts payable, and inventory worksheets.

Computer-based systems

If you already have a computer, using it to accomplish your bookkeeping and accounting functions almost always makes sense. (In the event that you don't have a computer, you're going to have at least two strikes against you as you work to grow your business.) Although the least expensive computerized software package available is a tad more expensive than a comparable manual system, the computerized system (if you use it properly) should save you time, provide you with more information, and establish a base for you to grow into a more sophisticated system as your business (we hope) expands.

You can consider four categories of computerized systems when shopping for your first accounting package. The system you ultimately select depends on the size and complexity of your business. A description of the four categories follows, along with several basic questions and a collection of tips intended to help you make the final choice.

Category 1: Quick and easy

Category 1 includes those quick-and-easy accounting systems used by many families, as well as by small businesses. The cost of these systems is usually around $50. They're basically an electronic checkbook register with the capacity to categorize and cumulate expenses and generate both profit and loss statements and balance sheets. Most Category 1 systems also include the capability to pay bills electronically. The most often used example of Category 1 is Quicken.

The primary shortcoming of Category 1 systems is that the software allows for the deletion of bookkeeping entries, so if you're interested in providing an audit trail for you or your accountant, you shouldn't purchase a Category 1 package. An *audit trail* enables you to track every dollar of income and expenses, thus making theft much more difficult. (Audit trails are required in all publicly held companies.) For this reason, most accountants don't recommend Category 1 systems to small-business owners who have prospects of future growth; these owners will eventually require the security that audit trails provide.

When your business is small and you know it's going to remain small, and you'll be the only person writing the checks, Category 1 systems may be satisfactory for you.

Category 1 systems don't include payroll systems. If you plan on eventually having employees and don't want to figure your payrolls or write your checks manually, you may as well spend another $50 to $100 and upgrade to Category 2.

TECHNICAL STUFF

A collection of accounting definitions

If you're interested in mastering a manual system (or if you just want to understand the basics of accounting, no matter what system you use), here are the key accounting terms you need to know:

✔ **Fiscal year:** A *fiscal year* is the specific 365-day period that you have chosen to begin and end your accounting period. Most businesses must choose a calendar year as their fiscal year; in other words, their year begins January 1 and ends December 31. (All personal service businesses are required to use a calendar year, as are all partnerships and sole proprietorships.) Some corporations, LLCs, and subchapter S Corporations may decide to use a fiscal year other than the standard calendar year; for example, many retailers choose not to end their fiscal year on December 31 because they're still too busy winding up their holiday season. As a result, many retailers select a non-calendar fiscal year of February 1 through January 31 (or any such non-calendar-year 365-day period).

✔ **Double-entry accounting and bookkeeping:** All accounting and bookkeeping systems are *double-entry*. For each entry made on the expense side, an offsetting entry must be made on the income side. Or, for every entry on the asset side, an offsetting entry must be made on the liability side. Every plus must be accompanied by an offsetting minus, or in accounting-speak, every debit to one account must be offset by a credit to another. For example, when a retail business sells goods from its inventory for cash, a credit is made to cash and a debit is made to inventory. Because of this double-entry aspect, such systems are always self-balancing. (The total debits will always add up to equal the total credits, hence the term *balance sheet.*)

✔ **Single-entry record-keeping:** The best example of *single-entry record-keeping* is your personal checkbook — one entry and the transaction is complete. Single-entry record-keeping systems aren't self-balancing. (Your checkbook doesn't balance until you've reconciled it to your statement.) Cash register tapes and the maintenance of internal ledgers are other examples of single-entry record-keeping systems.

✔ **Cash-basis accounting:** *Cash-basis accounting* records income at the time it's received and deducts expenses at the time they're paid. In effect, the date of the check and/or the deposit determines the date of the applicable bookkeeping entry. Most sole proprietorships and partnerships use the cash-basis accounting system because it's easier to understand and requires fewer year-end adjusting entries. However, you get much less useful information with which to manage your business.

✔ **Accrual-basis accounting:** *Accrual-basis accounting* records income at the time it's earned (when a sale is made as opposed to when cash changes hands) and deducts expenses at the time they're incurred (which may not necessarily be when cash changes hands). The IRS requires that businesses that have inventory use the accrual system. As a result, nearly all corporations utilize the accrual system.

If you have a choice for your business, consult with a tax advisor for advice as to which system will work best.

Category 2: Plus payroll and inventory

For about $100, *Category 2* systems provide a number of services that Category 1 systems don't. For example, Category 2 systems can perform the following functions:

- ✔ **Compute, write, and compile employee payroll:** Some small-business owners choose to outsource this function, but for those who are watching every penny, managing your own payroll is a good place to start.

- ✔ **Track and age *receivables* (monies your customers owe you) and *payables* (monies you owe your vendors):** *Aging* means determining the amount of time your receivables have been due to you or your payables have been due to your vendors.

- ✔ **Establish customer receivable ledgers:** These ledgers are, in effect, a timed listing of your customers' statements.

- ✔ **Maintain a basic inventory system:** Managing inventory is one of the small-business owner's most difficult and, thus, most unpleasant tasks. Using an automatic system to keep track of your inventory, especially when you have a large number of SKUs (stock keeping units), is the best way to make sure you're getting good numbers.

The primary disadvantage of Category 2 accounting software programs is that, similar to Category 1 programs, they don't provide an audit trail.

Examples of Category 2 accounting software packages include QuickBooks, Cashflow Manager, and Manage Your Own Business (MYOB).

Category 3: Following the audit trail

Category 3 programs provide their owners with all the benefits that Category 2 systems provide, as well as the audit trail, which is necessary for businesses in which someone other than the owners will be writing checks and maintaining the books. Additionally, Category 3 systems allow for multiple users: the bookkeeping department, the accounts receivable department, the inventory department, and so on. Prices vary, depending on the horsepower required, but they're generally in the range of $200 to $700.

Examples of Category 3 packages include BusinessWorks, Peachtree Accounting, QuickBooks Pro (an upgraded version of QuickBooks), and BPI.

Category 4: Modular power

Unlike the software packages in Categories 1, 2, and 3, which are purchased in a single package, *Category 4* systems are purchased in *modules,* or stand-alone units. However, Category 3 and 4 programs overlap to some degree because a few of the Category 3 programs also come with modules, thus making the choice between the two a bit complicated. Because Category 4 packages have more horsepower/bandwidth, as well as more module options, they work best for larger companies (more than 200 employees). See the next section for details on how to choose which system is the best option for you.

Category 4 software has the following module options:

- ✔ Basic system manager (the module that manages all the other modules)
- ✔ General ledger (otherwise known as the *chart of accounts* — the list of all the account titles that are tracked by every accounting system, including assets, liabilities, equity, and expenses)
- ✔ Financial reporting (profit and loss statement, balance sheet, and so on)
- ✔ Accounts receivable
- ✔ Accounts payable
- ✔ Payroll
- ✔ Inventory
- ✔ Job costing (a system that allows you to compute the exact cost of each of your products or services for pricing purposes)

The cost of each of these modules is approximately $500, but the total price for a complete system can begin at $2,000 and run all the way up to $10,000, depending on the bells and whistles you select. Good programs in this category are flexible and can support many types of accounting issues and business processes.

Examples of Category 4 accounting software packages include Microsoft Dynamics GP (formerly Great Plains and Dynamics), Sage Accpac, QuickBooks Enterprise Solutions, and MAS 90.

Choosing the system that's right for you

We explain the pros and cons of using a manual accounting system earlier in this chapter, so we focus on computer systems here. The first two questions you need to ask when choosing a computer-based system are

- ✔ How big is your business?
- ✔ What can you afford?

Generally speaking, the smaller the business, the more likely you are to use a Category 1 or 2 system. A home-office business can easily get by with a Category 1 system, while most non-home-office businesses with 50 employees or fewer can use a Category 2 system.

You also need to take into account how much inventory you'll be managing and whether or not you've decided to outsource your payroll. In other words, the more you ask of your system, the more horsepower you need.

When making your final system decision, consult with your CPA or computer professional and keep the following reminders in mind:

- ✔ **Don't waste your time purchasing and figuring out a system that you're going to outgrow in six months or a year.** We don't want you wasting money on a system you'd get such little use out of.

- ✔ **Don't buy a system that you think will take you three years or more to grow into.** That's too far out to accurately project. Buy a system that you think will work for you for the next two years.

- ✔ **In addition to considering the software system itself, consider the company behind the package you're buying.** Consider the following criteria: the support that the company provides, the history of its program updates (as a general rule, better companies provide more frequent updates), and the future of that company (will it be around to provide upgrades in future years?).

- ✔ **In the likely event that you can't answer these questions yourself, call the company (look for a toll-free number on the package) and ask direct questions.** Your tax advisor may also be able to give you an educated opinion.

- ✔ **Find out whether someone locally is trained to provide implementation and support services for the product you're considering.** Look in the Yellow Pages, ask an accountant, or call the manufacturer.

When in doubt, buy the highest category that you can afford and that you can picture yourself using within the next two years. After all, companies grow. Even if you think you want a Category 1 software package now, chances are you'll be in the market for an upgrade soon enough. The additional investment required to switch software packages isn't really the issue. The real damage comes from the time and staff retraining required to make the switch.

Controlling Your Expenses

The three ways to increase your business's profitability are

- ✔ Increasing sales (in which case, those increased sales may or may not have a positive impact on profitability)

- ✔ Increasing prices (in which case, the entire amount of the increase will have a positive impact on profitability, assuming that you don't lose customers due to the price increase)

✔ Decreasing — or controlling — expenses (in which case, the entire decrease will have a positive impact on profitability, assuming that you don't lose business due to the impact of the expense reduction on your product or service quality)

When you increase prices or cut expenses, a one-to-one leverage factor goes to work on your bottom-line profits. This is why successful small-business owners always look to the expense and pricing categories first when they're in a profitability crunch: Results can be instantaneous, and the impact is usually dollar on dollar.

Whether you're starting a new company or running an existing one, you must remember that controlling expenses is a cultural issue, and cultural issues begin at the top. We're talking about the old practice of leading by example. If you have overstuffed chairs in your office and idle secretaries in your foyer, your employees are going to demonstrate a similar penchant for spending unnecessary money.

Whenever we walk into a business's lobby or reception area and we're greeted by the gurgle of cascading waterfalls and the sight of bronze sculptures, we're reminded again of Sam Walton and Wal-Mart. Linoleum floors and metal desks were the order of the day at Wal-Mart's corporate offices in Bentonville, Arkansas. No wonder they could underprice and outperform such longtime competitors as Sears, Montgomery Ward, and J.C. Penney, whose overheads included the cost of maintaining plush corporate headquarters in the towering skyscrapers of Chicago and Dallas.

The following sections delve into the different types of expenses you need to control and explain the advantages of using zero-based budgeting.

Looking at fixed and variable expenses

As a small-business owner, you have to control two kinds of expenses:

✔ **Fixed expenses:** Those expenses that don't fluctuate with sales, including such categories as insurance, rent, and equipment leases. You usually negotiate them in the start-up stage and then leave them alone until the original negotiations lapse and you have to renegotiate them. Such periods may be anywhere from one year to five years.

Effective control of fixed expenses requires your skillful negotiation, because after they're established, renegotiation time probably won't come around for a while, which means you're stuck with them.

✔ **Variable expenses:** Those expenses that fluctuate with sales — as sales go up, variable expenses go up as well (and vice versa). These expenses include cost of goods sold, sales commissions, and outbound freight.

You can delegate the determination of the prices to be paid for variable expenses, as long as you remember that the responsibility for controlling them, in the early stages of a business anyway, should always rest with you (the owner). You need to approve all purchase orders and sign all checks that relate to variable expenses.

As the company grows, you may choose to delegate the responsibility for controlling expenses to other responsible individuals inside the company. Or you may choose to maintain control by continuing to sign the checks and questioning the invoices that support those checks (definitely our recommendation!).

A key to controlling expenses is keeping your employees cost-conscious. If your employees know that you and other key managers will question unreasonable or unnecessary expenses, they, too, will be motivated to be cost-conscious. You can also use incentives to help you cut costs. If you give your employees a reason (bonus, perks, recognition) to look for unnecessary costs, they're sure to find them.

As you manage your expenses, always be aware of the *80-20 rule,* which says that you can find 80 percent of your wasted expense dollars in 20 percent of your expense categories. For businesses that have a significant number of employees, the wages and salary account is usually the largest expense category and, thus, the most often abused.

We don't mean to say that you shouldn't challenge expenses in every category. You can usually find some wasted dollars by rooting around in such expense accounts as utilities, travel, insurance, and, of course, the compost heap — the "miscellaneous" expense account.

Effective expense control is not only a profitability issue but also an important element for controlling cash flow (see Chapter 14). Because lack of cash is usually the number one warning signal of a small business's impending troubles or failure, one of the best ways to build a solid foundation for your business is by controlling your expenses from the very beginning.

Understanding zero-based budgeting

Budgeting (also known as *forecasting*) is the periodic (usually annual) review of past financial information with the purpose of forecasting future financial conditions. If you've completed your business plan (see Chapter 4), you, in effect, prepared your first budget when you forecasted your profit and loss statement for the upcoming year. The only difference in preparing a budget for your ongoing business is that you now enjoy the advantage of having yesterday's figures to work with.

Incidentally, the process of budgeting is one that should apply not only to your business but also to your personal finances, especially if you have trouble saving money. If you aren't currently budgeting your personal revenues and expenses, start doing so now (see Chapter 2). After all, there's no better way to prepare yourself for running a business than to begin at home.

In your small business, you have two ways to budget expenses from year to year. The first — we call this *adjusted-for-inflation budgeting* — is to assume a percentage increase for each expense category, both variable and fixed. For example, say that you decide that your telephone expense (a variable expense) will increase by 5 percent next year, your rent (a fixed expense) will remain the same, and your advertising and promotion (a variable expense) will increase by 10 percent. Whoosh, a few multiplications later, and you've budgeted these expenses for the year. How much easier can budgeting get?

The other way to budget expenses is called *zero-based budgeting.* If you use this type of budgeting, you assume that last year's expenses were zero and begin the budgeting process from that point. For example, the zero-based formula assumes that your supplies' expense account begins at zero; thus, you must first determine who consumed what supplies last year, who will be consuming them this year, and how much will be consumed. Then you must determine what price you'll pay for this year's supplies. In this manner, zero-based budgeting forces you to annually manage your consumption at the same time that you review your costs.

The effect of zero-based budgeting is that you no longer include prior years' mistakes in the current year's budgets. For example, when you budget telephone expenses for the year, instead of increasing them by a flat percentage, zero-based budgeting demands that you make sure your prior year's bill was the lowest it could be. This assumption forces you to determine who's using your phones for what kind of activity and also to reprice your rates with telephone carriers. Instead of forecasting a 5 percent increase, you may well end up projecting a 5 percent decrease. The zero-based method also assumes that you'll check out prices with other vendors beside the ones that you're presently using.

Far too many small businesses don't budget expenses at all. Furthermore, of those small-business owners who do, few use zero-based budgeting, despite its many advantages. Not budgeting is truly one of the most expensive mistakes you can make as a small-business owner. Sure, zero-based budgeting may take more time than using a percentage, but it can pay big dividends in increasing bottom-line profitability — at home or in your business.

Managing Vendor Relationships

A small business's most underrated priority is working with its vendors (suppliers). Think about it. Without a good vendor, what would happen to your business? Say you own a computer retail store. Where would you be without Apple, Hewlett-Packard, and Microsoft on your shelves? Not into computers? Say you run a restaurant. Where would you be without a reliable baker, meat supplier, and fresh vegetable resource to depend on? Every successful business owner has learned the importance of having a cadre of loyal vendors standing behind his or her business.

Yet few small businesses have the muscle or the clout to demand any significant degree of vendor loyalty, which means that they must build strong vendor relationships the old-fashioned way — by earning them. The following tips provide information on how to earn favored relationships with your vendors:

- ✔ **Don't nickel-and-dime your vendors.** Agree on the details of your business arrangement (price, delivery, and terms) and then try to work within those parameters for the agreed-upon period of time. (Occasional exceptions will occur.) Whatever you do, don't use the low-ball pricing of the latest vendor on the street as leverage against the longtime reliable vendor unless you're prepared to lose or greatly annoy the longtime reliable one.

- ✔ **Pay your bills on time.** Paying your bills in the designated period of time helps maintain favored-customer status. After all, isn't prompt payment what you expect of *your* customers?

- ✔ **Save your special favor requests for when you need them.** Don't cry wolf on requests for out-of-the-ordinary service; save those requests for crunch time.

- ✔ **Treat your vendor's representatives (sales or customer service employees) as you want your own employees to be treated.** The Golden Rule is alive and well when it comes to maintaining vendor relationships.

- ✔ **Remember that relationships matter.** Everyone these days is preaching "relationships, relationships, relationships" when dealing with customers, right? Well, the same thing applies with vendors. Work to build a solid relationship with yours. If your vendor is a national supplier, build a relationship with its local or regional salesperson or representative or the person at the other end of the phone line. If your vendor is a local supplier, get to know him or her personally, just as you would a local customer. And remember, your bankers are vendors, too (perhaps the most important ones of all)!

Vendors — especially the good ones — can provide you with more than just a product or service. For instance, vendors can be a great source of new business referrals. They can also provide training to both your employees and, on some occasions, your customers — a form of assistance that the typical small businesses can't get enough of. For example, in coauthor Jim's sporting-goods business, the manufacturers of many of the products the company sold (fitness products especially) offered both on-site and off-site training programs at no charge. Be sure to ask your vendors what training programs and/or sales aids they offer and make use of them.

Not every prospective vendor will measure up to your standards. Be sure to check out your new vendors carefully, especially when they don't have a reputation or a track record. You can accomplish this inspection by touring their facilities, checking out the professionalism of their website, requesting customer references, and asking for financial statements.

The overriding point here is that creating a successful business takes a unique combination of human beings interacting together: you, your employees, your customers, your vendors, and a variety of outsiders (see the next section for details). No matter which of these you consider the most important, the others all have their roles in building your successful business.

Dealing with Bankers, Lawyers, and Other Outsiders

In the first two parts of this book, we discuss the loans that bankers make, the entities that lawyers initiate, the government agencies that interact with entrepreneurs, and the financial statements that accountants generate. But we haven't discussed the people behind all those activities.

This section is intended to help you understand the outsiders you must deal with, with the intention of helping you successfully manage the relationships that evolve with them.

Bankers

Ask the typical small-business owner what she thinks about bankers, and you'll usually get a reaction somewhere between a roll of the eyes and a hair-tearing tantrum. As a rule, bankers get a bad rap from the small-business community, especially since the banking problems of the 2008 financial crisis.

When bankers say no, they're only doing what they're trained to do — protect their depositors' money. For example, we know of a banker who, as part of his spiel to would-be borrowers, says, "I treat my bank's money as if it belonged to my parents." What this banker is really saying here is, "If there's a hint of a risk, you'll have to find your money elsewhere." After all, most of a typical bank's depositors are, in fact, *someone's* parents or grandparents.

A key part of the banker's job description is not taking big risks. Think about it: If bankers were creative and optimistic and prone to take risks, they'd be entrepreneurs, not bankers. Everyone has a role in a capitalistic system. Being safe and conservative just happens to be the role of the banker.

Make no mistake about it; start-ups are the riskiest of risks, which is why bankers don't usually consider financing them — unless the collateral is right. Meanwhile, especially in recent years, a variety of small-business below-market lenders have appeared on the scene, and today a number of viable alternatives exist for finding start-up capital.

Although bankers may not play an important role in the start-up, after the business is up and running, their role can become more crucial, especially when the small business experiences rapid growth. Expansion often requires operating capital in the form of outside financing, which is where bankers come in. (On occasion, of course, the entrepreneur may go back to her original source of operating capital; more typically, however, she gets her financing through bank loans.)

Here's how we recommend that you work with bankers:

- **Help your banker do her job.** Call her more often than she calls you — not just with the good news but also with the bad. Bankers don't like surprises, especially bad ones.

- **Always ask for more money than you think you need.** A little insurance never hurt anybody, and you usually won't get everything you ask for anyway. Besides, going back to the well a second time can be difficult, as well as embarrassing.

- **Prepare in advance for your banker's visits.** No matter what she says, your banker isn't paying social calls on you; she's kicking your tires. Include an agenda and a tour of your facilities and then review your financial results *before* she asks you for them. Finally, follow up your banker's visit with a letter outlining your discussion and thanking her for her time.

- **Recognize that you're probably going to have to *personally guarantee* (legally obligate your personal assets as collateral) your business's loans.** After all, you're asking your banker to, in effect, deposit her firm's money into your business. If you were in your banker's shoes, wouldn't you ask for such a guarantee? Remember, however, that your guarantee is only one of many issues that are up for negotiation when you're borrowing money. Try to use your guarantee to get an offsetting concession (something in return for your benefit) in the lending agreement.

✔ **Don't lose sight of the fact that a bank's interest rate, the collateral it requires, and the terms it outlines are negotiable.** What you settle on depends on the strength of your bargaining position. Don't blindly accept everything the banker offers; shop around among various banks that do small-business lending.

✔ **Be prepared to answer the bank's tough questions, especially where your assets are concerned.** The banker will want to know more about such hard assets as inventory, receivables, and equipment than you ever thought possible. But remember, those assets are the bank's insurance. The better your business's assets look to the bank, the better your negotiating position will be when the time comes to work out the terms of the loan.

The problem with bank committees

Several years after coauthor Jim purchased General Sports Corporation, the largest bank in Minneapolis granted his business its first line of credit. The relationship between Minneapolis's biggest bank (at the time) and its scrawniest entrepreneur (at the time) proceeded smoothly for the next several years, thanks to General Sports's profitable operations and the bank's capable account executive who handled the account. The account executive, who had become Jim's friend, knew everything that went on inside the business — Jim saw to that.

One day, the account executive stopped by unexpectedly to say good-bye (he had been promoted) and to pass on the news of a new bank policy: Jim's loan applications now had to be approved by "the committee." Apparently, General Sports's borrowing needs had exceeded some magic level and now required three loan-officer signatures instead of one. Jim was assured that this new procedure was only a formality.

A year or so later, the inevitable happened. "The committee regrets to inform you," the voice on the telephone began. And so ended the relationship between Jim and the biggest bank in town.

Jim and General Sports eventually survived, thanks to hard work and his working to develop a relationship with a neighborhood community bank. And as Jim's companies have grown over the years, he has learned to live with bank committees. Although the formula is simple (you depend on facts and figures and not on trust), the enactment is difficult and usually runs against human nature (against Jim's, anyway).

The problem, as Jim sees it looking back on the incident, is that committees don't spawn relationships; individuals spawn relationships. Jim found out the hard way that he would rather do business with a living, breathing human being than a committee.

Bankers and their conservative, close-to-the-vest ways are a fact of life. You can either learn to live with them or face life without being able to borrow their money.

Look at your local community banks first because they have historically taken the lead in small-business lending.

Lawyers

Lawyers used to be like FBI agents: You were aware that they existed, and sometimes you even met one, but you rarely had occasion to deal with them. They practiced their trade on someone else — never on you.

Today, lawyers are like pets. Everybody seems to have one. If you worked for General Motors, for example, lawyers would be part of the overhead — a fixed expense, similar to rent and depreciation.

But small-business owners don't work for General Motors. To you, lawyers are a large, additional expense. Lawyers' fees redirect your hard-earned cash, resulting in capital expenditures that you must put on hold, new employees that you can't hire, or trade shows that you can't attend. Additionally, spending time with them takes time away from work and results in lost productivity on the job.

All that said, consulting a lawyer has a time and a place. Lawyers provide protection (often against other lawyers) and force you to make plans to guard against the downsides that your entrepreneurially optimistic nature may overlook.

Yes, lawyers definitely have a time and a place. The place is always in the lawyer's office — you can't afford to pay a lawyer to travel to your office — or on the phone, and the times are

- ✔ When forming your corporation or LLC
- ✔ When taking in a partner or partners
- ✔ When creating shares of stock in your company — for you and for others
- ✔ When signing a lease, contract, or binding agreement
- ✔ When buying or selling a business
- ✔ When dealing with someone else's attorney on a conflictive issue
- ✔ When creating an employee handbook

✔ When designing employee bonus programs that result in company ownership for the employees

✔ When dealing with a situation that could result in expensive litigation (such as terminating a longtime employee)

✔ When considering bankruptcy (we hope that never happens)

No matter how much you want to avoid the expense of consulting with a lawyer, you should definitely hire one at the start-up stage and on the preceding occasions throughout the life of your business. When these occasions present themselves, we suggest you follow these tips for how best to find and utilize your lawyer:

✔ **When you absolutely, positively have to find a lawyer, don't shop just for price; shop for quality *and* price.** As with cars and quarterbacks, lawyers differ greatly in the way they perform, and that difference usually translates into winning or losing. Check references closely, just as you would when hiring a key employee.

✔ **Get a quote on your prospective lawyer's hourly fees and ask for an estimate of the total tab in advance.** The estimate may not hold up, but the lawyer will know that you're watching.

✔ **Always ask for itemized invoices.** A lump-sum invoice includes only time and rate, while an itemized invoice includes the date and time of each segment of work, the specific subject of each charge, and then the hourly rate. An itemized invoice also indicates work that was done by others — paralegals, for example — along with their hourly rates and charges for related materials.

✔ **Don't let lawyers chitchat about anything other than the business at hand if their meters are running.** Even though you enjoy talking about the latest sports or TV news as much as the next person, keep your discussions with your lawyer focused on your business. After all, we'd hate for you to pay $100 an hour to talk football!

✔ **Keep in mind that lawyers are human beings, too, which means they aren't always right.** Lawyers work in a gray profession, not a black-and-white one. The power of logic — theirs and yours — working in unison with their knowledge of the law will play a significant role in your business. You're capable of logic, too. Don't be afraid to use it in their presence. If your lawyers won't listen to you or ask for your input with important decisions, ditch 'em.

✔ **Don't be afraid to fire lawyers when they fail to perform up to your expectations.** They're no different from employees, accountants, or anyone else you hire to provide a service.

Lawyers aren't the only resource for settling disputes. Many small businesses today utilize mediation to resolve issues with customers, suppliers, and employees. Mediation is significantly less expensive than litigation and can take a fraction of the time (no court dates, no judges, and no miles of red tape). Nationwide providers of mediation services include the American Arbitration Association (www.adr.org; 800-778-7879) and JAMS (www.jamsadr.com; 800-352-5267), or you can look in the Yellow Pages under Mediation.

Tax advisors

Tax advisors, like lawyers, are professionals. The services they provide aren't rooted in conflict, but hiring and paying them can be equally discomforting and almost as expensive.

The role of tax advisors, in essence, is to provide you with the information you need to pay your taxes, make tax-wise business decisions, keep score of your progress, and manage your business. We cover the hiring of tax advisors/CPAs in Chapter 19.

Consultants

Hiring a consultant is akin to playing wild-card poker, meaning that fate will be a factor in determining whether you select the right one. That's not to say your success or failure is entirely in fate's hands, because the more effort you put into the hiring process, the better your chances will be to get the job done right.

Consultants can provide a wide array of services. Several of the areas where consultants can help the most include computer and information systems, tax issues, human relations, sales, and marketing.

You'll find more than one way to use and pay consultants. Some consultants offer their clients advice only; other consultants dive head-first into their client's business and get their hands dirty. Some consultants are paid by the hour, others by retainer (a fixed fee every month). It all depends on what you want and what you can afford.

Here are a few tips for how to get the most out of your consultant:

✔ **Search for a consultant as if you were hiring a key staff employee.** Network to find the best one and always check references carefully. Avoid consultants who have had only big corporate (as opposed to small-business) experience. Despite what they tell you, most don't understand what running a small business is like. Hire only consultants with plenty of small-business experience.

✔ **Whatever you do, don't hand over to your consultants the responsibility of making key decisions.** Also, never bet the house on the suggestions they make. Make your consultants prove themselves on smaller issues before you make the bigger changes they recommend. And never forget that you're in charge.

✔ **Don't offer any long-term contracts.** Build in a quick-exit option in the all-too-likely event that you don't get what you expected. And don't hesitate to show consultants the door when they aren't doing the job. Or, as the old adage goes, "Hire them slowly, fire them quickly."

✔ **Understand that their fees are only part of the ultimate cost of engaging ineffectual consultants.** Add misdirection, upset employees, and time lost, and consultants are capable of running up monumental tabs in surprisingly short periods of time.

Governments

If only entrepreneurs understood that the government is often an uncontrollable, random event, like a fire or a flood or a competitor moving in next door. This is especially true of the federal government, where the small-business owner may find it quite difficult to so much as talk to those officials who are the actual decision-makers, let alone get their problems resolved.

Come to terms with the fact that you'll sometimes have to comply with the government's unwieldy and often-unfriendly rules and regulations. Don't antagonize government employees (especially those who work for the IRS) — they can make your life miserable. Do what needs to be done to satisfy those sometimes-disagreeable government employees (you'd probably be disagreeable, too, if you had to spend your life in their environment), treat the agreeable ones like you'd want your own employees to be treated, and don't shoot the messenger — most government employees are only trying to do their jobs. In Chapter 18, we offer helpful advice for dealing with government regulations.

Chapter 11

Marketing: Products, Pricing, Distribution, Promotion, and Sales

*C*lose the door, turn off your phone and stereo, and put on your thinking cap. It's time to discuss the topic of marketing and the process that defines it. After all, marketing is the one facet of your business that will separate your product or service from the hundreds (or thousands) of competing products or services in the marketplace. Yet, marketing is typically either number one or number two on the small-business owner's list of the most difficult skills to master. (Managing employees is the other hard-to-master skill; see Chapter 16 for help on that one.)

Most small-business owners don't understand the process of marketing. Being a successful marketer requires a number of make-it-or-break-it skills that separate the mediocre (or failed) companies from the long-lived or fast-track ones. For proof of the importance of marketing as a business skill, look no further than those less-than-stellar products and services that are quite successful thanks to first-class marketing efforts (case in point: McDonald's certainly doesn't have the best hamburgers in the world). On the flip side, rarely are first-rate products successful through inadequate marketing efforts. Lucky for you, this chapter explains the five key elements of marketing to get you up to speed and on your way to a long, healthy business life. Along the way, we include tips and suggestions aimed at helping you develop your critically important marketing skills.

Marketing in a Nutshell

You aren't alone if you can't readily identify the difference between *marketing, sales,* and *distribution.* The definitions of these key terms (ones you'll hear over and over in the business world) are as follows:

✔ **Marketing:** The manner in which product development, sales, promotion, distribution, and pricing are bundled together to create an overall plan designed to communicate and deliver your company's products or services to the marketplace and, hence, to the ultimate customer.

✔ **Sales:** The manner in which your company either directly or indirectly connects with, convinces, and contracts with customers to purchase your products or services. Take note: Sales represents only one component of the marketing process.

✔ **Distribution:** The channels (such as retailers, wholesalers, and catalogs) that you use to deliver your product or service to your customers.

In large corporations, the senior executive in charge of marketing carries the burden; the work he does is pivotal to the success or failure of the business. In a small business, however, the marketing function usually rests on the shoulders of the owner.

The following five key components, which we discuss in detail in the following sections, make up the marketing process:

✔ Product and service development

✔ Pricing

✔ Distribution

✔ Promotion

✔ Sales

Tackling Product and Service Development

For most entrepreneurs, product and service development is the most enjoyable part of building a business. Whether refining an existing product or service or inventing a brand-spanking-new one, many entrepreneurs hang out their shingles in the first place because they believe they have valuable products or services to offer or have identified an unmet demand in the marketplace. They love the nuances of their products or services and are forever looking for ways to redefine and expand them.

Coauthor Eric is an excellent example of how product and service development can define the direction of a small business. From his work in the corporate world, Eric understands the financial services industry from the inside, and he sought to take that knowledge to help people improve their personal financial situations. Eric's initial service was personal financial counseling. Because he enjoys teaching, he soon began teaching personal finance courses through the University of California. He also began writing for a variety of publications and books. Today, somewhat to his surprise, Eric's writing (which now includes his books and website) takes most of his time; in the early stages of the business, Eric had envisioned reaching more people and growing his business through his financial counseling practice.

Coauthor Jim's second business had a similar growth pattern, resulting from the development of new products. His retail and wholesale sporting-goods company had spawned a screen-printing operation as he strove to add new lines of products. (He wanted to be able to number and letter the athletic jerseys that his company sold to teams.) Fifteen years later, his simple product development idea had grown into a stand-alone, $25-million business.

Despite the fact that most small businesses go about product and service development in haphazard ways, a defined process exists. That process goes something like this:

1. **Get an idea.**

   Someone (not necessarily you, the entrepreneur) hatches the idea. No matter where it comes from, though, you, the business owner, are always the one to *champion* (or support) the idea.

   New product and service ideas can come from a variety of sources, including vendors, trade publications, and, of course, employees. Unquestionably, however, the majority of new product ideas result from talking and listening to customers, both current and potential. After all, customers are the people who are most familiar with the use of the product or service, and customers are, in most cases, the same people who ultimately purchase new products.

2. **Evaluate the idea.**

   Work with the people responsible for product development to complete this step. Pay particular attention to issues such as profit potential, ease of manufacturing (where applicable), competition, and pricing.

   Not every idea turns into a workable or profitable product or service. You need to be critical and tough in the course of your evaluation. Be sure to ask the following questions:

   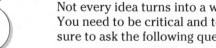

   - Do you have the staff and the cash (or can you assemble the resources) necessary to back the idea?

   - Does the idea fit your current product line, mission statement, and the values of your business, or can you build a new business or business unit around the idea?

- Is the competition already offering a comparable product or service? If so, is your idea distinctly better or more competitive?

Make sure that you can answer "yes" to these three questions before you move on to Step 3, as the product development process is expensive.

3. **Analyze your opportunity.**

Present the product or service concept to a few, select customers in an attempt to determine the size and scope of the potential market.

4. **Develop your product or service.**

At this stage, if the project is still a go, your goal is to develop the product or service. Time to dot the *i*'s and cross the *t*'s in preparation for the next step.

5. **Test the market/conduct market research.**

Test the completed product or service with a few prospective customers, with the intent of working out any bugs, in preparation for the product's official introduction to the marketplace.

6. **Introduce your product or service to the marketplace.**

Begin an advertising program, send the press releases, and start training the salespeople or manufacturers' representatives who will be responsible for selling the new product or service.

Because not every idea will turn into a workable or profitable product or service, you need to be tough as you proceed through these steps — especially when you reach the evaluation process (Step 2). Make sure that you thoroughly evaluate the pros and cons before moving on to the opportunity-analysis stage. The product development process is expensive, and you're better off cutting your losses early in the process rather than later.

Pricing: Cost and Value

Someone once made the observation that pricing is two-thirds marketing and one-third financial. This statement goes against the grain of common sense, which suggests that nothing could be more financial than price. But if your pricing isn't right, your marketing plan, no matter how well crafted, won't get off the ground. Prices too high? Your product won't sell. Prices too low? Your product may sell, but your company won't be profitable. The price, as the television game show proclaims, must be right.

To properly understand the role of pricing, you must first understand margin. *Margin* is the difference between how much it costs you to produce your product or service and how much you can sell it for. If your widget costs your company $2 to manufacture, for instance, and you sell it for $3, your margin is $1. Presented in terms of percentages, if you make a profit of $1 on each $3 sale, your margin is 33 percent ($1 divided by $3).

Developing your pricing strategy

Every business needs an overall strategy to guide it in making its pricing decisions. This means you need to plan your pricing strategy instead of just letting it evolve. Pricing shouldn't be a decision you make on a day-to-day basis, but rather an extension of an overall plan.

For example, you may decide (by planning) to be the lowest-priced company in your niche, thus attracting customers who think they're getting a bargain by frequenting your business. Or you may want to have the highest prices in your niche; high prices send messages of quality and distinction to some customers (witness art galleries, fine wines, or Brooks Brothers shirts). You may even want to sell some of your products at cost or even at a lower-than-cost price (these products are referred to as *loss leaders*) in order to attract customers who will then buy other products at higher prices.

As a small-business owner, you have the flexibility to determine your price points any way you see fit. Keep the following five factors in mind as you consider your pricing strategy.

Your marketing objectives

Marketing objectives vary with the product or service you're selling. If, for example, you have a new product to introduce, your short-term objective may be to gain market share and preempt competition, making your product well known to the consumer in the process. So you may discount your normal prices over the short-term, with profitability being shunted to the background, in order to achieve your long-term objectives. Another marketing objective may be to sell slow-moving inventory in order to generate cash. Similar to the example of new-product introduction, this objective also dictates short-term discounted pricing.

Be careful, however, not to get in the habit of continually discounting prices — unless, that is, you want to be perceived as a discounter. Most of the time, your marketing objective should be to maximize profit on your products without losing (too many) sales in the process. This objective should dictate your long-term pricing decisions.

The cost to produce the product or service

Cost is the total of all the expenses involved in generating your product or service — not only direct costs, such as wages and salaries directly involved in the product, materials, and freight-in, but also indirect costs, such as administration, accounting, and sales. Knowing the direct and indirect costs of your product or service is important in determining its *break-even point* (also called *break-even cost*), or the price below which you can't sell your offering without losing money.

Cost is one barometer of your break-even point, but it should never be the primary determinant in the pricing process.

The process of determining your break-even cost is quite simple — assuming, that is, that your accounting system is capable of gathering the necessary figures (see Chapter 10 for more on accounting systems). Here's how to determine your break-even cost:

1. **Determine the direct-cost allocation for each product or service.**

   Add all the direct costs (those directly involved in its manufacture — wages specifically involved in the product or service, materials, and incoming freight) associated with that particular product or service during a specific accounting period (preferably one month but no more than one quarter). Divide the total amount of direct-cost dollars by the total number of products manufactured or services provided during that period.

2. **Determine the indirect-cost allocation for each product or service.**

   Add the total dollars of your indirect costs (those indirect general and administrative costs that can't be specifically tied to a product or service) for the specific accounting period. Divide that number by the total number of products or services you provided in that period.

3. **Add the direct-cost allocation to the indirect-cost allocation to reveal your break-even cost.**

Amounts above the break-even cost represent your profit on that product or service; amounts below it represent your loss. If you offer more than one product or service, the process of determining a break-even point for each product or service can become complicated. Whether you succeed in arriving at an accurate break-even cost for each product or service depends on the sophistication of your accounting system.

Customer demand

The relative ease or difficulty of selling your product or service to the customer should play an important part in the pricing decision. What's the ratio of product on the market to supply available? The price points in all industries are subject to fluctuating supply-and-demand factors. (*Supply and demand* is basically a scarcity-of-goods/services equation. For instance, the more computer repair people you have in your area, the less the demand for their services. The consumer simply has too many choices.)

Comparative value to the customer

Just as beauty is in the eyes of the beholder, the value of a product is in the eyes of the customer. In addition to knowing what your product is worth in your eyes, you need to understand how much your product is *perceived* to be worth in the eyes of your customers. Set your prices at a level where your desired customers feel that they're getting their money's worth.

For instance, when Apple comes out with yet another new product, it doesn't set the price by arriving at the cost and then adding on a percentage of profit. Rather, Apple sets the price by attempting to determine where the customer will place the new product on the price scale of comparable products; then the company fits its new product's price somewhere in that vicinity. In other words, Apple attempts to determine how much the customer will perceive the new product to be worth, based on similar or competing products.

Competition

Who is your competition, and what's the price point of their products? How comparable are those products to yours? What are their products' perceived values compared to yours, and what factors affect their perceived values?

To determine the answers to these questions, you must first kick your competitors' tires by visiting the stores or websites where their products are sold or by picking up the phone and asking the right questions. Ask buyers of their products questions like the following:

- Why did you purchase the product?
- What is your perception of the relationship between value and price?
- Would you pay more for it if you had to?
- What do you like most about the product, and what do you like least about it?

 When comparing your product to that of your competitors, be sure to include all the criteria involved, not just the price. Additional criteria can include delivery, strength of brand name (image), packaging, quality, after-sales service, guarantees, return and trade-in policies, and much more. The rest of this chapter helps you decide what to do with this competitive information after you collect it, such as change your prices, better promote why your products and services are worth the extra price, and so on.

Picking the right price

After you understand the factors that go into making your pricing decisions and you've done your comparative shopping (see the preceding section), you need to pull all the pieces together to make the pricing decision. We explain how to make pricing decisions both for introducing a new product or service and for updating your price list for existing products or services in this section.

Pricing new products or services

When introducing new products or services, you have three pricing options. You may choose any one of the following three, depending on your predetermined pricing strategy:

- **Premium pricing:** Premium pricing is when you set your price higher than the competition or, in the event that you have no competition, higher than what's typical within the industry for that particular product. In this way, you skim the market, in effect appealing to the customers who are most motivated to pay a high price for products based on perceived value. Premium pricing may limit your unit sales, but it will also increase your profit margin.

- **Market penetration:** This pricing choice involves lowering your price to undercut competition, with the intent of gathering dominant *market share* (the percentage that you own of the total available market). This pricing strategy is designed to help maximize your company's name recognition in the marketplace and is frequently used by start-up businesses that want to attract low-cost buyers. Generally speaking, this is a short-term tactic that can't be maintained over the long term.

- **Meeting the competition:** This pricing decision is, as the name implies, designed to meet the price of your competition, thus encouraging the customer to compare your product or service to your competitor's — feature by feature, benefit by benefit. Before adopting this pricing decision, you must first make sure that your product or service can withstand the comparison and that you can offer a competitive price and value without threatening your survival.

Updating prices of existing products or services

Reviewing and altering prices on existing products or services is an ongoing procedure, not a once-a-year occurrence. Prices must never be cast in stone; they can and should change as market conditions change (consider gasoline prices). You can't always change prices — for instance, in those cases when you have to generate an "official price list" — but remember that pricing is primarily a marketing strategy; as markets change, so must your strategies for capturing those markets.

Distribution: Channeling to Customers

Distribution is how you get your product or service to the ultimate consumer. Distribution channels vary within the same industry and apply to all businesses.

No one right or wrong way exists to distribute your products or services; you can, however, usually find a way that works best for you.

Two basic categories of distribution exist, depending on whether a middleman comes between the manufacturer of the products (or the provider of the services) and the consumer: Direct distribution occurs when no middleman is involved; indirect distribution involves a middleman.

Each distribution channel has evolved for a reason, and each one has its own strengths and weaknesses. In the following sections, we discuss the various distribution options and offer tips for how to decide between them.

Direct distribution of products

The *direct distribution* of products involves establishing one-on-one relationships with the buyers, without passing any middlemen along the way. The following sections present the various channels of direct distribution.

Retail

What better way to avoid a middleman and be close to your customers than to physically interact with them in a retail environment? Knowing your customer is crucial to any small business's success, and a retail distribution system offers a perfect vehicle for doing just that. National retail chains like Gap and The Body Shop have chosen to sell their products through a direct distribution channel. Another advantage of retail distribution is that you retain the entire markup on your products. Still another advantage is that, in most cases, you don't have the expense of maintaining accounts receivable (as in, "Put it on my tab"), because these days retailing is primarily a cash — or credit/debit card — business. Although credit-card charges — Visa, MasterCard, American Express, and others — may not represent immediate cash, they do represent a dependable stream of cash, and you don't have to worry about collecting the funds. You do, of course, have to pay fees — up to 2 percent or more — for these privileges.

The disadvantage of retail distribution is that the costs of maintaining and staffing a retail store are high. Also, because you can't have your eye on the till and the door all the time (in most cases), retail is susceptible to theft of both cash and inventory. Finally, in most cases, you're required to sign a lease, a document that legally binds you to pay a landlord for a specified period of time, regardless of whether or not your store remains in business.

Direct mail

Direct mail refers to the mailing of flyers and advertisements directly to a specific audience. The success or failure of any direct-mail campaign is usually tied to the quality of both the mailing list and the promotional piece itself.

One of direct mail's advantages is its capability to directly target and reach *qualified prospects* (people who fit your demographic projections of who's most likely to want your product or service). Looking for a list of potential customers with two or more children, who own their own homes, and who have annual incomes in excess of $100,000? No problem. You can purchase a list and do the mailing yourself. Or you can hire a firm that will do it all for you.

One disadvantage of direct mail is the relatively high cost per contact. The cost per thousand of direct mailings is significantly higher than the cost per thousand to reach newspaper or magazine readers via advertising. The difference, of course, is that if your mailing list is good, every recipient represents a qualified prospect, whereas only a fraction of your advertising contacts may be qualified. A second disadvantage of direct mail is that some consumers simply don't like the direct-mail medium — so you can end up alienating potential customers when you use it.

Here's how to successfully develop your own direct-mail program:

- ✔ **Collect existing direct-mail pieces that you like and use them as examples for your own design.** Contact the business behind the materials that appeal to you the most and inquire who created the pieces and how they did so.

- ✔ **Concentrate on solving your customers' problems, not on selling them products.** Decide what offer you'll make to move your target prospect to take the action your mailer invites. For example, people don't want to pop pills; they want to increase their energy, so if your vitamins can help them do that, therein lies your message.

  This tactic is commonly known as *selling your product's benefits, not its features,* and it's quite possibly the number one rule of marketing!

- ✔ **Purchase or rent a mailing list by interviewing several different list companies.** Look in the Yellow Pages under Mailing Lists or call trade magazine reps and inquire about their subscription lists. Costs should vary from $25 to $75 per thousand names. Make sure you've defined the target market for your product or service and obtained a mailing list that includes only those who match the profile of your target.

- ✔ **Consider using a self-mailer when possible, thereby saving you the cost of an envelope.** More people throw away junk mail in sealed envelopes, anyway.

- ✔ **Stick with it; don't give up after the first mailing.** Many consumers need to see the same message several times before they react.

- ✔ **Follow up your mailings with phone calls.** When you intend to follow up the mailing with a phone call (which often helps to ensure better results), stagger your mailings so that you don't have to make too many calls during a short time period.

- ✔ **Maintain a complete record of the results of your mailing, detailing the number of responses and the number of orders that result.** A 2 to 3 percent response rate on a first-time direct mailing is usually considered good.

Mail-order catalogs

Mail-order catalogs, along with websites, have enjoyed a leap in popularity as the American shopper does more and more of her shopping from the comfort of home. Make no mistake about it, however: Catalog selling is an expensive channel for businesses, especially for start-ups. Creating and mailing a top-notch catalog can be off-the-charts expensive, depending on the size of the mailings. If you can't afford a top-notch catalog, you probably don't belong in this distribution channel.

Initial outlays include the charge for obtaining mailing lists, the costs of creating and developing the catalog, and the mailing expenses. And don't forget the additional cost (and risk) of maintaining sufficient inventory to be able to ship your orders within a reasonable amount of time.

Internet sales

Certainly the newer kid on the block, Internet selling (also known as *e-commerce*) is the most exciting development since the wagon trains headed west. In essence, Internet sales are another form of catalog sales. Customers simply connect to your company's website, click around until they find the items they're looking for, plug in their credit-card numbers, and wait for the packages to arrive by mail. Distribution via the Internet is easy on the shopper (no dodging traffic or fighting crowds) and easy on the vendor (no mall rent or expensive mailing lists).

Incidentally, this relatively inexpensive way of reaching customers also allows Internet prices for most products (except for those that are quite costly to ship) to be competitive. If you have any doubts, try undercutting Amazon's prices on anything it sells (which includes a lot more than books).

Internet selling works best for the small business when you have an off-the-beaten-path product that customers can't find anywhere else. Customers who are having trouble finding good products easily turn to Internet searches to locate alternative suppliers.

Trade shows

You may be in an industry that allows you to use trade shows to purchase your products from your vendors or to sell your products to your customers. Trade shows also provide the opportunity to network with other people who do the same thing you do and to check out the competition (see Chapter 15). Most of all, the information you glean from successfully working a trade show allows you to keep a firm pulse on your industry. (Don't overlook the training classes that are usually included with most trade shows.) Yes, trade shows can be expensive by the time you factor in travel and time away from the job, but they're usually a justifiable marketing expense.

Check out www.tsnn.com (Trade Show News Network) for an excellent resource that lists trade shows, seminars, and conventions all over the world for a wide variety of industries and organizations. The site covers everything from helping you find the best trade shows, conventions, and seminars to offering related travel information.

Indirect distribution of products

Indirect distribution is the process by which consumer products or services pass through a middleman before reaching the consumer. The following sections outline the channels you may use for indirect distribution.

Reaching your customers through other retailers

Traverse the aisles of a Wal-Mart or Target store and you'll find that every product on its shelves is from a manufacturer somewhere who has opted for the secondhand retailing method of indirect distribution. Meanwhile, Wal-Mart and Target are left to do what they do best: Sell retail to the consumer.

The advantage of selling to retailers is that you have to deal with only one, or a few, customers — the retailer's buyer(s) — which simplifies the distribution process immensely. This one-stop selling process enhances the *relationship building* process — that is, the establishment of a relationship between the vendor and the customer. (For more on relationship building, see "Sales: Where the Rubber Hits the Road" later in this chapter.) In this case, the relationship is typically between the manufacturer's salesperson and the retailer's buyer.

One distinct disadvantage of selling your products to retailers — especially those with multiple stores — is that they often use the size of the orders they place as leverage to become extremely demanding on such issues as price, payment, delivery, and packaging. Retailers, especially the larger ones, can keep their prices low for a reason, and more often than not, that reason comes at the expense of their vendors — especially the smaller ones that don't have the leverage the bigger guys have.

Relying on wholesalers or distributors

Wholesale distribution is a perfect example of how the middleman process works. The typical wholesaler/distributor buys large quantities of products from manufacturers, breaks them down into manageable quantities, sometimes repackages them, and then offers them to the consumer. Examples of wholesalers include plumbing- and electrical-supply businesses, whose primary customers are contractors, and grocery wholesalers, whose primary customers are grocery and convenience stores. Many manufacturers like working with wholesalers because they don't want the hassles associated with selling to consumers and smaller customers; after all, their expertise is in manufacturing.

Repackaging

Another common example of indirect distribution is *repackaging* — selling your products to another manufacturer or a developer of related products who offers them to its customers in another form. You often see examples of repackaging in the grocery business, where a grocery store chain sells products that bear the store's own name (the process is known as *private labeling*) on the containers of products someone else has manufactured. Many juices, frozen foods, and health and beauty products have been repackaged.

An advantage of repackaging is that, in most cases, the sales and marketing functions are left to your customer, allowing you to concentrate on the manufacturing part of your business. The disadvantages are that your profit margins are sure to suffer and you're likely to be overly dependent on one customer — the company doing the repackaging.

Deciding on distribution

No easy answer exists to the question of which distribution channels are best suited to your business. To help you answer this question, list the distribution channels that

- ✔ **Your competitors are using:** Rank the list with the most successful businesses at the top.

- ✔ **You can afford:** Distribution channels have differing costs; for instance, hiring your own sales staff costs more than creating a contract with a manufacturers' rep.

- ✔ **Your research and intuition tell you will be successful in your industry five years from now:** Given the continuing increase in web-based buying, yesterday's distribution channels will look different than today's.

Now compare these three lists, add a pinch of common sense, and determine the distribution channel(s) that you prefer.

Whatever you do, don't lock yourself into one distribution channel forever. Land's End, for instance, started in the catalog business, but today it also has consumer retail and Internet channels. Ditto L.L. Bean. Today's technologies are changing distribution channel options at warp speed. Small business is all about meeting change and staying flexible, so whatever distribution channel(s) you select should be subject to ongoing review.

Promotion: Spreading the Word

Promotion is the process of informing potential customers about your company and its products and services and then influencing them to purchase what you're selling. Promotional activities include word-of-mouth advertising, networking, media advertising, online communications, and publicity.

You'll use some of your promotions to generate immediate sales; you'll use other tactics to educate, inform, and plant the seeds for future sales.

Before you invest in any promotional effort, you must first determine the target market you want to reach and the objective you want to achieve. If you want prospective customers to call or visit your website, your ad must give good reasons to do so, and it better have a prominent presentation of your phone number and website address. If you want to create foot traffic, you have to put forward a time-sensitive, compelling reason to visit your business, such as a one-time discount or the appearance of a VIP.

To put everything you need to know about promotions in one sentence — know your audience and your objective and craft your messages accordingly. The following sections show you how to make use of the different promotional activities out there.

Networking (It's not what you know . . .)

Networking is connecting with people to make good things happen. Networking offers a host of benefits, the two most obvious being the opportunity to promote your products or services and the opportunity for you to learn from those with whom you network. These two benefits are the primary reasons that organizations such as the Chamber of Commerce, the Rotary, and Toastmasters exist.

But wait. Before you run out and join your local business organizations (see Chapter 15), think about using the networks you already have. Your friends, your relatives, your alma mater, your church, your children's school, your neighborhood, and the social organizations you belong to are all viable networks. With a little priming (being proactive), many of your existing networks will be happy to give your product or service a try. All you have to do is initiate the priming.

This priming can come in many forms — a telephone call, a flyer in the mail, an e-mail, or even a casual mention during a conversation following a school event. All these communication methods are viable parts of the network priming process, and all of them are available at little cost.

Be thoughtful and careful when networking with the people you know. People are busy and bombarded daily with tons of advertising, solicitations, and spam e-mail (aren't you?). The last thing most people want is to be accosted by a salesperson in what they thought were the friendly, safe confines of a school or church. Start with a low-key approach: Assemble a one-page summary or a simple flyer of your company's products or services and mail or e-mail copies to people you know.

You can improve your network priming with these additional tips:

- ✔ **At the beginning of every year, make a goal for yourself to add one more network to your current stable of contacts.** The most obvious way to do this, given today's web-based trends, is to start using social media tools, such as Facebook, LinkedIn, and Twitter.

- ✔ **Make sure that you have a professional-looking business card and don't be shy about handing it out.** Folks should be able to discern exactly what business you're in through the combination of your company name and your tag line, both of which should appear on your business card.

- ✔ **Be sure to follow up every networking opportunity.** A telephone call or a letter the next day reminds your networking prospects of your business and shows them that you manage it professionally.

- ✔ **Remember that networking works both ways.** Help another small business within your network, and you can usually expect that the other business will eventually help you.

Recognizing the power of referrals

What do you think when you hear a radio ad that says the Greasy Spoon Café serves the best burgers in town, but five minutes later, a friend tells you that Danny's Diner really serves the best burgers? Who are you going to believe — the radio ad or your friend?

If you're like most people, you'll believe your friend. After all, radio ads are scripted and paid advertising. Not so with friends; they have no script and generally no agenda, which makes them a credible resource. Such is the power of *word-of-mouth referrals*.

The problem, of course, is that you can't dictate the script of a referral the way you can a radio ad. If Danny's hamburgers aren't up to snuff, Danny's would be better off if its customers kept their mouths shut. Word-of-mouth referrals tell it the way the customer sees it, not as the business owner would like him to see it, so make sure your product or service is good before people start talking.

You don't have to hire an ad agency or media consultant to make word-of-mouth promotion work for you; you can do it yourself (for a price that's definitely right!). If you take care of your customers in the early stages of your business's life and provide an easy feedback mechanism, the referrals from satisfied customers should take care of you and your business in the future.

Every time you serve a satisfied customer, follow up the sale by calling the satisfied customer or asking her to fill out a feedback card (making sure she was satisfied with the transaction). Ask for the name of one referral (potential customer). Additionally, whenever a new customer does business with you, ask how he heard about your company. When the customer replies that he was referred to you by, say, Harry, make sure that the next time Harry stops by, he gets a sincere thank you and possibly a discount or some other offer of value. Rewarding Harry's behavior isn't necessarily a new trick in the promotional game, but it sure is an effective one.

Marketing with permission via e-mail

The Internet is the greatest direct-mail medium of all time, and e-mail is the engine that delivers the advertising message of Internet direct mail. We're not talking about the endless delivery of unrequested and unwanted e-mail — called *spamming* — that you see too much of these days. (That kind of e-mail is annoying, not to mention often illegal.) Instead, we're talking about sending targeted e-mails to lists of current and potential customers who have given you permission to communicate with them via this medium. You get such permission through personal contacts generated by phone conversations, sales calls, networking requests, and so on.

Small-business owners use the Internet for a number of reasons, including gathering information and purchasing products. However, customer or potential customer communication leads the list, with more than 80 percent of web users listing it as the main reason they go online. Research by the Direct Marketing Association (www.the-dma.org) indicates that the average advertising cost per sale of an e-mail campaign is $2. (Compare that to a direct-mail cost per sale of $71 and a banner-ad cost per sale of $100.)

Using e-mail allows you to do a number of marketing-related tasks that are directly related to building relationships with both current customers and potential customers. For example, you can

- ✔ Invite response to your e-mail so that you can e-mail the recipient back.
- ✔ Invite the recipient to visit your website.
- ✔ Provide information that will be noteworthy to the recipient.
- ✔ Simply keep in touch with your customer, as long as the content of the message is relevant to the permission you've been granted.
- ✔ Use e-mail to process a customer's order in the most efficient way possible.

Still not convinced that e-mail is a viable promotions avenue? Here are three more reasons why e-mail is such a rapidly growing direct-marketing tool and will continue to be for the foreseeable future:

- ✔ **Postage and printing are free.** Compare e-mail to the cost of creating (and then mailing) a brochure.

- ✔ **Frequency is free.** You can talk with your prospect over and over again.

- ✔ **Contact is fast.** Hit the Send button and your message is delivered.

Other Internet marketing opportunities

The Internet is one big promotions resource. Here are some of the best online opportunities for marketing small-business products and services:

- ✔ **Facebook:** Every small business should have a Facebook page, the primary purpose of which should be to build relationships with customers. (Go to www.facebook.com to start a page for your business now.)

- ✔ **Twitter:** You can use Twitter to keep customers alerted to special offers or product additions or modifications. (Find out more at http://twitter.com/.)

- ✔ **Groupon:** Groupon is a for-profit, web-based business that negotiates huge discounts — usually 50 to 90 percent off — for its small-business customers. Groupon sends the proposed deals to thousands of subscribers in a daily e-mail and (we hope) sends the business hundreds of new customers. (Check it out at www.groupon.com.)

For more on these digital marketing opportunities, take a look at the latest edition of *Small Business Marketing For Dummies* by Barbara Schenck (Wiley).

Media advertising

Our definition of *advertising* is a program of paid messages designed to inform large numbers of prospective consumers on the benefits of your product or service. Although the ultimate long-term purpose of advertising is to persuade the consumer to think well of your business and to purchase your product or service, some short-term advertising strategies may focus on the achievement of specific objectives. For instance, you may want to attract attendance at events, win sales within a certain time period, or gain name recognition for a new business.

Good advertising is about targeting the right message and the right market with repetition and consistency. Mention Nike and people think "Just Do It." Geico is where "15 minutes could save you 15 percent or more." And McDonald's has people everywhere singing, "I'm lovin' it." None of these slogans became implanted in consumer minds via a one-shot advertising blitz or a slogan-of-the-month effort. Rather, they became well-known thanks to focused and consistent message projection over time and through all forms of media, including traditional, social, and guerrilla marketing channels.

View advertising as an important investment rather than a dreaded expense. When you budget money to put your message in front of prospective customers with effective frequency, you're making an investment in your future success.

Because you're not a large company, you can't afford to spend buckets of money on media advertising. That's why we highly recommend that in the early stages of your business — when cash is generally scarce — you focus on networking and referrals as well as other low-cost, highly targeted advertising tools (such as e-mail) to get your first customers in the door. Then, when you're ready to venture out into the world of paid advertising, use one of these three methods of developing your advertisements to get the best results in a cost-effective manner:

- **Create your ads in-house, either by writing them yourself or by utilizing an employee who has advertising and creative talent.** Make sure, however, that you (and others) perform serious editing on everything that goes out your door. Mistakes or misspellings in advertising materials reflect poorly on the advertiser and will turn off some buyers.

- **Work with freelance copywriters, designers, media buyers, or other resource professionals.** Contract projects on an as-needed basis, and maintain responsibility for continuity, accuracy, and timeliness.

- **Hire an advertising agency to handle all your advertising needs.** Instead of calling a designer when you need a trade booth, a copywriter when you need an ad, or a direct-mail house when you need a mailing, turn to a single resource for all projects. A good agency can review all your communications needs, create a single campaign, and produce all the materials you need to prepare the message that works best for you.

  Yes, you'll pay handsomely for the expertise and service, but, in the process, you'll free yourself for other activities. Also, assuming the agency you select is a reputable and qualified one (check references carefully), your advertising program will give you the bang for your buck that you're seeking.

To find the advertising resource that's right for you, watch, read, or listen to media (radio, television, magazines, newspapers), select the ads you like, and then call the business that's doing the advertising and find out who produced or assisted in producing the ad. Or you can simply network with other noncompeting small-business owners who have advertised and ask questions to determine who and what worked for them. Also network with your vendors, with your customers, or within your business organizations. Be sure to check your prospective advertisers' credentials and get firm quotes on the cost of their services.

The media options we discuss in the following sections are the most widely used by small businesses for spreading the message.

Successful advertising requires focus, especially in terms of consumer demographics. If, for instance, you're selling opera star Placido Domingo recordings and advertising on a country-and-western radio station, you're focusing on the wrong audience.

Before you implement one or more of the following advertising techniques, be sure to devise a form or a procedure to track where your new business is coming from. This form should track new customers and find out how they heard about your business. That way, you'll know which of your advertising tools are working and which ones aren't. After all, you won't know whether your Yellow Pages option (or any other medium you've selected) is worth your time and money unless you ask.

Yellow Pages

The Yellow Pages were largely created for, and belong to, hometown retailers and service suppliers. Looking for a hardware store or somewhere to rent a tux? Many prospective customers head for the Yellow Pages first.

Be creative with your ad and remember that bigger (which is what the Yellow Pages sales rep will push for, thanks to the commission) isn't necessarily better. In the Yellow Pages, your ad will be placed right there with all your direct competitors, so your ad needs to set your product or service apart from the rest. Often, your product or service may fit in more than one category. Suppose that you sell screen-printed T-shirts. For an extra fee, you can get listed under T-shirts, Advertising, and/or Screen Printing.

If your primary customer audience comes from outside your local area, chances are you have little or no need for Yellow Pages advertising. Opt for a one-line entry, because you don't need any more. Yellow Pages ads can be expensive, especially when they aren't generating customer traffic. And remember, the importance of Yellow Pages advertising has waned as the wide-reaching tentacles of digital and Internet advertising have grown. The lesson? Don't earmark an inordinate amount of your budget to the Yellow Pages.

Newspapers

Newspaper advertising generally requires less cash outlay than other forms of advertising. Most ads are black and white, so production costs are low. Newspaper ads are excellent for specific geographic targeting (such as *zoned advertising*, in which areas of town are targeted for specific advertising content in news sections tailored to them). Most large metropolitan newspapers offer community sections with advertising targeted at local customers, as well as placement of ads on their websites.

Newspaper ads have a relatively short life span, don't offer the same quality of reproduction that other print advertising tools do, and are oftentimes quickly scanned (as opposed to read in detail) by readers.

Radio

Radio, along with magazines (see the later section), can help you target a specific demographic group. Also, similar to newspapers, radio focuses on a specific geographic area. Want to sell acne cream to teens (and their parents) in Albuquerque? Buy commercial time on the local pop or hard rock station.

Additional advantages of radio advertising include the following:

- ✔ Allows for short *lead times* (the time between when you decide to advertise and when your ad is heard by prospective customers).

- ✔ Reaches people when they're working, traveling in cars, and otherwise going about their daily activities.

- ✔ Provides a proven answer for speedy reaction. Studies indicate that approximately 75 percent of the responses to radio advertising occur in the first week after air time.

That same immediacy, however, is also the downside of radio advertising. If your prospects aren't tuned in at the exact moment that your ad airs, you're out of luck. That's why radio advertisers use the term *frequency* when planning their schedules. They aim to have the same ad run over and over, often on several stations in the same market area, hoping to catch the attention of prospective customers at least a few times.

Television

Television takes radio advertising one step further, adding video to the audio, and thus making more impact on the listener. TV also adds prestige to the business doing the advertising, although with significant costs. Finally, similar to radio ads, good TV ads can evoke a speedy response.

TV ad *buys* (another name for the buying of time to present your ads) come in two packages:

- ✔ **Network buys:** These involve running your ad on the entire network (think about the ads that run during the Super Bowl) — a very expensive proposition.

- ✔ **Spot buys or local time buys:** These are the ad time slots the network makes available, even during the Super Bowl, for use by local stations. These ads are priced based on the size of the audience reached by the local station and the time of day the ad runs.

As with radio ads, TV ads, especially those on a local basis, usually involve a frequency strategy — that is, the ad is intended to be viewed frequently over relatively short periods of time. TV ads also work best when the message is clear, simple, and entertaining.

The cost for producing a TV ad can run the gamut. You can have the local station assemble a simple 30-second ad relatively inexpensively; you can have an ad agency produce the ad (the same freelance professional or ad agency that does your print advertising); or you may be able to produce the ad yourself.

After your ad is produced and you're ready to buy time slots on the local station, approach the scheduling process with your facts in hand. Know the age, gender, and programming preferences of your customer prospects. Then either your station representative (the salesperson representing the TV station) or your media buyer (the ad agency that's putting together your ad program) can show you the viewer demographics and other viewing patterns for various programs to help you select a schedule that will target the right audience. Discuss your overall strategy with your media buyer, making sure that she also understands your budget constraints.

Local and national magazines

The primary benefit of magazine advertising is that the advertiser can target specific audiences, as opposed to newspaper ads, where anyone and everyone may be the reader. Run an ad in *Scientific America,* for example, and you'll attract one kind of audience; place an ad in *GQ,* and you'll reach another.

An additional advantage of magazine ads is that they have a longer life than the other forms of advertising media, because magazines are often passed from reader to reader. Compare this longer-life benefit to radio or television, whose ads are gone after their broadcast cycle.

If you're a manufacturer, for example, a trade magazine can offer a rare degree of consumer-targeting potential. Readers of trade magazines are more than likely potential consumers; in many cases, readers peruse a trade magazine with the specific intent of studying its ads. Check out the reference book *Small Business Sourcebook* (Gale; www.gale.cengage.com), which includes lists of trade publications for all types of businesses.

The downside of magazine advertising is that it's a high-budget item relative to other media, especially if you use high-profile publications. The cost of a full-page, full-color ad in a national magazine can easily hit five figures.

Here are a few other interesting notes on magazine advertising:

✔ **You must plan your magazine ads well in advance.** Often, magazine ads must be submitted more than two months before the publication hits the mailbox or newsstand.

✔ **Cross your fingers when it comes to placement of your ad.** Everyone wants front-of-the-magazine, right-hand-page placement, but at some magazines, those prime locations usually go to long-standing, multiple-page advertisers who have built up clout over the years.

✔ **The more upscale the magazine and the bigger its audience, the more expensive the space.** Plan accordingly.

Online advertising

An increasingly viable advertising option for many small businesses today is a company website. Websites — particularly those intended to be "brochure-ware" only (and not interactive) — are relatively inexpensive (several hundred dollars and up) to establish and maintain.

One distinct advantage of online advertising is that it levels the playing field. Even without massive monetary outlays, smaller companies can compete with the big boys by building websites and maintaining them diligently.

As with other advertising media, the success of your online strategy depends on how many people are introduced to your company and how frequently your message falls on their eyes. Following are several tips on how to build a strong web presence and keep your web customers coming back for more information:

✔ **Provide up-to-date content.** You need to update your website's information on a regular basis (at least monthly and preferably weekly) so that your visitors have an incentive to come back.

✔ **Commit to functionality.** A wide variety of Internet tools are available to take your business beyond a basic brochure-ware-intended web presence — enabling you to communicate and collaborate with both customers and potential customers. Ask a local website designer for a list of these tools.

✔ **Allow for easy navigation.** Keep the look and the layout clean. If information is difficult to come by, if the flow of your site isn't intuitive, or if the font or the background makes information difficult to read, visitors will move on to the hundreds of other choices on the web.

✔ **Differentiate your site.** Your site needs to stand out by being creative, including both the content and the graphics. When visitors arrive at your home page, make sure they understand what it is that makes your site (and your products or services) different from the crowd.

✔ **Promote your site.** Just because you build a site doesn't mean that consumers will visit it. You need to let people know what your site address is and why they should visit your site. Promote your site via your traditional communication efforts and online communication strategies, including Facebook and Twitter.

Other advertising vehicles

A wide range of other, usually less-expensive advertising options are available. This range includes such media as billboards and bus ads (and other transportation-oriented media), as well as less-professional advertising tools such as flyers, posters, and handbills. Ultimately, the description of your target market, the nature of your message, the depth of your pocketbook, and your own expertise will determine the medium that's best for you.

Publicity

Publicity ("free advertising" through news sources) is especially effective as a promotional tool because people (specifically, prospective consumers) tend to give more credibility to what they read or hear when it comes from news sources, whereas their belief in advertising messages is often tainted with varying degrees of suspicion (understandably). Unlike advertising, you don't pay for publicity. You do, however, have to spend time and money generating it.

Typical examples of publicity include feature stories and product (or service) announcements distributed in media resources such as newspapers, business periodicals, television and radio stations, magazines, websites, and blogs — including online magazines and newsletters as well as links to and from sites that serve those in your target audience. And don't limit your search for publicity to only the business-oriented outlets; oftentimes, exposure in the news or in human-interest stories is even more beneficial.

The downside to publicity is that, similar to word-of-mouth advertising, you can't control what's said about your company or your product or service. So make sure that what you're about to publicize can withstand media scrutiny.

The following tips can help you develop "free advertising" for your business through publicity:

- ✔ **Write an article for your local newspaper on a subject that relates to you or your business.** If the article is well written and has a special hook, it could bring you the publicity you seek.

- ✔ **Give talks or teach classes about your profession or business to local groups.** You can go to places such as the Chamber of Commerce, Rotary Club, civic associations, and other groups.

- ✔ **Hire a public relations (PR) firm.** PR firms are to publicity what ad agencies are to advertising. (Unfortunately, their fees are similar, too!)

Whenever appropriate, send a professional-quality photo of yourself (and of your event, if there is one) along with any publicity requests. Photos personalize the request, and many papers will use them. As a start-up business owner, you should always have a high-quality photo of yourself available, in the event that a sudden PR opportunity presents itself.

The following sections provide more details on two important aspects of publicity: the news release and the hook.

Sending a news release

One frequently utilized tool of publicity is the news release. A *news release* is a notification of something newsworthy that you send to appropriate newspaper, magazine, radio, and television editors and/or reporters. News releases are appropriate for such occasions as the opening of a new store, the introduction of new products and services, or the procurement of an important new customer or key employee.

For the most part, you should send your news releases to the business editor or business reporter; in some cases, however, you may want to send them to the editor of a specific department, such as sports or lifestyle.

The best way to determine which editor or reporter to send your news releases to is to look at the bylines on newspaper or magazine public-interest articles that are about companies similar to yours. You can also listen for the name of the reporter on public-interest radio or TV stories.

Work diligently to build a relationship with the employee who's the gatekeeper of the kind of publicity you're looking for. Try to make his job easier. Prepare the news release carefully, make sure all the relevant information is included, and write it (and then rewrite it) until you're sure it's as professional as you can make it. Also, don't abuse this relationship after you've established it — make sure that whatever it is you're submitting is newsworthy and factual.

Creating a hook

In most cases, you need some sort of hook to attract publicity. A *hook* is the characteristic that makes you or your product or service unique and of publicity value. Examples of hooks include an excellent Italian restaurant where the waiters are intentionally rude to patrons or an antique shop with goats in its lobby for visitors to feed. (Visit Las Vegas if you're looking for examples of hooks. Every hotel on the strip has a hook, from belching volcanoes to golden Sphinxes.)

A secondary advantage of having a hook is that it makes your attempts to find publicity easier. A bona fide hook, which of course doesn't need to involve rudeness or something bizarre, will interest most reporters, because media writers will perceive it as something of interest to their readers or viewers.

What exactly is your business's hook? If you can't think of a hook, perhaps you need to do some reflecting on your overall approach to marketing.

Sales: Where the Rubber Hits the Road

Coauthor Jim spent the majority of his business career in Minneapolis. One of that city's most successful entrepreneurs, the late Curt Carlson (known for Radisson Hotels, TGIF Restaurants, and Carlson Travel), coined a phrase years ago that Minneapolis business veterans know by heart: "Nothing happens until a sale is made." What Curt was saying is that a product or service, no matter how good it may be, will live or die based on the ability of the sales and marketing staff to generate sales.

Because sales are so critical to the success of your small business, we dedicate this entire section to the topic. Read on to find out how to make sales a top priority in your business.

Pitting in-house versus outsourcing

Face it: Someone has to sell your products or services. The question is who that selling-someone should be:

- ✔ Should the seller be you, an employee hired by you, or a team of employees hired by you? (These are examples of an *in-house* sales force.)

- ✔ Should the seller be an outsider — someone who's already calling on your potential customers with related products? (This is known as *outsourcing,* and the people who do it are typically called *manufacturers' representatives,* or *reps.*)

The following sections are designed to help you make the decision about whether to sell in-house or to outsource.

Using an in-house sales force

An *in-house sales force* is comprised of employees of the company whose products they sell. In-house salespeople are usually hired, trained, and compensated by the company itself. Thus, their mission is to sell only the company's offerings.

The advantage of hiring and maintaining your own sales force is that you can exert direct control over your salespeople, and they, in turn, can direct all their energies toward selling your products or services. The disadvantage of hiring an in-house sales force is that you're picking up 100 percent of the expenses involved in employing and deploying your salespeople; therefore, you must be able to find enough sales potential within any given geographical area to financially support the salesperson assigned to it.

Most in-house salespeople today are compensated on a commission basis, and you can choose from a wide variety of ways to pay that commission. (For more on compensation plans, see Chapter 16.)

Using manufacturers' reps

Manufacturers' reps (also called *independent agents*) are independent salespeople who carry a "line of products" from different manufacturers and get paid a percentage of every sale they make. The collection of products they choose to sell usually is aimed at customers within a given industry. For example, the sales rep who calls on photography stores will pitch products, such as film, tripods, and scrapbooks, from varied manufacturers. The collection of products from any one manufacturer is called a *line,* and a typical rep may have anywhere from 1 to 30 lines of products in her bag.

Always ask how many lines the rep you're considering is carrying; the more lines in her bag, the less attention yours will get.

Some reps are part of a larger rep agency; others work solo. Manufacturers' reps are paid only for what they sell (in other words, straight commission), and they often cover a large geographic territory, depending on the density of population. The commissions they charge vary with the product and the areas they cover; commissions can range anywhere from as low as 5 percent (on big-ticket sales) to as much as 25 percent (on small-ticket, difficult-to-sell items).

The primary advantages of using manufacturers' reps include the following:

✔ You don't have the out-of-pocket expense of maintaining a sales force: no salaries, benefits, or travel expenses. Because the reps are paid solely on commission, if they don't sell your products or services, they don't get paid — period.

✔ Because reps can spread their costs over a number of manufacturers' lines, they can cover a wide geographical area for minimal expense. Networks of manufacturers' reps, both individuals and firms, cover every state in the nation; you can pick and choose until you find the combination you need.

✔ Reps can make *small-ticket* (low-price-tag) sales as a result of their ability to spread their time and expenses over a number of products. This means that when you have a small-ticket product, your reps can afford to sell it to customers in outlying areas, whereas in-house salespeople, with only one manufacturer's product in their bag, usually can't afford to make the sales call in the first place.

The primary disadvantages of hiring manufacturers' reps include the following:

✔ You lack control over your reps' activities. After all, you aren't employing them; they're employing themselves.

✔ Due to the reps' distance from and noninvolvement in your day-to-day business, they can't possibly know your product as well as an in-house sales staff — especially if your product is technical in nature.

✔ Manufacturers' reps, like all salespeople, have limited time in front of each customer. The products the reps choose to sell during that designated time depend on their perception of how easily they can sell a given product, as well as how much commission they can generate from the transaction.

If your product or service is well established and relatively easy to sell and your customer base is widespread, manufacturers' reps may work well for you. In these cases, the reps will be sure to pull your product out of the bag during the course of a sales call. On the other hand, if you have a relatively new product or one without an established customer base, manufacturers' reps may not give your product the time or attention it needs.

Where do you find manufacturers' reps? Look in your industry's trade magazines or visit a trade show within your industry and ask for the manufacturers' rep bulletin board. Or contact the Manufacturers' Agents National Association for the latest directory containing the names of manufacturers' rep organizations around the country (visit www.manaonline.org or call 877-626-2776).

Making the decision

In short, you sacrifice control for expense when you employ a manufacturers' rep in lieu of an in-house sales force. Not surprisingly, the correct decision depends on your situation. The following "equations" can help you decide which of the two options is best for you:

Easy products to sell + Limited finances = Manufacturers' reps

Difficult products to sell + Adequate finances = Your own sales staff

Small-ticket item + Wide territory = Manufacturers' reps

High-ticket item + Small territory = Your own sales staff

Becoming a sales-driven company

Today's owners and leaders of sales-driven companies know that to be truly sales driven, every employee — from the person who answers the telephone to the one who drives the delivery truck — must understand the overriding principles of a sales-driven company:

- ✔ **Sales-driven companies sell solutions, not products.** Product-driven companies focus on the product, which is only a part of the solution. Sales-driven companies focus on the entire solution, which is what the customer is really seeking. The result is that the company that provides solutions builds relationships with its customers, while the company that sells products only sets itself up to be undersold by its competitors.

- ✔ **Sales-driven companies sell benefits, not features.** The sales-driven company's sales force sells the benefits that a product provides, not the product's features. For example, it doesn't matter how light the razor is, or what color it is, or how easy it is to change blades. What matters is the ease and quality of the shaving experience.

- ✔ **Sales-driven companies respect their sales force.** One sure sign of a sales-driven company is the manner in which its salespeople are perceived by the other employees. Because salespeople are the voice of the customer and because they're responsible for making the sale — without which "nothing happens" — salespeople in sales-driven companies are held in high esteem. And yes, they're usually paid more than the other employees.

- ✔ **Sales-driven companies build relationships; they don't just sell products or services.** The typical business's primary sales goal used to be to get the order. Everything that the company did was in response to that goal. If the salesperson wrote the order, the sales call was a success; if he didn't, the call was a failure.

Today, the sales-driven business's primary sales goal is to establish an ongoing relationship with the customer. Relationships come from employees understanding the value of the relationship with the customer and doing whatever they can to foster that relationship.

Incidentally, whether it's you, your employees, or your manufacturers' reps who are dealing with the customer doesn't matter. Every employee in the business chain — from customer service to the shipping department — must be in tune with the relationship-building principle when dealing with customers.

Today's successful companies have learned this lesson well: You can put a price on a product or service, but you can't put a price on a customer relationship.

Understanding the Business Triangle

To be a successful sales-driven company, you must first create a mindset within your company that everyone needs to be a winner in the sales transaction, the customer included. To understand how to develop this concept within your company, consider the Business Triangle model.

Visualize a triangle with three equal sides. This triangle represents the relationship among the three principals of the business: the company itself, its employees, and the company's customers. When the three sides of the triangle are equal and stable, you have a balanced triangle. However, when one side is significantly longer or shorter than the other two, the triangle — and thus the relationships among its principals — becomes unbalanced and precarious.

The benefits that each party derives from the relationship determine the length of each side of the triangle. Because those benefits are measured against expectations, you need to consider what each of these three parties expects from a business relationship:

- **Customer expectations:** Solutions to problems and promises kept regarding quality, delivery, and pricing

- **Employee expectations:** Fair wages, reasonable job security, and courteous treatment

- **Company expectations:** Fair profit, good professional reputation, and opportunity for continued growth

Your job as a small-business owner is to make sure that you and your employees understand how this Business Triangle works and then see to it that the three legs remain balanced. The overriding principle here is that, in the long term anyway, everybody must win.

If you're looking for a resource that picks up where we leave off and delivers the best marketing advice available from a small-business perspective, we recommend Barbara Schenck's *Small Business Marketing For Dummies* (Wiley).

Chapter 12

Tapping Technology

....

In This Chapter

▶ Ramping up your business's efficiency by using technology and the Internet

▶ Researching business ideas and finance options online

▶ Using the web to market your business

....

M ost of the time, technology enables small-business owners to run their businesses more efficiently and profitably. Hence, we encourage you to keep a finger on the pulse of technology and its role in your type of business. In fact, if you fail to track and take advantage of useful technology, your business could end up getting thumped by your competition (for more on the needs of a growing business, head to Chapter 20). However, like any tool, technology can be misused or overused and become more costly than it has to be.

Using technology effectively can help you do many things for your business:

✔ Save you and/or your employees time

✔ Stimulate ideas that can help make your business grow larger and more profitable

✔ Manage your personal and business finances (think online banking and accounting software)

✔ Deliver advertising and marketing to targeted sectors

Never buy expensive new business hardware and software until you talk with several other small-business owners who've used the product for at least a year. Be sure to exercise self-discipline when you're surfing the web to find small-business services or to identify software you may want to purchase. Computers and handheld time-management hardware, for instance, are incessantly sold as time and money savers, but anyone who has dealt with those products knows that they can also make things more difficult and stressful and can end up costing more than they save if you use them inefficiently.

Few websites offer useful information for the sake of offering information; more often, websites offer "free" small-business services and business news, business plan advice, and so on in order to keep you clicking through the site. The goal, of course, is to sell you something, not to educate you. Don't get sucked into these time-wasting and money-burning sites.

Now that we've addressed the warnings, we can proceed with the good stuff — the ways in which you can use technology to better conduct your business and separate your company from the pack. This chapter contains our suggestions for the best ways to utilize technology in your small business, including our recommendations for software programs and websites.

Improving Your Business's Efficiency

Technology costs money to buy and implement. So the simple promise of making your business more efficient isn't enough of a reason to spend your hard-earned cash on technology. For you to buy a particular technology resource, the improvement offered by that resource must more than pay for the cost of buying it.

In this section, we discuss where we see you getting the best bang for your buck in terms of improving your business's efficiency through technology.

Managing your time

In the early stages of your business, only one person can make or break your business. That one person is you, which means that every minute of your time is valuable. Because time is finite, if you waste an hour, that hour, along with whatever you could've accomplished during the course of it, is gone forever. Thus, the management of time — especially the time that belongs solely to you — is potentially the most valuable service that technology can provide.

Every small-business owner manages his or her time differently. Some owners still use the ubiquitous manual methods — to-do lists, calendars, and various forms of the good old-fashioned Day-Timer. Today, however, more and more successful small-business owners are turning to technology to manage their time, whether via computer-based calendars, e-mail, or scheduling programs on cell phones and smartphones.

Smartphones such as Blackberrys, Droids, and iPhones, which double as cell phones and e-mail devices, are increasingly considered a must-have time-management device for today's fast-paced entrepreneurs. Despite the addictive nature of such devices, they enhance your opportunity to manage schedules, multitask, and get the most out of your day. Every small-business owner should at least experiment with the use of smartphones because, when used appropriately, they can make the user undeniably more efficient.

Another great time-management tool is computer networking. For example, you can network your computer at home to the one at your office so that you can manage your calendar and be on the job from either location. Just be careful not to let technology turn you into a workaholic.

Finally, e-mail is the second most efficient communication device of them all. No waiting for someone to pick up the phone, no wasting time with idle conversation, no telephone bills at the end of the month. Just type your message, click Send, and wait for the response. Communication doesn't get much more efficient than that. Just don't make the mistake of using e-mail for important issues like selling to customers, providing feedback to employees who report to you, or resolving any kind of conflict. In those cases, more personalized communication, such as in person or by phone, makes greater sense.

Providing supplemental web services

In addition to using your website for marketing purposes (see Chapter 11), you can use your website for various operational and customer-service functions that would otherwise require the time and energy of you or one of your employees. For instance, your website, when properly configured, can

- **Provide order-entry service for your customers:** A few clicks of the mouse by your customer and his or her purchase order can be entered, printed, subtracted from inventory, and invoiced, all without the involvement of you or any other human being. Yes, someone still has to pack the order and ship it, but stay tuned; someday maybe even that function will be automated. For those of you with small businesses in the hospitality industry (restaurants, bed and breakfasts, and so on), you can also use your website to take reservations and send confirmations.

- **Accept payment for products and services:** When a customer completes an order online via your website, your credit-card company or an online service like PayPal either accepts the customer's account number or denies it. That means no more bounced checks, no endless phone calls, no unheeded promises, and no collection agencies.

- **Solicit customer feedback:** Are you interested in what your customers think about your company but don't want to go to the expense required in mailing a printed questionnaire? No worries! You'll get a better response rate, the responses will come faster, and the costs will be less if you e-mail your questionnaire to the proper people.

Lowering your administration costs

Computers, when configured and used properly, can provide a number of administrative services, reducing the time and manpower needed for such tasks. Consider how computers can make the following administrative tasks more efficient and less expensive:

✔ **Letters and memos:** Type the letter or memo, print it, sign it, and mail it instead of dictating it, having someone else type it and send it back to you to edit and sign, and then mailing it. Computers make this task quicker, less expensive, and more private (no administrative assistants nosing around in your hallowed company secrets).

✔ **Communications:** E-mail is the quickest, easiest, and least expensive way to communicate.

✔ **Filing:** Electronic filing of letters, worksheets, financial statements, and so on is quicker, neater, less expensive, and less space-consuming than manual filing.

Just make sure that you back up your files daily in case your computer crashes — which it inevitably will!

✔ **Worksheets:** When you know how to work with the software, you can develop and fill out electronic spreadsheets in half the time (or less) that it takes you to fill out manual spreadsheets. As an added bonus, electronic spreadsheets are more professional looking, easier to file, and easier to update and change. Given their pre-programming ability, they're also much less prone to error.

✔ **Office supplies:** Why waste your time and aggravate yourself driving to an office-supply store when you can more quickly and cheaply buy most office supplies for your business online? Our favorite sites include www. pcconnection.com, www.staples.com, and www.officemax.com, which offer competitive prices and good service (including by phone if you need it).

✔ **Mailing:** Printing computer-generated mailing labels is much faster than creating hand-addressed postcards or envelopes. Remember, direct mail is only "junk mail" when it doesn't seem relevant and personal! For all its bad press, mass mailing, when done right, can lead to increased sales.

Of course, computers and the accompanying technology can also waste your time if you happen to get hooked on surfing the Internet, fiddling with the latest presentation software, or reading endless computer manuals. As with any other item that's part-tool/part-toy, you need to keep your computer usage (and that of your employees) in check and focused on your business.

Scanning and managing inventory

Inventory scanning is especially useful for retail- and manufacturing-based small businesses that include extensive, and expensive, quantities of inventory.

Handheld, wireless scanners make counting inventory a relatively easy task — especially when compared to the tried-and-true, yet slow and less accurate, manual method. The best small businesses we know take frequent inventories — quarterly or even monthly. Without the requisite scanning technology, the process of tabulating inventory can be time-consuming and inaccurate. And the more SKUs (stock-keeping units) you have in your inventory, the more important inventory scanning becomes.

Scanning devices are proliferating within the inventory-carrying small-business sector. For instance, one scanning device is designed to measure the amount of beer that has been consumed from a keg; that's certainly a valuable tool for the bar and restaurant industry. Check with your industry trade association; it can make you aware of the latest technologies available in scanning.

Inventory scanning technology for small-business owners in the retail industry can be either a stand-alone function or part of a complete management software system (see Chapter 20). For instance, one national vendor we know offers a system that includes a bar-code scanner, a credit-card reader, a receipt printer, and a cash drawer. Such a configuration of products allows the retailer to track inventory, create purchase orders, determine sales taxes, and avoid many of the time-consuming minutiae that often plague the typical retailer.

Managing finances

Online banking has a number of benefits in addition to the time and money you save:

- You can check your account balances 24 hours a day.
- You can view your account activity and history whether you're at home or on the road.
- You can transfer money immediately.
- You can reorder checks instantly.
- You can perform a number of general banking functions without having to leave the comfort of your home or office.

✔ You can cut down on late fees because you can pay your bills instantly.

✔ You can utilize most online banking services free of charge — and *free,* in the world of the profit-conscious small-business owner, is usually good.

Certainly, some small-business owners have valid reasons for being reluctant to make the switch to online banking. The ever-present web scammers continue to find creative ways to trick the unwary web user, including fake e-mails and phony websites. But the careful online-banking customer has learned how to recognize today's scams and has thus made the decision to go with the efficiency, timeliness, and transparency of online banking.

The banks, of course, want their customers to opt for online banking, too. Electronic banking is less expensive than paper transactions, online customers require less customer service, and, as experience has proven, a bank's online customers are less likely to switch banks. (*Tip:* Incidentally, you can apply the same logic to why you should be looking for ways to entice your customers to conduct their e-business on your website.)

Expanding Your Research Possibilities Online

Although the Internet can be a vast time waster, when used well, it can be a powerful research aid. In this section, we discuss common uses for the Internet, such as brainstorming business ideas, finding financing, and researching businesses or franchises that you may be interested in buying.

Brainstorming business ideas

The Small Business Administration (SBA) offers the most extensive array of information and services to aspiring and current small-business owners at www.sba.gov. This site also has a compilation of useful business information and regulations from the dozens of federal agencies that assist or regulate business (for more on business regulations, see Chapter 18). If you're trying to develop and research a list of possible business opportunities, be sure to peruse the SBA site.

Trade association sites can be a great resource for getting information on a specific line of work. Try adding *.org* to the type of business you're interested in and plug that into the address bar in your web browser; you'll be amazed how often this little trick works. If you're skeptical that a site is available for a particular kind of business, remind yourself that www.coinlaundry.org exists for all those interested in the Coin Laundry Association! (For more on trade associations and the like, see Chapter 15.)

If you don't yet have a computer or Internet access, try the public libraries in your area, many of which can perform computer searches (sometimes for free and sometimes for a nominal fee) for small-business owners and help you get on the Internet. Most also have banks of Internet-connected computers available for public use.

Finding and obtaining financing

Type the words *small business financing* into your favorite search engine and you'll see dozens of links to organizations eager to loan money to small-business owners. Those web-based organizations are many, and the kinds of loans they offer are all over the map: SBA loans, unsecured business loans, equipment leasing loans, and business credit cards with significant lines of available credit. You name the loan that works best for you and you'll find an offering for it on the web.

We've seen online companies that offer loans requiring no collateral, no business plans, no doc or full doc (*doc* is short for documentation), APR from 6 percent up, and loans from $10,000 to $250,000. That's too good to be true, you say? Well, maybe it is, but if you haven't been able to find your money locally, if finding financing is a matter of life or death for this idea of yours, and if you absolutely, positively won't be deterred, we suggest you let your fingers do the searching and see what you can find online. After all, given the number of names that will emerge as a result of your search, it's obvious that some of those opportunities have worked for other small-business owners.

After you've honed in on a possible online resource, you need to do a thorough background check on the financing business you'll be working with. And never sign any loan document or guarantee without having your attorney review it first. In other words, tread extra-carefully because, unlike your local bank, which has been in the same bricks-and-mortar location for decades, most of these online businesses are relative newbies. They don't have a track record, they don't have an inventory of customers that you can readily compare notes with, and they don't have an office where you can look into the eyes of the people who work there.

While we don't want to discourage you from utilizing these online resources, especially when you can't find anything else, we encourage you to first try to get funding from your local, traditional resources: banks, credit unions, angel investors, and other financial organizations and individuals who have a history of working with local businesses (we discuss all these resources in Chapter 5).

The thing about working with local resources is that, in the case of banks and credit unions especially, they offer an inventory of other services you need, in addition to an operating loan. Try lines of credit, letters of credit, checking accounts, and money transfers for starters. Right or wrong, banks and credit unions are more disposed to working hard for those customers who choose to do *all* of their business with them than they are for those customers who do only *part* of their business with them.

Along the same lines, remember that personal relationships are critical to managing your business's financial future. While maintaining a personal relationship exclusively via e-mail or telephone isn't impossible, it isn't the same as sitting in front of a living, breathing person — someone who knows you, knows your business, understands your community, and, as a result, can help you resolve the many financial issues you'll face as your business prospers and grows.

Finally, and this we can guarantee, your business's financial future will have ups and downs, and working through those ups and downs is much easier to do with someone who can shake your hand and pat you on the back.

Bottom line: Don't let your idea die because you can't find financing. If the web is the only place you can find it, that's where you should go. But first, look closely at home.

Buying a business or franchise

The Internet still has a ways to go before it becomes a major meeting place for business buyers and sellers, but you may find some promising leads with the following two sites:

- **BizBuySell** (www.bizbuysell.com): This site has all the ingredients for a good business-for-sale online database — a pleasing design, a smooth search engine, and a decent description of each listed business that includes the asking price, gross income, cash flow, year established, number of employees, facilities description, details on the competition, and growth possibilities. We've seen such entries as a smoothie franchise in Texas and a pet store in California. Not surprisingly, this site can really help jog your entrepreneurial imagination!

> ✔ **Franchise Advantage** (www.franchiseadvantage.com): If you're interested in owning a franchise business, check out this website, which matches up its client franchise companies with your selection criteria and profile as a potential franchise owner. The site gives good specs on each franchise, including the company history, number of stores, description of company support, franchise fee, and necessary capital to get started.

For more details on buying an existing business, check out Part II of this book.

Marketing Your Business Online

Successful marketing is one of the keys to running a successful small business, which is why we cover the marketing topic in depth in Chapter 11. We don't want to be redundant here, so in this section, we highlight a few specific online uses for marketing — for networking and for using e-mail and e-newsletters.

Networking online

Ask any small-business owner the question, "Whose advice do you trust the most?" and you'll likely hear that his or her most valuable and trusted advice comes from another small-business owner — preferably one who's experienced in his career field and has one or more successful businesses to his credit. Hence, the concept of online business networking among small-business owners (receiving advice from your peers) makes sense.

Online business networking involves the virtual (online) assembling of small-business owners with the intent of identifying other owners, meeting them, and sharing information. Oftentimes, such networking groups include small-business owners operating within the same industry sector — retail, technology, manufacturing, and so on. The most effective business networking results when you can work with other small-business owners within your specific niche — outdoor retailers, computer printing service providers, or widget manufacturers, for instance.

You can access a number of popular online business-networking providers, including LinkedIn (www.linkedin.com), Ryze (www.ryze.com), and Tribe. net (http://newjersey.tribe.net/welcome). To find other business-networking providers, simply type the term *online business networking* into your favorite search engine and take your pick.

You don't have to be a techie to participate in a networking group. You can do it by phone, e-mail, or online subscription. Or for those tech geeks among you, you can use more advanced online collaboration tools, such as Skype, forums, blogs, and even wikis — all tools that can take business networking to the next level.

One other advantage of networking online with other business owners is that the trusted advice you receive on how to run your business is free (other than the cost of belonging to the website). Imagine: Trusted advice at no cost. That's a match made in heaven for the cost-conscious small-business owner.

Marketing over e-mail

E-mail marketing has proven to be more efficient and less expensive than any other form of marketing (see Chapter 11). Of course, for such a virtual tool to be successful, you, as the marketer, must first garner some sort of "permission" from the target audience to accept your e-mail advances. This "permission" is what separates e-mail marketing from spam.

Think about it: If you receive an e-mail from someone you know or are familiar with, you're likely to open the e-mail. On the other hand, you're less likely to open an e-mail that you get from a stranger. Thus, the e-mail marketer's goal is to turn those otherwise strangers into acquaintances and then those acquaintances into friends.

Most often, the best source for e-mail marketing is your existing customer base. Using that base, you have a number of ways to expand it, including events, opt-in gifts, and, most of all, an effective website that encourages visitors to sign up for, say, your newsletter, marketing program, or latest product release.

Effective e-mail marketing is based on the concept of *one-to-one marketing* — marketing to an individual who's already known to the marketer — as opposed to the more typical shotgun-based marketing methods, like direct mail, which reaches a long list of prospects who match a predetermined target customer profile, and the various forms of mass-media advertising that reach one and all in a radio, television, newspaper, or magazine audience. After you establish a one-to-one relationship with your potential customers, the success of your marketing program rests on making sure that the products or services offered are relevant to your customers' needs. Remember, no marketing medium, no matter how inexpensive and efficient, can overcome poor offerings and/or poor quality of products or services.

Educating with e-newsletters

The ultimate purpose of an e-newsletter is to enhance the relationship between your business and whomever it is that you're sending it to, with the intended result of increasing awareness and regard for your business and ultimately increasing sales.

Because the initial glimpse of your e-newsletter is when the recipient decides whether or not to hit the delete button, the first rule of e-newsletter success is that it must be pleasing to the eye and professional in appearance. You can find numerous e-newsletter templates to help you achieve these goals, including those available from MyNewsletterBuilder (`www.mynewsletter builder.com`), Topica (`www.topica.com`), and eNewsletterPro (`www.enewsletterpro.com`).

After you've captured your readers' attention with the look and feel of your e-newsletter, the next step is to provide enticing content. A recent survey showed that e-newsletter readers are more likely to become avid readers when you provide the following:

- ✔ Specific information on whatever subject you happen to be writing about

- ✔ Timely, up-to-date facts and figures on the topic

Failure to provide this information on an ongoing basis will result in your e-newsletter being regarded as just another piece of unwanted spam.

Sure, an e-newsletter is really just another e-mail marketing tool, but if the recipient doesn't perceive it as an educational opportunity, your e-newsletter won't be around very long. So your e-newsletter must include informative news and relevant commentary on subjects that will be of interest to the people receiving it. In other words, you must include educational benefits in your newsletter.

In addition to providing enticing content, you need to do the following if you want to have a successful e-newsletter campaign:

- ✔ Make sure that your mailings aren't too frequent (once every two months is our recommendation).

- ✔ Don't send other e-material to your e-newsletter recipients if they haven't signed up for it.

- ✔ Don't include pop-up ads in your e-newsletters.

- ✔ When purchasing an e-newsletter template, make sure that the software tracks a variety of relevant statistics, including the number of views, opens, and clicks on each link.

You can measure the degree of interest created by your newsletter by gathering data on the number of visits to your website, tracking the number of sales made to the e-newsletter recipients, or tracing the number of phone calls by recipients to your sales department. Whatever measure of success you deem to be most relevant, be sure to track it diligently.

Chapter 13

Keeping Your Customers Loyal

. . . .

In This Chapter

▶ Knowing how to satisfy customers so that they keep coming back to you

▶ Communicating with unhappy and difficult customers

. . . .

A huge factor in your business's long-term success is not only attracting but also satisfying and retaining customers. As a small-business owner, you may be on the front lines of dealing with your business's customers. However, if you have employees, they'll likely be dealing with customers, too. Therefore, the importance of providing excellent customer service must be clear to everyone in your organization who has any impact (direct or indirect) on customer satisfaction. This includes the receptionist, the accounts receivable clerk, the delivery truck driver, and many others.

Although the level of customer service in many American businesses leaves much to be desired, only a foolish business owner would assume that unhappy customers will continue to tolerate poor service or buy products that don't perform. Consumers generally have many choices, so if you and your employees don't satisfy your customers' needs, you'll likely face these unpleasant results:

✔ **Competitive threats:** Now more than ever, customers have many options for buying what your company has to offer. For the vast majority of businesses, competition is intense at the global, national, state, regional, and local levels. It's only a matter of time before your unhappy customers become your competitors' newest customers.

✔ **Negative word-of-mouth:** Even worse than losing dissatisfied customers to the competition is *negative word-of-mouth*, whereby unhappy customers talk and tell other consumers why they wouldn't buy your products and services. Furthermore, your competitors are more than happy to recount the negative stories they've heard from your disgruntled customers. All this talk will certainly tarnish your business's reputation.

✔ **Potential lawsuits:** As if losing customers and tarnishing your business's reputation aren't enough, disgruntled customers can initiate (gasp!) lawsuits. Even if those litigious customers don't prevail in court, they can cause you to face large legal bills, and your business can suffer further damage to both its profitability and its reputation.

In this chapter, we offer some helpful advice for providing excellent customer service. Here, you discover many strategies for keeping your current customers, whether they're satisfied or dissatisfied.

Retaining Your Customer Base

As the owner of a small business, you need to keep your customers happy. How? Well, you have an enormous impact on your customers' satisfaction through your company's products and services and the way in which you present them. This section provides you with the keys to keeping your customers satisfied. Of course, not all customers will stay satisfied and loyal to your business. So we also explain how you can learn from customer defections to minimize their happening in the future.

Getting it right the first time

As a small-business owner, if you don't get your product or service right the first time, you may not have a second chance with customers. Customers aren't stupid, and if you sell them inferior merchandise — especially when better merchandise is available from other sources — they won't come back the next time they're in the market for the products and services you offer. What's more, they'll tell others of their lousy experience with your company. Large companies usually have enough cash reserves built up to weather a storm, but the typical small-business owner does not.

Think back to the 1970s and 1980s, when the big U.S. auto manufacturers (Ford, Chrysler, GM, and AMC) made a major mistake: They ignored the competitive threat of foreign automakers. Despite having a relatively small market share in the early 1970s, the foreign auto manufacturers had intensely loyal customers. Why? Because the best foreign automakers made quality cars that rarely had problems. And when the rare problem did occur, they generally provided excellent service.

Domestic automakers, on the other hand, upset customers by producing subpar cars. Sure, their cars looked nice on the auto dealers' lots, but after a short time in use, many of them developed problems. To add insult to injury, U.S. auto customers didn't get particularly good customer service when they brought in their cars for needed tune-ups and repairs.

The bottom line is that the chief bean counters and the management of the major U.S. automakers weren't considering the bigger picture when they analyzed their companies' financial statements. They were too focused on short-term profitability and didn't consider the after-sales service that was required as a result of their initially shoddy products. As a result, they couldn't stand up against the up-and-coming foreign automakers, who worked on getting their cars right the first time.

Continuing to offer more value

Getting your product or service right the first time isn't enough to keep customers coming back in the long run. Like life, the business world keeps changing. Because of the ever-present threat of competition, resting on your laurels is foolish — and perhaps fatal. In addition to initially developing a top-notch, quality product or service, you must regularly examine how you can offer even more value — improved products or services at the same or lower cost. If you don't, competitors who faithfully keep up with market forces will gradually eat your lunch.

Suppose that you're a dry cleaner. A new dry-cleaning technology that allows dry-cleaning establishments to get their work done 20 percent faster and 30 percent cheaper has been introduced in the marketplace. If you fail to take advantage of this improvement in your industry, you may discover the hard way, when your customers leave you for your competitors, that they want the value this new technique offers. As your competitors cut prices and reap greater numbers of customers and profits, you lose business and experience shrinking profit margins.

Remembering that company policy is meant to be bent

Flexibility is paramount in any organization, but it's especially important in a small business, where responsive and personally tailored service can set you apart from the larger companies. One place where you should be flexible is in your company policy. If a customer has a problem but you have a rule or regulation preventing you from resolving that problem, forget the rule or regulation. Bend it. Skirt it. Find a loophole in it.

To see what we mean, put yourself in the following situations:

- ✔ You're an electrical contractor who needs material to complete a job. Your electrical wholesaler tells you that he has a backlog in the order-entry system and can't process your order right now, so you'll have to come back tomorrow to place your order.

✔ You're a regular customer at a dry cleaner. It's Wednesday and you need your tuxedo dry-cleaned by Friday night. The dry cleaner informs you that it won't be ready until Saturday because of the firm's three-day turnaround policy.

What are the common threads here?

✔ The electrical wholesaler and the dry cleaner apparently have cast-in-stone rules and regulations that dictate the way they do business, and they won't bend those rules to solve a customer's problem.

✔ The two businesses are in danger of alienating a customer.

How can these business owners become more flexible to satisfy the customer? The electrical wholesaler can give the contractor the material today and run the transaction through his order-entry system tomorrow. The dry cleaner can put the customer's tuxedo in front of someone else's order, no matter what the company's operations manual dictates.

These are the moments of truth in any business — the times when what the business says it will do conflicts with what the business actually does. These times differentiate the business that *says* the customer is king from the business that *acts* as if the customer is king.

We're not saying that you should always provide extra service casually or for free. In some situations, you may want to charge more for a special service. Consider the special favor and the one-time transaction when you set your pricing strategy (see Chapter 11 for details on pricing). Also, you don't want to tell your employees to feel free to break any rule at any time; that's the road to chaos and lack of profitability. But flexibility helps keep customers feeling happy and coming back — and recommending you to others. Let your managers and employees know that you stand behind this philosophy, and you'll empower them to always provide good customers with top-notch service.

Learning from customer defections

The costs of acquiring a new customer are huge. After spending the marketing effort and dollars needed to secure a new customer for your business (see Chapter 11 for the skinny on marketing), you need to keep that customer coming back to your business for many years. If you experience much customer turnover, your cost of doing business will rise significantly as you try to attract replacement customers, so you need to take action quickly. After all, customer turnover can indicate major problems with your company's products or services and customer service.

A popular action within a business is to celebrate successes rather than examine failures. However, as a small-business owner, you'll stick around much longer if you scrutinize your failures and make positive changes to correct them. Take the time to examine customer defections and their underlying causes. The following sections dig deeper into this topic.

Examining the value of customer loyalty

Frederick Reichheld is a management consultant who specializes in understanding, and working with corporations on, customer loyalty. He's the author of several books on customer loyalty, and his research has produced the following powerful insights and facts:

- The average company today loses half of its customers in five years.

- The typical *Fortune* 500 company has an average annual *real growth* (that is, growth in excess of the rate of inflation) of 2.5 percent. If such a company retained just 5 percent more of its customers each year, its real growth would jump to 7.5 percent.

- A 5 percent increase in customer retention in a typical company generally translates into an increase in profits of more than 25 percent. In some industries, good, long-standing customers are worth so much that reducing customer defections by 5 percent can double profits.

Clearly, retaining customers — particularly your best customers — has an enormous bottom-line impact. Given how important and valuable retaining customers is, you may think that if a business were losing many of its customers, it would seek to understand why and to correct the underlying problems. Well, if that were the case, customer loss wouldn't be as high as it is in many businesses.

Tracking customer defections

In his consulting work and research, Reichheld has also found that, not surprisingly, many businesses don't learn from their customer losses. He says,

> Psychologically and culturally, it's difficult and sometimes threatening to look at failure too closely. Ambitious managers want to link their careers to successes; failures are usually examined for purposes of assigning blame rather than detecting and eradicating the systemic causes of poor performance.

The good news for you, the small-business owner, is that you don't have to be concerned with bosses and organizational politics when addressing the problem of customer defections. After all, you're the boss. However, it's a natural human tendency to spend more time chasing and celebrating successes than investigating and learning from failures and losses.

Make a commitment to tracking the customers that you lose and asking why. (This is the customer equivalent to the exit interview that you should always perform with departing employees; see Chapter 16.) Knowing that you've lost customers isn't enough; you must find out *why* you lost them. Doing so can help keep you in business and help keep your business growing (see Chapter 20 for more on growing your business).

Consider, for example, the automotive oil-change business that coauthor Eric used to frequent. The business boasted that you could get your oil changed within ten minutes and be on your merry way. On one visit to the establishment, Eric pulled into the entrance and got out of his car. He was then ignored for the next ten minutes — and not because the business was too busy. The people who were checking in new customers moved at a snail's pace, and one employee even spent several minutes on a personal phone call.

When it was Eric's turn, the employee who checked him in was rude. Eric left during the oil change to do some shopping nearby rather than sit in the poorly ventilated, exhaust-infested garage. Upon his return, he had to wait another ten minutes because, although his car had finally been serviced, the paperwork wasn't done. The same employee who checked Eric in took another 15 minutes to finish the paperwork and kept his unfriendly and surly attitude all the while.

Throughout this poor-service experience, Eric didn't utter a word of complaint, but guess which shop he bypassed the next time his car needed an oil change? A gas station closer to Eric's home started offering oil changes, which were about 20 percent less costly than the other place. The attendant who checked Eric in at the service station was friendly and polite, and his car and paperwork were ready when promised.

Make it part of your company's culture that you don't expect employees to be perfect and that making mistakes won't necessarily lead to an employee's immediate firing. However, make it clear that you won't tolerate employees who repeatedly drive good customers away from your business. (For more employee tips, refer to Chapter 16.)

Recognizing and practicing customer service

All businesses have products or services to sell. Sometimes businesses get too focused on those products and services, giving short shrift to the accompanying customer service that customers expect.

Maybe you can't readily define the term *customer service,* but we bet you know what it is when you get it or don't get it. For example, you surely recognize customer service in a company you do business with when

✔ Its telephone operator (or at least its telephone system) connects you with your party quickly and efficiently

✔ Its bookkeeper politely answers a question you have about an invoice

✔ Its shipping clerk quickly traces your order and tells you exactly when to expect it

✔ Its salesperson gets back to you quickly with the quotes and delivery schedules you requested

In each of these situations, the company is solving your problem or addressing your need in a manner that meets or exceeds your expectations, which is, after all, the definition of *customer service.* Customer service = solving your customers' problems or meeting their needs.

When you ask an employee for help in a business that you frequent, have you ever felt that his or her behavior was essentially saying to you, "That's not my department or responsibility"? In a business — large or small — that recognizes the value of customer service, the correct response to a customer question is, "Let me find the solution for you." The solution may ultimately rest in the hands of another employee, another department, or even another business, but the employee has accepted responsibility for solving your problem.

Some larger companies have distinctly identified *customer service departments* — a person or group of people whose sole purpose is to solve customer problems. In such a company, all customer telephone calls are routed through to the customer service department. In smaller companies, however, many — perhaps even all — employees are involved in customer service. In the examples from the previous bulleted list, the telephone operator, the bookkeeper, the shipping clerk, and the salesperson are providing customer service. If you, the boss and Grand Poobah, get involved in solving a customer's problem, you, too, are focused on customer service. The same is true for the janitor or the night watchman.

The challenge is for your employees to understand that they're on the job to solve your customers' problems. After all, they may believe (because this is the way their job descriptions read) that their role is simply to answer the telephone, keep the books, ship products, or sell services. Although these functions accurately describe the employees' assigned *activities,* they don't define the employees' assumed *responsibilities.*

You and your employees are on the job — just as your entire company exists — for one reason and one reason only: to solve your customers' problems.

Smart business owners know that customer service (and the accompanying problem solving) begins before a sale is made, continues during the sale, and continues long after the sale is complete. Remember that customers aren't just coming to your business for your products and services. The attentiveness you show toward your customers' needs — before, during, and after the sale — that comes with what you sell is an integral part of the package. Treat your customers as you would a good friend.

The following sections break down the stages of customer service so that you can see what you and your employees need to do to keep your customers coming back.

Customer service before the sale

When a customer goes to buy a product or service, part of what can close the sale or blow the deal is the quality (or lack thereof) of the customer service before the moment the customer decides to buy. When a customer schedules an appointment, she's buying not only the service provider's expertise but also the "proper care and handling" before the service is provided. And when a potential customer enters your store for a product, she wants the store to be clean, well maintained, and conveniently arranged. That's all part of the customer service experience.

Consider the last time you bought something, whether it was a car, a bag of groceries, a medical exam, or a haircut. With each of these purchases, you interacted with the business provider before you committed to buy the product or service.

If you're like most people, you probably have some bad memories about slick salespeople who accosted you the moment you walked onto an auto dealer's lot. Many car salespeople spend more time selling than they do listening and educating. The salesperson isn't trying to solve *your* problem — figuring out which car to purchase. He's trying to solve *his* problem — how to make a hefty commission to meet his next mortgage payment. Because of poor customer service at the point of sale in the car business, many people turn around, checkbooks in hand, and take their business elsewhere.

Customer service during the sale

After a customer commits to buying a product or service, the customer service must continue. Never halt your efforts to satisfy customers. When a customer forks over the dough for your wares and you don't meet the customer's service expectations, even if the sale is finalized, you may lose repeat business and the opportunity for referrals to other customers.

For example, after your doctor arrives in the examination room, you'll pay close attention to how well she listens to you and how she treats you. If the doctor is abrupt, bad at listening, and arrogant in asserting her opinion — instead of showing a willingness to discuss options and consider your needs — you may choose to find another physician.

Likewise, after you decide to buy a car, you won't be overjoyed if completing the transaction takes several hours. Even though you may be happy with the selection of the car, the hassle in getting on your way may make you less glowing in your recommendation to others.

Customer service after the sale

After a customer has purchased your company's products or services, your relationship with that customer, at least as it relates to that transaction, isn't over. The customer may have follow-up questions that you need to answer or problems down the road with your products or services.

If you or your employees treat your customers as if they're bothering you and you aren't attentive to after-sales service, you may discourage customers from making more purchases and referring others to your business. Poor after-sales service communicates to your customers that after you have their money, you don't really care what happens to them.

In addition to being attentive to all your customers' questions and concerns, be sure to solicit feedback (possibly through a formal survey) from your customers as to the quality of the customer service that your business offered them.

In some businesses, you must be careful not to give away valuable support that you can and should charge for. For example, if follow-up exams or appointments are expected, you should build the cost of those expected services into your upfront pricing or set a pricing schedule for the cost of the follow-up. Be sure that at the time customers buy from you, they know the cost of such follow-up work. Customers don't like negative surprises, especially when they affect their pocketbooks. (See Chapter 11 for more on pricing.)

Showing that you care — the old-fashioned way

In the age of technology, you may be tempted to discard some of the personal touches that today's customers still appreciate. Although technology certainly answers many of your business's needs, it can never replace the following personal touches in the eyes of customers:

✔ **Handwriting notes:** A handwritten note is always the best way to say "thank you."

✔ **Thanking customers personally:** Having the owner of a company call and say "thank you" (as opposed to having an assistant or salesperson send out an e-mail) makes a positive impression.

✔ **Handling mistakes honestly and quickly:** Don't waste one second trying to cover your tracks after mistakes are made. Come clean, fess up, and solve the problem. Provide personal customer service representatives — not voicemail boxes that allow you to avoid dealing with problems. Approached correctly, mistakes can provide an opportunity to improve your business, impress your customers, and reward their loyalty.

Dealing with Dissatisfied Customers

You can have the best products and services, offer competitive prices, and provide terrific customer service and you'll still end up with the occasional unhappy customer. How you handle complaints — both justified and unjustified — is vital to the long-term reputation and health of your business. The following sections contain our time-tested advice for dealing with your unhappy and sometimes troublesome customers.

Here's a tip to help you maintain your sanity: Keep in mind that you have your own way of doing things, that yours isn't a perfect product or service, and that you can't meet *all* your customers' needs and expectations *all* the time.

Listen, listen, listen

Most people like to believe that they're terrific listeners. The reality is that most of them aren't. And even if you *are* a good listener, you have moments when, for any number of reasons, you don't listen well. You get busy and stressed out with the competing demands on your time from work, family, friends, daily chores, and obligations. You also have days when you're tired, not feeling well, or have been on the receiving end of bad news or bad experiences.

Another impediment to good listening is that you may be convinced that an upset customer is simply being a troublemaker. As with all personal relationships, however, your preconceived notions about others can keep you from hearing legitimate and real concerns and reasons for being dissatisfied.

Before you (or one of your employees) lose your temper with a complaining customer, take a deep breath. Try to set aside all your personal issues, your opinions about the situation, and your preconceived notions about the customer and her right to be unhappy. Stop and listen. Try to find out what the customer is unhappy about and why. Different people, not surprisingly, get upset about different things. You have no way to know and understand what's upsetting a particular customer until you take the time to ask and truly listen.

To ensure that you've really heard what your upset customer has said, paraphrase the concerns you've heard and tell the customer that you're sorry that she's unhappy. (Keep in mind that this isn't an admission of wrongdoing or guilt on your part, especially if you're worried about landing in court and being sued for product liability.) Then work on developing a solution with the customer (see the following section for how to do so).

The absolute worst thing that you (or your employees) can do to a customer with a complaint is to interrupt and argue when she's trying to convey dissatisfaction with your products or services. And don't be defensive. We realize that this is easier said than done, but you'll do far more long-term damage to your business's reputation by further upsetting an already-unhappy customer. Even if you're 100 percent certain that the customer is the biggest yahoo you've ever dealt with and that you don't want her as a customer, treat her with respect and try to solve her problem. Otherwise, you may end up with negative word-of-mouth advertising and possibly a lawsuit.

Develop a solution

When a customer complains, remember that he's complaining because of dissatisfaction with the deal that he received. The next step, after listening to the customer's complaints, is to develop a solution that addresses the complaints.

You have two ways to arrive at a solution:

✔ **Ask the customer what solution he would propose and then see how it compares with what you can do.**

The advantage of asking the customer for a solution is the same as with any other form of negotiation (which, after all, is what's going on in this situation). If you let the dissatisfied customer make the opening offer, you know exactly where you stand and what you have to do to satisfy him.

Imagine the benefit you can derive when the customer's solution is less costly than what you were about to offer. In such a circumstance, the opportunity suddenly exists for you to take an unpleasant situation and turn it into an opportunity to strengthen the complaining customer's loyalty to your business.

✔ **Propose a solution yourself and then wait for the customer to counter with a solution that he thinks is better.**

If you go this route, you don't propose a solution until the customer doesn't have, or refuses to come up with, one.

For example, suppose that you run a professional service business and you're responsible for missing a customer's appointment — either because of a scheduling mistake or because you're behind schedule and the customer simply couldn't wait any longer. You quickly determine that the customer is really angry about having been stood up after he had taken valuable time out of his workday.

Your solution to ease the customer's unhappiness could go something like this:

1. **Apologize for the time he wasted.**

2. **Ask for his recommended solution.**

3. **If he doesn't have a solution, offer a discount (perhaps 15 or 20 percent off the appointment price when he reschedules).**

4. **When the customer returns for the rescheduled appointment, be absolutely certain that he's seen on time and provided with the best possible service.**

The key to understanding your customers' complaints (and your employees' complaints, really) is your ability to put yourself in their shoes. After you've figured out how to view your business through the eyes of a customer, you'll find that you can solve problems the vast majority of the time.

Now suppose that your company sells products, and a customer comes in to say that a product you sold her broke and isn't worth the packaging it came in. In this case, you could offer a replacement product, fix the broken one, or offer the customer a refund. But if you're certain that the customer misused the product and that her mistake subsequently led to the breakage, you have a dilemma on your hands. You have to decide whether this person adheres to your definition of what a "good" customer should be.

Even in those situations in which you determine that this person isn't what you consider to be a good customer, try to make the parting of your ways as harmonious and conflict-free as possible. It's okay if an unmanageable customer doesn't do business with you anymore. Just do everything you can to ensure that he doesn't go away angry and tell others that your business offers a lousy service or product.

If you want to delve into more details about what makes for good customer service, we highly recommend reading the latest edition of *Customer Service For Dummies* by Karen Leland and Keith Bailey (Wiley).

Chapter 14

Managing Profitability and Cash

In This Chapter

▶ Figuring out what cash flow is

▶ Reading and interpreting profit and loss statements and balance sheets

▶ Reviewing the key ratios and percentages of profitability

▶ Overseeing your inventory and accounts receivable

▶ Controlling your costs and improving your profits

*A*lthough people drive the business of doing business, money fuels the engine. That money can be counted, compiled, and presented in a number of different ways — ways that, in the right hands, can provide a steady flow of financial information with which you can accomplish a number of key business functions, including the following:

✔ **Maintaining bookkeeping information:** The bookkeeping process includes keeping records of physical inventories, monies due from others (accounts receivable), and monies due to others (payroll and accounts payable).

✔ **Paying taxes:** Federal, state, and local governments require not only that every business pays taxes but also that it keeps records to back those payments (see Chapter 19).

✔ **Keeping score:** To determine whether you'll be able to meet next month's expenses or whether your business's profitability and cash are trending in the right direction, you need to keep track of the results of doing business.

✔ **Providing a management information tool:** Information fuels the decision-making process, and the more information you have as a small-business owner, the better your decisions will be.

This chapter is about collecting and using financial information. Fortunately, you don't have to be a financial expert to understand the numbers. (Do you have to understand how a thermometer works to take your temperature?)

After a thorough review of this chapter, some time spent with your tax advisor, and several months of closely reviewing your personal financial statements (see Chapter 2), you'll be able to properly use the financial information your business's accounting system generates.

Although we discuss three of the four previously mentioned key business functions in this chapter (we deal with the subject of taxes in Chapter 19), our primary emphasis is on the use of financial information as a management tool. Specifically, we focus on information that you can use to manage your cash flow, increase your profitability, and improve your chances of staying in business for the long haul.

Cash Flow: The Fuel That Drives Your Business

In order to pay your bills, you need to manage the money/cash you have going out and coming in — that is, your *cash flow*. Before you can have cash flowing out, you must have cash flowing in. When your cash flows out in excess of what flows in, your business is heading for trouble.

To understand the basic concept of cash flow, you first need to distinguish between the following two oft-confused terms:

- ✔ **Cash flow:** An operating term that describes the movement of money (cash, checks, electronic debits, and credits) in and out of your business
- ✔ **Profitability:** An accounting term that refers to the capability of your business to generate more sales dollars than the cost of operating expenses

When a business is *profitable,* profits don't necessarily accumulate in the form of cash. Instead, they can take the form of an increase in other noncash assets, such as inventory, accounts receivable, equipment, or real estate. Yes, those profits may once have been in the form of cash, but somewhere along the line, the owner made the decision to shift that cash into another asset — purchasing additional inventory or buying a piece of equipment, for example. In this manner, a business can be profitable in accounting terms but still be short of cash in the checkbook.

Although an increase in cash is only one of the many possible results of profitability, it is, by far, the most important result because cash fuels the day-to-day operation of your business. If you've chosen to spend too much cash on purchasing inventory and equipment or you've been slow in collecting your accounts receivable, you may not have enough cash to pay your vendors and compensate your employees. After all, you can't pay them with inventory or equipment!

Ironically, some profitable (in accounting terms) businesses have entered bankruptcy because their owners made the wrong choices when allocating cash. Instead of accumulating it, they (knowingly or unknowingly) accumulated other nonliquid assets, and then, lo and behold, the bills came due and the cupboards were bare.

Your business's bank account (or money market fund) is the obvious measure of today's cash. Do you have enough money in it to pay today's bills and meet today's payroll, and will you still have money left over when the day is done?

The difficulty comes in projecting tomorrow's cash flow. Because every business has to be concerned with more than just what's happening today in terms of cash availability, projecting tomorrow's cash flow is an important task. To do that, you need to consider questions like the following:

- Will you have enough cash to meet next Friday's payroll?
- Will you have enough cash to pay that big vendor invoice that's due the following Monday?
- Will you have enough cash to pay the bank-loan payment, the upcoming utility bills, and the real estate taxes that will be due at the end of the month?

Questions like these, and the answers they beg, point out the need for preparing *cash flow projections* — forecasts of how much cash you'll have over a given future time frame. Some businesses project cash flow for 30 days out, some for 180 days, and some for an entire year in advance. To project cash flow accurately, you need to polish up the old crystal ball because you're about to make a number of important predictions. For example, you must predict

- Your future sales
- The rate at which you'll collect the money that's due you as a result of those sales
- The dollar amount of your upcoming payrolls
- The dollar amount of vendor invoices to be paid in the next day, week, month, six months, or even year

The better your predictions, the more accurate a forecast you can prepare. Table 14-1 shows a sample worksheet for making cash flow projections.

Table 14-1	Cash Flow Projections	
Period of time (days, weeks, months, and so on)		_____
Total current cash (checking, money market, and petty cash accounts)		$_____
Add expected cash sales for time period		$_____
Add expected receivable collections for time period		$_____
Subtotal		$_____
Subtract payroll		$_____
Subtract taxes		$_____
Subtract all other accounts payable		$_____
Total = Expected cash balance at end of time period		$_____

You can prepare your cash flow projections for the next day, next week, next month, next year, or any combination thereof. Predictions for longer time periods, although more useful, are likely to be fuzzier and less accurate than predictions for shorter time periods. We recommend that you make your cash flow projections for at least six months out and then update them at least once each month, always staying six months out. That way, you'll spot problem periods earlier and be able to adjust to them more quickly.

Although most small businesses don't generate cash flow projections on a daily basis, you should be tracking cash on a monthly basis. (You say you do generate projections daily? Then you're our hero.) After all, no matter how small or uncomplicated your business happens to be, cash is key. We can guarantee you one thing: At some point in your business career, you *will* have cash flow problems. Wouldn't you rather anticipate the problem than let it blindside you?

Most accountants have a preformatted cash flow projections worksheet available for their clients to use. Whether you use their worksheet or the one we provide in Table 14-1 (or something you create on your own), make sure you understand the concept of cash flow because it's one of the most important (and least understood) financial concepts that a small-business owner must know.

Don't let cash flow intimidate you. The concept is as simple as the concept behind maintaining a checkbook. Cash flow is nothing more than a few new wrinkles on an old, familiar face.

Making Sense of Financial Statements

Whether manual or computer based, the accounting system you use should ultimately generate two financial statements: the profit and loss statement (also known as the *income statement*) and the balance sheet. Both of these statements are produced at the end of a business's accounting period, usually monthly, quarterly, or annually. (See Chapter 10 for an explanation of the different accounting systems you have to choose from.)

We recommend that you prepare (or have prepared) your financial statements as frequently as possible, with monthly statements usually being the most useful. If your accounting system allows you to generate your financial statements internally, we suggest that you generate your statements monthly. If monthly statements are impossible for some reason, quarterly statements will do, but don't fall into the trap that many small businesses do by generating your statements only once or twice a year.

Financial statements function primarily as a management tool, and you can't go 365 days without paying attention to the information they provide. The following sections discuss the profit and loss statement and the balance sheet.

The profit and loss statement

The *profit and loss statement* (P&L) adds all the revenues of your business and subtracts all the operating expenses, thereby providing you with a figure that represents what's left over: the profits. (If the total expenses exceed the total revenues, your business would have a loss rather than a profit.) The P&L measures the results of operations of your business over a given period of time — typically a month, a quarter, or a year.

Choosing a P&L format

When you sit down with your bookkeeper and/or tax advisor to design your financial statement format, always remember the cardinal rule of business numbers: Any given number is meaningful only when compared to another number. For instance, say you're the CEO of IBM and your company shows a profit of $500 million this year. Most outsiders would see that as a positive result, but if IBM showed a profit of $1 billion the previous year, a $500-million decline spells big trouble. And so it is with your business. You need to compare the current year's figures to other numbers — last year's actual performance or this year's budget or, preferably, both.

In Figure 14-1, we offer a sample P&L to help you understand how to construct one and how to effectively use it in managing your business.

TIP

You can use a wide variety of formats in presenting a P&L. We recommend that you use the four-column format shown in Figure 14-1 for both the P&L and the balance sheet (we discuss the balance sheet later in this chapter). This four-column format allows you to quickly and easily compare the three key figures: prior year, budget, and current year. The fourth column measures the percentage increase or decrease (in parentheses) between the current year and prior year.

Big Spenders Corp.
Profit and Loss Statement
For the year ending December 31, 2011

	Prior Year	Budget	Current Year	Percent Change Compared to Prior Year
Sales (revenues)	$450,000	$475,000	$500,000	11%
– Cost of goods sold	$200,000	$210,000	$225,000	12.5%
= Gross margin	$250,000	$265,000	$275,000	10%
Expenses				
Wages and salaries	$75,000	$77,000	$97,000	29%
Rent	$50,000	$52,000	$54,000	8%
Selling expenses	$55,000	$58,000	$61,000	11%
Telephone	$10,000	$11,000	$11,000	10%
Utilities	$10,000	$11,000	$11,000	10%
Total expenses	$200,000	$209,000	$234,000	17%
Net income (pretax)	$50,000	$56,000	$41,000	(18%)

Figure 14-1:
A sample four-column profit and loss statement.

The process you use to arrive at a P&L's net income conclusion isn't difficult to understand. Just follow these two easy steps:

1. **Subtract from the gross sales (in Figure 14-1, $500,000) the cost of the goods that were included in those sales (in Figure 14-1, $225,000).**

   What's left is the *gross margin* on those sales — the difference between what it costs you to produce your product or service and the price you charge for it (in other words, the gross income before subtracting operating expenses). Figure 14-1 shows this figure to be $275,000.

2. **Subtract from that number all the operating expenses incurred during that accounting period — including all selling and administrative expenses.**

In Figure 14-1, $234,000 is the number you subtract. The number left over is — how easy is this? — the net income. Ta-da! Our sample company had a net income of $41,000.

As you can see, the trick is not so much in assembling the P&L but in retaining and retrieving all the figures that go into it. In essence, the better your accounting system, the easier this process will be. (See Chapter 10 for more on accounting systems.)

Deciphering P&L information

Deciphering important information from a P&L (formatted like the one in Figure 14-1) is easy:

✔ Go to the net income figure under the Current Year column — the P&L number that every small-business owner is most interested in. Using the percentage in the next column, you can quickly determine how profitable Big Spenders Corporation has been this year compared to the previous year. (Profits are down by 18 percent.)

✔ A quick glance at the top row of the statement reveals that the profitability decrease isn't due to falling sales, which are up by 11 percent, nor is it due to a declining gross margin, which is up by 10 percent. Because sales and gross margin are both positive, you can assume that the problem must be related to expenses.

✔ Moving down the expense items, you see that wages and salaries are up by 29 percent. This means that, although sales have increased by 11 percent and the gross margin is up by 10 percent, the whopping increase in wages and salaries has caused the problem. A quick comparison to the wages and salaries budget reveals that the 29 percent increase wasn't budgeted; therefore, whatever has happened wasn't planned for. You can then delve into your wages and salaries account to determine what caused the problem.

Some companies may include an additional three columns on the P&L. These three columns represent the percentage of the total for the Prior Year, Budget, and Current Year categories. For example, using the sales total as 100 percent, every figure in each column would represent a percentage of that total. Thus, continuing with the Big Spenders Corporation example from Figure 14-1, the percentage of the total for the Current Year column would reveal a gross margin to sales of 55 percent ($275,000 divided by $500,000), wages and salaries to sales of 19 percent ($97,000 divided by $500,000), and net income to sales of 8.2 percent ($41,000 divided by $500,000). The only disadvantage of adding these three columns is that it clutters up the P&L and makes it more difficult to read.

After you have your P&L prepared in an easy-to-read, four-column format, you can relatively easily determine what your business has done and where it currently needs to improve. For example, as a result of comparing the columns, the P&L allows you to quickly answer the three questions that define any business's profitability:

- ✔ **Have you controlled your costs?** For Big Spenders Corporation, the answer appears to be no.

- ✔ **Have you maintained or improved your gross margin?** In this example, the answer is yes.

- ✔ **Have you maintained or increased sales?** In this example, the answer is yes.

Although the answers to these three questions provide significant help in managing your business, the answers aren't the only information the P&L provides. See the section "Turning the Numbers into Action" later in this chapter for even more uses of the figures generated by the P&L.

The balance sheet

The *balance sheet* provides a snapshot of a company's financial position at any given point in time. As with the P&L, the concept behind a balance sheet isn't complex. Quite simply, the balance sheet is a list of what your business owns *(assets)* minus what your business owes *(liabilities),* with the resulting difference being what your business is worth *(net worth).* This net worth figure is also commonly referred to as *book value.*

The P&L is designed to analyze profitability issues: sales, margins, and expenses. The purpose of the balance sheet, on the other hand, is to analyze an entirely different issue: resource allocation. Did you decide to allocate your dollars to increasing inventory, to paying off loans, or to accumulating cash? The small-business owner makes many asset-allocation decisions over the course of the year; the balance sheet provides a year-end snapshot that summarizes the history of those decisions.

In Figure 14-2, we provide a sample balance sheet to help you understand how this important financial statement works.

We've prepared the balance sheet in Figure 14-2 in the same four-column format that we use in the P&L (refer to Figure 14-1). This format is designed to simplify the comparison of the prior year, budget, and current year figures. Although we suggest that you consider this format when preparing your own balance sheet, we should note that the vast majority of businesses don't budget their balance sheets but still operate successfully.

Big Spenders Corp.
Balance Sheet
For the year ending December 31, 2011

Assets	Prior Year	Budget	Current Year	Percent Change Compared to Prior Year
Current assets				
Cash	$25,000	$35,000	$5,000	(80%)
Accounts receivable	$50,000	$55,000	$55,000	10%
Inventory	$50,000	$55,000	$85,000	70%
Total current assets	$125,000	$145,000	$145,000	16%
Fixed assets				
Land, buildings	$100,000	$95,000	$95,000	(5%)
Furniture, fixtures	$50,000	$47,000	$47,000	(6%)
Equipment	$50,000	$47,000	$47,000	(6%)
Total fixed assets	$200,000	$189,000	$189,000	(5.5%)
Total assets	$325,000	$334,000	$334,000	4.9%
Liabilities				
Current liabilities				
Accounts payable	$75,000	$69,000	$80,000	6.7%
Short-term notes payable	$10,000	$10,000	$10,000	-
Total current liabilities	$85,000	$79,000	$90,000	6%
Long-term liabilities				
Mortgages payable	$70,000	$65,000	$65,000	(7%)
Long-term notes payable	$45,000	$0	$20,000	(55%)
Total long-term liabilities	$115,000	$65,000	$85,000	(26%)
Total liabilities	**$200,000**	**$144,000**	**$175,000**	**(12.5%)**
Owners' equity (net worth)	$125,000	$190,000	$159,000	27%
Total liabilities & net worth	**$325,000**	**$334,000**	**$334,000**	**4.9%**

Figure 14-2:
A sample
balance
sheet.

In the example in Figure 14-2, Big Spenders Corporation completed the current year with an increase in net worth of $34,000 ($125,000 to $159,000) over the prior year. By comparing the Current Year column on the balance sheet with the Prior Year column, you can readily determine what has happened to the mixture of assets and liabilities during the course of the year — in other words, how Big Spenders Corporation's management decided to allocate the company's resources.

To give you another example of how easy it is to glean information from this four-column balance sheet format, take a look at the Percent Change Compared to Prior Year column. Note that although the total current assets didn't change appreciably, two of the categories within the Current Assets category — cash and inventory — did. The cash account, as of December 31, is only $5,000, while inventory has ballooned to $85,000. Sometime during the course of the current year, a larger inventory has built up, depleting the company's cash reserves in the process.

An examination of the Budget column confirms the fact that this inventory accumulation was unplanned and unbudgeted. (Incidentally, this is a perfect example of how a company can be profitable and still get into financial trouble.) As evidenced by the balance sheet, Big Spenders Corporation currently has $90,000 in short-term liabilities but only $5,000 available in cash. As a result, despite being profitable, Big Spenders is in a classic cash crunch.

The only other percentage on this sample balance sheet that should attract immediate attention is the 55 percent decrease in long-term notes payable. Sometime during the course of the year, management decided to pay off a portion of its long-term debt — a decision that, in light of the company's present cash shortage, they would now probably like to reverse.

Turning the Numbers into Action

Here's an exercise that every small-business owner should attempt: Try figuring out exactly how much money it costs to produce your financial statements every year. Go ahead, we dare you! Add up the wages and salary costs of the people responsible for collecting the data, the depreciation of the accounting hardware and software involved, and the cost of any outside services you contract (tax preparers and advisors and so on). Now add the figures together and what do you have?

You probably have one costly process for determining how much income tax you have to pay — especially if that's all you use your financial statements for (see Chapter 19 for the lowdown on small-business taxes). On the other hand, if you use your financial statements as a management tool to guide and direct your business, the picture changes. In some cases, your financial statements may even pay for themselves if the actions you take because of the lessons they provide result in increased profits and/or cash flow.

For example, in the Big Spenders Corporation P&L (refer to Figure 14-1), if the business owner had plugged the salary increases into the budget before making them and been fully aware of the impending negative impact on the company's profitability, she may have given a second thought to this decision. Ditto with the balance sheet example (refer to Figure 14-2), where the owner made the decision to increase inventory and pay down her long-term debt. Had the owner plugged those figures into the balance sheet budget, she would've understood the impact these decisions would have on the company's cash account and probably would've altered her decisions.

Such is the power of using financial statements and budgets. They allow you to see the results of your decisions — before you make them! Every small-business owner should use the numbers and statistics that the business generates to help make important decisions.

Financial ignorance isn't bliss

Ed owned a successful construction company. In business for 15 years, Ed's company employed 20 people, did several million dollars in annual sales, and provided a comfortable living for Ed. During the course of a meeting between Ed and coauthor Jim, who was a consultant with Ed's company at the time, Ed confided that he had been embarrassed by a question the bank had asked when he recently inquired about a loan.

"They asked what my current ratio was," Ed said sheepishly. "And I not only didn't know the answer; I didn't know where on my financial statements to find it."

As it turned out, that wasn't all Ed didn't know about his financial statements. He also didn't know where to find his return on sales, how to determine his days in accounts receivable, or how to compute his debt-to-equity ratio (see the section "Understanding Key Ratios and Percentages" for details). And he didn't have year-to-year comparison figures with which to properly compare the line items on his profit and loss statement and balance sheet. In short, Ed didn't know how to read his financial statements, much less utilize the information that was on them.

Unfortunately, Ed is typical of many small-business owners who use their financial statements for little more than keeping score and paying taxes. Ironically, Ed employed a well-paid controller to maintain his books, keep score, and pay the business's taxes. Not much of a return on a $75,000 expense!

Understanding Key Ratios and Percentages

Before you can take the numbers generated by the P&L and balance sheet and turn them into meaningful management tools, you need to consider two overall points about the numbers, ratios, and percentages that come from those financial statements:

- ✔ **Comparisons work best.** Numbers, ratios, and percentages are most useful when compared to other numbers, ratios, and percentages. Your company may have what appears to be a respectable percentage of net profit on its sales, but if that percentage is less than it was during the same period the preceding year, danger may lie ahead. Numbers are most effective when you can use them to identify trends — and identifying trends always requires a comparison of numbers over time.

- ✔ **The industry matters.** Acceptable numbers in one industry may not be acceptable in another. Industries vary widely in the numbers they generate. For example, if you're in the software business, you may be disappointed with a 15 percent profit return on your sales dollar (we explain what that means in the next section). If you're in the grocery store business, however, you'd probably be ecstatic with a 5 percent profit return on sales.

If you don't know the acceptable ratios and percentages in your industry, contact your appropriate trade association. Most trade associations can give you the benchmark ratios and percentages that you need to know to compare your own business to industry averages. Check out the *Small Business Sourcebook* (Gale) to find a list of the trade associations applicable to your profession.

We strongly suggest that you learn how to extract the key ratios and percentages from your financial statements by yourself instead of depending on your bookkeeper or tax advisor to do so. The process itself gives you a better idea of where the numbers come from and how you can use the financial statements for other ratios and percentages that may be meaningful to your individual business. Although any ratio or percentage alone won't give you all the information you need to become a sophisticated financial manager, the knowledge of how they all work together will make you much more effective.

In the following sections, we explain the most common percentages and ratios that a small-business owner needs to consider.

Return on sales (R.O.S.)

Return on sales (R.O.S.) is a percentage determined by dividing net pretax profits (from the P&L) by total sales (also from the P&L). The resulting figure measures your company's overall efficiency in converting a sales dollar into a profit dollar. R.O.S. very much depends on what type of business you operate.

R.O.S. is an excellent figure on which you and your employees can focus. It's relatively easy to track, understand, and explain. Some businesses use this percentage as a company-wide scorecard to help their employees understand how the businesses make money, thus motivating them to do their part in assuring and improving profitability. (Most employees think their businesses make much, much more money than they really do.)

Return on equity (R.O.E.)

Return on equity (R.O.E.) is a percentage determined by dividing pretax profits (from the P&L) by equity/net worth (from the balance sheet). The resulting figure represents the return you've made on the dollars that you've invested in your business (your equity).

Over several years, if your return on equity isn't higher than 5 percent or thereabouts (which is the average return on money invested in such secure investments as short-term, high-quality bonds), you may want to consider selling your business and investing the proceeds in bonds. Your return would be similar, but your risk and the work involved would be much less.

This assumes, of course, that you're in business to make money. If, however, you're motivated by something else — creativity, growth, independence — or if you simply like owning your own business, you may be content with minuscule earnings despite the fact that you could make a similar or better financial return elsewhere.

Note: Both R.O.S. and R.O.E. are impacted heavily by the amount of money the owner decides to take out of the business in the form of salaries, bonuses, and benefits. Obviously, the more taken out, the lower the R.O.S. and R.O.E. percentages will be.

Gross margin

Gross margin is a percentage determined by subtracting your cost of goods sold (from the P&L) from total sales (also from the P&L). This figure represents your business's effective overall markup on products sold before deducting your operating expenses.

How good your gross margin is depends on your industry, your business, your pricing strategy, and the products or services you're selling. Trend is especially important here. Over a period of time, you want to see an increasing rather than decreasing gross margin.

Current ratio

Current ratio is a ratio determined by dividing current assets (from the balance sheet) by current liabilities (also from the balance sheet). The resulting figure measures your business's *liquidity* (the ability to raise immediate cash from the sale of your assets); thus, this ratio is of great interest, especially to your lenders.

The higher the current ratio, the more liquid your business. As a general rule, current ratios in excess of 2 to 1 are considered very healthy; anything less than 1 to 1 is in the danger zone. Again, trend is especially important here. Over any period of time, you want to see an increasing rather than decreasing current ratio.

Debt-to-equity ratio

The *debt-to-equity ratio* is a ratio determined by dividing equity/net worth (from the balance sheet) by debt/total liabilities (also from the balance sheet). The resulting ratio indicates, in effect, how much of the business is owned by the owners (represented by equity/net worth) and how much is owned by its creditors (represented by debt/total liabilities).

As a general rule, a 1-to-1 ratio is considered healthy; anything less is questionable. To further illustrate this point, refer to the Big Spenders Corporation balance sheet in Figure 14-2. Note that Big Spenders owes its creditors and debtors $175,000 (its total liabilities), while the company's net worth is $159,000 (the owners' equity). This means that as of the date that this balance sheet was assembled, Big Spenders Corporation's creditors and debtors had $16,000 more working for the company than the owners did (the difference between $175,000 and $159,000); therefore, its debt-to-equity ratio was slightly less than 1 to 1. If the owners needed another loan to make ends meet, they'd have a hard time showing that their financial stake in the company justified another loan.

Keeping the debt-to-equity ratio within the healthy 1-to-1 parameter is of paramount importance. For example, when the debt-to-equity ratio falls below 1 to 1, such cash-draining options as adding inventory, hiring new employees, and buying new equipment should be put on hold until the ratio becomes more lender friendly.

Inventory turn

Inventory turn is the number of times your inventory turns over in a year. You determine the number by dividing your cost of goods sold (from the P&L) by your average inventory (beginning inventory + ending inventory ÷ 2). For example, if your beginning inventory (on January 1) was $100,000 and your ending inventory (on December 31) was $150,000, your average inventory would be $125,000. Your inventory turn shows how well you're managing your inventory. The higher the number, the more times your inventory has turned, which is always preferable.

The number of times your inventory turns is highly dependent on your industry (manufacturer, wholesaler, or retailer) and your role in it. Typical inventory turns can range anywhere from 5 to 20 times a year (see the section "Managing Your Inventory" for details). Consult your trade association for inventory turn ratios that apply to your industry.

Number of days in receivables

You determine the *number of days in receivables* — that is, the average length of time between selling a product or service and getting paid for it — by first computing your average sales day. Divide your total sales for the period (from the P&L) by the number of days in that period (for a year, use 365). Then divide your average sales day into your current accounts receivable balance (from the balance sheet). The resulting figure gives you the number of days in your receivables.

Generally speaking, fewer than 30 days in receivables is considered excellent, between 30 and 45 days is acceptable, and more than 45 is cause for concern. (See the later section "Collecting Your Accounts Receivable" for more advice on this topic.)

Managing Your Inventory

The opportunities to improve profitability by the efficient handling of inventory are endless. Inventory isn't gray, like marketing, or in the future, like sales; it's here today and resting on your shelves, available to touch and feel and count. As a result, if you improve your efficiency at handling inventory, your business can have a double financial benefit:

✔ **Profitability:** The less inventory you have to write off, the more profitable you become.

✔ **Cash flow:** The fewer dollars you have invested in inventory, the more cash you have in your bank account.

Aside from texting while driving, accumulating excess inventory is the quickest and easiest way we know of to get into trouble. Excess inventory and its long list of hidden horrors have turned many a healthy small business into an ailing one. Unlike getting rid of employees who aren't performing, you can't give inventory that isn't performing a pink slip and send it out the door. Nor can you step up your collection effort with your inventory, as you can with slow-moving receivables, and expect it to turn into cash. Nonperforming inventory just sits there, collecting dust, at the same time that you're paying interest on the money you've invested to purchase it.

Yes, sometimes inventory disappears, but not always in the manner intended and not always in exchange for a customer's money. Inventory can disappear in a number of unsatisfactory ways, including internal theft (by your employees), external theft (by your customers), and at the hands of the most virulent scourge of them all — obsolescence.

If inventory is an integral part of your small business, use the following tips to manage it effectively:

✔ **Gather information on past purchasing and sales transactions.** Preventing inventory accumulation starts with the person doing the purchasing. The more information on past purchasing and sales transactions that person has, the better his future purchasing decisions can be. To gather this information, do the following:

• Make sure that you buy the best inventory-tracking software you can afford because inventory's past performance is usually the best indicator of how it will perform in the future. A good small-business tax advisor should be able to help you decide which software choice is best for you. (If you aren't computerized, ask your accountant to help you develop a manual system.)

• If you plan to enter the retail business, make sure that you also buy a *point-of-sale program* (a system that makes adjustments to inventory as a result of cash-register transactions). The system should be sophisticated enough to capture the information needed for you to accurately track your inventory.

✔ **Divide your inventory into small, manageable pieces.** Pay especially close attention to those pieces where you have the most financial exposure. Remember, inventory is subject to the *80-20 rule:* You usually get about 80 percent of your sales from 20 percent of your inventory units. Pay special attention to tracking that 20 percent.

✔ **Make sure that you have a workable system and qualified employees in place at the inventory-handling corners: shipping and receiving.** Most inventory disappearance problems can be identified at one of these two positions. If your inventory system is manual, ask an experienced tax practitioner to help you establish a workable digital or electronic system.

✔ **Take frequent physical inventories.** To determine whether you're having inventory-shrinkage problems and, if so, how significant they are, count the items in your inventory and compare your physical count to your financial records. (If you divide your inventory into small, manageable pieces, you can more readily determine where the shrinkage is occurring.) Taking a physical inventory is the only way to ensure that the gross margin figures on your P&L are correct. We suggest that most businesses take a thorough physical inventory at least twice a year and preferably four or even six times.

✔ **When selecting suppliers, don't simply settle on the supplier with the lowest price.** Include delivery time and shipping dependability at or near the top of your criteria. After all, the shorter the delivery time and the more dependable the vendor, the less of that vendor's inventory you'll have to carry.

Some vendors take returns on inventory you've purchased from them, often charging a restocking fee of some sort. In most cases, a vendor's willingness to take back items that don't sell is an added benefit, assuming that the restocking fee isn't too high.

Collecting Your Accounts Receivable

Banks aren't the only institutions in the business of lending money; most small businesses lend money, too. The primary difference between the two, however, is that when banks lend money (known as *loans*) to their customers, they charge interest; when small businesses lend money (via *accounts receivable*) to their customers, they usually don't charge interest.

Think about it: When customers buy your product (unless your business deals only in cash), you usually give them 30 days to pay the invoice. During those 30 days, the customer not only has your product but also retains the cash that's due to you — the same cash that you could otherwise use to reduce your debt, pay your bills, or invest to your benefit.

Today's business culture places the customer on a pedestal, as well it should. After all, someone has to purchase your products or services. But the word *customer* is incomplete; the correct phrase should be *paying customer*. Today's successful entrepreneurs know that a customer isn't a desirable customer until she has paid the bills.

Finding paying customers

The following list presents our time-tested collection of tips on how to find and do business with paying customers:

- ✔ **Use a credit application.** Design and use your own credit application. Ask one of your vendors if you can use its application as a sample. Make sure that every potential customer fills one out before you ship an order or provide your service. The credit application you use should include, among other things, the customer's references (other vendors used by the customer), the name of the customer's bank, the person responsible for accounts payable, and the name of the owner/president/CEO (the person ultimately responsible for the customer's debts). And be sure to check the references provided in the application.

- ✔ **Evaluate every applicant.** Ask yourself these questions about every prospective customer who submits a credit application, and if the answer to any of these questions is no, feel free to wave good-bye to the prospective sale:

  - • Does this applicant have the ability to pay?

  - • Has she indicated by her past actions a willingness to pay on time?

  - • Can you make a reasonable profit on sales to this account?

- ✔ **Ask for a financial statement.** Don't be afraid to ask for a financial statement before shipping to a first-time customer. Can you imagine a bank lending you money for your business without first asking you for a financial statement?

- ✔ **Check credit.** You can bet that your good vendors checked your credit; you should check your customers' credit, too. Remember that the granting of credit is a privilege; in effect, you're lending money to the person requesting it. Grant credit the way banks do — with care.

- ✔ **Establish terms.** No sale should be made without first establishing credit terms. Terms should work for both parties, but remember your signature on the bank's guarantee when a customer wants you to carry his or her receivables for long periods of time. Your bank won't back off its terms — why should you?

Managing your accounts receivable

Every successful small business needs someone dedicated to the collection of accounts receivable. In the early stages of the business, that someone is almost always the entrepreneur or founder. In later stages, that responsibility may be delegated to a bookkeeper, controller, or Chief Financial Officer (CFO). But whoever that person happens to be, he must be passionate about collecting the monies due the business.

After you've properly established your accounts receivable record-keeping functions (see Chapter 10 for details on bookkeeping systems), you need to figure out how to manage them. The following tips can help you do just that:

- ✔ **Bill promptly.** Bill the same day you ship or, in the case of a service business, the same day you fulfill the customer's order or the terms of the contract. If you wait until the end of the month to prepare and/or mail invoices, you further increase the number of days before you'll receive the cash.

- ✔ **Track the time it takes your customers to pay their bills.** You need to *age* all outstanding receivables at least once a month. (In other words, you need to compute the number of days that every receivable has been outstanding. Companies where money is tight run agings every day.) Creating an aging list reminds you who's in control of a large amount of your company's cash. An acceptable age of a receivable (in most industries, anyway) is 30 days; danger signals should appear after a receivable exceeds 45 days.

- ✔ **Begin collections promptly.** Don't wait until your receivables are more than 90 days old to kick in your collection procedures. Do so while the invoice is still warm (no more than 45 days).

- ✔ **Utilize a carrying charge or interest charge.** Why shouldn't you charge interest on overdue balances? After all, you're expected to pay a carrying charge when you exceed your payment terms (review your credit-card agreement if you have any doubts on this one). Don't charge anything less than 12 percent. A relatively high interest rate will ensure that you get the overdue account's attention.

- ✔ **Don't ship to nonpayers.** Don't continue to ship to customers who don't pay in accordance with your terms.

- ✔ **Involve the boss.** Pick up the phone yourself when the bill-paying stalling becomes noticeable. A call from the owner or boss is always more effective than a call from the bookkeeper.

- ✔ **Use a collection agency only as a last resort.** Collection agencies are expensive, charging up to 50 percent of the receivable for their services. Also, collection agencies aren't known for their consideration and politeness. Be prepared to kiss your customer good-bye forever if you choose to hand your slow-paying account over to an agency.

Your accounts receivable represent cash, and cash is the ultimate measure of your business's liquidity. Liquidity is the first place lenders and investors look when appraising the health of a business. Make sure that your receivables are current before showing your financial statements to people who have a reason for reading them.

The Three Ways to Improve Profits

Every small-business owner spends a significant amount of time trying to increase the business's *profitability* — the difference between revenue (the money you take in) and expenses (the money you pay out). No one succeeds in increasing profitability all the time, no matter how hard he tries. Some succeed often enough to grow a small business into a larger one. Some succeed just often enough to survive. And, unfortunately, some don't succeed at all.

The three ways to increase your business's profitability are

- ✔ To decrease expenses
- ✔ To increase margins
- ✔ To increase sales

You can do all three at the same time — that is, if luck and the time you have to devote to the task are on your side. However, our advice would be to pick the easiest avenue first (decreasing expenses). Then proceed to the second easiest (increasing margins) and then, finally, to the toughest (increasing sales). Unfortunately, too many entrepreneurs start with sales first (after all, increasing sales is a lot more fun than cutting expenses). While we applaud their gusto, they're approaching the process from the wrong end and won't see the same results they'd get if they started with expenses.

Instead of proceeding by trial and error, you can use a thorough understanding of how these profitability-improving options work to determine exactly what to do when your profits aren't what they should be. In the sections that follow, we explain what you need to know about each of these three options.

Decreasing (or controlling) expenses

The biggest advantage that comes from decreasing, or controlling, your expenses is that appropriate expense cuts have a direct short-term impact on the bottom line. For every dollar you save by eliminating an expense, you earn an extra dollar of profit. (Sure, increasing sales is another way to increase profits, but an extra dollar in sales may bring in only 25 cents of profit. We explain more about that shortly.)

Of course, not all expense cutting is equal. There's a world of difference between reducing the expense of your phone bill, for instance, by switching to a company with a lower cost but comparable long-distance service and reducing the cost of your product by switching to a supplier that offers lower cost *and* lower quality. Higher returns from disgruntled customers — or, worse, lawsuits stemming from harmful products or services — will do more harm than good to your business's long-term profitability.

So although we're strong advocates of operating a lean business, you must be thoughtful about where and how you reduce your expenses. You need to consider all the effects of cost cutting — not just the short-term, bottom-line effects — before you make any cuts.

 Controlling expenses is a cultural issue, which means that it's a lead-by-example issue that begins with you, the business owner, and carries over to your employees (presuming that you've hired the right ones; see Chapter 16 for details on how to do so). From the day you open your business's doors, you must pay close attention to managing its expenses, being careful not to spend money carelessly and being tactfully critical of those who do. If the boss sets the right example, the rest of the company is certain to follow. That's how a company culture is established and flourishes.

The following sections give you guidelines for successfully controlling expenses.

Zero-based budgeting

After you determine what kind of expense-controlling culture you want to set up in your business (and then make the commitment to act accordingly), your next step is to introduce a zero-based budgeting program. *Zero-based budgeting* requires that you begin each year's annual budget process by set-ting each expense category to zero. In other words, you don't assume that the dollar amounts in the preceding year's expense account were legitimate; you question every dollar that went into that expense account — hence, the term *zero-based.*

The zero-based budgeting approach contrasts with the manner in which many businesses budget expenses. Most businesses add a percentage increase to the preceding year's expenses, with the rate of the prior year's inflation increase being the most frequently used common multiplier. If last year's inflation rate was 3 percent, for instance, many businesses just plug in 3 percent increases to arrive at this year's budget.

The primary advantage of budgeting by the percentage-increase method is that it's quick and easy. The primary disadvantage is that it carries last year's fat into this year's menu. Ditto with next year's menu, and so on, forever — unless that particular expense category is eventually purged through the zero-based budgeting technique.

Here's an example of how zero-based budgeting works: Suppose it's time to budget your telephone expense for the year. The quick-and-easy solution is to take the preceding year's telephone expense figure, add 3 percent (or whatever inflation is), and move on to the next line item on the P&L. However, the zero-based budgeter's job is to examine and evaluate the company's telephone needs — to determine what kinds of calls need to be made in the course of business and then to call alternative carriers, collect quotes on their services, and award the business to a less-expensive but comparable-quality provider.

More often than not, the additional time you spend budgeting will be rewarded with a decrease in expenses, as opposed to an inflation-based increase. (Check out Chapter 10 for more on controlling expenses and zero-based budgeting.)

Trimming costs

In addition to zero-based budgeting, effective control of expenses requires understanding the 80-20 rule as it applies to expenses. The *80-20 rule* maintains that you can usually find 80 percent of wasted expense dollars in 20 percent of the expense categories.

As you create your budget, challenge expenses in all categories, large and small. You can usually find quick-and-easy dollars to save by rooting around in such overlooked expense categories as utilities, travel and entertainment, insurance, and the compost heap of them all, the miscellaneous category.

The following tips provide a framework in which you can effectively control your expenses:

✔ **Avoid overstaffing.** Finding and hiring a good employee is costly, and after you've hired one, unhiring her is not only difficult but also expensive. Use outside contractors, temporary services, and part-timers if you're on the fence about the need to hire a full-time employee.

✔ **Automate where possible.** Technology is usually cheaper than people (and it can be depreciated). When possible and when doing so won't compromise the quality of your products or services, purchase software in lieu of hiring additional employees. Functions such as accounting, inventory control, accounts receivable, and payroll lend themselves to automation. Let technology do your detail work.

✔ **Don't wait until a crisis arrives to do something about your expenses.** Institute an expense-control program when things are going well; you don't have to wait until the roof caves in. Be motivated by efficiency, not by fear.

✔ **Put the responsibility for controlling expenses where it belongs — in the hands of the employees who spend the money.** Also, make them accountable for their actions. Reward them when they meet their goals and provide corrective feedback when they don't (that's Management 101!).

The preceding tips are intended to provide you with an overview of how to control your expenses. Following are several cost-controlling measures, intended not only to give you specific ideas but also to put you in the frame of mind for getting serious about managing your expenses:

✔ **Ask for price quotes before you obligate yourself to services.** This is true for everything from lawyers, accountants, and financial advisors to computer repair people, plumbers, and consultants. (Often the quotes won't hold up, but they'll give you a basis on which to negotiate subsequent charges.) Also, make sure that you always ask for itemized invoices.

✔ **Don't pay unnecessary bank charges.** Question the fees on your statements. Shop around if your bank is charging more than competitors for services. Just about everything is negotiable, including bank charges.

✔ **Shop your telephone service every year or so.** Everyone is discounting telephone services as technology and deregulation make prices more competitive.

✔ **If you have employees, review your experience modification factor with your insurance agent.** Your *experience modification factor* is the tool that determines your workers' compensation insurance payment (see Chapter 10 for details).

Speaking of insurance agents, how long has it been since you've shopped for insurance, both liability and health? Given the relentless upward trend of health insurance and the seemingly endless changes in the health-care system, our recommendation is that you annually price your business's health-insurance policies (and compare those prices with other polices out there).

We're not suggesting that price should be your only consideration or that after you've found a lower price you should automatically wave good-bye to your current supplier. Rather, we're suggesting that you be aware of the going rate in the marketplace and, where appropriate, either change suppliers or press your current supplier to reassess the prices it's charging you. Squeaky wheels get the grease, and the effective control of expenses is no exception to this rule.

The preceding tips are a few of the many possible ways for you to control your business's expenses. Remember that effective expense control isn't a one-time event; it's an ongoing occurrence whose success or failure lies entirely in your hands. Read the rest of this book for more smart business ideas that are cost effective.

Increasing margins

As we've mentioned, *margin* is the difference between sales price and the cost of the goods or services sold. (*Gross margin* is the accounting term you see on the balance sheet to mean the same thing.) Here's a simple illustration of how to understand what the margin is on a given transaction: If your product sells for $15 and the cost of that product (including shipping charges) is $10, your margin is 33 percent — the $5 in markup divided by the $15 gross sales price. Your margin dollars are $5 (the difference between the $10 cost and the $15 sales price).

You can increase margins in three ways:

- By raising prices
- By lowering the cost of the goods or services sold
- By doing both

Regardless, the magic of increasing margins is that, similar to decreasing expenses, every dollar of income derived from the margin increase ends up as additional profit, assuming no reduction in sales.

Continuing with the preceding example, if you raise the price of the product from $15 to $16, the margin jumps from 33 percent to 37.5 percent, and the margin dollars increase from $5 to $6. Because increasing prices generally costs very little, nearly the entire $1 of the price increase will be realized as profit, again assuming no reduction in purchasing from customers.

Increasing margins by lowering the cost of goods or services sold is a little more difficult. If you're a manufacturer, you must decrease the cost of manufacturing your product either by cutting your labor costs or by reducing the cost of the raw materials you purchase from vendors. If you're a wholesaler or retailer, you must reduce the cost of the goods you purchase for resale. Similar to reducing prices, this method of increasing margins also results in a dollar-on-the-dollar recapture of profitability.

Consider the case of the small business that does $500,000 in sales in a year. If the owner, at the beginning of the year, decides to increase the prices of his products by an average of 1 percent, that would mean an additional $5,000 in profits at the end of the year. An average increase of 2 percent would add $10,000, and 5 percent would add a solid $25,000 (again, all this assumes that the price increases don't reduce sales).

Generally speaking, small-business owners are more reluctant to raise prices than they should be. Too many times, your humble authors have witnessed reluctant small-business owners tremble in the course of reasonably raising prices, only to learn that their customers don't care as long as the quality of the relationship endures. The tolerance of your customers to accept price increases depends on such issues as competition, alternative products, and, most of all, the customer relationships you maintain. (See Chapter 13 for tips on keeping your customers happy.)

We strongly recommend that every small-business owner review the margins on every product or service at least once a year. Determine a time of the year when raising prices makes the most sense (usually at the beginning of the business's fiscal year), mark that date on your calendar in permanent ink, and when the time comes, start with your lowest-priced item and work up. Analyze the percentage of price increase on each individual item. Don't simply increase prices by using an across-the-board percentage increase. Also, be sure to aim for higher margins on the lower-priced items (those that aren't as likely to be price-shopped by your customers) and on those products that don't need to be as competitively priced.

But realize that you don't have to wait until the end (or the beginning) of the year to consider increasing your prices. You may want to consider a price increase when the demand for your product suddenly increases. Perhaps a competitor has raised its prices, or perhaps the law of supply and demand is hard at work — in other words, maybe more demand than supply for the product in question can provide a perfect scenario for raising prices. Don't feel guilty for taking advantage of such situations — you'll encounter plenty of occasions when the law of supply and demand works in reverse and you have to cut your prices.

Increasing sales

After you have decreased (or controlled) your expenses and increased your margins, you can focus on doing what every entrepreneur worth her weight in loan guarantees loves to do: increase sales.

After all, increasing sales is what most small-business owners are born to do, and besides, offense (increasing sales) is always more enjoyable than defense (cutting expenses). Everyone loves to roll out a new product, hire a new salesperson (it's always more fun to hire a salesperson than it is to hire a bookkeeper), or develop a new sales promotion. What's more, you can easily measure the results of a plan to increase sales.

In most cases (the operative word here being *most*), the act of increasing sales adds profits to your bottom line, assuming that those sales are priced at a high enough level to make them profitable. We stress the word *most* here because small-business owners too often attempt to solve their profitability problems by focusing only on increasing sales. What they fail to realize is that if their sales aren't at a price high enough to generate a profit, then adding more sales will only serve to increase their cumulative losses. Or stated another way, sales alone don't beget profitability; only profitable sales do. (Turn to Chapter 11 for loads of advice on how to make sales a top priority in your business.)

Chapter 15

Learning from the Experiences of Others

* *

In This Chapter

▶ Connecting with mentors and peers who can help

▶ Assembling a board of advisors

▶ Finding a partner

▶ Tapping into trade associations and business incubators

▶ Surveying other business resource options

* *

*W*hat do you think the number one cause of small-business failure is? Do you think it's lack of capital? How about poor location? Maybe inadequate marketing or distribution?

Answer: none of the above. Rather, the answer is isolation, as in the small-business owner's isolation.

A lack of capital, a poor location, and inadequate marketing and distribution aren't causes of small-business failure; they're just symptoms — symptoms of the dreaded disease Owner's Isolation Syndrome. The symptoms of this syndrome affect every small-business owner at one time or another, but if you commit yourself to preventing the disease, you can avoid many of the symptoms.

In light of our status as charter members of the Never-Bring-Up-a-Problem-without-an-Accompanying-Solution Club, we use this chapter to present a collection of options that will help you do away with the trial-and-error method of small-business management and learn from the experiences of others.

Utilize Mentors

We know two things for sure:

- If we had our small-business careers to live over again, the first thing we'd do is find more mentors.
- Somewhere within your reach, you can find a veteran small-business owner who will agree to be *your* mentor if you approach him or her correctly.

Effective *mentors* are basically consultants — who usually work for free. What they have to offer is the ability to draw upon their extensive experience, one of the best teachers of all. You can go to a mentor to deal with strategic issues — you know, the long-term, fundamental, and always-critical issues, like strategy, vision, and finances. (Note that most mentors prefer to focus primarily on your strategic concerns, as opposed to your operational issues.)

So get the help of a mentor. Sounds simple, right? Unfortunately, most small-business owners don't know how to find those veterans who will agree to become mentors, nor do they know how to cultivate good mentor-mentee relationships after they do find them.

Finding your mentor

Here's our three-step Mentor Search Plan:

1. **Compile a list of prospective mentors.**

   Ask your banker, your accountant, your lawyer, and folks around town who are wired into the small-business community (people at the Chamber of Commerce, Service Corps of Retired Executives, and Small Business Development Centers) for the names of veteran small-business owners who may be interested in helping you succeed.

2. **Contact the person that your research and intuition indicate may be the best mentor for you.**

   The best mentor is typically someone who has current or previous experience within your chosen industry, although this isn't a prerequisite. (General business experience/knowledge, however, *is* a prerequisite.) Oftentimes, a good mentor is retired and, thus, may be motivated to help others as a way to stay involved in business.

The best way to approach a prospective mentor is to write him or her a letter introducing yourself, your business, and the reason for your interest. Follow up the letter with a phone call. Don't use e-mail for the initial contact; it's too informal and doesn't convey how important the mentorship is to you.

3. **Persuade your prospective mentor to sign on.**

   Proceed as follows:

   • "Mr. (or Ms.) Veteran, my name is Wanda Wannabe. Mr. Legal Beagle, a mutual friend of ours, suggested I call you."

   • "Mr. (or Ms.) Veteran, I'm not looking for your money, but I am looking for your advice. Would you agree to spare a small amount of time each month to meet with me if I promise not to waste one nanosecond of it, if I provide you with a complete agenda in advance of every meeting, if I follow up on the suggestions you make, and if you can name the place and time of our meetings?"

   • "Mr. (or Ms.) Veteran," you conclude, with just a touch of a plea in your voice, "As you have probably surmised, I am looking for a mentor. Would you consider being that person?"

Don't rush into the relationship; have a lunch or a dinner together first. (You buy, of course!) Remember, this is a relationship you're seeking here; you want to make sure that you and your mentor will be compatible.

Building the mentor-mentee relationship

After you've found a mentor who matches your needs and requirements and is willing to work with you, work at fostering your relationship. Here are several tips that will help you retain your mentor and make the most of the relationship:

✓ **Understand that mentoring is a personal experience, not a business one.** If the chemistry is right, the relationship will work well. If the chemistry doesn't work, the relationship won't work either.

✓ **Follow up.** Drop your mentor a note after your meetings. Or the next time the two of you talk, let your mentor know how implementing her advice turned out and how much you appreciate the help.

✓ **Be honest with your mentor about the problems and issues you face.** No sugarcoating allowed. Your mentor will see through the fluff anyway, and he won't hang around for long if he thinks you aren't being completely truthful with him.

✔ **Leave your thin skin at home.** Good mentors speak their minds and aren't shy about shooting down poor ideas.

✔ **Don't blindly follow all of your mentor's advice.** Your mentor may have different priorities, ethics, and needs than you do. So, in the end, follow your heart as well as your head in making decisions based on your mentor's input.

Network with Peers

Nobody knows the business of small business better than a retired veteran (see the preceding section), but finishing a close second in the antidote-to-lonely-decision-making competition is the current small-business owner — a peer who is facing the same day-to-day issues that you face.

Imagine the power of putting a dozen or so current small-business owners in the same room. Imagine the wealth of solutions that may appear when one of the members presents a nagging problem or a thorny issue and asks for help. Do you have a problem with an employee who can't seem to get to work on time? Surely, another business owner has had the same problem before; don't be afraid to discover from your peers what has worked for them. (See Chapter 16 for our two cents on the employee issue.)

Peer networking works because, as we say throughout this book, a small business's problems are generic — that is, they're usually not unique to your industry or niche. Thus, the solutions are often generic, too.

Second only to a good mentor, peer networking is the best of the small-business owner's learning devices — *if* you can locate the right networking resource. (Sorry, we're not talking Rotary Clubs or Chambers of Commerce here, although these are steps in the right direction.)

Some cities already have for-profit or nonprofit peer-networking programs up and running, and they're spreading the word of the value of the concept. You can ask at your local Chamber of Commerce or your city's or state's small-business magazine or newspaper to find out what and where these programs are in your area. Here are just a few of the peer-networking organizations that you may find helpful:

✔ **Vistage International, Inc. (formerly The Executive Committee):** www.vistage.com

✔ **American Business Women's Association:** www.abwa.org

✔ **The Alternative Board (TAB):** www.thealternativeboard.com

✔ **President's Resource Organization (PRO):** `www.propres.com`

✔ **Opportunity Knocks (OK):** `www.opp-knocks.org` (founded by co-author Jim)

One or more of these organizations (or another with a similar agenda) may surface in your city if one hasn't set up shop already. Keep your eyes peeled.

Form a Board of Advisors

Boards of advisors are like breath mints: Almost everybody could benefit from one, but too few people partake.

Similar to a mentor, a board of advisors provides you with an affordable, outside perspective. Boards replace trial and error with experience and knowledge. They act as sounding boards, rebound boards, and boards of inquiry. They open needed doors and close unnecessary ones, while giving you an inside look at the outside business world.

Incidentally, we're not talking about a board of *directors* here; we're talking about a board of *advisors*. Directors are responsible for directing the company; advisors are responsible only for advising the president or Chief Executive Officer (CEO) — that's you!

Reaping the benefits of a board

The primary benefits of having your own board of advisors include the following:

✔ **Credibility:** Having a board is an indicator that your business is serious about its direction. Also, board members with solid reputations can bring additional credibility to your organization.

✔ **Lead generation:** Your board can play an integral role in networking sales leads.

✔ **Connections:** Your board will open a variety of doors that you can't open by yourself.

✔ **Advice:** You can diversify the skills of your board and then look to your board members for advice in their specialties.

In fact, there aren't many valid reasons not to have a board of advisors. Yes, a board does take time to organize and coordinate, but that time will be repaid many times over if your board is a good one. A board is also inexpensive; most board members will gladly donate an hour or two of their time every three months or so for the price of a lunch.

Of course, you can reap these benefits only if your board meetings are well organized, if the board members feel that you're not wasting their time, and if they feel that you're heeding their advice.

Forming your advisory board

Most small-business advisory boards consist of three or five members, excluding the owner. (If you're a home-office business or a truly small, small business, you may select the three-board-member size.) Here are some tips on how to assemble, utilize, and treat your board of advisors:

- ✔ **Select advisors from outside your company.** No board of employees here, all nodding their heads in unison. You want knowledge and perspectives that don't already exist in the company.

- ✔ **Balance your skills with the skills of the board members.** If your strengths are sales and marketing, make sure that you cover the finance and operational bases through your other advisory board members. Could you use a banker on the board? A lawyer? An accountant?

- ✔ **Include a customer as a board member.** No viewpoint can equal the viewpoint of a customer — especially one who knows your industry, pays his bills on time, and considers vendors to be partners. Never go to a board meeting without that viewpoint.

- ✔ **Round out your board with someone from your industry.** After you've selected the banker, lawyer, accountant, and/or customer, and you still have a slot or two left over, feel free to include someone from your industry — someone with potential mentoring skills and/or someone with financing contacts that may eventually aid your growing business.

- ✔ **Schedule meetings regularly and well in advance.** Give at least one month's notice, maybe more. Quarterly meetings usually are the best; anything more frequent is asking too much from your board members.

- ✔ **Limit the meetings to two hours.** Keep them meaty and keep the advisors interested.

- ✔ **Avoid surprises.** Send out an agenda in advance of the meeting and then stick with it unless an emergency prompts some last-minute changes. Board members, like bankers, don't like surprises.

✔ **Focus on strategic and overview issues.** Board meetings take up valuable time, so make sure your board members spend each meeting resolving issues that have long-term impact.

- *Strategic issues* are issues of business direction and positioning; they include such subjects as distribution systems, marketing plans, and sales initiatives.

- *Operational issues* include specific problems such as administrative snafus, shipping and receiving roadblocks, and invoicing issues.

Typically, businesses don't discuss operational issues in the course of board meetings. If you have an operation-related problem and a board member with the skills to help resolve it, approach him during non-board-meeting hours.

What about the most important issue of them all — cash flow? Although a shortage of cash really is an operational problem, it always results from a strategic problem — not enough sales, inadequate margins, or out-of-control expenses, for example. So your board should definitely deal with cash flow issues during board meetings.

✔ **Be truthful.** Lose your credibility, and you'll lose your advisors. Be candid — no sugarcoating or truth bending allowed.

✔ **Follow up on suggestions.** Follow up on all your board's recommendations, not just those that you consider to be valid. You don't have to *implement* every recommendation; you should, however, have the courtesy to *respond* to all seriously considered recommendations and ideas.

✔ **Pay the board.** If you can afford to do so, pay board members anywhere from $50 per meeting on up. If you're a start-up and money is tight, at least buy your board members lunch until you can afford to compensate them.

After your advisors get comfortable with you and your business, you can ask to use their credibility and contacts to help you gain new customers, new vendors, and new sources of financing.

Get a Partner

Here's a fact that not everyone knows: Partnerships outperform sole proprietorships by a wide margin. This statement is nothing more than simple math at work: One plus one equals at least two. Sometimes, one plus one equals significantly more than two if the partners can blend their skills and talents. (Google, Apple, and Hewlett-Packard are examples of companies that began as partnerships.)

So why might a partnership make sense for you? Here are just a few reasons:

- **Complementary skills:** Although you're probably aware of your own strengths, you may overlook your weaknesses. Ask those who know you well — family, friends, and current or previous coworkers — what complementary skills you should seek in a business partner.

- **Additional capital:** Two savings accounts are better than one.

- **Greater problem-solving capacity:** Two heads are (usually) better than one.

- **More flexibility:** One partner goes on vacation or gets sick; the other one minds the business.

- **Ease of formation:** Partnerships are easier and less expensive to form than corporations (but not as easy or inexpensive as sole proprietorships; see Chapter 5).

- **Less risk:** Profits aren't the only thing partnerships share. They share problems and losses, too.

For sure, you may have plenty of reasons not to want to take a partner (or multiple partners) into your business. Everyone knows juicy horror stories about business partnerships that turned sour and even ended up in court, destroying the business in the process (assuming anything was left to destroy). After all, warring partners seldom go down alone.

The success ratio of partnerships is highest when the two partners have complementary skills. You're a salesnik? Find an operations type for a partner. Your skills are in product development? Find someone who has experience in getting the product to the marketplace and subsequently sold. You're a mover and a shaker? Find someone who can count the beans that you'll be moving and shaking.

How do you find a partner (or partners)? The same way you locate a key employee, a consultant, or a mentor (see the first section of this chapter): Identify what it is that you need (in this case, the skills you're looking for) and then network your available resources. (Go to Chapter 16 for the skinny on finding superstar employees.)

When forming a partnership, you're beginning what you hope will be a long-term relationship — a long-term relationship that often rivals a marriage in terms of complexity. If you're smart, you'll determine a way to test the chemistry of the partnership *before* you get so far involved that you can't get out. Otherwise, you may learn the same lesson that too many marriages teach — a lifetime can be a long time. (See the nearby sidebar for more on testing your partnership chemistry.)

Testing the partnership waters

How can you test a partnership before you get in so far that you can't get out? First, ask your attorney or accountant for the names of partners who currently own a business together. Meet with them (without your prospective partner) and ask questions to find out the pros and cons of partnering. Ask your attorney or accountant for the names of people who have been involved in failed partnerships, too. You can learn just as much from failures as you can from successes.

We also suggest that you give your partnership a trial run before you open your business.

For starters, write your business plan together; doing so gives you an immediate insight into whether you're capable of working side by side. Next, investigate your financing options together, meet with probable vendors, and interview potential customers — in essence, do everything just short of hanging out your shingle. Sure, the time involved in testing a partnership may cost you a month or two of doing business. But we can guarantee you this: No matter how time-consuming and messy the formation process may be, it will never be as time-consuming and messy as the dissolution of a failed partnership.

The number one rule of a partnership is this: Don't enter into one without first consulting an experienced small-business lawyer. Have the attorney advise you and your prospective partner about the many obstacles that lie in the path of a successful partnership. Then ask the lawyer to assist you in drawing up an ironclad, airtight, cast-in-stone, buy-sell Partnership Agreement to overcome those obstacles — a Partnership Agreement, by the way, that will be tested many times throughout the life of your business. (For more on partnerships and Partnership Agreements, see Chapter 5. For more on legal issues, head to Chapter 18.)

Join a Trade Association

Thousands of trade associations exist in the United States, and we wholeheartedly recommend that you join one. No matter who you are or what industry you're in, a trade association is probably available for you. The best trade associations offer a wide range of potential benefits — everything from business contacts to skill-building workshops to industry-specific information to group insurance programs. In addition, most trade associations host industry-wide trade shows at least once a year, during which you can mingle with suppliers and peers.

The two kinds of trade associations are industry-specific trade associations and small-business-specific trade associations. The following list breaks down these options:

✔ **Industry-specific trade associations:** Consult your local library to find the trade association or organization that caters to your industry. Flip through the *National Trade and Professional Associations of the United States* (Columbia Books), which lists more than 7,500 associations in the United States today. Your local library should have a copy of this $269 annual publication. Or you can search the web by opening a search engine and keying in the name of the specific industry you're in, followed by the word *association* — as in *sporting-goods association.*

✔ **Small-business-specific trade associations:** These trade associations include the following:

  • **National Small Business Association (NSBA):** This association watches congressional actions and reports on issues affecting small businesses. Visit the NSBA website at `www.nsba.biz` or call 202-293-8830 for details.

  • **National Association for the Self-Employed (NASE):** NASE offers resource materials and a monthly magazine. Visit its website at `www.nase.org` or call 800-232-NASE for details.

  • **National Association of Women Business Owners (NAWBO):** This association brings together women entrepreneurs for support and assistance. Surf its website at `www.nawbo.org` or call 800-55-NAWBO for more information.

  • **National Federation of Independent Business (NFIB):** The NFIB is the largest lobbying organization for small businesses in the country. Visit its website at `www.nfib.com` or call 800-NIFB-NOW for details.

Trade associations aren't without their warts. First, don't assume that products and services marketed to the association's members are necessarily the best of what's out there. Many associations, for example, offer insurance programs to their members — programs that the members could purchase at a lower cost elsewhere. *Remember:* The programs a trade association offers are only as good as the people who determine what that association will and won't offer its members.

Don't limit yourself to providing a product or service only in the manner that people in the trade association recommend. For example, when coauthor Eric began offering personal financial counseling services, he chose to do so exclusively on an hourly basis, even though most other financial advisors worked on commission or managed money for fees. Eric knew that their way wasn't the only way, and the path he chose reflected his belief that a financial counselor should have no personal financial stake dependent on any of the products or services that he or she recommends. This policy worked well for him.

Find a Business Incubator

Business incubators provide new small-business owners with a friendly location to set up shop. An incubator offers its start-up customers a mixture of the following benefits:

- ✔ Below-market rent
- ✔ Free or discounted access to a variety of office services
- ✔ Discounted administrative services
- ✔ The opportunity to network with other entrepreneurs who are in the same knee-knocking, start-up boat

Because entrepreneurs are most inclined to trust the advice of their peers, what better place to receive your advice and locate your business than within an incubator?

For more information on incubators, log on to the National Business Incubation Association (NBIA) website at www.nbia.org or call the association at 740-593-4331.

Locate a Small Business Development Center

Small Business Development Centers (SBDCs) are cooperative programs designed to provide current and potential business owners with advice and information on running their businesses. SBDCs are sponsored by a partnership between the Small Business Administration (SBA), a local college or university, and often your state's Economic Development Department. Every state has a central SBDC, and the United States has nearly 1,000 service centers, most of which are located on college or community college campuses.

As with any type of consultant, the quality of SBDC counseling varies widely from one SBDC office to another. Tread carefully and don't bet the farm on their advice.

To locate the SBDC nearest you, visit www.sba.gov/sbdc or call 800-8-ASK-SBA.

Give SCORE a Try

The *Service Corps of Retired Executives* (SCORE) is affiliated with the SBA and offers one-on-one counseling through its 10,000+ experienced counselors across the country. SCORE is a wonderful concept, but its offerings sometimes fall short of its potential. The quality of SCORE's advice varies widely and depends on the individual counselor. Similar to the SBDCs, proceed cautiously when accepting advice from SCORE volunteers.

SCORE volunteers (usually *Fortune* 500 graduates) will probably be most helpful to you if you're trying to determine whether to leave your day job and make the risky leap to business ownership.

SCORE offices are easy to locate. Log on to `www.score.org` to find the chapter nearest you.

Tap into Small-Business Information

Magazines and books (and associated videos, audiotapes, and CDs) that focus on helping the small-business owner are everywhere. Where small business is concerned, you name it and a book has been written about it — including this one! Read your industry trade publications (which you can often find through your industry's trade associations, a resource we discuss earlier in this chapter). Also, we suggest that you check out the *Small Business Sourcebook* (Gale), a huge reference that you can find in most public libraries.

On the technological front, DVDs, podcasts, and webinars are often produced and offered by larger companies that service your industry or by technology vendors that sell products within the small-business sector. Intuit and Microsoft are two examples of companies that offer a wide variety of technology-based informational offerings.

The number of websites and small-business blogs available online have grown to a near-infinite number. We suggest that you put the online medium to work to keep up to speed on new trends and offerings under the small-business category. (See Chapter 12 for our top Internet resource recommendations and check out Chapter 3 for helpful government resources, such as the Small Business Administration.)

Part IV
Keeping Your Business in Business

The 5th Wave   By Rich Tennant

"It's an extension of the open-kitchen concept. We call it our open-owner's office area where patrons can watch the owner fend off creditors, haggle with suppliers, and reprimand the staff."

In this part . . .

After you start your business, the real fun begins — staying in business and growing your business. This part puts you through your paces, covering employee issues like hiring and benefits, government regulations, taxes, and special issues for fast-growing businesses.

Chapter 16

Finding and Keeping Superstar Employees

*I*f you're like most small-business owners we know, you may work without any employees for a period of time as you transition through the start-up stage. Then after you decide to hire employees, you may find that you need or want only one or two. However, if you have ambitions to really grow your business, you'll probably end up hiring many employees. After all, employees mean *leverage* (increased means of accomplishing your mission) in the world of business, and leverage opens up all kinds of opportunities for growth.

The concepts and suggestions in this chapter are designed to help you hire top employees and keep them happy and, in the process, exactly where they belong: working for you, not your competition.

Every business has a number of *game-breaker* positions (key positions that will make or break your company). When you're just starting out, the game-breaker position may be yours alone because you may be the only employee. In larger, established small businesses, those game-breaker positions may include the president/CEO/Grand Poobah (that's you), the financial person, the sales manager, the marketing manager, the production manager, the office manager, the purchasing agent, the art director . . . well, you get the idea. Every successful, growing small business must have a team of super-stars filling its game-breaker positions. A *superstar* is an employee who

✔ Is capable of taking on increasing responsibilities and contributing to the company's continued growth

✔ Is loyal to your vision

✔ Shares your ethics and principles

✔ Is creative within his or her area of expertise

✔ Adds to the synergy of the team by working effectively with other team members

✔ Welcomes positive change

Assembling your team of superstars is a three-part process — hiring, training, and motivating. Unfortunately, in the process of hiring people you hope are superstars, you'll sometimes stumble and hire someone who doesn't work out. Sadly, that calls for a related process that's equally as important: firing. We discuss all this and more in the coming sections.

Assembling a Top Team

Hiring is mostly science, not art. It's a methodical, repetitive, and often drawn-out process, but it's one that most small-business owners have to go through eventually. The first step in the hiring process is to collect a roster of worthwhile applicants for the position, likely through one of the following methods:

✔ By running an ad

✔ By putting out a sign or a website posting

✔ By encouraging referrals from employees, vendors, and customers

Referrals are almost always the best option. After all, referred applicants are more likely to be skilled, hard-working applicants (because the people doing the referring don't want the embarrassment of referring a weak applicant), and they cost next to nothing. Just get the word out that you're looking and then let your employees, vendors, or customers do the talking.

Never accept an applicant for a responsible position (one responsible for managing employees, handling money, dealing with customers, and so on) without first obtaining a professionally prepared resume. If the applicant hasn't taken the time to create such a resume, you know right away that he's not right for the position. *Exception:* When hiring for a part-time position or a minimum-wage job, you may receive applicants who don't have resumes. Make sure you have an application form ready for them to fill out. (Ask your accountant or any active business for a copy of the form it uses.)

The tough part comes after you've collected the resumes: You must interview, then reinterview, and then reinterview again. You must check those often-camouflaged references, whose primary function, you soon discover, is to tell you as little as possible about a candidate's faults in between glowing adjectives aimed at his strengths. Keep reading to find out what you need to know to be a successful hirer.

Taking hints for hiring

The best employees go to the entrepreneur who's willing to go to the most trouble to find them. Following is a list of hiring tips to help you locate and hire those elusive superstars:

- ✔ **When running an ad, remember that you're selling an opportunity, not just offering a job, and write the ad accordingly.** You want (we're assuming) to attract a career-minded employee who wants to grow with your company, so you need to paint your company, and the position, in an attractive light. Review a large number of existing ads carefully, and then use bits and pieces of the best ones.

- ✔ **Establish a reward system to encourage your employees to refer qualified candidates.** The best candidates often come from inside-the-company referrals. Rewards can include anything from cash to vacation days.

- ✔ **Always prepare a job description, which we now call *performance expectations*, before you post a job ad.** Good applicants want to know exactly what the job entails and what's expected of them. As part of the ad, include the job definition, expectations of work, salary, expected bonus, perks, and your business's chain-of-command, as it relates to the position being offered (see the section "Motivating: Pay and Performance Issues" for details).

- ✔ **Review each applicant's resume, looking for the names of businesses or people you may know who aren't listed as the candidate's official references.** The most informative references may be those that the applicant doesn't list. Because of a variety of legal ramifications, such third-party references are usually more candid with their comments than the official references are.

- ✔ **Try to open the door to more candid conversations when you're talking to an applicant's references.** Look for areas of commonality in order to put the person at ease. Tune in for the little things as you listen. Ask about the applicant's weaknesses and then multiply — most references are prone to sugarcoating. Just because a reference is reluctant to provide information on the applicant doesn't necessarily mean that the applicant has problems; the reference may simply be protecting herself.

✔ **Have every applicant complete a job application in addition to submitting a resume.** Resumes + applications = more information on candidates. Most applications ask questions about topics that don't appear on resumes, such as citizenship, green card, felony arrests, and so on. It's perfectly okay for applicants to write "see information on resume" for applicable sections of the application.

Use the U.S. government's E-Verify system, if appropriate. *E-Verify* is an Internet-based system that compares information from an employee's Form I-9 (Employment Eligibility Verification) to data from the U.S. Department of Homeland Security and the Social Security Administration to confirm employment eligibility. You should use E-Verify when you have a reasonable doubt of an employee's legality. While participation is voluntary for most businesses, certain states require it and more may begin doing so. (Arizona and Mississippi currently require it.)

✔ **Look for the applicant's ability to listen during the interview.** If he doesn't listen well during the interview, he's unlikely to listen well after you hire him and he's on the job.

✔ **Find out what research the applicant has done on you and your company.** If she comes to the interview unprepared and devoid of knowledge about your company and industry, you've discovered something about either her work habits or the depth of her desire for the job.

✔ **Remember that the hiring process usually requires you to wear two hats:**

 • The detective's hat, to be donned as you interview and separate potential superstars from the rest of the pack.

 • The salesperson's hat, to be donned after you find your prospective superstar. Most superstars have other options, so part of your job is that of a salesperson.

Don't forget to prepare for the second role and don't incorrectly assume that your company is the only, or the best, opportunity in town. Like any good salesperson, remember to sell the benefits of the job as opposed to its features; in other words, show your prospective superstar how working for you will make her life better.

Hiring right brings you an endless list of benefits. The biggest is that the better the employee you hire, the less time you have to spend managing him. Instead, you can spend your time on product (or service) development, business-building activities, such as marketing and sales, hiring more employees, supervising the production floor, or doing the other things you enjoy most.

Considering the employee-leasing option

More than 2,000 employee-leasing companies — also known as *professional employer organizations* (PEOs) — exist in the United States today, which means that at least one is probably located near you. The employee-leasing company's primary customer is the small-business owner because most large businesses develop a wide variety of human resource services in-house.

Employee leasing means that the leasing company assumes the paperwork and administrative responsibilities of dealing with employees, allowing you to concentrate on the operational activities. Thus, in effect, you're outsourcing your human resource needs. In this way, you and your PEO become *co-employers* of the employees. In return for the services the PEO provides, it charges its customers an administrative fee (its markup over costs) that's usually between 2 percent and 8 percent, depending on the dollar amount of the transaction.

We aren't advocating employee leasing for every small business; whether to lease or not is a gray area. Here's why leasing employees makes sense for some small businesses:

✔ PEOs do what they do best (hire and handle the administration of employees), and you do what you do best (run your business). You can focus on developing your product, selling your product, servicing your customers, and improving profitability.

✔ You write one check and the PEO does the rest.

✔ PEOs can serve as unofficial employment agencies. You can eventually hire the best of the temporary employees they send you and return the rest.

✔ By pooling employees, PEOs can cut costs in such areas as insurance rates.

✔ PEOs worry about regulatory compliance so you don't have to.

At the same time, leasing has the following disadvantages:

✔ When a PEO goes under, it can take your payroll cash (including tax payments) and prepaid insurance along with it. This leaves you, the employees, or both holding the bag.

✔ If you can provide comparable employee services at the same cost, you can, in effect, cut your expenses by hiring your own employees. Remember that every dollar saved by not paying a leasing-company fee results in an extra dollar of profit.

If you do decide to lease your employees, be extremely careful in selecting the company you use as your co-employer. Check references thoroughly and remember that everything is negotiable when signing a leasing contract. You may even want to customize the leasing agreement to meet your specific needs. Also, you may want to check with the Employer Services Assurance Corporation in Little Rock, Arkansas (www.esacorp.org), to verify that you're dealing with an accredited PEO. This self-regulating industry group has accredited PEOs in all 50 states. When in doubt as to where to look for a PEO, this is a helpful resource.

In the final analysis, most small-business owners make the decision to lease employees based on whether they think they can save all or part of that 2 to 8 percent administrative fee by taking care of the hiring process themselves. They also evaluate how much of their time and energy they want to spend on human resource issues. The fact that the employee-leasing industry is growing at a rapid rate indicates that increasing numbers of small-business owners have made the decision that the 2 to 8 percent charged in fees is worth the expense.

Mastering the interview process

Yes, the interview process is time-consuming and will take you away from other projects that may appear to be more meaningful and that are certainly more enjoyable. But remember, the price you'll pay for doing a second-rate job of hiring is that you'll have to do the costly, time-consuming process all over again — sooner rather than later.

The process of hiring superstar employees (that is, all employees who aren't in line for part-time or minimum-wage positions) should proceed along these lines:

1. **Interview #1:** This interview takes place in your office. During it, you ask probing questions, and the interviewee does about 90 percent of the talking. (If he doesn't do that much of the talking, *you're* talking too much.) Immediately following the interview, assuming it goes well, begin the reference-checking process while the details are still fresh in your mind.

2. **Interview #2:** Meet on neutral turf this time, maybe for breakfast or lunch. Relax the interviewee, loosen him up, and get a look at his social and personal side. Ask any puzzling questions that may have emerged as a result of the reference checks.

   Simply observe the applicant's behavior. Don't ask personal questions that may get you into areas that you legally can't enter. For instance, don't ask the applicant's age, race, religion, nationality, or political per-suasion. And don't inquire about his marital status, parental status, or wealth. Doing so could land you in court.

3. **Interview #3:** If all has gone well, have the applicant go through the interviewing process with other key employees who have a stake in the hire. Ask for their opinions and compare notes. If the applicant doesn't mesh with your key employees, finding out now is better than finding out later.

4. **Interview #4:** Review, negotiate, and seal the deal — if the applicant still passes muster. Then cross your fingers; employees don't come with guarantees, no matter how thorough a job you do. (Fortunately, your odds will improve with your hiring experience.)

When you interview an applicant, be sure to ask open-ended questions. *Open-ended questions* are those that can't be answered adequately with a simple yes or no; the questions are designed primarily to get the interviewee talking. Here are a few of our favorite open-ended questions that can help you discover those superstar job applicants:

✔ **What's the number one trait that differentiates you from other applicants?** You want something measurable here — specific accomplishments, specific skills, or specific prior jobs. Get inside the general statements like "I'm a people person" or "I meet my deadlines" or "I'm a hard worker" by asking specific questions: "What makes you a people person? Give me an example." Watch out for egotistical and egocentric responses; large egos usually get in the way of becoming a team player.

✔ **What's your most significant business achievement?** Again, look for specifics. If this is the applicant's first job, ask for her most significant achievement in whatever else she has done — schooling, homemaking, and so on.

✔ **What was your biggest failure and what did you learn from it?** Look for honesty here. Everyone has had failures. Promising applicants have no trouble admitting theirs and are quick to tell you what they learned from them. Insecure applicants have trouble admitting failure and, thus, may have a difficult time learning from it.

✔ **What are your weaknesses?** Everyone has weaknesses (including your humble authors). The honest and mature applicant readily admits his or hers. If the applicant can't come up with any, soften the question to "What kind of work do you dislike?" or "What aspects of this job will you enjoy the most and what will you enjoy the least?"

✔ **What are your strengths?** Look for specifics — again. Ask for examples. Do the candidate's strengths match the needs of the position?

✔ **Who's the best boss you've ever worked for and what made him or her so good?** The answer to this question will give you an insight into what it takes to motivate the interviewee. Also, it should indicate whether he could, and should, work for you.

✔ **Who was the worst boss you've ever worked for and what made him or her so bad?** Watch for whining and the blame game here. The answer to this question will give you a good idea of how the interviewee deals with adversity.

✔ **What do you want to be doing five years from now?** The "right" answer to this question is determined by the position you're hiring for and your own personal goals for the company. For game-breaker positions in a growing company, for instance, you may look for an answer signifying that the candidate wants increasing responsibility over the next five years. On the other hand, if you're hiring someone into, say, a truck-driver position from which you don't anticipate promotion possibilities, you may hope that the candidate's response is that he wants to be doing the same thing five years from now that he'd be doing today — driving a truck.

Training: An Investment, Not an Expense

Training is generally recognized as the most efficient and least expensive answer to employee improvement. Unfortunately, however, training remains close to the bottom of too many small-business owners' priority lists. Too often, small-business owners view training as an expense rather than as an investment that comes back in the form of increased productivity.

We've heard too many small-business owners complain about the cost of training, especially when that training results in the employee moving on to greener pastures — and taking her knowledge with her. Although such occurrences definitely do take place, part of the reason that employees move on is because they don't get the opportunity to receive the training they need. Besides, as the old saying goes, "If you think training employees and watching them leave is expensive, try not training them and watching them stay!"

Training comes in many forms and from various sources. Unlike many large companies, which generate much of their training from in-house sources, small-business training usually comes from the outside. Here are your major training options:

- ✔ **Consultants and coaches:** Although consultants and coaches have the most potential as trainers, they're also the most expensive and risky (see Chapter 10).

- ✔ **Vendors:** Vendors can be an excellent resource for training, and they're less costly than consultants. Some vendors even provide free training on their products or services (see Chapter 10).

- ✔ **Seminars:** Seminars can be expensive in both dollars and time, and their potential value is difficult to predict. Good seminars are great bargains; bad ones are outlandish scams. The seminars with the best potential (and usually the least expensive) are those put on by your trade association at its annual trade shows, which are geared to the industry you're in (see Chapter 15).

- ✔ **Schooling:** This category includes universities, colleges, night schools, and vocational training. Although schooling is probably more dependable than seminars, the value is also difficult to predict. The benefit of the course depends largely on the quality of the instructor.

Consider offering a tuition-reimbursement program, whereby you reimburse employees' expenses for outside studies related to the business. The benefits to the company from such a program include goodwill, the development of a self-improvement culture, and the infusion of new ideas in its employees. Require a B grade (or better) for reimbursement, to be paid after the course is completed.

✔ **Books:** Books are a great value. In fact, a good book is the ultimate training bargain. Read it (or have your employees read it) between projects, put it down when you please, and refer to it always. Keep it forever or pass it on to a friend or another employee. If you extract and implement one good idea, no matter how small, the $20 you spent is quickly repaid, many times over. Every good idea after the first one is a bonus. (Audio and video courses fall into this same category.)

✔ **The Internet:** The web is becoming an increasingly valuable training tool for both small-business owners and employees. More and more training classes are appearing on the Internet — some are for pay and some are for free. Be sure to investigate the agenda of the course sponsor. Is the sponsoring organization trying to sell you something, or is it interested in improving your business?

Motivating: Pay and Performance Issues

People who study such things tell us that the typical employee is motivated by the following (in this particular order):

1. Recognition or appreciation

2. Interesting work

3. Wages

4. Awareness of what's going on in the company

5. Good working conditions

6. Job security

7. Feeling that management cares about the employee

Meanwhile, the typical entrepreneur is motivated by one or more of the following (in no particular order):

✔ Creativity or growth

✔ Money

✔ Power

✔ Freedom

✔ Survival

Although the two lists have some overlap, the lesson here is that what motivates you, the employer, is, in most cases, quite different from what motivates your employees. So if you expect your employees to perform as you want them to, you must figure out how to motivate them differently than you motivate yourself.

To be a successful employer, you must adjust the way in which you envision the motivational process. The biblical Golden Rule needs its own special twist for employers: "Do unto your employees as they would have done unto themselves."

The following sections discuss the tools that play a primary role in the motivational process: compensation, goal-setting, performance expectations, and performance reviews. Look for the differences between you and your employees as you read.

Designing a compensation plan

Compensation (wages and/or salaries) is number three on the typical employee's list of key motivators. Although this news may be encouraging to the U.S. economic future, as well as to that of your own business, it becomes irrelevant when salary-review time comes around — Pee Wee Herman suddenly turns into Mike Tyson when his wages are on the line.

Finding out what employees really want

Employees are like spouses: Just when you think you have them figured out, they do or say something that leaves you scratching your head. Here's what we mean.

An acquaintance of ours is the local manager of a small wholesale business with 20 employees. One day, the home office sent a consultant to his branch to conduct an employee survey. The home office wanted to delve deeper into its employees' wants and needs, to find out what they liked and didn't like about the company, and to determine ways to improve the workplace environment. "A waste of time and money," our friend groused, as some managers (and owners) are prone to do when consultants come bearing suggestions. "I already know what my employees want: more money, more benefits, more vacation, and longer coffee breaks."

Well, the results from the survey came in and guess what? The employees asked for more of only one thing: training. That's a pleasant commentary on human nature, if you ask us — most people want to discover more about their jobs, improve their skills, and, in the process, be better off tomorrow than they are today. Most thinking employees (especially your potential "superstars") recognize that ongoing training is what gives them the opportunity to realize their goals.

Our friend went on to increase training, whereupon his company's 15 percent growth in profits doubled to 30 percent. And then, because the company paid its employees monthly bonuses (that's right, monthly!) based on profits, each employee received some healthy bonus dollars over the course of a year.

Training — it's a win-win situation, if ever there were one.

The next time the annual salary-setting time comes around in your company, try saying no to a few expected (and deserved) raises among your employees. Or try cutting the salary for a few of your good employees. Number three on the list suddenly becomes number one!

Nothing is more important than compensation on the day that you tell your employee whether he's getting a raise and how much it will be. Why? Because compensation is a black-and-white issue; your employees can look at it, compare it, and show it off to their loved ones. Compensation states what a particular employee is worth, in your — the boss's — eyes, anyway. Oh yes, and compensation can also be the first foot in the door when competitors come snooping around to hire away your best employees. (A healthy salary increase is usually the opener in negotiations between an employee and a prospective new employer.)

In the following sections, we dig deeper into the types of compensation you can provide and the best plans you can create for your company and employees.

Reviewing the types of compensation

You can compensate employees in a number of proven ways:

✔ **Hourly:** The original tool of the "paying for time" compensation method. It works for Honda and Wal-Mart, and it can work for you, too, especially for your part-time and entry-level employees.

✔ **Salaried:** The long-term version of "paying for time." Salaries usually come with annual cost-of-living raises and bonuses, typically ranging anywhere from 3 percent to 25 percent of base salary. (These bonuses should be based on performance and/or achievement of goals.) As a rule, salaries represent security to their recipients, and security is number six on the employee motivation list.

✔ **Commission:** Always the best compensation method for the hungry, hard-charging, sales types. Security isn't important to these folks; money, open ends, and opportunity are.

✔ **Pay-for-performance:** An increasingly popular alternative to the traditional "paying for time" compensation plans. Also called *gain-sharing* or *success-sharing,* pay-for-performance usually involves a relatively small base salary — often without annual cost-of-living adjustments — with all other compensation based on either individual or team performance (or a combination of both). Specific pay-for-performance plans are as varied and creative as the small businesses that use them, and they always require an efficient measuring system to back them up.

✔ **Hybrids:** A mix of annual salary, pay-for-performance, annual bonuses, stock-option plans (see Chapter 17), and whatever else you can devise.

Creating a plan that works for your business

The subject of compensation is one of those eye-of-the-beholder kinds of issues. If you view compensation as an expense when you establish a plan for your business, that's exactly what it will turn out to be — an out-of-pocket, painful expense, with all the downsides that the term implies. On the other hand, if you view your compensation plan as a motivational tool, you won't be creating and managing an expense account; you'll be developing an instrument to increase your employees' performance.

The best employees are the ones who believe they're valued and treated fairly. The best *measurable* (key word here!) method of that valuation is their salary. If your employees believe their wages are consistent with the value they deliver to your business, you won't have to motivate them because they'll motivate themselves. Poof! The salary expense account suddenly becomes a salary investment account. A huge difference!

The following list outlines our advice for devising a compensation plan that will work for *your* business:

- ✔ **Design your compensation plan *before* you hire your first employee.** Doing so ensures that you have a defined plan in place so you don't set precedents for your first employee that you'll later have to reset.

- ✔ **Make sure that your employees thoroughly understand whatever method you use to compensate them.** Paying for performance may make all kinds of motivational sense, but it works only if the employee understands what performance formula you're using and how she can impact the results.

- ✔ **Make sure that you can measure whatever needs measuring before you agree to pay for it.** Measurement is always easier said than done.

- ✔ **Be consistent within employee groups.** For example, with your salespeople, have one compensation method and be consistent within that group.

- ✔ **Remember that benefits are an important part of the compensation package — important to your employees' security and to your bottom line.** Consider them carefully and be sure that you (and your employees) know what they're worth (see Chapter 17).

- ✔ **Keep the time between bonus payments as short as possible.** Rewards, financial and otherwise, lose their impact when stretched out too long. The timing on when to give bonuses varies, but for most employees, in most cases, quarterly bonuses are the most effective. For some (high-impact managers), semi-annual or annual bonuses work better, since top management's accountability is typically more long term in nature. Avoid monthly bonuses; the administration is too much of a burden.

- ✔ **Contact your industry trade association if you're unsure of how much to pay your employees.** It may have information on what similar-sized businesses are paying employees in comparable positions.

- ✔ **Make any period-ending bonus meaningful in size.** We suggest that you make each bonus at least 3 percent of the employee's annual salary. We also recommend that you give it to the employee personally.

Your employee compensation plan is one area in which you don't want to be the early adopter. Make sure that other small businesses have successfully adopted the compensation plan you're contemplating. Changing compensation plans midstream can be quite detrimental to a team of employees, so try to get it right the first time. If you think you need to make changes, ask people who are cognizant of small-business compensation issues whether the changes you want to make can accomplish your objectives.

Bottom line: You can willingly spend a fortune compensating your employees, but if the dollars don't help motivate the people to whom you pay them, your compensation plan may be less than effective. The possibility exists, too, that you hired the wrong employee for the position. If that's the case, see the earlier hiring section for tips on upgrading your hiring skills, as well as the later section on firing.

Get SMART: Goal-setting that works

Everyone can use goals as a motivational tool — and not just when relating to the workplace. You can also use goals in raising kids, pursuing financial security, and improving your golf game. And we're not talking lighthearted New Year's resolutions here; we're talking *goals,* as in commitments to objectives.

Although the purpose of this section is to assist you in working with your employees to set goals that will motivate them, these suggestions can also help you with your own personal goals.

LIFO, FIFO, CRM, TQM — acronyms are everywhere these days. Even goal-setting comes with its own acronym — SMART — and here's how it works:

- ✔ **S = Specific.** Goals must be clear, direct, and definable.

- ✔ **M = Measurable and meaningful.** Goals must be measurable, in the sense that both employer and employee can assess whether the goal is achieved. And, of course, goals must be meaningful to both parties.

- ✔ **A = Appropriate.** Goals should be appropriate to the employee's experience, training, potential, and responsibilities.

✔ **R = Realistic.** Goals should challenge but be achievable. Eighty percent of the goal should be relatively easy to meet; 20 percent should be a stretch.

✔ **T = Time limit.** Goals should be achievable within a specified time frame.

The two biggest mistakes business owners make when setting goals for themselves, their businesses, and their employees are creating goals that aren't measurable and including a nonspecific time frame for the goals. Consider the following examples:

Non-SMART goal: "Increase sales and increase profitability by working smarter and harder." This goal isn't measurable, and it doesn't specify a time frame in which to measure it.

SMART goal: "Increase sales by 15 percent and increase profitability by 20 percent by the end of this fiscal year." Are these goals measurable? Yes. Is a workable time frame given? Yes. Are they achievable? You make the call.

Solve your employees' problems to solve your own

Joe, the owner of a small machine parts business, tells the following story:

Fred, my shipping and receiving supervisor, had been unusually quiet — bordering on morose — for the past several weeks. As a result, the rest of my employees started doing whatever they could to avoid communicating with him. Fred was also making an unusual number of mistakes, and whenever I corrected him, Fred shrugged his shoulders and would make the same mistake again. Finally, I called Fred into my office.

"Fred," I began, "you've worked for me for four years now, and I know the quality of work you can do. What you've been doing lately isn't up to your usual standards. This can't continue."

Fred's shoulders slumped, but he didn't argue. "I know," he whispered, his eyes gazing at the floor. "I'm sorry, Joe, but I can't keep my mind on my work."

"Okay, Fred, 'fess up. What's the trouble?"

"It's the IRS. I owe them $1,200, and I don't have the money. I don't know what they're going to do if I can't pay them by Friday."

I briefly excused myself, walked into the adjoining office, and returned with a check for $1,200 made out to Fred. "Fred, here's an interest-free loan," I said, handing him the check. "I'll deduct $25 a pay period until the loan has been repaid."

That was six months ago. Fred went back to being a great employee and enjoying his job again. Best darn investment I ever made.

"Hey, it was a no-brainer," Joe laughed, explaining why he decided so quickly to write Fred the check. "$1,200 is a small price to pay to keep a good employee. Aside from the fact that I owe Fred for his past performance, think how much I would spend hiring and training a new supervisor to replace him."

The following list outlines how you and your employees can set and achieve SMART goals:

- ✔ **Never set goals without first planning how to reach them.** For instance, wanting to increase sales by 15 percent isn't enough; you must have a game plan for how to do so.

- ✔ **Don't wait until the end of the goal-setting period to do the measuring.** Check progress informally as the mood strikes and formally at defined time intervals between now and the end of the goal-setting period.

- ✔ **Allow for the unexpected.** Changing goals midstream is acceptable if the reasons are right. Because the success of a small business is in part due to being able to make changes faster than its larger competitors, you should always build the likelihood of change into your goal-setting procedures.

- ✔ **Make a public announcement within the business (occasionally outside of the business when the goals reached are extraordinary) as soon as your business or your employees have achieved goals.** Let the celebration begin, let it be spontaneous, and let it be loud.

- ✔ **Understand that an employee may occasionally come up short on his goals.** What's not okay is for an employee to consistently come up short. In that event, something is wrong with either the employee or the goal-setting process (see the later section on firing if the employee is the issue).

Effective goal-setting should be a communal, bottoms-up process. The more involved your employees are in establishing their goals, the more committed they'll be to achieving them. Ask each employee to prepare her goals first, and then review them together, hone them together, and be sure to write them down, giving one copy to the employee and adding a second to her personnel file. Documenting goals makes the goal-setting process official and minimizes potential misunderstandings when performance-review time comes around.

Writing performance expectations

Many years ago, this section would've been called "Writing job descriptions," but in these days of empowered and enlightened employees, the term *job description* is a remembrance of the past. Today the correct term is *performance expectations*.

Although some companies may get by without using performance expectations (or the old-fashioned job descriptions), we think that most small-business owners would agree that employees need some degree of structure in their jobs. Performance expectations provide that structure; used correctly, they provide a loose but reliable framework to help the employee focus on the *results* of his activities, not on the activity itself. That's the key difference between job descriptions and performance expectations: *Job descriptions* focus on the activity of the position; *performance expectations* focus on the anticipated results.

For example, say a typical job description states that a salesperson is responsible for selling the company's products at the published prices, writing sales orders correctly, and making sure that the sales orders are submitted within a specified time. A performance expectation for the same position would require the salesperson to represent her company professionally (it would define the word *professional*), build ongoing relationships with customers and buyers, and assist the entire business team in realizing the specified departmental goals.

Writing performance expectations isn't as difficult as you may think. Here's how the writing process works:

- ✔ **Include a brief explanation of what the position's objective (or mission) is and how the position relates to the business's overall mission.** This explanation should appear at the beginning of the performance expectations.

- ✔ **Describe the position's location on the organization chart.** Include the immediate supervisor's title and the positions (if any) of those being supervised (see the later section "Designing Flexible Organization Charts" for details).

- ✔ **Define the performance evaluation process.** Who will perform the evaluation, when will it be done, and on what basis will the employee's performance be appraised?

- ✔ **Concentrate on output, not activity, and be careful not to limit the ways in which the job can be accomplished.** Define the responsibilities and allow the employee the freedom to make the job work.

- ✔ **Be flexible.** The world and your business will change, and your performance expectations need to change right along with them.

Employees aren't robots; the biggest mistake you can make is to develop performance expectations that restrict the employee's performance options. You should write the performance expectations before you advertise for the position; then after you've hired the new employee, review the performance expectations together and agree on the expected results. Try to avoid the number one headache of most employees: micromanagement. Give your employees the leeway to achieve the desired results without constantly looking over their shoulders.

Reviewing an employee's performance

How important is the performance review? Consider this: You're assigning a value to someone's existence in a place where he likely spends more than 50 percent of his waking hours during the workweek. If performance reviews aren't important, breathing isn't either!

The biggest problem with performance reviews is that the typical entrepreneur perceives the review as an opportunity to criticize the employee's performance rather than to improve it. Sure, criticism of past performance may be part of the review process, but so is the positive critique of performance. Everything you do in the performance review (including criticizing past performance and increasing compensation) is a means to improving future performance, not punishing or complaining about past performance.

Ensuring a successful review process

Good performance reviews don't just happen. They evolve as a result of a well-defined evaluation process that includes

- ✔ **Writing performance expectations:** Before you even hire an employee, you must establish written, meaningful standards by which to measure performance (see the preceding section for details).

- ✔ **Setting goals:** You must work with each employee to establish — and agree on — applicable SMART goals. You should develop these goals as soon as the employee is comfortably settled in her new job. (See the section on goal-setting earlier in this chapter.)

- ✔ **Creating critical-event memos:** You must document all critical events in an employee's day-to-day performance and file them in the employee's personnel file at the time they occur. That way, you can use them at review time to add objective support to your subjective observations.

These critical-event memos should include occurrences of positive as well as negative behavior. Because the purpose of reviews is to improve performance, you can usually earn more motivational mileage by pointing out the employee's successes than you can by itemizing her failures.

- ✔ **Providing interim feedback:** In between performance reviews, you should informally and regularly give employees feedback. Thus, by the time the next performance review comes around, the employee shouldn't have any surprises. If you're consistent in providing feedback to your employees, you'll give them plenty of time in between reviews to work on improving their behavior.

✔ **Conducting the annual performance and salary review:** At last, the main event! Now's the time to compare actual performance with expectations and goals, review critical-event memos, assign new wages, and agree on bonuses and perks, all while discussing goals and expectations for the future. Remember that the purpose of all these tasks is to motivate the employee to improve her performance in the upcoming period.

✔ **Scheduling the follow-up review:** You should hold follow-up reviews either quarterly or semiannually (although if the situation is dire enough, you can hold them monthly until the employee's performance has improved to your expectations). These follow-up reviews should be informal but well prepared, and during them, you need to provide feedback on the employee's progress since the annual review.

Holding effective reviews

The employee evaluation process is a natural progression that begins with performance expectations and goal-setting and ends with the performance and salary review and the follow-up review. The performance review itself is but one piece of the process; without the other pieces, the evaluation is incomplete. Don't expect earth-shattering results from performance reviews if you aren't willing to adopt the entire process.

Following are guidelines for providing effective performance reviews:

✔ **Hold the official review once a year.** Conduct the review on the employee's hiring anniversary or sometime around the beginning of your business's fiscal year.

✔ **Schedule the review well in advance, giving both parties plenty of time to prepare.** No phones, no interruptions. Go off-site if you expect the review to be stressful.

✔ **Prepare for the review with the same thoroughness as you would for any other important business meeting.** Keep in mind that reviews are benchmarks in the employee's career.

✔ **Begin each review with a generous helping of compliments, citing specific accomplishments and good work.** Get things off to a positive start. Reinforce the intent of the review early — to improve the employee's performance.

✔ **Evaluate the employee based on the past year's performance, not just the past month's.** We're talking careers here, not short-term trends.

✔ **Back up subjective comments with objective facts and stories.** These should come from the critical-event memos you've retained in the employee's personnel file.

✔ **Keep it a performance review, not a character review.** Keep personalities out of it.

✔ **Discuss changes in compensation after you critique the employee's performance but before you solicit feedback from the employee about the company.** Ask how he feels about the way the company is being run and what aspects could be better managed.

The timing here is important. You won't get frank feedback from most employees until they have the assurance — in the form of a pay change commitment from you — that negative comments won't get in the way of their pay increase. But if you discuss pay changes first, the employee may not be in the mood to listen well to the review.

When no pay increase is on the agenda, make sure during the course of the review that the employee knows exactly why an increase won't be forthcoming, and then conclude the review by asking the employee if he understands why. Also, be sure he knows when the next opportunity for pay increases will come and what he (and the business) must do to get his performance up to the level where he can expect an increase.

Dealing with failure

The best way to judge the immediate results of a performance review is by observing and asking how the employee feels about the review and change in compensation. If the employee is visibly upset and goes away angry, the review is a failure. If she goes away appearing to be motivated, the review is a success.

If the review is a failure — if you perceive that the employee doesn't go away motivated — one of two things may have happened:

✔ **You didn't conduct the review correctly.** If this is the case, we recommend that you try again a week or so later — after upgrading your presentation and explaining to the employee that you made some mistakes you'd like to correct. Yes, bosses and owners are human; they make mistakes, too!

✔ **You performed the review correctly, but the employee falls into the category of people who simply can't take criticism, constructive or otherwise.** If this is the case, the employee may not be the right person for the job. Observe the employee's performance over the next few weeks to watch for signs of improvement. If you don't see any, you may need to schedule a formal follow-up review or start considering termination (see the following section).

Parting Company: Firing an Employee

Firing an employee, as much as you'd like to avoid it, has its place in the growth of a successful business (though if you hire right, train right, and motivate right, it won't happen frequently). As long as employees are people, you'll occasionally have to fire them. As a matter of fact, if you *never* fire an employee, you're bound to have a handful of nonperforming employees on your payroll — a financial burden few small businesses can afford and a condition that won't be acceptable to the rest of your employees who *are* performing.

The small-business owner's fear of the dismissal process is usually worse than the event itself. After all, most employees know when they're not performing, and they're usually as unhappy in their jobs as you are in having them there. Yet, they're too afraid or insecure (or motivated by unemployment compensation laws) to make the first move, leaving the difficult work to you.

Using exit interviews to gain fresh perspective

Inevitably, your company will have employees who quit their jobs for one reason or another. These employees can be a valuable resource for you to tap into before they leave. During an *exit interview,* as the name implies, you interview the exiting employee to gain insights into the company that a current employee may be reluctant to provide. Exit interviews can be an excellent tool for seeing your business through the eyes of others, especially because you — the person at the top of the organization chart — have a unique perspective that may be narrow or skewed.

Be sure to include at least the following questions in an exit interview:

✔ What was the main factor in your decision to quit?

✔ What did you like the most about our company?

✔ What did you like the least?

✔ How do you rate such issues as working conditions, cooperation and teamwork, on-the-job training, supervision, opportunity for promotion, and communication?

✔ If you could change one thing about this company, what would it be?

Always interview employees who quit of their own volition. When possible, also give employees you fire an exit interview, remembering that the terminated employee may exaggerate your business's shortcomings. Never exit-interview an employee at the same time you're firing him; wait until later, when he returns to pick up a severance paycheck or personal belongings. Not every terminated employee is a candidate for an exit interview, of course; select only those who depart under circumstances that aren't overly combative.

Having to let an employee go is a fact of business life and, in the end, can be justified by your obligation to your business's existence and to your team of employees who are performing. After all, you have an obligation to them to build a cohesive team that's as good as it can be, and you can't meet that obligation when nonperforming employees are on board. You're not passing judgment on the person being dismissed; rather, you're passing judgment on the performance of the employee in that particular job. His or her talents, which may be many, may simply lie elsewhere — within or outside of your company.

Here's our advice to help you get through the unpleasant task of firing an employee:

- ✔ **Explore all the alternatives before settling on dismissal.** Alternatives include demotion, grace periods, personalized retraining, and consultant contracts (hiring the employee as a consultant outside of the business to do only specific, one-time jobs). When the alternatives won't work, record the reasons why. The employee may ask.

- ✔ **Do the firing as soon as possible after you make the decision to terminate.** The longer you wait, the more likely it is that word will leak out to the soon-to-be-fired employee.

- ✔ **Know the laws of your state.** For example, do you need to provide documentation? Check with your attorney before firing a longtime employee or a member of a minority group if the reasons for the termination may appear vague to the person being terminated. You also need to involve your attorney when the firing is for an offense (sexual harassment, fighting, and other such incidents) that may wind up as a lawsuit.

- ✔ **Prepare the firing package in the same organized and documented manner in which you prepared the hiring package.** Include, where applicable, severance pay, continuance of health insurance, duration of benefits and perks (memberships, subscriptions, and so on), and return of company assets (keys and computers, for example).

- ✔ **Plan the firing meeting as you would any other important business meeting.** Organize in advance, outline your presentation, and have handouts prepared if necessary. Make the dismissal as businesslike as possible, and, above all, avoid sentimentality and reminiscing. Keep emotions subdued; they only make matters worse.

- ✔ **Perform the termination first thing in the morning.** Doing so allows the employee to leave the company and have the rest of the day to gather his composure. At a minimum, pay the employee through the end of that day and perhaps even the rest of the week or month to help him stay on his feet financially.

✔ **Don't argue.** State the reasons and the facts surrounding the termination. Show the supporting documents. Arguing will only further incense the person being fired. Let the employee rant and rave if he chooses; he may feel better when he's done, and, as a result of your listening, you may find out something about how to be a better manager for the future.

✔ **Arrange for outplacement services.** Small businesses can learn this lesson from watching their *Fortune* 500 cousins perfect the ritual of downsizing. You can soften the firing by helping the employee get back on his feet again.

Firing an employee plays an important role in the process of building a company, but it will never be an enjoyable part, no matter how much practice you may have at it. When you're feeling especially sorry for yourself because you have to fire an employee, keep in mind that the situation is a heck of a lot tougher on the person sitting on the other side of your desk.

Designing Flexible Organization Charts

Some say that *organization charts* — a graphic depiction of your company's chain of command — are out of style. All you have to do, these people tell us, is empower your employees and then step aside while the jobs get done. No layers, no politics, no people caught in the middle — or so the story goes. Today's empowered employees don't require management, they conclude; they simply need a flexible and lenient work environment.

We respectfully disagree. We're firm believers in organization charts and in the chain of command, but only when the person at the top of the chain is worthy of the position. We further believe that someone must manage employees, motivate them, and help them improve their performance. Someone must also promote them, demote them, and, on occasion, fire them. Like it or not, employees, we believe, have to work for somebody.

Even so, organization charts — especially in small business — shouldn't be carved in stone. You don't want to live or die by the constrictions of your organization chart. It should serve as a structural guideline for making decisions and assigning responsibility — nothing more. So use it administratively, but bend it and mold it to fit the skills of your employees and the ever-changing needs of your company. For instance, feel free to assemble creative and temporary secondary charts from time to time to accomplish those complicated projects and one-time jobs.

Here's how to construct your business's organization chart and use it effectively:

- ✔ **Construct the organization chart based on the employees, not the "organization."** For instance, if one person is particularly knowledgeable about the project-du-jour, give her the senior responsibility for that job. (This structure means that your sales manager may be working on a project headed by a computer clerk — if the computer clerk knows more about the project than the sales manager.)

- ✔ **Pay by the quality of each employee's performance and his contribution to the team, not his position on the organization chart.** So although the sales manager and the operations manager may be on the same tier of the chart, they may be compensated quite differently, based on the degree of difficulty of the position, the number of people being managed, and the relative importance of sales and operations to the overall success of the company.

- ✔ **Determine how many employees one person can supervise.** The answer depends on the quality of the team you've assembled. One is plenty if that one is like some people we've seen over the years. On the other hand, eight employees may be a snap to manage if those eight are good ones. Typically, an experienced manager can handle managing five to seven employees.

Flatter organization charts (those with fewer tiers) are better, especially when you have the right employees. Flatter organization charts mean better communication — from top to bottom and bottom to top — because the communication doesn't have to pass through intermediaries. The more tiers you have in your organization charts, the more chances you have for the message to be garbled or misconstrued.

Valuing Employee Manuals

In terms of excitement, the employee manual ranks right up there with ordering toner cartridges for your copy machine. Most entrepreneurs don't rank it in the top ten list of Things We Can Hardly Wait to Do.

However, as soon as employees are on your payroll, you need to add employee manuals to your business's preventive medicine kit. A well-prepared manual can save its user pain later. The employee manual is important because of the varied and important functions it fulfills. Behold what a well-prepared employee manual can do for you:

- ✔ **The employee manual provides the first opportunity to define your corporate missions and goals to your new employees and sets the tone for what's to come.** Imagine the message that a well-prepared employee manual sends to the recently hired employee when her questions are succinctly answered in an organized and thorough manner. (Imagine the message you send when those questions *aren't* answered!)

- ✔ **The employee manual saves time — time spent on resolving problems that established policies in a manual would've prevented in the first place.** The employee manual also saves time spent by explaining the basics of the job, such as hours of work, vacation and sick days, and termination policies.

- ✔ **The employee manual saves time, effort, and money spent on lawyers by establishing company policies for all to see.** By stating company policies publicly and in writing, you quickly and succinctly alert potential problem employees to the fact that they must either find a way to work within your policies or seek employment elsewhere.

The best way to assemble your employee manual is to use someone else's as a template — a neighboring small business, a vendor, or a small business that you've frequented over the years. Worthy employee manuals tend to make the rounds from small business to small business — with good reason. The ones that have survived have already been tried and tested and can serve as a guide for constructing yours.

When compiling your employee manual (whether you prepare it yourself or you use someone else's as a template), be sure to do the following:

- ✔ **Include a statement of your company's mission and goals.** Keep it brief, make it specific, and put it at the beginning of the manual where you know employees will read it.

- ✔ **Include an *employment-at-will statement* (which says that you aren't restricted to firing only for cause) if you reside in a state where it's applicable.** An attorney experienced in small-business management can advise you on the laws of your state.

- ✔ **Declare early on that the employee manual isn't a contract and that it can, and undoubtedly will, change.** Don't overlook the employee manual, or it will quickly become out of date and out of mind.

- ✔ **Include an equal-opportunity statement.** An equal-opportunity statement is a clause that states that qualified applicants are considered for all open positions for which they apply and for advancement without regard to race, color, religion, sex, sexual orientation, national origin, age, marital status, the presence of a medical condition or disability, or genetic information.

✔ **Spell out the benefits you offer, such as health insurance, maternity leave, profit sharing, company-reimbursed education, and so on.** Where applicable, include the details of the insurance plans in attachments.

✔ **Define policies regarding the workday.** Also include policies regarding overtime pay, time off, and breaks, as well as those concerning performance reviews, promotions, and wage increases.

✔ **Develop and define a drug and alcohol policy, including pre-employment screening and post-accident testing (if any).** Given the many negatives that result from alcohol and drug use in the workplace, you need to let your employees know exactly how you feel on the subject, what the rules are, and how transgressions will be dealt with.

✔ **Define standards of conduct such as dress, timeliness, and consideration of others.** Include causes for disciplinary action and termination, along with severance pay policies.

✔ **Keep the employee manual current as you go and keep your employees abreast of the changes.** Post any changes on the bulletin board at the same time that you hand out or e-mail revision attachments for your employees' manuals. You may also consider posting a copy online in a portion of your website that's accessible only to employees.

Before you distribute the completed manual to employees, have an attorney who's experienced in working with small businesses and employee handbooks review and edit it. That review, while potentially costly, could save you a great deal of grief and money down the road.

Turning the Tables: Characterizing Successful Employers

No two small businesses are alike. The reasons behind one small business's success are often greatly different from the reasons behind a second one's success. One succeeds because of its marketing efforts, another because of its product or service quality. One focuses on customers, another on employees. One has an awesome in-house sales force, another utilizes an eye-catching catalog to sell its products.

However, every successful small business (one that includes employees, anyway) has three identifiable characteristics, no matter its niche, product, or service: flexibility, accountability, and follow-up.

Flexibility: The bending of rules

Consider the following examples of when flexibility should play a big role in your management decisions:

- ✔ **Employees:** You say you have a good employee who needs additional time off to resolve a family situation? Nuts to the rules. Give him the time off and help him solve his problem. You say you have a good employee who needs a flexible work schedule to honor her responsibilities at home? What are you waiting for? Create a flexible work schedule and help her solve her problem.

- ✔ **Loyal, paying customers:** Rules are meant to be bent when it comes to loyal, paying customers. You say you have a good customer who needs an additional 30 days to pay an especially large invoice? Then 30 more days it is. You say you have a good customer who needs his products individually shrink-wrapped rather than bulk-wrapped? Then shrink-wrapped it is. (Yes, you may have to adjust your price to cover the additional cost.)

- ✔ **Organization charts:** As we say earlier in this chapter, you should use organization charts only for administrative and structural purposes. If you look at your business as providing solutions rather than merely following rules, you'll be better able to meet the demands of today's ever-changing business life.

Don't get us wrong; we're not saying that you should flexibly manage everything in your business. To the contrary, a small business does need to include a number of inflexible rules and regulations among its management tools. For instance, you need inflexible rules and regulations to manage such things as

- ✔ **Ethics and principles:** If ethics and principles are flexible, they aren't ethics and principles.

- ✔ **Expense controls:** The best small businesses are those that are as aware of their expenses as they are of their sales. You need to control your expenses inflexibly.

- ✔ **Quality:** Quality can't be flexible. The product or service is either fit for your most-demanding customer or it's unfit for any of your customers. There's no middle ground.

But where people enter into the picture, flexibility is the order of the day, because people are different and unique and, well, flexible. One employee's reward may be another employee's punishment. Just as no two people are alike, no two responses to management are the same.

Accountability: So the buck doesn't get passed

Your employees really have two options when you ask them to perform a task: Either they do it or they don't. When they don't perform the designated task, the question you must ask is "why didn't they do it?" The answers to that question can include the following:

- ✔ **The employee is incapable of performing the task.** Your options are to reassign the task, reassign the employee, or replace the employee.

- ✔ **The employee isn't properly trained.** In this case, you must train the employee.

- ✔ **The task and its priority weren't clearly communicated.** Your job is to communicate the task more clearly.

- ✔ **The employee saw no good reason to accomplish the task and, thus, elected not to do it.** In this case, either your company doesn't include accountability as part of its culture or you made a serious hiring mistake.

Accountability — being responsible for your own actions — is a cultural issue. It begins with you holding your employees accountable and then trickles down through your organization. In the process of creating an accountable culture, you must provide a system of rewards when employees perform and consequences when they don't.

To determine whether your small business has an accountable culture, answer the following four questions:

- ✔ Do your employees have the motivation to achieve what you want them to achieve?

- ✔ Does achievement make a difference in the success of the team, and do you and your employees know how to recognize that difference?

- ✔ Can the other members of the team tell when an employee has achieved or not achieved?

- ✔ Do your employees know that they have to achieve, or is achievement only one of their options?

In the process of answering these questions, you'll quickly recognize the four elements required to differentiate an accountable culture from an unaccountable one:

- ✔ Employees have to have a reason to achieve.

- ✔ Achievement has to be recognized throughout the company.

> ✔ Employees should receive rewards when they do achieve.
>
> ✔ Consequences have to be in place when employees don't achieve the goals you've agreed on.

Put these elements together and you can, within a relatively short period of time, create a culture that promotes accountability. Although the manner in which business owners install these elements may vary, all businesses have one thing in common: They always begin at the top — with you.

Follow-up: The more you do it, the less you need it

Why should you follow up? After all, you've already gotten whatever it was off your desk the first time. Why must you do it all over again? After all, if *you* were an employee, you sure wouldn't have to be followed up. But (and this is the last time you'll hear this) you aren't an employee. You're an entrepreneur, and if you don't remember the difference, you may not be in business for long. If you don't follow up with your employees, missions and goals won't be missions and goals anymore; they'll be hopes and wishes. And hopes and wishes don't build businesses; they only create dreams.

The good news is that when your employees know that follow-up is coming, the need for it decreases. Translation: When you have an accountable culture firmly in place, you won't have to follow up as much anymore.

In the beginning, when your business's culture is being established, you have to follow up on every commitment made, large or small. You can do so by making a simple notation on the calendar and transferring it to the to-do list on the appropriate day.

Never stop trying to collect that team of superstars we mention earlier in the chapter. After all, superstars don't need to be rigorously followed up (if they do, they're not superstars!), which means that employing them will allow you to spend more time doing the things you want to do (like growing your business; see Chapter 20).

Chapter 17

Providing Employee Benefits

. . . .

In This Chapter

▶ Selecting a retirement plan for you and your company

▶ Exploring the option of sharing equity with your employees

▶ Designing and securing a quality health-insurance plan

▶ Making sense of disability, life, and other insurance plans and benefits

. . . .

*W*hat do you think is the most valuable benefit an employee can receive from an employer? If you answered health insurance, you have plenty of company. According to the Employee Benefit Research Institute (EBRI), by a 3:1 margin, American workers view their health insurance as their most prized employee benefit in comparison to retirement benefits.

However, if you examine the monetary value of all benefits that employers offer, retirement plan benefits are actually the most financially valuable in the long run.

This chapter is all about benefits, so read on to find out which ones may make sense for your company to offer.

Seeing the Real Value in Retirement Plans

For sure, other benefits such as life and disability insurance may be important to many employees. These benefits, however, are far less valuable (and far less costly) than retirement plan benefits, and employees often can easily purchase them on their own as long as they don't have a preexisting medical condition. Although health insurance is usually more costly to replace than disability or life insurance, employees can purchase it, too.

If retirement benefits are so valuable, why do so few workers recognize that fact? Several reasons may explain why people value their health benefits above their retirement benefits:

- ✔ **The absence of health benefits can be financially catastrophic if a major illness arises.** If you do have a preexisting health condition, being able to jump into an employer's group plan without a health evaluation can mean the difference between getting health-care coverage and going without.

- ✔ **Younger employees view retirement as something far in the future and intangible.** Consider this testimonial from a baby boomer named Alice: "I personally believe in the importance of retirement savings and wish I had started sooner. While some younger employees may not value these benefits, eventually they probably will and will be grateful."

- ✔ **Employees often don't know what retirement benefits are worth because many companies do a poor job of educating and promoting their value.** For example, with a *pension plan,* an employer sets aside money separate from an employee's salary to fund the monthly pension payment to be paid during the employee's retirement years. Unlike with a *retirement savings plan,* such as a 401(k) — where you can see the current account value — employers generally don't prepare individual pension statements showing the total amount contributed for each employee and the investment returns on that money.

The lesson here: If you aren't getting sufficient bang from your benefit dollars, you probably aren't communicating the value of those benefits properly. After all, most employees don't come armed with the basic knowledge they need to understand the value of the benefits you're offering; you need to educate them.

If you're still dreaming about starting your own business, don't view your current employer's benefits package as a ball and chain tying you to your current job. As a small-business owner, you can replace the benefits provided by your former employer on your own, and you can establish a SEP-IRA or Keogh retirement plan to tax-shelter your self-employment earnings. In fact, SEPs and Keoghs, which we discuss later in this section, may allow you to shelter far more money than most corporate retirement plans do.

Getting the most value from your plan

Retirement plans are a terrific way for small-business owners and their employees to tax-shelter a healthy portion of their earnings. If you don't have employees, regularly contributing to one of these plans is usually a no-brainer.

With employees, the decision is a bit more complicated, but contributing is still often a great idea because it helps you attract and retain good employees.

Self-employed people may contribute to Keoghs or SEP-IRAs. Small businesses with a number of employees should also consider 401(k) and SIMPLE plans. The following sections walk you through these and other options you have when providing yourself and your employees with retirement benefits.

With SEP-IRA and Keogh plans, if you have employees, you're required to make contributions on their behalf that are comparable to the company owners' contributions (as a percentage of salary). Some employees who are part-time (working fewer than 500 or 1,000 hours per year) or newer (with less than a few years of service) may be excluded. Small-business owners often set up plans for themselves but fail to cover their employees because either they don't know about this requirement or they choose to ignore it. Be forewarned — the IRS and state tax authorities may discover that you've neglected to make contributions for eligible employees, sock you with big penalties, and disqualify your prior contributions. Because self-employed people and small businesses get their taxes audited at a relatively high rate, don't take risks in this area (see Chapter 19 for more on small-business taxes).

Don't avoid establishing a retirement savings plan for your business just because you have employees and you don't want to make contributions on their behalf. In the long run, you build the contributions that you make for your employees into their total compensation packages, which include salary and other benefits like health insurance. Making retirement contributions doesn't have to increase your personnel costs.

SEP-IRAs

Simplified Employee Pension Individual Retirement Account plans (SEP-IRAs), which are geared to owners, require minimal paperwork to set up. They allow you to sock away up to 20 percent of your *self-employment income* (business revenue minus expenses) up to a maximum of $49,000 (for 2011) per year. Each year, you decide the amount that you want to contribute; the plan has no minimum requirement. Your contributions to a SEP-IRA are deducted from your taxable income, saving you on federal and state taxes. As with other retirement plans, your money compounds without taxation until you withdraw it.

Keoghs

Keogh plans require a bit more paperwork to set up and administer than SEP-IRAs. The main difference, and attraction, of Keogh plans is that they allow you, the small-business owner, to maximize contributions relative to employees in two ways that you can't with SEP-IRAs:

- ✔ **Vesting schedules:** Keogh plans allow *vesting schedules,* which require employees to remain with your company for a specified number of years before they earn the right to their full retirement account balances. *Vesting* refers to the portion of the money in a retirement account that's owned by the employee. After a certain number of years, employees become fully vested and, therefore, own 100 percent of the funds in their retirement accounts. If they leave prior to being fully vested, they lose the unvested balance, which reverts to the remaining plan participants. Thus, when you offer Keogh plans, you give employees a good reason to stay rather than leave.

- ✔ **Social Security integration:** Keogh plans allow for *integration,* which allows high-income earners at your company (usually you and the other owners or executives) to receive larger percentage contributions than the less highly compensated employees. The logic behind this idea is that Social Security taxes top out after you earn more than $106,800 (for 2011). Social Security integration allows you to make up for this ceiling.

Defined-benefit plans

Defined-benefit plans are for people who are able and willing to put away more than the $49,000 per year currently allowed (as of 2011) with SEP-IRA and Keogh plans. As you can imagine, only a very small percentage of people can afford to do this. Consistently high-income earners older than age 45 or so who want to save more than $49,000 per year in a retirement account should consider these plans. If you're interested in defined-benefit plans, ask your tax advisor or hire an actuary to crunch the numbers to calculate how much you can legally contribute to such a plan.

401(k) plans

Many for-profit companies offer *401(k) plans.* The silly name comes from the section of the tax code that establishes and regulates these plans. The 401(k) plan allows you to stash away up to $16,500 per year (for 2011). (***Note:*** An individual plan's contribution limits may be lower if not enough employees save enough in the company's 401(k) plan.) Those employees who are 50 and older may put away an additional $5,500 per year.

Your contributions to a 401(k) are generally excluded from your reported income and, thus, are free from federal and, in most cases, state income taxes, but not Social Security and Medicare taxes. An employer may make contributions to an employee's accounts as well. Similar to the employee's contribution, these contributions are tax deferred until retirement.

Because of the cost of establishing and maintaining a 401(k) plan, such plans generally make the most sense for larger (20 or more employees) and consistently profitable small companies. You may want to make employees wait a year following employment before contributing to a 401(k) plan to make sure that the employee is one that you want to keep over the long term and to ensure that you have adequate time to educate them about the virtues of your plan so that they'll view it as a valued benefit. To encourage participation, consider matching a portion of the employees' contributions.

The best investment companies through which to consider establishing a 401(k) plan are the bigger and better mutual fund companies, such as T. Rowe Price (www.troweprice.com; 800-492-7670), Vanguard (www.vanguard.com; 800-662-2003), and Fidelity (www.fidelity.com; 800-343-0860). In some cases, your company may need to work with a separate — usually local — plan administrator, in addition to one of these investment firms. These excellent investment companies can also recommend an administrator to help you with all the tedious aspects of 401(k) plan paperwork and accounting.

403(b) plans

If you happen to be running a nonprofit organization, you can offer a *403(b) plan* to your employees. As with a 401(k), contributions to a 403(b) plan are federal and state tax deductible. Unlike a 401(k) plan, a 403(b) plan includes virtually no out-of-pocket setup expenses or ongoing accounting fees. The only requirement is that the organization must deduct the appropriate contributions from employees' paychecks and send the money to the investment company handling the 403(b) plan.

Nonprofit employees generally are allowed to contribute up to 20 percent or $16,500 (for 2011) of their salaries, whichever is less. Employees who are 50 and older can contribute more — up to $22,000 in 2011 — and employees who have 15 or more years of service may be allowed to contribute a few thousand dollars beyond these limits.

The best place to establish a 403(b) plan is through the leading mutual fund companies that we mention in the preceding section — Vanguard, Fidelity, or T. Rowe Price — all of which offer proven mutual funds and 403(b) plans to invest in.

Don't invest through *tax-sheltered annuities,* the name for insurance-company investments that satisfy the requirements for 403(b) plans. Such plans have higher fees and worse investment performance than the better mutual fund companies' 403(b) plans.

SIMPLE plans

If you think that the people in Congress have nothing better to do with their time than to keep tinkering with tax laws and cooking up even more retirement plan options, you may be right! Yet another retirement plan, the *SIMPLE plan,* was introduced in the late 1990s. *SIMPLE* stands for Savings Incentive Match Plans for Employees.

SIMPLE-IRAs have a contribution limit of $11,500 per year (for 2011). Older workers (age 50 and over) can put away even more — $14,000 in 2011. As compared to 401(k) plans, SIMPLE plans offer somewhat easier reporting requirements and fewer administrative hassles.

Employers are required to make small contributions on behalf of employees. The employer can either match, dollar-for-dollar, the employee's first 3 percent contributed or contribute 2 percent of pay for everyone whose wages exceed $5,000.

Interestingly, if the employer chooses the first option, the employer has an incentive not to educate employees about the value of contributing to the plan because the more employees contribute, the more it costs the employer. And unlike a 401(k) plan, greater employee contributions don't enable higher-paid employees to contribute more.

Convincing employees that retirement plans matter

The single biggest mistake that people at all income levels make with regard to retirement planning is not taking advantage of retirement accounts. For folks in their 20s and 30s (and for some even in their 40s and 50s), living for today seems a whole lot more fun than saving for the future.

Assuming that you don't want to work your entire life, the sooner you start to save, the less painful saving for retirement will be each year, because your contributions have more years to compound. Each decade that you delay approximately doubles the percentage of your earnings that you need to save in order to meet your financial goals. For example, if saving 10 percent per year in your early 30s would get you to your retirement goal, waiting until your 40s may mean putting away about 20 percent of your pretax (gross) earnings.

The longer you wait, the more of your income you have to save for retirement and, therefore, the less you have left over to spend during your earning years *and* your retirement years. As a result of not starting soon enough, you may not meet your retirement-savings goal, and your golden years may be more tarnished than golden.

So instead of waiting to set up a retirement account, consider all the benefits that you and your employees can reap by saving and investing in some type of retirement account now. These benefits include the following:

  ✔ **Contributions offer immediate tax savings.** Retirement accounts should really be called *tax-reduction accounts.* If you're a moderate-income earner, you probably pay about 35 percent in federal and state income taxes. Thus, with most of the retirement accounts described in this section, for every $1,000 you contribute into them, you save yourself about $350 in taxes in the year that you make the contribution.

✔ **Investment earnings accumulate tax-deferred.** Inside a retirement account, contributions accumulate interest, dividends, and appreciation without being taxed. You get to defer taxes on all the accumulating gains and profits until you withdraw the money, presumably in retirement. Thus, more money is working for you over a longer period of time. Even if your retirement tax rate is the same as your tax rate during your employed years, you still come out ahead by contributing money into retirement accounts. In fact, because you defer paying taxes and have more money compounding over more years, you can end up with *more* money in retirement even if your retirement tax rate is higher.

As we mention earlier in the chapter, most people don't value retirement plan benefits for the simple reason that they don't understand them. So, as an employer, to get the most employee appreciation from your retirement plan, do the following:

✔ **Educate your employees about the value of retirement savings plans.** For example, people, on average, need about 75 percent of their pre-retirement income throughout retirement to maintain their standard of living. See the latest edition of Eric's book *Personal Finance For Dummies* (Wiley) for helpful background information about why people should be planning ahead financially for the golden years. Get your employees to understand and appreciate your investment in their financial futures.

✔ **Use your plan as an incentive to retain employees.** Many small businesses have trouble with employee turnover. But with particular types of Keogh plans, for example, employees must stay a certain number of years to become vested in their contributions. (For more on vesting, see the section "Keoghs" earlier in this chapter.)

✔ **Select the plan that best meets your business needs.** Consider offering a 401(k) or a SIMPLE plan, which allows employees to contribute money from their paychecks.

Deciding Whether to Share Equity

As we discuss in Chapter 5, one decision that all small-business owners must confront in the early days is whether to go it alone or take on partners. If you decide to have partners, you'll probably share ownership with some or all of those partners. Even if you go solo, over time you may benefit from sharing equity with key employees or even all your employees.

Why would you want to consider sharing equity with your employees? The answer is simple: Doing so aligns their incentives with yours. After all, one of the reasons that you may have started a small business is to benefit from the economic rewards of your work. Sharing equity allows others to benefit along with you. If your employees simply draw a standard paycheck, they have less incentive to work toward boosting the short- and long-term profitability of your business.

Not surprisingly, sharing equity also has downsides. One is that some small-business owners end up giving away too much too quickly and too easily. If you give away too much ownership to employees or outside investors, you may find yourself a *minority shareholder* (owning less than 50 percent of your business) and no longer in control of the destiny of your enterprise or your own job security.

Additionally, as a result of their ownership, minority shareholders have rights and, therefore, interests that may not always align with yours. (The extent of their rights depends on the state in which you live.) This disparity in interest is especially true when a minority shareholder leaves the company either on his own or with a push from you.

In Chapter 16, we discuss the importance of hiring the best people that you can into key positions in your company. In order for you to attract and retain superstar employees for the critical positions in your company, you may need or want to offer some equity to those employees. Just be sure to use a lawyer when creating an ownership position (no matter how small) within your business, and be sure to consider the downsides of sharing ownership. For info on the types of equity and tips for how to handle them, keep reading.

Stock and stock options

Shares of ownership in a company are known as *stock*. The number of shares of stock in a company is an arbitrary item. Suppose, for example, that your company is *capitalized at* (viewed to be worth) $500,000. You could have 1,000 shares of stock, 10,000 shares of stock, 100,000 shares of stock, or any number of shares of stock your heart desires. If you have 1,000 shares of stock, the price or value per share is $500, whereas if you have 100,000 shares, the price per share is $5.

When hiring a key employee, you can simply grant that person a certain number of shares of stock that he or she will receive after staying with you for a certain period of time. Alternatively, you can grant *stock options,* which allow the key employee to buy a specified number of shares of your company's stock at a predetermined price within a defined future period.

Continuing with the previous example, suppose you have 100,000 shares of stock in your company and the price is $5 per share, for a total value of $500,000. You've been interviewing a prospective star marketing manager, and you want to offer her some financial upside if she's able to help you expand your company. After some conversations, you decide that you'll offer her stock options to purchase up to 5,000 shares of your company's stock (5 percent of the total company stock) within the next five years at a price per share of $5. Five years from now, if your marketing manager and other key players have done their jobs, your company should be worth a whole lot more than it is now, and your stock should be worth much more than $5 per share, thus enriching the stock-option holder's compensation.

Here are some tips for offering stock and stock options to key employees:

✔ **Make sure that the employee is a keeper.** Just as you should date a person before marrying, make sure that you've had ample opportunity to observe firsthand an employee's abilities and shortcomings before you offer him equity. Just because someone has an impressive resume and comes across well in a job interview doesn't mean that he'll work well in your company and is worthy of equity from day one.

✔ **Make 'em earn it.** In most cases, vesting your key employee(s) in a certain portion of the stock per year makes good sense. (See the earlier section "Keoghs" for more on vesting.)

✔ **Get expert help.** Issuing stock and granting stock options can get complicated fairly quickly and, once consummated, is irrevocable unless agreed to by both parties. Get good tax and legal advisors on your team (see Chapter 10 for tips on working with lawyers and Chapter 19 for tips on working with tax advisors).

Employee Stock Ownership Plans (ESOPs)

The Washington, D.C.–based Employee Stock Ownership Plan (ESOP) Association defines an *ESOP* as "an employee benefit plan which makes the employees the owners of stock in a company." ESOPs are most often used when the owner of a privately held small business readies for retirement, has no family successor, and wants to pass on the company to the employees. The federal government encourages small-business owners to consider ESOPs by granting tax breaks. The only big expense is the eventual cost to the company of buying out retiring employees.

ESOPs work only when a company has a strong balance sheet and a sustainable record of being profitable. ESOPs aren't for the start-up or for the small business that isn't performing.

You can obtain more information on this unique, equity-sharing tool by contacting The ESOP Association at 1726 M Street N.W., Suite 501, Washington, D.C. 20036; 202-293-2971; or www.esopassociation.org.

Buy-sell agreements

In the event that you and a minority shareholder have a dispute (and you can bet that you'll eventually have one — especially if you have more than one minority shareholder), a buy-sell agreement is a vital legal document for your business.

Buy-sell agreements specify the terms under which owners/shareholders must sell their stock upon separation from the company. They also establish a method to determine the price of the buy-back and make provisions for the death of a shareholder.

As we say earlier in this book, you need to involve an attorney several times in the life of a business — and making equity decisions is certainly one of those times. Never create a minority shareholder without one!

Including Insurance and Other Benefits

A variety of insurance and related benefits are tax deductible to corporations for all employees. If your business isn't incorporated, as the owner, you can't deduct the cost of the insurance plans discussed in this section, with the exception of health-insurance plans, for yourself, but you can deduct them for your employees.

Health insurance

Employees usually value their health-insurance coverage over other traditional employee benefits (see the earlier section on retirement plans for details). Of course, not all your current and prospective employees will value health-insurance coverage the same. For example, some married employees may already be covered through their spouses' plans and may not need or want health coverage through your small business. Similarly, younger, unmarried employees, who think they're indestructible, may place a greater value on flexible work schedules than they do on health insurance.

One hundred percent of your health-insurance premiums are deductible for yourself and your covered family members.

We cover the ins and outs of providing a health-insurance plan for your business in the sections that follow. But first, we provide a brief synopsis of the new federal laws affecting health insurance that were signed into law in 2010.

Making sense of the new federal health-insurance rules

As this book goes to press, the 2010 Patient Protection and Affordable Care Act (PPACA) and the Health Care and Education Reconciliation Act of 2010 are being challenged in court. The outcome of the 2012 elections may have some impact on these new laws if a new president is elected. In the meantime, however, a number of provisions of these bills have kicked in or will soon be taking effect; that's what we discuss in this section.

Effective in 2011, employer group health plans

✔ Must offer coverage to adult children up to age 26 (regardless of whether they qualify as the employee's tax dependent) who are not eligible for coverage under another employer's health plan. The coverage isn't taxable to the employee or dependent, and as it stands now, beginning in 2014, the requirement that the nondependent child must not be eligible for coverage under another employer's plan will no longer apply.

✔ May not impose lifetime limits and can impose only "restricted" annual limits. No annual limits will be permitted beginning in 2014.

✔ May not impose preexisting condition exclusions on children under 19. No preexisting conditions will be permitted for any participants beginning in 2014.

✔ Are required to disclose the value of each employee's health coverage on the employee's annual Form W-2 that's filed with the IRS.

✔ Must provide preventive care without cost sharing and cover certain child preventive care services as recommended by the government. Apparently, plans already in existence on the enactment date of the PPACA are grandfathered — in other words, they need not comply.

The following additional group-health-plan provisions are set to commence in 2014:

✔ Employer "pay or play" responsibility begins, meaning that employers must offer minimum essential coverage to full-time employees or make nondeductible payments to the government.

✔ Employers must remove all annual dollar limits on all participants.

✔ Employers must limit cost sharing and deductibles to levels that don't exceed those applicable to HSA-eligible, high-deductible health plans (*HSA* stands for health savings account; see the later section for details).

✔ Employers must remove all preexisting condition exclusions on all participants.

✔ Employers must remove waiting periods longer than 90 days.

✔ Permitted wellness incentives in group health plans will increase from 20 percent to 30 percent of plan costs and up to 50 percent if determined to be appropriate.

✔ Plans must cover clinical trials for life-threatening diseases. This provision overcomes plan restrictions on out-of-network providers; however, plans in existence at the enactment of the PPACA are grandfathered.

Knowing what to look for when establishing a health-insurance plan

Shopping for a quality health-insurance plan requires patience and time to understand the myriad attributes of plans, as well as to address your needs and those of your employees. Here are some issues to consider when establishing a health-insurance plan:

✔ **Commitment of the insurer to its health-insurance business:** Some insurance companies have their fingers in various pots — they may dabble in many lines of insurance, including health insurance, for instance.

Although you won't receive a guarantee that any particular insurer is going to stay in the health-insurance business for the long haul, we suggest that you choose among the biggest plans offered by the most experienced companies in your area. Besides the increased likelihood that they'll stay in the business, the larger players can usually negotiate better rates from providers.

✔ **Comprehensive, catastrophic coverage:** So-called major medical coverage pays for potentially large expenses such as hospitalization, physicians, and ancillary charges (such as lab work). Health-insurance plans specify the maximum total benefits *(lifetime maximum benefits)* that they'll pay over the course of the time that you're insured by their plans.

✔ **Choice of health-care providers:** Increasing numbers of health-insurance plans contract with specific health-care providers, which restricts your choices but helps keep costs down. Health maintenance organizations (HMOs) and preferred provider organizations (PPOs) are the main plans that restrict your choices.

The major difference between HMOs and PPOs is that PPOs pay the majority of your expenses if you use a provider outside their approved list. If you use an outside provider with an HMO, you typically won't be covered at all.

If you and your employees want to be able to use particular physicians or hospitals, be sure to find out which health-insurance plans they accept as payment. If you can't use their services in the restricted-choice plans, ask yourself if the extra cost of the open-choice plan is worth being able to use preferred services.

Selecting higher deductibles and copayments

As with other insurance policies, the more you're willing to share in the payment of your health-insurance claims, the less you'll have to pay in premiums. To reduce your health-insurance premiums, choose a plan with the highest deductible and copayment that you and your employees can comfortably afford. Most policies have annual deductible options, such as $250, $500, or $1,000, as well as copayment options (typically 20 percent or so).

Note: A 20 percent copayment doesn't mean that you would have to come up with $10,000 for a $50,000 claim. Insurers typically set a maximum out-of-pocket limit on your annual copayments of $1,000 to $2,000 and then cover 100 percent of medical expenses over that cap. With HMO plans, most insurers offer copayment options such as $5, $10, or $20 for a physician's office visit. Again, the higher the per-visit charge you're willing to accept, the lower your health-insurance premiums will be.

Sharing costs with your employees enables you to provide better policies at a fair price for all. We suggest that you, as the employer, pay at least half of the cost of the health-insurance premiums and have your employees pick up the other half (to attract and retain superstar employees, you may want to pay a greater portion, especially if your competitors are doing so).

Utilizing health savings accounts

A terrific way to slash your health-care costs is to establish and utilize *health savings accounts* (HSAs). Like many types of retirement accounts, when you contribute to an HSA, you gain an upfront tax break because the amount contributed reduces your taxable income. Also, the money compounds free of tax over time. If you use the funds to pay health-care expenses, withdrawals are also free of tax.

The list of eligible health-care expenses is generally quite broad — surprisingly so, in fact. You can use HSA money to pay for the following expenses, among other things:

✔ Out-of-pocket medical costs not covered by insurance

✔ Prescription drugs

✔ Dental care (including braces)

✔ Vision care

✔ Vitamins

✔ Psychologist fees

✔ Smoking cessation programs

IRS Publication 502 details permissible expenses; find out more at `http://www.irs.gov/publications/p502/index.html`.

To be eligible to have an HSA, your health plan must have a high deductible, which is defined as at least $1,200 for individuals and $2,400 for families (in 2011). The contribution limits for HSAs are $3,050 for individuals and $6,150 for families (in 2011).

In the pleasant event where you don't need to tap the HSA to pay health-care costs, the money can compound without taxation over time in the investments you've selected (mutual funds are a good choice). After age 65, you may withdraw HSA funds to use toward non-health-care costs and simply pay income tax at that time on the withdrawal.

Shopping around for the best plan for your business

Most health-insurance plans are sold through insurance agents, but some are sold directly by the insurer. If a plan is sold both ways, going through an agent shouldn't cost you any more. Start by getting plan proposals from the larger health insurers in your area. Also, check with professional or other associations that you belong to. A competent, independent insurance agent who specializes in health insurance can help find insurers who would be willing to offer you and your employees coverage.

In most cases, you should shop around for health insurance at least every two years. Why? Health-insurance costs have risen dramatically in the last decade or more, there appears to be no end in sight to those increases, and the effect on your bottom line is significant.

Health-insurance agents have a conflict of interest common to all financial salespeople working on commission: The higher the premium they sell you, the bigger the commission they earn. So an agent may try to steer you into higher-cost plans and not suggest some of the available strategies to reduce the cost of your company's coverage (see the previous sections).

Disability insurance

The purpose of disability insurance is to protect your income and that of your employees from being lost in the event of a disability. Anyone who's dependent on his or her own income should have disability insurance. After all, if you suffer a total disability, you probably won't be able to earn income or as much income, but you'll have the same or higher living expenses.

As an employer, you may be required by your state to pay into a state disability or workers' compensation program (the latter only covers injuries and disabilities suffered on the job). Additionally, through the Social Security system, you and your employees have minimal disability benefits. Although coverage through government disability programs often isn't sufficient, it's better than nothing, so you as the employer shouldn't beat yourself up for not offering disability coverage to your employees.

One good reason to offer disability coverage to your employees, however, is that your competitors offer their employees coverage and/or you can afford to pay for such coverage. As with health insurance, we strongly encourage you to share the cost of disability coverage with your employees — perhaps you could pay 50 percent.

If you're in the market for disability protection for you and your employees, here's how to get the best coverage at a competitive price:

- **Replace about 60 percent of income.** People generally need enough disability coverage to provide them with sufficient income to live on until other financial resources become available.

  If you pay for a portion of your employees' disability coverage, that portion of the benefits becomes taxable. You may also get a policy with a so-called "residual benefits" feature, which pays a partial benefit to someone with a disability that prevents him from working full time. Lastly, consider getting a cost-of-living adjustment rider, which increases a benefit payment by a set percentage or in accordance with changes in inflation and helps retain the purchasing power of a policy's benefits.

- **Get benefits through age 65.** A good disability policy should pay benefits through an age at which the employee becomes financially independent, which for most people occurs around age 65 (the approximate age at which Social Security retirement benefits begin).

  If you'd like to offer your employees disability coverage but find that policies until age 65 are too costly, you can get five-year benefit policies instead.

✔ **Use an adequate definition of disability.** An *adequate definition of disability* in a policy is that the policy pays benefits if you can't perform work for which you are "reasonably trained." *Own-occupation policies,* which pay benefits if you can't perform the duties of your current occupation, are the most expensive because there's a greater chance the insurer will have to pay out benefits.

✔ **Buy policies that are noncancelable and guaranteed renewable.** These features ensure that the disability policy can't be canceled because an employee develops health problems.

✔ **Accept a lengthier waiting period.** The *waiting period,* which can also be thought of as the deductible on the policy, is the time between the onset of your disability and the time when you begin collecting benefits. Accepting a longer waiting period — at least three months, and preferably six months — greatly reduces the cost of the disability insurance.

✔ **Shop around.** In addition to soliciting proposals from insurance agents who specialize in disability coverage, check the professional associations to which you already belong or can join.

Life insurance

We recommend that you not waste your precious compensation and benefit dollars on life insurance. Why?

✔ **Few small-business employers offer life-insurance coverage.** Why waste your precious benefit dollars on something that your competitors are unlikely to provide?

✔ **Many of your employees won't need it.** Those who don't have financial dependents don't need life insurance. The vast majority of your single employees, childless employees, and employees with grown children won't have the need for life insurance, either. Hence, it isn't a wise benefit to offer.

If you decide that you really want to offer the Cadillac of benefits packages, buy term life insurance, not cash-value life insurance. With *term life insurance,* you pay an annual premium for a set amount of life-insurance coverage. During the term of the policy, if you stay alive, your beneficiaries collect no death benefit and you're out the premium, but of course, you're eternally grateful you're not deceased! With *cash-value life insurance* (also known as whole life, universal life, or variable life), you pay a much higher premium for a combination of life insurance coverage and a savings-type account. For the same amount of coverage, cash-value policies cost a whopping eight times more than comparable term policies.

Employee Assistance Programs

Employee Assistance Programs (EAPs) provide support for employees' mental and physical health beyond what a traditional health-insurance plan provides. Specifically, EAPs help employees struggling with

✔ Substance abuse (alcohol and drugs)

✔ Marriage and family problems

✔ Stress

✔ Workplace concerns (including layoffs, reorganizations, and workplace violence concerns)

Although far more common to large employers, EAPs are increasingly found in smaller businesses. A basic EAP involves simply providing printed material, usually in the form of pamphlets, to interested employees. More sophisticated EAPs provide confidential telephone hot-line services to employees in need and counseling referrals to psychological professionals. Larger businesses sometimes include counselors on staff.

Just about everyone is touched by the problems addressed by EAPs, so such plans do get utilized and are appreciated by employees — so long as confidentiality is ensured and the quality of services is reliable. To find out more about EAPs, check out `http://supporting employees.com/`. For referrals to EAP professionals, contact the Employee Assistance Professionals Association at 703-387-1000 or visit `www.eapassn.org`. Health-insurance providers can also submit suggestions for EAPs.

Dependent care plans

A *dependent care plan* enables you and your employees to put away money from your paychecks on a pretax basis; you can then use that money to pay for child-care expenses or to care for an ill or aging parent. Dependent care plans save you federal, state, and even Social Security taxes, and they allow you to put away up to $5,000 per year in a reimbursement account to be used to pay for eligible dependent care expenses ($2,500 for those who are married and filing separately).

Dependent care spending accounts are a "use it or lose it" benefit. If you or your employees aren't able to spend the money for child-care expenses in the current tax year, at the end of the year the IRS forces you to forfeit all the money you haven't used.

Vacation

We all need downtime, and weekends just aren't enough. A full week or two off can do wonders for you and your employees.

Two weeks of paid vacation is the norm for new hires in the world of small business. For key employees and employees who have been with you for several or more years, three weeks is the norm. Many small businesses offer a graduated vacation schedule that may, for instance, offer four weeks after 10 years and five weeks after 20.

Some employees may value vacation flexibility and more time off, so if your business allows, try to accommodate such wants to keep good employees happy. For example, if an employee would rather have an extra week's vacation each year than a 2 percent pay raise, you should be indifferent financially — unless, of course, that employee is difficult or impossible to replace during that extra vacation period.

Flexible hours

A wide variety of options are available when it comes to offering flexible hours. Families with children are especially starved for time, and most employed parents greatly value flexible work hours and the ability to take additional time off, even without pay. Sensitive employers who create a family-friendly work schedule and business environment reap enormous benefits, including happier, more loyal employees.

Here are a few options that are becoming more popular for some small-business owners:

- Four 10-hour days (flex time)
- A flex time option that allows employees to vary their working hours depending on personal requirements (for example, employees with health or child-care issues)
- A work-from-home option (telecommuting)

Finally, offering flexible hours in advance of or during holidays also makes a lot of sense because, by and large, worker productivity falls off drastically during these times anyway. We know of one business, for instance, that, during the week between Christmas and New Year's, works only four-hour days (from 8:00 a.m. to noon).

Flexible benefit plans

Flexible benefit, or "cafeteria," *plans* allow employees to pick and choose the benefits on which to spend their benefit dollars. (These plans are also known as *Section 125 plans,* after the part of the IRS tax laws that sanctions such plans.) Under a flexible benefit plan, your employees can choose to receive a portion of their compensation as pay or to put those dollars toward purchasing benefits of their own choosing from a menu you offer.

The virtue of a flexible plan is that it allows employees to customize their benefit packages to suit their needs and wants. For example, a married employee with young children may prefer to spend his benefit dollars on dependent care expenses or more vacation days, whereas a single employee may prefer simply to receive more cash compensation.

Another significant advantage of a flexible benefit plan is that the associated tax benefits produce greater value for employees from their compensation dollars. Rather than receiving some of their annual pay as taxable income, employees can elect to purchase benefits with pretax dollars, thus saving on income taxes.

Unless and until you offer a number of insurance benefits to your employees, offering a flexible plan won't be appropriate or worthwhile. However, if you're offering a generous number of benefits and would like to offer your employees maximum flexibility in using their benefits, a flex plan may make sense.

Among the types of benefits that you may want to consider offering to your employees in a flexible plan are

- ✔ Health insurance and health-care spending accounts
- ✔ Group life insurance
- ✔ Disability insurance
- ✔ Vacation days
- ✔ Employee contributions to a 401(k)
- ✔ Dependent care plans and spending accounts

Don't bother including the following benefits in your flexible benefit plan:

- ✔ Dental and vision insurance
- ✔ Group legal insurance plans

These insurance programs ultimately cover small-potato items. You should spend your insurance dollars on coverage options that protect you and your employees against potentially financially catastrophic losses, such as those that could be incurred from a long-term disability or major medical problem.

Because flexible benefit plans are time-consuming and fairly costly for small businesses to establish and administer, your small business likely won't have one, especially if you have fewer than ten employees. If you have a large-enough small business and you decide to establish a flexible benefit plan, hire competent tax and benefit advisors to help you design your plan and to help you comply with the myriad tax issues that you must deal with on an ongoing basis with such a plan.

If you're going to go to the trouble and expense of putting a flexible benefit plan in place at your company, also invest the necessary time and cost to describe the specific benefits in the plan and explain how employees can choose among them. For many employers, small and large, too many employees don't understand the flexible plan, which hampers them from making good use of, and appreciating, the plan.

Chapter 18

Handling Regulatory and Legal Issues

---

*O*ne of the least-pleasant aspects of starting and running a small business is comprehending and adhering to the myriad government regulations that affect how and where you do business. Not to mention the plethora of legal issues that can blow up in your face and culminate in a lawsuit. So we understand that you probably have a strong desire to skip this chapter. But please don't; doing so could ensnare you in government fines and legal fees that could prove disastrous to your business.

And if the thought of these penalties isn't enough, we have what we hope is an incentive for you to familiarize yourself with the issues raised in this chapter: We can save you time and headaches by showing you how to efficiently and correctly complete important legal and regulatory tasks.

Navigating Small-Business Laws

You may think that if you're starting or operating a truly *small* small business, you don't need to know much on the legal and regulatory fronts. We wish that were true, but it's not. Consider the following types of issues that most small-business owners must grapple with, both in the early years of their businesses and on an ongoing basis:

✔ **Selecting a name for your business:** You can't simply choose any name and start using it for your business. After all, you may select a name that another business is already using, and that owner could take legal action against you. Besides, you'll probably spend a lot of marketing money over the years to distinguish *your* business from the masses, and you don't want people (especially your customers) to confuse your business with someone else's.

✔ **Complying with government licensing and permit requirements:** Federal, state, and sometimes even local governments regulate and license certain types of businesses, such as restaurants, taxicabs, and beauty shops.

If you're operating a business that requires registration with particular government entities, the passing of certain exams, or the satisfaction of specific licensing requirements (see the later section "Complying through licensing, registrations, and permits"), you'll be breaking the law and may be put out of business if you don't comply. The possible penalties for running afoul of business laws can be steep and can include monetary fines and outright prohibition against practicing your line of work for months or even years. And if that isn't bad enough, your transgressions may become public knowledge (and permanently etched into the Internet), which can hamper your ability to get your business up and running again when you're legally able to do so.

✔ **Protecting your ideas and work:** If you prepare a business plan and distribute it for comment or to raise money (see Chapters 4 and 5), you don't want anyone to steal your ideas, do you? If you invent or brainstorm something new and unique, you don't want someone else to copy your creation and profit from it, do you? Well, if you don't properly protect your ideas, work, and other creative developments through trademarks, copyrights, and patents, someone could rip you off and you'll have little, if any, legal recourse. (See the later section "Protecting ideas: Nondisclosures, patents, trademarks, and copyrights.")

✔ **Establishing a retirement plan:** Perhaps you've heard of retirement plans such as profit sharing, money purchase pension plans, SEP-IRAs, and so on. Over the years, these plans can slash tens, and maybe even hundreds, of thousands of dollars off your tax bill. However, if you have employees, they're entitled to certain retirement benefits that are subject to federal regulations. Your reward for violating retirement-plan rules can be the disallowance of your contributions into the plan, thereby causing you to owe the IRS taxes and penalties — ouch! (We cover retirement plans in Chapter 17.)

✔ **Filing your taxes:** As a business owner and self-employed person, you're responsible for properly filing all federal, state, and local taxes for yourself and your business. And when you employ others, you must withhold appropriate taxes from their wages and submit the withheld taxes in a timely fashion to the various tax regulatory authorities. More than a few small businesses have failed because the owners fell behind on taxes and subsequently were buried by past-due payments. (Chapter 19 helps you stay in the good graces of the tax authorities.)

✔ **Hiring and managing employees:** Employment law is a vast and growing area of the legal profession. When you hire and employ workers, you must be careful about what you say to them and how you manage and behave around them. If you're not careful, you can face big legal bills and possible lawsuit damages, while the reputations of you and your hard-earned business are dragged through the mud during legal proceedings. (See Chapter 16 for more on finding and hiring employees.)

✔ **Preparing contracts:** In many ways, contracts make the business world go 'round. When properly prepared, contracts function as legally binding, enforceable agreements that your business makes with suppliers, employees, and others relating to the operation of your business. If you offer a contract to another person or business or seek to change the terms and conditions of an existing contract, you must first understand the legal ramifications. If you don't understand these ramifications, at a minimum, you'll have to deal with upset parties on the other end of the contract; in the worst cases, you could end up in court with soaring legal bills and potential lawsuits (see the later section "A business prenup: Contracts with customers and suppliers" for more).

Suffering through Start-Up Regulations

Before you begin working with your first customer, you need to invest time and money into getting your legal and regulatory ducks in a row. In the start-up phase of a small business, however, few business owners have the luxury of spending hard-to-spare time and money on these issues. So in this section, we assist you in saving some of both while helping you protect your business.

Complying through licensing, registrations, and permits

Years ago, when Eric started his financial counseling practice, the first thing he did was investigate what government regulatory organizations he needed to register with. To his surprise, he had to register with both the federal Securities and Exchange Commission (SEC) and his state's Department of Corporations. He was surprised because he figured that a profession as full of deception, conflicts of interest, and outright cases of corruption as the financial planning profession would've had less government oversight. (Then again, government "oversight" of a profession can literally result in oversights!)

To discover the various ways in which different government bodies regulate your line of business, we suggest you check with the following:

✔ **Trade associations for your business or profession:** Most lines of business have active trade associations, whose management and members can share war stories and information about regulations. Obviously, association members in your local area will have far more relevant experiences to share, assuming they aren't competitors. Turn to Chapter 15 for information on how to locate a trade association in your industry or check out the *Small Business Sourcebook* (a useful reference publication published by Gale), which you can probably find at your local library.

✔ **Peers in your profession:** Those who have been there and done that can save you time by sharing their experiences. The simplest way to network with others in your line of work is to attend conferences or conventions for your industry or profession. Again, trade associations can help you locate such events, or you can network in your local area.

A downside of the local-area strategy is that people in the same line of work in your town may view you as competition and be less than forthcoming with assistance. Also, keep in mind that others may or may not have done a thorough job of researching regulatory requirements and may have chosen not to comply with certain regulations.

If you're fortunate enough to live in a community that has a business incubator (see Chapter 15), stop in and inquire about one or more of its lessees. They are, by definition, people who recently went through the same thing you're going through now.

✔ **The state agency that oversees corporations and/or small businesses:** Check out the state government section in your local phone directory or peruse your state's website to find the right number to call. Look for any of the following state government agencies: Economic Development Department, Department of Commerce, or the Office of Small Business. When you make the call, be persistent, because if the person who answers the phone is poorly trained or having a bad day, you may not get the information you need and you may have to start over again with a different department.

✔ **Other relevant local government agencies:** Let your fingers do the walking through the government (city, county, and federal) section of your local phone directory. For tax issues, look under Tax Collector. For real estate issues, look under Planning Department or Building Inspection Department. For health-related issues, look under Health Department. If you get stuck and can't reach the correct department, most cities and towns have a city clerk or town clerk who can transfer you to the right department.

✔ **Trade publications:** You may be surprised at how many specialized occupational publications exist. (See Chapter 7 for tips on how to identify and locate them.) You can research past articles on industry regulations in such publications. (You may need to contact the publication for a listing of topics covered in prior issues, or you can check out the publication's website for an internal search engine.)

✔ **The local Chamber of Commerce:** Most communities have a local Chamber of Commerce; the better ones have helpful information for prospective and current small-business owners (including the applicable government organizations you need to check in with and the other people you need to speak to).

✔ **Small Business Development Centers (SBDCs):** Every state has an SBDC, and most SBDCs have extensive small-business libraries, as well as a wide variety of pamphlets and brochures, compliments of the applicable government organizations.

✔ **Experienced small-business advisors:** Tax and legal advisors, as well as consultants experienced with businesses like yours, can help point you in the right direction. Although such advisors generally charge a hefty hourly fee, the advice can be well worth the price if you select a good advisor. An advisor may even be willing to offer free tips on general regulatory issues in order to cultivate your future business.

✔ **Real estate agents and building contractors:** If your business will operate in a commercial or retail space, you can acquire knowledge by conversing with agents who sell or lease space and/or contractors who develop and renovate space similar to what your business will occupy.

In the next sections, we dig deeper into the realities of compliance and the local, state, and federal regulations you must follow.

The realities of compliance

Various government agencies — at the local, regional, state, and federal levels — impose all sorts of licensing, registration, and permit requirements on small-business owners. If you've ever arrived in a new city without a map and tried to get around by yourself in a car, you already know what it may be like as you try to discover all the agencies and paperwork required for the type of business you want to operate.

If you overlook applying for one important permit or license, the government can slap you with hefty fines, and disgruntled customers can sue you, using your lack of compliance with government regulations as an indicator of slipshod business practices. And even if you're a good enough detective to ferret out and understand the government regulations with which you must comply, you may tear out your hair trying to determine the right order in which to obtain your permits and licenses.

Okay, so life could be worse — you could live in a communist country where such permits are available only to the highest bidders! Just remember to keep your eyes and ears open. Talk to as many people as you can and remember that the burden for compliance falls on your shoulders. Don't toss your hands in the air, say that compliance with government regulations is too hard to figure out, and just wing it.

The success or failure of a business often lies in the details — or, more specifically, in the owner's willingness to pay attention to them. Complying with all applicable regulations is an early test!

Local regulations: Taxes, zoning, and health

The town, city, and county in which you operate your business more than likely impose some requirements on businesses like yours. Even if you operate a home-based business, you can't assume that you can do what you want when and where you want to do it because home-based businesses often are even more restricted than their office-park counterparts.

Some common local regulations that affect small-business owners include the following:

✔ **Taxes:** In most areas, if you're selling products through a retail store, you have to collect sales tax. In fact, even if you don't operate a retail store, you may have to collect sales tax on products you sell, and some cities tax all revenue from small businesses. Plus, you may be surprised to discover that some communities levy an annual property tax on certain business assets such as inventory, equipment, and furniture.

✔ **Fictitious name:** If the name of your business is different from your own name, you need to file what's known as a *fictitious name* or *doing business as* (DBA) form. You usually file your DBA form through the county, and you may have to publish your DBA filing in a local newspaper.

✔ **Real estate:** All real estate is affected by *zoning,* which restricts the use of a given property. If you don't like the idea of local government telling you what you can and can't do on your property, consider how you'd feel if your next-door neighbor opened a chicken and pig farm on his property! Whether you're leasing or buying a property, you'll have to deal with zoning ordinances.

You need to investigate whether you can operate your business at a given location, as well as plan on dealing with the good folks in City Hall if you want to do any renovations to your place of business. If those renovations raise any environmental concerns — such as disturbing or removing potentially hazardous substances like asbestos — you may need to involve your local health department as well (see the next bullet). Zoning and renovation issues often come into play when a home-office business steadily grows and the owner finally decides to add on to his house or garage in order to hire another employee or carry more products in inventory or when the business generates a level of activity that affects noise levels, traffic, and parking demands.

✔ **Health and safety:** Small-business owners whose enterprises involve food are subject to all sorts of regulations from the local health department. For instance, you may need to have your water tested occasionally if you live in a less densely populated area that uses well water. And don't overlook the myriad safety regulations, such as local fire codes and elevator inspections.

State regulations: More taxes, licensing, insurance, and the environment

In addition to regulations at the local level, states impose requirements on businesses, and you need to be aware of, and comply with, these requirements. Most states have established agencies to assist business owners with doing business in the state. After all, states do have some vested interest in trying to attract and retain businesses because business tax revenues fill their coffers.

Here are the primary issues that may affect your small business due to state regulations:

✔ **Licenses:** State licensing is primarily intended to reduce the consumer's likelihood of being fleeced or victimized. Although some occupations (such as doctors and lawyers) are universally required to be licensed, each state has a unique list of occupations that it regulates.

State licensing requirements vary by occupation and by state. In some states, you can get certain licenses after you complete a few forms and pay the state a fee. In most cases, however, you have to take a test or complete some form of certification in order to get a license.

✔ **Taxes:** As we discuss in the local regulations section, some businesses, such as retailers, have to collect sales tax on products sold. In most states, all businesses must pay income taxes at the state level (see Chapter 19 for more on taxes).

✔ **Insurance:** To you, the small-business owner, having to pay for employee-related insurance will feel like another tax. Common state-required coverage includes workers' compensation, which compensates workers for lost wages due to job-related injuries, and unemployment insurance, which pays laid-off employees for a certain period of time or until they secure another job.

✔ **Environment:** If you're a manufacturer and your plant emits unsavory smoke, particles, or odors into the air or water, you can be certain that your state (and possibly other government agencies) will regulate your activities — and for good reason. Left to their own devices, some unsavory business owners would knowingly pollute because installing control devices would add to the cost of doing business, effectively reducing profits.

Federal regulations: Still more taxes, licenses, and requirements

In addition to local and state regulations, small-business owners must comply with U.S. federal government regulations, which cover taxes and licenses as well as the health, safety, and welfare of your employees.

Not all federal labor laws affect all small businesses because some issues apply only to employers with a specific number of employees. So the good news may be that your small business is small enough that you don't have to concern yourself with all the issues we cover in the following list. (Find out what issues apply to your business by consulting the resources listed in the section "Complying through licensing, registrations, and permits.")

Here are the key federal regulations most small-business owners need to consider:

✔ **Licenses:** Most businesses that require a license or permit to operate generally obtain the documentation at the state level. Some businesses, however, receive permits and licenses at the federal level. These businesses include alcohol and tobacco manufacturers, drug companies, firearm manufacturers and dealers, investment advisors, meat packing and preparation companies, radio and television stations, and trucking and other transportation companies.

✔ **Taxes:** All incorporated businesses, or their owners if the business isn't incorporated, must file a federal income tax return. Additionally, most small-business owners — especially those who hire employees — choose to apply for and utilize a federal Employer Identification Number (EIN). See Chapter 19 for the lowdown on small-business tax issues.

✔ **Americans with Disabilities Act (ADA):** This legislation prohibits employers with 15 or more employees from discriminating against prospective and current employees or customers with disabilities. Such discrimination is barred in the hiring, management, and dismissal of any employee. For example, during the process of interviewing job applicants, you can get yourself into a heap of legal hot water if you exclude from consideration qualified candidates who are in some way disabled.

✔ **Family and Medical Leave Act:** This legislation requires employers with 50 or more employees (within 75 miles) to provide up to 12 weeks of unpaid leave to employees who desire or need the leave for personal health issues due to a serious medical condition that affects the employee's ability to perform the regular duties of his or her job; to spend time with a newborn or adopted child; or to care for a family member who has a serious medical condition.

During the term of an employee's leave, the employer must continue to cover the employee under the company's group health-insurance plan under the same conditions as when the employee was working.

Eligible employees (who have been with the employer for at least one year and who have worked at least 125 hours over the previous year) who take a leave under the Family and Medical Leave Act generally can do so with the understanding that they can return to their same positions with the same pay and benefits. So-called highly paid "key" employees aren't guaranteed the same positions and compensation packages if their returns would lead to significant economic harm to the employers. (The Department of Labor defines a *key employee* as a salaried employee ". . . who is among the highest paid 10 percent of employees within 75 miles of the work site.")

✔ **2010 federal health-insurance legislation:** Congress passed sweeping health-insurance legislation in 2010 that affects and will affect many small businesses. Turn to Chapter 17 for the details.

Selection of a business entity

In the start-up phase of your business, be sure to consult your attorney or tax advisor about what type of organization or business entity — for example, sole proprietorship, partnership, corporation, or limited liability company (LLC) — makes sense for your enterprise. Although the different corporate entities that you may form for your business can provide some legal protection for you and your personal assets, establishing such entities involves significant time and expense and doesn't completely insulate you and your company from lawsuits.

Given the excitement and stresses inherent in the early days of running a small business, we can understand why you may not care to spend your precious time and money on researching and consulting with legal and tax experts about what type of organization you should establish. As we discuss in Chapter 5, however, because of taxes and other issues, you should choose which entity will best serve your needs sooner rather than later.

Protecting ideas: Nondisclosures, patents, trademarks, and copyrights

Your business idea and business plans probably aren't 100 percent unique. Some business owners, however, have taken a different twist on something or have created a truly unique product or service. But even if you don't have a unique or different product or service to offer, you don't want others to steal your plans and ideas. By circulating copies of your business plan (see Chapter 4), you may be giving away much of your hard work and ideas to an individual or another business that can end up being a competitor.

The following sections explain what you need to know about protecting your business and ideas in general and specifically through nondisclosures, trademarks, patents, and copyrights.

General tips for protecting your ideas

Here are some tips for how to protect your business plan and ideas:

- ✔ **Be careful about who sees your business plan.** A friend or advisor who happens to know a lot about your type of small business, or small businesses in general, is unlikely to have unfriendly motives in looking at your plan. On the other hand, an industry insider or a potential competitor who peruses your plans may not have your best interests at heart.

- ✔ **Keep proprietary information out of your plan.** Don't include product designs, manufacturing specifications, unique resources, or other information unique to your company in the copies of your business plan that you distribute to others. Share such information with serious investors only if needed to gain their investments, and do so with a nondisclosure agreement attached (see the next section).

- ✔ **Place a nondisclosure statement in the front of your business plan.** If your plan does fall into the hands of someone who may be inclined to steal your ideas, a nondisclosure statement (which we discuss in the next section) should scare them off.

- ✔ **Get legal assistance when necessary.** If your work and ideas are proprietary and protectable, speak with an attorney who specializes in intellectual property, including copyrights, trademarks, and patents. We explain these important legal protections in the upcoming section "Patents, trademarks, and copyrights."

Nondisclosure agreements (NDAs)

Always be sure to attach a *nondisclosure agreement* (NDA) to the beginning of your business plan before you circulate it for review. The purpose of the NDA is to warn the reader that the enclosed contents are private property and are not to be spread around without your consent. (***Note:*** You don't need an attorney to craft this agreement.)

Simply including the NDA with your business plan isn't enough; never hand out your plan without first having the recipient sign the NDA.

Following is a sample nondisclosure agreement:

> This confidential Business Plan has been prepared in order to raise financing for Wowza Widgets, Inc. This material is being delivered to a select number of potential investors, each of whom agrees to the following terms and conditions:
>
> Each recipient of this Business Plan agrees that, by accepting this material, he or she will not copy, reproduce, distribute, or discuss with others any part of this plan without prior written consent of Wowza Widgets, Inc.
>
> The recipient agrees to keep confidential all information contained herein and not use it for any purpose whatsoever other than to evaluate and determine interest in providing financing described herein.
>
> This material contains proprietary and confidential information regarding Wowza Widgets, Inc., and is based upon information provided to Wowza Widgets, Inc., by sources deemed to be reliable. Although the information contained herein is believed to be accurate, Wowza Widgets, Inc., expressly disclaims all liability for any information, projections, or representations (expressed or implied) contained herein from omissions from this material or for any written or oral communication transmitted to any party in the course of its evaluation for this financing. The recipient acknowledges that this material shall remain the property of Wowza Widgets, Inc., and Wowza Widgets, Inc., reserves the right to request the return of the material at any time and in any respect, to amend or terminate solicitation procedures, to terminate discussions with any and all prospective financing sources, to reject any and all proposals, or to negotiate with any party with respect to the financing of Wowza Widgets, Inc.
>
> The projections contained in the pro-forma Financial Section are based upon numerous assumptions. Although Wowza Widgets, Inc., believes that these assumptions are reasonable, no assurance can be given as to the accuracy of these projections because they are dependent in large part upon unforeseeable factors and events. As a result, the actual results achieved may vary from the projections, and such variation can be material and adverse.
>
> Signature (print): _____
>
> Signature: _____

Patents, trademarks, and copyrights

You may have created a product, service, or technology unique enough that you want to prevent others from copying it. Or maybe you simply want to restrain others from using and profiting from the name of your business or literary, musical, or artistic creations.

Welcome to the wonderful and often confusing world of patent, copyright, and trademark law. You'll be relieved to hear that this isn't a legal book, in part because your two humble authors are, happily (for us at least), not lawyers. And most small-business owners don't need to spend much time or legal expense on these issues.

If you do need to deal with patents, copyrights, or trademarks, you have to be familiar with the following very important terms. For more information, consult a lawyer who specializes in intellectual property.

- ✓ **Patent:** If you've invented something (such as a new type of toy or computer disk), you may want to explore patenting your invention. The reason: By filing a *patent* with the federal government, you have exclusive rights to manufacture, sell, and use the patented invention. You can, if you so choose, license usage of the patent to others.

- ✓ **Trademark:** Companies invest significant time, effort, and money into creating brand names (for example, Coca-Cola and *For Dummies*), marketing strategies, advertising slogans (Making Everything Easier!), logos (the Dummies Man on this book's cover or the Nike swoosh, for instance), and so on. The point of the *trademark* is to protect your brands and prevent other enterprises from using and profiting from the recognition and reputation you've developed through your business's brand names, marketing/advertising images, and the words associated with your product.

  Trademarked items can also include things such as the packaging, shape, character names, color, and smell associated with a product. If you think your business has identifying characteristics that you don't want copied by competitors, think about applying for trademark protection. *Note:* Patents and trademarks are handled by the U.S. Patent and Trademark Office (www.uspto.gov); copyrights are the domain of the U.S. Copyright Office (www.copyright.gov).

- ✓ **Copyright:** *Copyright* laws cover such works as musical and sound recordings, literary works, software, graphics, and audiovisuals. The owner of the copyright of a work is solely allowed to sell the work, make copies of it, create derivations from it, and perform and display the work. The creator of the work isn't always the person or part of the organization that holds the copyright, though. For example, writers sometimes do freelance writing for publications that hold the copyright to the work that their writers create for them.

In the less complex cases, you can copyright your idea, product, or authorship yourself to save money. A two-page form is available from the U.S. Copyright Office (www.copyright.gov/forms; 202-707-3000). Follow the directions and you can register your copyright yourself. You must pay a modest filing fee for each request, but you can put similar works on one form.

No copyright cops are out there searching for people who are violating your patents, trademarks, or copyrights. The burden is on you to perform the detective work yourself; if you detect a violation, head immediately for an attorney.

A business prenup: Contracts with customers and suppliers

All small businesses have customers as well as suppliers (or vendors). In both of these relationships, small-business owners often engage in contracts, whether formally written or verbal. Here are our tips for dealing with contracts with your customers and suppliers:

- ✔ **Get it in writing.** Otherwise, you have little or no recourse if someone (such as a supplier) doesn't deliver as promised.

- ✔ **Don't make promises verbally that you aren't willing to put into writing.** What you say can get you into trouble, especially in terms of your customers and advertising.

- ✔ **Get a legal perspective.** As we discuss in Chapter 10, you need to seek legal assistance for small-business operation issues at various times in the life of your business. When you're drafting contracts is one of those times.

Whether or not you should develop a contract with a vendor or a customer depends on the situation. If, for example, you're working with a local customer or vendor — especially someone you know — and you think he may be offended by your request for a formal contract, sticking with handshakes is fine. If, however, you happen to land a whale for a customer or you order products from a large vendor, neither of whom you have a personal relationship with, you should definitely initiate a formal contract.

In fact, most large companies — whether they're customers or vendors — expect a formal contract as part of the package. If they don't get one, they may wonder about your ability to work with them on a professional level. If the professionalism issue isn't enough to convince you to develop a formal contract, let self-preservation be your motivator. After all, large businesses don't always have small businesses' best interests in mind. Why not lock in your safety with a contract?

Laboring over Employee Costs and Laws

When your business begins to hire employees, the good news is that it has probably gotten off the ground sufficiently well enough to afford the costs associated with hiring and managing them. The bad news is that, besides the salary you pay your employees, you'll encounter several significant "hidden" costs, including the following (see Chapter 16 for the lowdown on finding and hiring employees):

- ✔ **Taxes:** On top of your employees' salaries, you're also responsible for paying Social Security taxes on their earnings, as well as other taxes, such as unemployment insurance. When hiring, you must be careful about whether you hire people as employees or independent contractors. Many small-business employers prefer to hire people as independent contractors because doing so lowers their tax bills, but the IRS has strict rules for who qualifies as an independent contractor. If you classify someone as a contractor who should be considered an employee, you could end up facing stiff penalties. (We cover small-business tax issues in detail in Chapter 19.)

- ✔ **Employee benefits:** Various insurance programs, paid vacation, and retirement plans help attract and retain employees. The smallest small businesses can't afford to offer many employee benefits, but you should know your options and be aware of what your competition is offering. (We cover employee benefit programs in Chapter 17.)

- ✔ **Government regulations:** Are you surprised that a host of local, state, and federal government regulations dictate, mandate, and cajole your hiring, management, and dismissal of employees? You shouldn't be if you've read this chapter all the way through!

- ✔ **Employee lawsuits:** Don't think that just because you're not running a billion-dollar enterprise you can't and won't be sued. Although some employee suits are frivolous, others are caused by employers not exercising proper care when dealing with employees. Check out Chapter 10 for info on working with a small-business-experienced attorney.

Chapter 19

Mastering Small-Business Taxes

· ·

In This Chapter

▶ Managing your business taxes and maintaining sound financial records

▶ Identifying and managing your tax bracket

▶ Understanding employee tax issues

▶ Using sensible tax write-offs

▶ Choosing a tax-friendly corporate entity

· ·

*O*ne of the more painful aspects of owning your own business is the amount of time you have to spend on doing tax-related bookkeeping chores and on completing and filing numerous tax forms. In addition to federal income tax requirements, most states assess income taxes, and as we discuss in Chapter 18, some local governments levy taxes on small businesses, too. This chapter is all about helping you understand small-business taxes.

When you were an employee, you probably took for granted how simple your tax life was. As a wage-slave, you had the appropriate taxes withheld by your employer from each of your paychecks, and your employer submitted the money to the required government entities. When it was time to file your annual tax return, your employer provided you with Form W-2, which neatly summarized your total pay for the year just passed, as well as the dollar amount of taxes paid at the federal, state, and local levels. Being a wage-slave, from a paperwork standpoint anyway, has benefits!

By contrast, as a small-business owner, you're the employer, and you have many more tax responsibilities. Throughout the year, you're personally responsible for paying estimated taxes as you earn money, and you must withhold and submit payroll taxes for all your employees. And then, when the time comes to file your annual tax return, the real fun begins. For all these reasons, many small-business owners (justifiably) seek help from tax professionals to complete their annual income tax returns and to file their payroll tax payments throughout the year. As we discuss in Chapter 10, after your company starts growing, you may choose to hire an in-house bookkeeper. Even then, however, you probably won't be able to go it alone on your income and payroll taxes and still be assured of avoiding errors and taking advantage of legal ways to minimize your tax bills.

That last point is important because whether you hire professional tax help or not, we don't want you to pay more taxes than you're legally required to pay. Although you may have heard tales of small-business owners who cheated on their taxes, we know some small-business owners who pay *more* taxes than they should. Either they haven't taken the time to understand the tax laws or they (or their tax preparers) are being too conservative in preparing their tax returns. Also, some small-business owners don't want to claim legal deductions if doing so will trigger an audit. Frankly, we find that approach foolish. As long as you stay within the boundaries of the tax laws, you have no reason to fear an audit, except for the hassle of time and possible out-of-pocket expense for representation if you so choose. So throughout this chapter, we highlight strategies for reducing your small-business taxes.

One final point before we get into discussing specific tax solutions: Cash may become tight at some point in your business's growth. When that happens, you have a number of options for generating, or saving, cash (see Chapter 14 for more details):

- ✔ Collect your receivables faster.
- ✔ Convert your inventory into cash faster.
- ✔ Pay your vendors more slowly.

Notice that paying your taxes late is *not* an option — not a viable one, anyway. Although just about anything else goes when the cash flow blues arrive, the tardy payment of taxes is a no-no. The government has too many options to collect their due and it can nail you with stiff costs for late and missed payments, so be sure to pay the government's share of your taxes on time. Of course, you can certainly make your tax payments just before the due date, but make sure you've earmarked the cash for those payments.

Getting Smarter about Taxes

Whether you decide to hire tax advisors or deal with taxes completely on your own, your best strategy for reducing your small-business taxes and complying with tax laws is to educate yourself. If you can afford to hire outside bookkeeping and tax preparers or advisors (and you'd prefer to do so), go ahead. But take note: We believe it's a mistake to seek such assistance without first investing a small amount of time to better understand what the tax laws are and how they fit into your small-business and personal financial situations.

Just by understanding the tax system, you can legally reduce your tax bills by tens of thousands of dollars during your working years. Compound these savings over the life of your business and you'll see why we're so adamant on the subject of figuring out how to play the tax-saving game. In this section, we cover resources that can help you deal with taxes on your own, and we offer tips for how to hire tax preparers and advisors.

Reading income tax guides

The following helpful booklets are available for free from the Internal Revenue Service (IRS; www.irs.gov):

- **Publication 17, Your Federal Income Tax:** Designed for individual tax-return preparation

- **Publication 334, Tax Guide for Small Business:** Designed for small-business owners to use in their tax-return preparation of Schedule C or C-EZ

Not surprisingly, the IRS doesn't go out of its way to suggest ways for you to cut your income tax bill and doesn't exactly have a knack for clearly and concisely stating things in plain English. If it did, people wouldn't get so frustrated and annoyed when completing their tax forms.

Fortunately, you don't have to rely solely on IRS booklets to understand taxes and file your tax returns. You can obtain tax-preparation, -planning, and -advice books that highlight wise and legal tax-reduction moves. We're partial to J. K. Lasser's *Your Income Tax* (Wiley). You can also access many tax articles on Eric's website, www.erictyson.com.

Using tax-preparation software

Good tax-preparation software offers many benefits, including the following:

- Explains how to complete your tax return

- Highlights what could trigger an audit

- Suggests some tax-reduction strategies

- Enables you to quickly recalculate all your tax numbers if something changes

Among the major programs out there, our favorites are H&R Block At Home (www.hrblock.com/tax-software/index.html) and TurboTax (www.turbotax.intuit.com). If you use bookkeeping software, check to see whether the tax package you're interested in allows you to transfer data easily from your financial program into the tax-preparation program.

Hiring help

Hiring a tax preparer or advisor — particularly when you're completing a tax return as the owner of your own business for the first time — can save you time *and* reduce your tax bill. If and when you end up seeking the services of a tax practitioner (as most small-business owners do), do your homework to find a good one. Like any other professional consultant and/or advisor, the quality and competence of tax preparers and advisors vary widely. Hire them with the same care, concern, and due diligence as you would a key employee (see Chapter 16 for details on hiring superstar employees).

When searching for tax help, as with seeking other competent professionals, take the time to get the names of several leads and interview your prospects. Then check their references carefully. Word-of-mouth referrals are useful places to start. For instance, networking with other small-business owners is the best way to find an experienced and capable professional (although law-yers and bankers can also be good sources for referrals).

What should you be looking for and asking about? We're glad you asked! Here are our suggestions:

✔ **Small-business focus:** As a small-business owner, you have unique income tax requirements, quite different from those of a retired person or an employee who draws an employer's paycheck. As a result, one of the first things you need to ask a tax person you're interviewing is to describe the makeup of his practice in terms of income, assets, and client occupation. Don't say that you're a small-business owner because that may bias his answers.

Another way to verify the tax advisor's experience with businesses like yours is to ask specifically for small-business references.

✔ **Tax focus:** The U.S. income tax system can get complicated. Good tax advisors will tell you that keeping up with it is a full-time job. Thus, you should seek the services of a tax person who focuses full time on tax preparation and advice.

Some tax preparers who are struggling to build their businesses or seeking fat commissions try to sell financial products under the guise of performing financial planning for their clients. You don't want or need a sales pitch for investments and insurance products. Hire professional tax advisors who are selling their time and tax expertise — and nothing else.

✔ **Solid training and experience:** As we discuss in the sidebar "What's in a tax pro title?" tax advisors come with varying credentials. Far more important than a credential is the relevant training and experience the tax advisor brings to the table.

✔ **Tax advice, not number crunching:** Some tax practitioners only complete tax returns and don't offer advice or much other assistance throughout the year. We suggest that you seek out the services of a tax advisor — someone who has a broader view of the job than simply plugging numbers into your annual tax return and then forgetting about you until the next spring. A good tax advisor should help you plan ahead to reduce your taxes and help you file other important tax documents throughout the year. He should also make sure that you don't overlook deductions or make costly mistakes that may lead to an audit, penalties, or interest.

If your current tax advisor isn't checking in with you every November or December for planning purposes, you're probably using the wrong person. Tax planning for the upcoming year and last-minute tax planning for the current year are as much a part of the tax process as crunching the numbers. The small incremental cost of a tax-planning session can be well worth the investment. If you aren't currently planning, get busy now!

✔ **Reasonable prices:** As you interview prospective tax advisors, ask them what their hourly billing rates are and what total fees they expect to charge you for specific services (such as completing your annual income tax returns, helping with employee payroll tax issues, preparing financial reports, and so on). Then hold them to their quotes — unless you dump more work on them than you originally planned. Also, make sure their invoices break down their billings into hourly charges. More-experienced advisors charge a higher hourly rate, but they should be able to complete your work more efficiently than someone less experienced. Ask exactly who will prepare your return and what the fees are; if someone other than the person you're interviewing will prepare your return, also ask who will review the preparer's work.

✔ **Insurance:** When interviewing prospective tax advisors, ask if they carry liability, or what's sometimes known as *errors and omissions* (E&O), insurance. If your tax advisor makes a gaffe, especially a major one, E&O insurance increases your chances of being compensated for your damages.

✔ **Glowing references:** Ask a tax advisor candidate to provide you with three clients who do similar work to yours and who have used the advisor's services for the past couple of years. As you check references with these clients, ask them such questions as what they like or don't like about working with that tax advisor and how aggressive and proactive the advisor is with regard to tax-reduction tactics.

✔ **An ability to speak your language:** Advisors who use a lot of confusing jargon and don't give straight answers are a waste of your time and money. Sure, taxes can get complicated, but a good advisor should be able to explain your situation in plain English. If he can't, you'll be going on blind faith that the advisor is taking the best path for you.

You can be your own best tax advisor. Understanding how the income tax system works and how to make it work best for you can save you tens of thousands of tax dollars, as well as tax advisor fees. Use advisors to increase your knowledge and save you money, not as replacements for your own responsibility. And if you have a static tax situation year after year or if you take sufficient interest in understanding the income tax system, we don't believe you need to hire a tax person, unless you feel you have something better to do with your time.

What's in a tax pro title?

In the income tax field, you'll find practitioners who go by all sorts of names and titles. Here are the common ones you'll encounter, along with our take on when each may be appropriate for you to hire:

✔ **Tax preparers:** Tax preparers (such as those who work for large chains like H&R Block and Jackson Hewitt, as well as scads of sole practitioners and small partnerships) tend to focus on tax preparation and sometimes don't work in the tax field year-round. Although they're among the least costly of tax people, most preparers don't have adequate expertise to handle the typical small-business owner's tax returns and other tax questions. As is the case with so-called financial planners, no regulations or licensing applies to tax preparers. A good preparer who has completed an adequate training program makes sense for small-business owners with simple situations and businesses.

✔ **Enrolled agents (EAs):** Enrolled agents tend to focus their practices on income tax return preparation. EAs, whose prices tend to be higher than those of preparers, complete significant training as well as continuing education. Unlike a preparer, if you ever get audited, an EA can represent you before the IRS or state tax authorities.

✔ **Certified public accountants (CPAs):** Similar to enrolled agents, CPAs go through significant training and examination to receive their credentials and then must complete continuing education. CPA fees tend to be a bit higher than EA fees.

✔ **Tax attorneys:** Most tax attorneys don't prepare tax returns; instead, they typically get involved in court cases dealing with tax problems. Attorneys with sufficient small-business experience can also help you with buying or selling a business.

Note: A tax person with a credential isn't necessarily competent, ethical, or cost-effective. Whatever credential a given tax advisor has should have little impact on your decision about whether to retain her services.

Keeping Good Financial Records Leads to Tax Benefits

As small-business owners who've survived more than a few years running our own shops, we know from experience the value of tracking and documenting business financials. Along with our word, consider the following tax benefits when you find yourself wondering whether keeping good records and staying on top of your business bookkeeping are worth your time and effort:

- **Reduced taxes:** The better the financial records you keep for your business, the better able you are to come up with legal, tax-reducing deductions when the time comes to fill out that dreaded annual tax return. Also, good records enable you to stay on top of your income tax payments for yourself and your business and payroll tax payments for your employees throughout the year — saving you late interest and penalty charges.

- **Easier and less costly income tax return preparation:** If you don't keep a proper accounting of your income and expenses during the tax year, you won't be able to accurately complete the necessary tax forms when the time comes to file them for your business. A tax preparer may actually be happy with your slipshod practices, however — the more time she has to spend assembling and organizing your documentation, the fatter the tax-preparation fee you'll have to pay.

- **Documentation for audits:** Because the IRS uncovers more mistakes and fraud on small-business returns than on ordinary employee returns, small-business owners get audited at a much higher rate than employees who draw a paycheck. The better records you keep, the better able you'll be to effectively substantiate your tax return in the event that you do get audited.

- **Better planning for subsequent years:** The better your records from last year, the better the decisions you'll make when planning for the coming year.

We discuss how to establish a bookkeeping system for your small business in Chapter 10.

Knowing (And Managing) Your Tax Bracket

Over the years that you own and operate your small business, your income will, we hope, increase; most likely, it will also fluctuate from year to year. Because of the way the IRS and most states tax income, your changing income will probably place you in different tax brackets from year to year.

The good news is that you may be able to legally shift some of your business's income and expenses from one tax year to another, saving yourself some tax dollars — perhaps even thousands of dollars — in the process. For example, if you operate your business on a *cash basis* — meaning that you recognize or report income in the tax year in which that income was received and expenses in the tax year that you paid them — you can exert some control over the amount of profit that your business reports in a given tax year.

Sole proprietorships, partnerships, S Corporations, limited liability corporations (LLCs), and personal service corporations, for instance, can typically shift revenue and expenses. On the other hand, C Corporations (and partnerships that have C Corporations as partners) may not use the cash accounting method.

Suppose that, like most business owners, you expect your next year's income to be higher than this year's, and you expect to be in a higher tax bracket next year. In this case, you can likely reduce your total tax bill for both this year and next by paying more of your expenses in the following year, thus reducing your next year's taxable income, which you expect to be taxed at a higher rate. Although you can't expect your employees to wait until January for their November paychecks, maybe you can delay buying a new photocopying or fax machine or paying a December invoice for expenses (as long as no penalties are involved) until the beginning of the next tax year.

Staying on Top of Employment Taxes

As we discuss in Chapter 16, hiring and keeping good employees is no small challenge. One of the administrative unpleasantries that comes with hiring employees is needing to withhold proper taxes for various government entities. This section contains our advice for dealing with the sometimes sticky issues of employee taxes.

Be aware of your benefit options

As a small-business owner, you can deduct the cost of various benefits — including retirement savings plans and insurance — which are there for you and any other employees in your company. As a self-employed person, you may find thinking of yourself as an employee odd, but you are, in fact, an employee in addition to being the owner. You have to look after your own benefit needs as well as those of your employees.

Peruse Chapter 17, which covers the ins and outs of benefits, to find out which benefits are tax deductible as expenses related to your business.

Stay current on taxes

When you're self-employed, you're responsible for the accurate and timely filing of all taxes owed on your income. Without an employer and a payroll department to handle the paperwork for withholding taxes on a regular schedule, you need to make estimated tax payments on a quarterly basis.

If you have employees, you need to withhold payroll taxes on their income from every paycheck you cut them. You must then make timely payments to the IRS and to the appropriate state authorities. To discover all the rules and regulations of withholding and submitting taxes from employees' paychecks, contact the IRS (www.irs.gov) and your state agencies for informational brochures (and see Chapter 18).

In addition to withholding federal and state income tax, you need to withhold and send in Social Security and any other locally or state-mandated payroll taxes from your employees' paychecks.

If you doubt your ability to stay current on taxes for yourself and your employees, you should hire a tax advisor and/or payroll service who will force you to jump through the necessary tax hoops. (Good tax advisors can usually recommend payroll services, and such firms often offer a bevy of other human-resources-related services, too.) Falling behind in taxes has sunk too many small businesses. See the earlier section "Hiring help" for tips on how to hire the right tax advisor.

As we note in Chapter 18, all businesses except certain sole proprietorships are required to obtain an Employer Identification Number (EIN) from the IRS. The application form, known as an SS-4, is available at your local IRS or Social Security office; you can also go to the IRS website at www.irs.gov or call 800-TAX-FORM.

Report your work with independent contractors

Many small businesses start off hiring people as part-time independent contractors rather than full-time employees. Why? Because hiring a contractor is less of a financial commitment:

- ✔ **If you hire an employee:** Your business must withhold federal (including your share of the employee's Social Security taxes) and state taxes, as well as any other mandated taxes, and then send those tax payments to the appropriate tax authorities.

- ✔ **If you hire an independent contractor:** You don't have to offer him benefits, such as health insurance or a retirement plan.

Although you, as the small-business owner, may benefit from hiring people as contractors rather than employees, the people you hire may also prefer to be classified as independent contractors for the following reasons:

- ✔ Contractors have a greater ability to write off business expenses on their personal income tax returns.

- ✔ Being self-employed, contractors can establish and fund retirement savings plans, such as SEP-IRAs or Keoghs (see Chapter 17), which allow them to tax-shelter as much as 20 percent of their employment income.

The IRS dislikes independent-contractor arrangements because it believes contractors tend to underreport their income and inflate their business expenses. Not surprisingly, the IRS has rules for determining whether someone you hire should be classified as a contractor or as an employee. The general rule is that unless the person doing the work is clearly another business, you have an employee. Neither the length of employment nor how much you pay matters. Even if you and the other person both agree that you're using an independent contractor, the only thing that matters is whether the business (person) meets both state and federal guidelines.

Here are some of the many guidelines for making the determination:

- ✔ **Amount of employer's direction:** Employers direct employees in their work. Independent contractors largely figure out for themselves — without much instruction from the employer — how to accomplish the work that they're hired to do. Employees also usually have established hours of work, whereas independent contractors have more freedom in setting the hours that they'll work for a given employer.

- **Number of employers:** Independent contractors tend to perform work for many employers at the same time; they may even have their own employees. Employees typically work for just one employer.

- **Where the work is performed:** Employees typically do their work at the employer's place of business; independent contractors usually do much of their work elsewhere.

IRS Publication 15, Circular E, Employer's Tax Guide, spells out all the parameters to consider in classifying someone who works with your firm as an employee or an independent contractor. If the distinction still confuses you — and you're not alone if it does — seek out the help of a tax advisor experienced in working with small-business owners (see the earlier section "Hiring help"). You can also allow the IRS to make the determination by completing Form SS-8, Determination of Worker Status for Purposes of Federal Employment Taxes and Income Tax Withholding, and mailing it to the IRS.

If your business legitimately hires independent contractors to perform work, the contractors are responsible for paying their own taxes. However, you, as the small-business owner, still have to report on the independent contractors that your firm works with. In fact, you're required to file Form 1099 with the IRS (and some state tax agencies), which details the amount of money paid to companies (that aren't corporations) that receive $600 or more from your business for services (not the product provided).

Hire your kids!

If your kids can perform a useful job in your business, consider hiring them. Here's why:

- You'll be showing them firsthand the value of their efforts.

- You may get an important bonding opportunity with your kids.

- If you're a sole proprietor, you could save your family taxes. Your kids are surely in a lower income tax bracket than you, so by paying them some of your income, you're effectively lowering your income tax bill. Also, if your kids are under the age of 18, they won't have to pay the same Social Security on their earnings as you do.

To make the most of hiring your kids, follow these guidelines to keep the IRS off your back and to keep you and your kids happy:

- Give them real, tangible work. Don't make the work part of their household chores.

- Pay fair-market wages (given their experience level and productivity).

✔ Highlight the value of working for work's sake and for the accomplishment of broader goals, such as saving for college, a home, or major purchases.

✔ Treat your child as you treat your other employees when she's on the job. Keep your business relationship businesslike. (Doing so will keep both the feds *and* your nonrelative employees happy.)

Spending Your Money Tax-Wisely

As a small-business owner, you have many opportunities for how and where to spend your start-up funding and the cash you generate from your business's operations. In this section, we explain how you should base part of your spending decisions on tax factors.

Take equipment write-offs sensibly

When you buy equipment — such as computers, office furniture, bookshelves, and so on — each item can be *depreciated,* meaning that each year you can claim a tax deduction for a portion of the equipment's original purchase price. Alternatively, through a so-called *Section 179 deduction,* you can deduct the entire amount you spent on the equipment as long as the deduction doesn't contribute to showing a tax loss. You must also be within the current IRS limits for the amount of equipment purchases deducted for your business.

Although you may want to deduct the full amount of an equipment purchase in the tax year that you made the purchase, doing so isn't always the best option. Looking ahead, if you expect your business profits to increase and push you into a higher tax bracket, you may be able to reduce your taxes by *depreciating* (over a period of time) rather than deducting (immediately); in other words, you can push more tax write-offs into future years when you expect to be in a higher tax bracket. See the section "Knowing (And Managing) Your Tax Bracket" earlier in this chapter for more details.

Don't waste extra money on a business car

If you use your car for business, you can claim a deduction. Some small-business owners mistakenly buy a costly car for business use. The reasoning is that a splashy car will impress clients and customers and, because auto expenses for businesses are tax deductible, the IRS is helping to foot the bill.

Don't waste your money buying a costly car. Instead, buy a car within your means — just as you should buy any other piece of business equipment within your means. You can then spend the money you don't spend on an expensive business car on marketing, customer service, a new computer system, and so on — all of which are much more important to your business's success than a nice-looking car.

Realize that the IRS limits the depreciation write-off you can take for a car, thus negating some of the potential tax write-offs on more expensive cars. Without boring you with the details, suffice it to say that, for tax purposes, you shouldn't spend more than about $25,000 on a car for business use.

Minimize fun and travel expenditures

With meal and entertainment expenditures, only 50 percent of your business expenses are deductible. The IRS doesn't allow deductions for club dues, such as health, business, airport, or social clubs, or entertainment facilities (like executive boxes at sports stadiums, apartments, and so on).

The IRS has clamped down on writing off travel, meal, and entertainment expenses because of abuse by business owners and employees who try to write off nonbusiness expenses.

Grasping the Tax Implications of Your Entity Selection

As we note in Chapter 5, corporations are taxed as entities separate from their individual owners. This situation can be both good and bad. Suppose that your business is doing really well and making loads of money. If your business isn't incorporated as a C Corporation, all the profits from your business are taxed on your personal tax return in the year that you earned those profits.

If you intend to use your profits to reinvest in your business and expand, incorporating can potentially save you some tax dollars. If your business is incorporated (as a regular *C Corporation*), the first $75,000 of profits in the business should be taxed at a lower rate in the corporation than they would be on your personal tax return (see Table 19-1 for details). One exception to this rule is personal service corporations, such as accounting, legal, and medical firms (which pay a flat tax rate of 35 percent on their taxable income).

Table 19-1	Corporate Tax Rates for C Corporations
Income	*Tax Rate*
$0–$50,000	15%
$50,001–$75,000	25%
$75,001–$100,000	34%
$100,001–$335,000	39%
$335,001–$10,000,000	34%

Another possible tax advantage for owning a corporation is that corporations can pay — on a tax-deductible basis — for employee benefits such as health insurance, disability, and up to $50,000 of term life insurance (see Chapter 17 for the lowdown on employee benefits). Sole proprietorships and other unincorporated businesses can take tax deductions for these benefit-related expenses only for employees. Benefit expenses for owners who work in the business aren't deductible.

Resist the temptation to incorporate just so you can have your money left in the corporation, which may be taxed at a lower rate than you would pay on your personal income. Don't let this seemingly short-term gain motivate you. If you want to pay yourself the profits in the future, you could end up paying *more* taxes. Why? Because you pay taxes first at the corporate tax rate in the year your company earns the money and then again on the profits (this time on your personal income tax return) when you pay yourself from the corporate till in the form of a dividend.

Another tax reason not to incorporate — especially in the early days of a business — is that you can't immediately claim the losses for an incorporated business on your personal tax return. You have to wait until you can offset your losses against profits. Because most businesses produce little revenue in their early years and have all sorts of start-up expenditures, losses are common. With all entities except C Corporations, the business profit or loss passes through to the owner's personal tax returns. So if the business shows a loss in some years, the owner may claim those losses in the current year of the loss on the tax returns. If you plan to take all the profits out of the company, an S Corporation may make sense for you (see Chapter 5 for more on the different business entities).

The only significant advantage for most small businesses to incorporate in their early years is that the corporate "shield" protects owners from some liabilities, such as lawsuits against the company — if the corporation is properly organized. Because incorporation has legal and tax consequences, we recommend that you consult a tax preparer and an attorney before making your entity decision. See Chapter 5 for a full discussion of the pros and cons of incorporation.

Chapter 20

Cultivating a Growing Business

· ·

In This Chapter

▶ Understanding the evolution of a growing business

▶ Addressing issues in human resources

▶ Managing time in a budding business

▶ Pairing the right management tools with your growing business

▶ Finding solutions for business problems

▶ Making the transition from entrepreneur to manager (or moving on)

· ·

Given the choice, most small-business owners would prefer that their companies grow rather than not grow, stagnate, or even fail. After all, growth *is* the American way — not to mention it's also one of the typical entrepreneur's primary motivators.

This chapter is for you if your business is presently on a growth track or (you hope) soon will be. In it, we provide you with insights into what awaits you on your journey, along with tips on how to survive the trip and prosper as you go. We warn you, however, that growth — especially that of the consistent and relentless variety — can feel like a climb up an uncharted mountain. And the climb becomes even steeper if you set out on the journey unprepared to make the change that has eluded so many small-business owners before you: the transition from entrepreneur to manager.

The changes to your growth-fueled business will be apparent everywhere. Five years from now, your customers will be different, their demands and needs will be different, and many of the products and services you offer them will be different. You'll also have a number of brand-spanking-new superstar employees, and employee-related matters will take up more and more of your time. (Sadly, some of your earlier hires will have departed or won't have the necessary skills to keep up with your growth.)

Finally, you — Mr. or Ms. Grand Poobah — will be constantly in the midst of change, engrossed in the not-always-enjoyable-but-always-necessary process of personally making the transition from entrepreneur to manager. Along the way, you'll adopt skills such as delegation, focus, and holding people accountable — skills that every successful manager must eventually acquire to effectively lead a growing team of employees. And your financial, communication, and leadership skills will be tested and, we hope, improved. In other words, you won't be the same Grand Poobah you are today!

The only characteristics of your business that won't change as your company grows are its ethics and principles. However, if your top management (which is probably just you at this point) changes during the business's growth years, as happens in so many growing entrepreneurial companies, even your company's ethics and principles may be subject to change. Growth holds nothing sacred!

Recognizing Growth Stages

Small-business success doesn't just happen. Some fairly predictable but not very orderly stages characterize its evolution. Most entrepreneurs caught up in the day-to-day goings on in a business don't recognize these stages until they've passed. Well, it's time to open your eyes. The following sections describe the three stages of business evolution.

The start-up years

The *start-up years* are the period when survival motivates your thoughts and actions. Everything that happens within the business is dominated by you; words such as *delegation, team,* and *consensus* generally are not yet part of the business's vocabulary. These are the hands-on years. For some owners, they're the most enjoyable years of the business; for all owners, they're an integral part of the learning process.

The work during this time is hard — often the physically and emotionally draining kind of hard. The hours are long and sometimes tedious, but by the end of the day, you can see, touch, and feel the progress you've made. The gratification is instantaneous.

The duration of this first stage varies greatly from business to business. Some fly through the start-up stage in less than a year, but most spend anywhere from one to three years growing out of this stage. Others — often those in the more competitive niches — spend as many as five or more years in the start-up stage.

You know you've graduated from the start-up stage when profitability and orderliness become a dependable part of your business. The hectic days of worrying about survival are replaced by the logical, orderly days of planning for success.

The growth years

The *growth years* are the years when your business achieves some sense of order, stability, and profitability. Your evolving business has survived the mistakes, confusion, and chaos of the start-up years, and now optimism, camaraderie, and cooperation should play an important role in the organization. Key employees surface, efficient administrative systems and controls become part of the business's daily operating procedures, and the need to depend on you for everything that happens diminishes.

The business of doing business remains fun for most small-business owners in this stage, because increasing sales translate into increasing profits — every small-business owner's dream. The balance sheet puts some flesh on its scraggly bones as you generate cash as a result of profitability. You learn to delegate many of those unpleasant tasks that you performed in the past. And survival is no longer your primary motivator. At last, the daily choices you make can be dictated by lifestyle goals rather than survival.

We have more good news: This stage can last a long time if the growth remains under control and if you manage the business and its expanding population of employees properly. (For information on out-of-control growth, see the sidebar "Is your business growth healthy growth?") More than likely, however, this stage will last anywhere from a few years to six or seven years or so before the next stage raises its ugly head.

The transition period

The third stage, the *transition period,* can also be called the *restructuring stage* or the *diversification stage.* By the time this stage begins, something basic to the success of the growth years has changed or gone wrong. As a result, in order for the business to survive, a strategic change in direction, or transition, is required. (See the later section "Redefining Your Role in an Evolving Business" for more on this topic.)

Many factors can bring about the transition period, including the following:

- ✔ **Relentless growth:** Relentless sales growth requires relentless improvement in the business's employees, systems, procedures, and infrastructure, and many businesses simply can't keep up with such pressures.

- ✔ **Shrinkage of sales and the disappearance of profits, or even prolonged periods of stagnation:** This is the opposite of growth. The causes for this shrinkage or stagnation can come from anywhere and everywhere, and they often include such uncontrollable factors as new competitors, a changing economy, new technology, and changes in consumer demand.

Is your business growth healthy growth?

Growth is good, as long as it's healthy growth. Here are two ways to figure out whether your business's growth is trending toward healthy or unhealthy:

✔ Using your profit and loss statement (see Chapter 14), compute the percentage growth of your sales. Then compute the percentage growth of your earnings. If your sales are growing faster than your earnings, your business is showing an early sign of unhealthy growth. (The bigger the spread, the more unhealthy the trend.)

✔ Using your balance sheet (see Chapter 14), compute the combined percentage growth of your key noncash asset categories: accounts receivable, inventory, and equipment. If the combined percentage growth of these three categories exceeds the percentage growth of your sales (see the preceding bullet point), your business is showing another early sign of unhealthy growth. (Again, the bigger the spread, the more unhealthy the trend.)

For your business's long-term growth to be trending in a healthy direction, two things should be taking place:

✔ Your percentage growth in earnings should keep up with, or exceed, your percentage growth in sales.

✔ The combined percentage increase in the key asset categories (accounts receivable, inventory, and equipment) should be less than your percentage increase in sales.

The financially astute small-business owner is no different from the financially astute homeowner. The homeowner must figure out how to keep his expenditures in line with his income. The small-business owner must figure out how to keep her income in line with her sales (which amounts, in large part, to controlling her expenses), all while controlling the purchase of those key assets (inventory, receivables, and equipment) — the increase in which must be paid for by cash generated through future earnings.

The solution to transition-period problems lies in making a strategic change — a transition — in the fundamentals of the company. This transition often involves a change in top management. It isn't unusual for a rapidly growing company to outgrow its founding entrepreneur (that's you!). Additionally, the transition may involve the introduction of new products or services, the establishment of new distribution systems, the adoption of new technology, or the paring of underperforming parts of the business.

The good news to a displaced founding entrepreneur: If yours was a profitable company and you can sell it on the way out, you can then afford to go back to what you do well and what you enjoy. You can go back to the life of an entrepreneur and start all over again. Or, if you're financially able, you can move on to other pursuits.

Handling Human Resources Issues

As we discuss in Chapter 16, the day that you hire your first employee is the same day that the bottomless pit of human resources (or HR) issues appears on your path. After all, that newly hired employee has needs, privileges, and rights — the last of which, lest you forget, are protected by a host of watch-dog government agencies. In the following sections, we raise some important HR concerns and suggest how to handle them.

Identifying some important HR concerns

Consider, if you will, a partial list of HR issues, the mere mention of which can make a government inspector's mouth water:

- ✔ Sexual harassment
- ✔ Discrimination
- ✔ Wrongful discharge
- ✔ Hiring violations
- ✔ Workplace safety violations
- ✔ Working conditions violations
- ✔ Wage and hour violations

Unfortunately, much of the concern for the employee's welfare that you hear about today is well founded and necessary, because too many greedy and uncaring business owners over the years have created the need for such government scrutiny. This means that law-abiding and people-caring small-business owners like you must pay the price in the form of red tape and regulations. And the more your company grows, the larger that price becomes. (We deal with legal and regulatory issues in Chapter 18.)

Dealing with HR issues in three stages

How do you deal with such a wide spectrum of HR issues? The answer depends on which of the three stages of HR development your company happens to be in.

Stage 1: Dealing with HR issues yourself

Stage 1 is the start-up stage when your business has, for example, fewer than ten employees and you have no one on the payroll to whom you can delegate the wide variety of HR issues. In this stage, you must interrupt the activities that you probably prefer performing (sales, product development, and customer service) and deal with those that you don't (working conditions, drug and alcohol policies, and employee conduct).

Stage 1 is the hands-on stage when you're up to your eyeballs in the day-to-day details of running a business (see the earlier section "The start-up years"). The good news is that the HR lessons you learn at this stage of your business will benefit you forever. The bad news is that dealing with some HR issues may consume an extraordinarily large part of your time.

If you're struggling through Stage 1 right now, turn to Chapter 16 for helpful advice on coexisting with employees. Also, when dealing with those sticky issues that have the potential to become even stickier — harassment, wrongful termination, employee theft, and the like — consult a professional (a human resources consultant or lawyer) before you act (see Chapter 10 for details on finding a good lawyer).

Stage 2: Delegating HR responsibilities to others

As the number of employees in your company grows in Stage 2, you should look for the opportunity to offload some HR details onto someone else in the business — most likely a full-time bookkeeper or the person who manages your office — or to outsource to a professional employer organization. Whatever option you choose, the basic HR functions will remain as a part of your day-to-day business procedures until your business enters Stage 3.

Stage 3: Hiring an HR director

You may think you're in heaven when your business grows to the point when you can finally afford the small-business owner's greatest luxury: your very own HR director. (Our experience is that this will happen when you have somewhere in the neighborhood of 50 to 100 employees.) We know that it's hard to believe that people actually make a 9-to-5 living dealing with and actually enjoying the seemingly endless details involved in HR. Imagine, someday you could have that person on your payroll!

Strangely, people capable of becoming HR directors are similar to consultants: There seems to be one on every street corner. Run an ad for an HR director in the newspaper or on one of the many online resources (national organizations such as Monster or Craigslist or regional/local sites) and measure your responses in the dozens. Among those dozens, you can reasonably expect to find a number of quality applicants. (See Chapter 16 for tips on how to hire the best one.)

Addressing Time-Management Issues

The faster a company grows and the bigger it becomes, the more important time-management issues become. The increased size of an organization requires increased communication between its members — which in turn increases the demands on your time and that of your employees.

Time, and the efficient use of it, is one of those cultural issues that starts at the small-business owner's desk. You, by way of your actions, determine how your business utilizes its time. If you ensure that meetings start on time, that the workday begins at 8 o'clock sharp, and that prolonged gatherings around the copy machine are unacceptable behavior, your company is bound to develop a culture of efficient time management. On the other hand, if you don't pay attention to such issues, human nature will take its natural course, which doesn't bode well for your business's efficient use of time.

Here are just a few of the ways that a small-business team can waste time:

- Missed deadlines and appointments
- Meetings that last an hour when they should last only ten minutes
- People who arrive late to meetings
- Meetings that shouldn't be held in the first place
- Long voicemail messages, unreturned phone calls, unanswered phone calls, and unnecessary calls
- Unnecessary or long-winded e-mails
- Employees who conduct personal matters on the job (making calls to friends, shopping online, surfing their Facebook page, and so on)
- People who take 15 minutes to say what could be said in 5
- Time spent waiting — in waiting rooms, outside offices, or for someone to get off the phone or fax machine or away from the copier
- Equipment that malfunctions, systems that don't work, and supplies that run out of whatever is needed at that instant

Imagine what your company would be like if everyone practiced effective time management. How much additional work would each employee get done? How much time would he or she save? Five hours a week? Ten? What could every employee do with another five hours a week — 250 hours a year? And what could your company do with those 250 hours a year, multiplied by the number of employees you have?

To increase efficiency in your small business, you can insist on employee attitudes and behavior that value rather than abuse time. For example, you can insist on a culture within your business that

- ✔ Requires people to be on time for the start of the day, for meetings, for conferences, for whatever.

- ✔ Never holds an unnecessary meeting.

- ✔ Requires every employee to use some kind of time-management system, whether it's a simple to-do list, an intricate store-bought system, or the latest handheld device.

- ✔ Has definitive rules governing such issues as surfing the Internet for personal purposes and playing computer games on company time.

- ✔ Deals with its in-house nonstop talkers and time abusers (every office has them).

- ✔ Requires that telephones be picked up after the first or second ring, voicemail messages be shortened, and telephone calls be returned promptly.

- ✔ Respects visitors' time. (How do you like it when you visit another business and you have to wait in the lobby for half an hour?)

- ✔ Encourages thoughtful delegation. (Don't waste your time doing a task that someone else can do faster — and often better.)

- ✔ Understands that shorter and quicker is better when it comes to meetings, memos, letters, manuals, and rules.

- ✔ Insists on employee accountability. (Count on employees to perform such tasks as keeping the supply inventory at adequate levels, maintaining equipment to minimize downtime, and designing and implementing workable internal systems and controls.)

- ✔ Uses time-proven technology.

Time management itself is impossible to measure. What you *can* measure are results — results when compared to plans, budgets, and goals. You can usually figure that whenever you see improving results in the areas you *can* measure, your management of time is improving, too.

You alone can make effective time management a part of your company's culture. After hiring the best people that you can (see Chapter 16), you have to set the right example. Your employees will take it from there. (If they don't, you've hired the wrong employees.)

Choosing Your Management Tools

Little is new in the world of small business. Other organizations have needed restructuring, other employees have needed motivating, and other cultures have needed change.

So what are you, the small-business owner who's looking for ways to continue growing your company, supposed to do when you think your business is ready for a dose of something new? What management tools should you use to ensure continued growth? Whose advice should you take? And how can you possibly know which of the latest fads to glom onto?

The truth of the matter is that no one management tool will turn your company around. Just as no one strategy will produce profitable customers, no one tool will change your culture, correct your infrastructure, or unite your employees.

When you're considering adopting the latest management system or tool, we suggest that you wait and let someone else be the pioneer. (Like someone once said, "You can always tell the pioneers — they're the ones with the arrows in their backs.") In other words, be aware of the fads making the rounds of the small-business arena, but don't bet the farm on the latest one. Feel free to cherry-pick a fad's key components that make the most sense to you and your business.

Use the following tips to help you determine whether the tools inherent in a given management system will work for you:

- ✔ **Don't be the first kid on the block.** Determine which similarly sized businesses have already pioneered the system and/or utilized any of its most appropriate tools and then solicit their suggestions and advice. This step is particularly important when you're considering new, costly, software-driven applications. Make sure the program you're considering has been time-tested and has many satisfied users. Also do your due diligence to ensure that the software company will be around to service and upgrade the system you buy.

- ✔ **Make sure that your key employees agree with the need for and the basic elements of the new tools before you introduce them.** Include your key employees in the purchasing, planning, and especially the implementation processes.

- ✔ **Consider the downsides as well as the upsides of utilizing the new tools.** Be sure you know what it will cost to pull the plug midstream if the tools don't work as you planned.

✔ **Understand the time frame needed to implement the tools and measure their success.** Ensure that you can live within the time frame. (Whatever figure you come up with, you generally can multiply that number by two.)

✔ **Be certain that you, the owner and chief culture-setter of your business, have the time and energy to devote to the proper implementation of the new management tools.** The implementation of new tools always requires total commitment from the Grand Poobah; if you aren't willing — or able — to make that commitment, don't even think about introducing any new tools.

If your business is working well (as measured primarily by profitability), don't break it. (You can, however, bend it.) If your business isn't working well, consider a change. One of your many responsibilities is to be the systems and tools matchmaker. Be sure to stay current with the latest and greatest management systems and the tools within them and then match your business's need for change with the applicable system.

Consider, for instance, the management fads in the following sections. Each of the fads has at least one key management tool that makes sense — ranging from setting goals to redefining processes, from paring expenses to sharing financial information. Every fad offers a degree of management wisdom and an accompanying management tool, but that doesn't mean you need to adopt the entire system. Cherry-pick as you see fit.

Management by objective

An old-timer for sure, the basic components of *management by objective* (MBO) — setting and reaching goals — have endured and are still used, to one degree or another, by many successful businesses. We discuss the process of goal-setting at length in Chapter 16. Most successful businesses — small and large — use the management tool of goal-setting in some form; so should yours.

Participatory management

The primary characteristic of *participatory management* is that all employees take part in determining the direction and policies of the company. Great in theory, this approach can work wonders when organized carefully and phased in over long periods of time. The participatory tools inherent in such a system work for two reasons:

✔ Given a voice in the decision-making process, employees are much more likely to make a personal commitment to the decisions reached.

✔ Given the fact that employees see the business through different eyes than the owners, their input enhances the quality of the decisions made.

But don't give away the keys to the car too soon. Figuring out how to drive a small business takes years of training and preparation. Besides, not all employees *want* the responsibility that goes with being behind the wheel. Finally, employee participation takes time and patience, neither of which is available in huge quantities to most entrepreneurs.

Employee ownership

Although we're certainly proponents of the motivation tool inherent in offering employees the opportunity to own a piece of the company (in other words, *employee ownership*), sharing the pie isn't always as easy as it sounds. Sometimes you don't have enough pie to go around; sometimes the pie isn't divided the way everyone would like it to be; and sometimes your employees would rather bet their futures on T-bills than on small-business pie. Besides, minority shareholders can be a pain in the rear.

But for many people, ownership is one, if not the best, motivator out there. That's why, despite the problems that come with sharing the pie, we see more and more pie-sharing going on today than ever before. Even the federal government recognizes this fact, which is why it offers a number of incentives to companies to establish such employee-empowering tools as Employee Stock Ownership Plans (ESOPs). For much more on offering employees equity in your company, see Chapter 17.

Quality circles

Quality circles are ad hoc groups or temporary teams (also known as *ad hoc committees*) of employees assembled to solve specific problems. Most successful businesses use forms of this team approach to problem solving every day. In many cases, businesses assemble specially formed teams to solve a problem and then quickly disband them after the issue has been resolved.

The appeal of the problem-solving tool inherent in quality circles is the age-old theory that two heads are better than one. This is especially true when those two (or more) heads are focused on solving a specific problem and when those heads bring differing perspectives to the problem-solving table.

Total Quality Management

Total Quality Management (TQM) is an all-encompassing phrase that means "the involving and empowering of employees to increase profits by increasing quality, increasing focus on the customer, and decreasing costs." Whew. Sounds like a synonym for *sound business practices* to us.

The faster the growth, the harder it is to keep up

Joan, a friend of coauthor Jim, owned what had been (for its first five years) a very successful sign company. Her sales had grown at an annual rate in excess of 25 percent and had reached $15 million per year in less than eight years. As a result of Joan's previous job in sales, she'd developed an effective sales staff within her company, a group that kept the orders coming — and coming.

Unfortunately, her business's systems and controls had not kept up with the 25 percent annual increase in sales. Neither of these functional areas had the skills of her managerial, administrative, and production employees. As a result, despite the consistent increase in sales, Joan's inefficient business lost money in its sixth, seventh, and eighth years, eventually forcing her to file for bankruptcy.

"The more rapid the sales growth," Joan told us later, "the more difficult it is to keep up. A 5 percent sales-growth rate provides ample time for the employees to learn and react. A 25 percent sales-growth rate and the accompanying crush of new problems do not."

Here are some lessons to take from businesses like Joan's that get consumed by sales growth:

✔ **Unless your business has large fixed costs that you can lower, don't try to grow yourself out of profitability difficulties.** Consequently, never try to throw more sales at profitability problems. More sales generally magnify existing deficiencies. Forget

focusing on sales growth. Focus instead on improving profitability (see Chapter 14).

✔ **Be willing to make a strategic change (that is, a transition) at this stage in your business.** Evaluate your business's missions, goals, and strategies and change them accordingly. Evaluate your current systems and controls and repair or, more often, replace them when necessary. Review and upgrade the organizational structure to fit your business's current needs. Most importantly, train and, when necessary, replace key employees — this includes, when the shoe fits, you, the founder. (See the advice in the sections "The transition period" and "Redefining Your Role in an Evolving Business" for more.)

✔ **Don't give yourself, your managers, and your key employees cheerleading speeches when they require training.** A fight for life is going on here, and the fight will be won or lost by you and your employees.

✔ **Be willing to go outside of the organization for management help.** A promote-from-within strategy in the face of exploding sales may mean a team of more secure employees, but it can also mean that their secure days will be numbered if your staff doesn't have the objectivity to honestly evaluate the business's weaknesses. Most employees of rapidly growing but struggling companies welcome the infusion of new blood.

After all, the tool involved in managing quality, focusing on customers, and controlling expenses is nothing more than plain-old common sense, which, come to think of it, is what TQM is all about. What makes it an ongoing fad is beyond us.

Reengineering

Called *process analysis* by some and *Business Process Reengineering* (BPR) by others, *reengineering* refers to putting each of your business's functions under the microscope and refining it. Given the choice, we'd call reengineering either *expense management par excellence* or *fat cutting extraordinaire.* The primary tool is, of course, the management of expenses.

Similar to TQM, reengineering is just another fancy word for "managing your business efficiently and logically," which makes the fad itself another excuse for consultants to write books on the subject.

Open-book management

Open-book management says that informed employees are capable of making key decisions usually reserved for management — within, that is, their areas of expertise. An *informed employee* is one who's privy to nearly everything that goes on within the company, including a variety of tools usually reserved for management, such as financial statements.

Similar to any other management system, the open-book management system has an upside and a downside:

- ✔ The downside is that your employees may find out things that you'd prefer they didn't know, like how much you spend on travel and entertainment in a year and how much your new Lexus costs the company.

- ✔ The upside is that informed employees tend to make better day-to-day decisions than uninformed ones. Informed employees are also more likely to be committed to the cause — in this case, to increasing the profitability of the company.

Troubleshooting Your Business

From time to time, businesses call in small-business consultants to troubleshoot. Although troubleshooting can be an effective tool any time, many small-business owners use it only when their growing business suddenly slows down. Consultants can help a struggling business by evaluating important areas of the business — such as finances, employee morale, and business appearance — and then making suggestions for improvement. Find out how in the following sections.

Filling out a troubleshooting checklist

Most consultants use checklists to help them determine the seriousness of a business's problems. Here's a checklist that one troubleshooting consultant we know uses.

Rank each of the following categories from 1 to 10:

_____ **Quality of cash-management procedures (cash flow reporting and forecasting) (1 = poor, 10 = excellent)**

_____ **Quality of financial reporting (profit and loss statement and balance sheet) (1 = poor, 10 = excellent)**

_____ **Quality of financial forecasting (budgets) (1 = poor, 10 = excellent)**

_____ **Dependence on borrowed funds (1 = heavy, 10 = none)**

_____ **Late with payroll tax deposits (1 = often, 10 = never)**

_____ **Lag between sales growth and profit growth (1 = substantial, 10 = none)**

_____ **Employee turnover (1 = heavy, 10 = nonexistent)**

_____ **Quality and frequency of strategic planning (1 = never, 10 = regular and dependable)**

_____ **Owner has more work to do than time to do it (1 = too much work, 10 = balances time efficiently)**

_____ **Owner's feelings about the business (1 = hates it, 10 = loves it)**

If you were your own troubleshooting consultant, how would you rate your business overall? What areas would you target for improvement? Use this checklist to determine how your business checks out. How many items would receive close to a 10? How many areas would receive something less than 5?

Although there's no overall key to grading your answers, we suggest that you give immediate attention to upgrading the number of any answer that received a 5 or below. For the 6s and 7s, put the issue on your long-range to-do list. For the 8s and above, pat yourself on the back and make sure that, where applicable, the employees responsible for the rating are publicly recognized and, where possible, rewarded.

Taking the five-minute appearance test

Your business's appearance is important. With this in mind, we devised a simple appearance test. Five minutes are all you need to take it. (For more on the importance of appearance, see the later sidebar "You *can* judge a business by its cover.")

Start with a business other than your own. For instance, you can offer to give a friend's business the following five-minute appearance test. Simply drive into the parking lot, walk into the general office area, peek into a few offices here and there, step into the restroom for a quick look around, and then check out the areas around the coffeemaker and fax and copy machines before you go.

Note the following as you go, ranking your observations from 1 (poor) to 5 (excellent):

THE EXTERIOR

_____ **Parking lot:** Well cared for and clean

_____ **Grounds and exterior:** Well maintained, trimmed, and inviting

_____ **Windows:** Clean, unsmeared, and uncluttered when viewed from the outside

_____ **Signage:** Well maintained, readable, and understandable

THE INTERIOR

_____ **General neatness:** Desks and working areas neat and uncluttered

_____ **Restrooms:** Neat and clean

_____ **Expense awareness:** Unnecessary lights and unused equipment turned off, no original Van Goghs in the lobby

_____ **Time management:** Employees appear focused and busy, no gossipy gatherings around the coffeemaker or copy machines

_____ **Employee attitudes:** Polite, alert, attentive, and focused

_____ **Employee appearance:** Neat, clean, and dressed appropriately

_____ **Sense of urgency:** Employees going about their business at a pace that indicates they don't have time to waste

THE BEST AND THE WORST

The one thing I saw that impressed me the most:

_____

The one thing I saw that bothered me the most:

_____

You *can* judge a business by its cover

Most people who work with small-business owners have discovered that you can often (but not always) accurately prejudge the health of a business by its physical appearance. Here's a telltale example of how a few simple details can provide a surefire indication of what a growing business's culture is really like and how it can be translated into the health of that business.

Coauthor Jim was asked to visit an automobile recycling business (also known as a junkyard) to help the owner devise a commission plan for his sales employees. Driving into the parking lot, Jim noticed the well-kept wooden fence, the neat landscaping lining the front office, and the freshly asphalted and well-marked parking facilities. Upon entering the office, he was immediately struck by the neatness and cleanliness of the facilities, the professional counter and wall displays of the company's "recycled" products, and the staff of employees with matching, embroidered shirts. The busy atmosphere and the prevailing sense of urgency impressed Jim.

Well, Jim could tell you one thing about this man's business within 30 seconds of walking into the place, without so much as talking to its owner or glancing at its financial statements. The business looked, felt, and, yes, even smelled like a profitable business.

And so it was. The financial statements revealed rapidly growing sales and robust profitability in excess of a 10 percent return on those sales. Additionally, the company boasted a low employee turnover, excellent employee benefits, and an inventory system that was second to none that Jim had seen in any small business.

In short, this business's financial performance lived up to its appearance, a relationship that almost always goes hand in hand.

Give the questionnaire to the owner. Ask your friend to repay you the favor. Your business could use the five-minute appearance test, too.

Redefining Your Role in an Evolving Business

Owning a business is like raising a teenager: As it grows, the business is sure to get into trouble, yet you can never be sure what the trouble will be, how severe it will be, and how the company will weather the experience. Whether the business (and the teenager) will survive and subsequently thrive or fail depends on the quality of leadership provided.

That leadership, in the case of your business, anyway, must come from you.

So why is growth, especially that of the rapid variety, so hard on the typical small-business owner? The reasons are twofold:

- **Most small-business owners aren't prepared for the managerial demands of a growing business.** In most cases, the owner's expertise is in a specialized area, such as sales or accounting, or is related to his craft or to the product or service that the company offers. As a result, he's untrained and unskilled in the management aspects of running a business. To make matters worse, many of the management skills required to run a growing business are usually counter to the way the owner is accustomed to doing things.

- **The bigger your company becomes, the farther you fade from the center of the action.** Visions get blurred as a result of that distance, missions fade, and communications falter. Also, the more the business grows, the more layers you have between you and your customers, vendors, and employees. With this distance comes misdirection — unless your management skills, as delegated to your key employees, can keep pace with the growth.

A proficient manager requires a number of traits, but most of these traits aren't required for a successful start-up; they only come into play as a company grows. The ability, or inability, of the entrepreneur to adopt these skills determines the ultimate success of the business.

Making the transition to manager

Here's a popular entrepreneurial axiom: "The day you hire your first employee is the same day you begin making the transition to manager." This transition isn't an easy one to make because many of the personal traits of the typical small-business owner run counter to those of a successful manager. Consider the following required traits and job descriptions of the successful manager — traits that aren't always near the top of the typical entrepreneur's list of skills:

- **Focus:** The successful manager focuses on the project at hand, no matter what else is going on around him. The typical entrepreneur stops in the middle of the task to respond to the latest opportunity or crisis.

- **Attention to detail:** The successful manager devoutly dots her *i*'s and crosses her *t*'s. The typical entrepreneur is often too busy or is simply not the type that enjoys dealing with details.

- **Follow-up:** The successful manager understands that employees need to know that their work will be evaluated. The typical entrepreneur doesn't think that employees' work should have to be followed up; he believes that the employees should do it right the first time.

> ✔ **Conflict resolution:** The successful manager views resolving conflict as an important part of her job description. The typical entrepreneur sees it as an intrusion on her time.
>
> ✔ **Training:** The successful manager views training as an investment. The typical entrepreneur sees it as an expense.

Of course, not all small-business owners fit this entrepreneur's profile. You can make changes in some, if not all, of the managerial traits that you lack. However, the transition to manager isn't an easy one, and it involves some basic — and often wrenching — changes in the entrepreneur who originally founded the business.

Implementing strategic changes

The *Peter Principle* (which says that, sooner or later, everyone peaks and ends up in a job beyond his or her capabilities) constantly creeps up on all small-business owners as their companies grow. For one entrepreneur, it may arrive when his company has only one employee; for others, it may creep up when their companies reach 1,000 employees. But everyone has limitations — managerial and otherwise. Having limitations doesn't make you a bad person; it only means that, where the management of your business is concerned, there may come a time when you should either move over or move on.

When you notice that the Peter Principle is hanging over your management skills and you're having a difficult time making the transition from entrepreneur to manager (you'll know it's happening when your business isn't fun anymore), take some time to consider the four alternatives in the following sections.

Downsizing your business

Downsizing involves shrinking your business back to the point where you're able to spend your time doing those things you enjoy and are best at. For example, you may decide to limit your customer base to only those within your market area, thereby cutting your sales and allowing you to shrink the number of employees you must manage.

Before making the decision to downsize, ask yourself the following questions:

> ✔ What are the downsides of shrinking the business (losing income, reducing the market value of the business, letting go of customers, and possibly laying off employees)?
>
> ✔ Will you be able to emotionally and financially cope with these losses?

If the answer to either of these questions is no, consider the alternative in the following section.

Taking a personal inventory

Taking a personal inventory includes assembling your own *managerial defect list* — a list of your personal traits that make managing your business difficult, such as inattention to detail or fear of conflict. Consider which entries on the list you could, and would, change in order to make the managerial transition.

Ask your spouse, friends, and key employees to help you make your managerial defect list.

After you make your list, ask yourself the following questions:

- ✔ How many of the traits on your managerial defect list can you hire around?
- ✔ How many of the traits can you train around?
- ✔ How many of the traits can you delegate around?
- ✔ Of those traits that you can't hire, train, or delegate around, which ones can you reasonably expect to change?

This exercise will tell you what you need to do to improve your managerial skills and how you can go about doing so. Assuming that, as a result of the answers given, you decide you can make the transition, get busy! Start hiring, training, delegating, and, where applicable, making changes in your organizational structure (see the earlier section "Choosing Your Management Tools").

If you decide that you can't — or won't — make the managerial transition, consider the following alternative.

Hiring a replacement

Hiring a replacement includes hiring a president or Chief Operating Officer (COO) to run your company while you become Chief Executive Officer (CEO). The president or COO takes control of the day-to-day management of the business, while you concentrate on long-range, strategic matters. (See Chapter 16 for details on how to hire the right person for the job.)

Before hiring a replacement, ask yourself the following:

- ✔ Is your company big enough and profitable enough to afford a president or COO?
- ✔ Are you capable of letting go and keeping your nose out of the day-to-day operating functions of your business? In other words, can you keep yourself from micromanaging your company?

If the answer to either of these questions is no, you have two options:

- ✔ Go back to the preceding alternatives (downsizing your business or making personal changes) and decide how to adapt one (or both) of them to your situation.
- ✔ Consider the fourth alternative.

Selling the business

Before you decide to take such a big step as selling your business, ask yourself the following questions:

- ✔ Will you emotionally be able to sell and walk away from the company you've built?
- ✔ Is your company salable at a price that works for you?

Ultimately, you may decide to sell your business and move on to something you're better suited for or more ready to do.

Part V
The Part of Tens

The 5th Wave   By Rich Tennant

"The investors liked our business plan —
particularly the in-depth assessment of our
competition, which is who they've decided
to invest with."

In this part . . .

This part provides lists of things you need to know in order to build your business and keep it growing. We provide wisdom on such topics as common mistakes you don't want to make and tips for small-business success.

Chapter 21

Ten Mistakes You Don't Want to Make

. . . .

In This Chapter

▶ Getting the most out of your financial statements, annual budget, and accounting services

▶ Making marketing work for your business

▶ Knowing when to hire new employees and when to let nonperformers go

▶ Taking advantage of available resources and staying organized

. . . .

*Y*ou can learn the lessons associated with starting and growing your business two ways. The first is by making the mistake and then cleaning up the mess afterward. The second is by observing others' mistakes, learning from them, and then not making them yourself. Fortunately for you, we've made and observed many of the mistakes we're about to talk about. It's up to you to take the lessons we present in this chapter and apply them to your business. After all, why go through the pains of trial and error when you can get what you need from the experiences of others like us?

Failing to Use Financial Statements to Manage Your Business

A wise old sage once said that if you can't measure it, you can't manage it. That statement is certainly true in business. After all, your business's financial statements (the ultimate in measurement) can provide all the information you need to make the best decisions when managing your business. Nevertheless, too many small-business owners believe that, because they can look at the bottom line of the profit and loss statement (P&L) and locate the net income figure, they know everything they need to know about their financial statements. Meanwhile, they overlook such tools as the balance sheet, cash flow statements, cash flow projections, and budgets, along with myriad valuable percentages and ratios that evolve from all those financial statements (see Chapter 14 for the skinny on these financial tools).

Every business transaction generates a number, and every number contributes to a story that gets told within the pages of your financial statements. To fully understand your business (and, in turn, successfully manage it), you absolutely must know how to compile (or have someone else compile), read, and understand those financial statements.

While managing the direction of your business is certainly the most important use of financial statements, it isn't the only one. A recent *Inc.* magazine survey indicated that 56 percent of the poll's respondents shared their financial statements with their employees. Thus, a secondary purpose of generating financial statements is to use them to help educate your employees on how the business works, with the underlying purpose of motivating them to do what they can to improve profitability.

Finally, in the event that you should decide to sell your business, no sophisticated buyer will consider purchasing a company that doesn't generate accurate and professional financial statements.

Failing to Prepare an Annual Budget

Budgeting is one of the most underrated, underutilized, and yet potentially valuable tools available to the small-business owner. Certainly, the budgeting process is a detail-oriented, laborious discipline, and yes, it's fraught with assumptions, but the benefits you reap from developing an annual budget make the process eminently worthwhile. The two primary benefits you get from developing a budget are

- ✔ **Accurate planning:** An annual budget is really nothing more than a projected profit and loss statement for the upcoming year. Making the necessary assumptions is always the most difficult part of preparing a budget. Some of the assumptions are easy to make (think rent, office supplies, and telephone services), while others are more difficult (think total revenues, gross margins, or profitability). The only way to come up with the right assumptions is to plan for them, thus accurate planning is a prerequisite for accurate budgeting.

- ✔ **Expense control:** Expense control is a cultural issue, and a business's culture is determined by the leader, which means that the small-business owner is ultimately the one who determines whether or not the business will be mindful of its expenses. The best way to begin developing an expense-control culture is by adopting a zero-based budgeting system as you create your annual budget. (*Zero-based budgeting* means that at the beginning of every year you start with zero and justify every dollar of every expense instead of just adding a fixed percentage to last year's expenses. See Chapters 10 and 14 for more on this type of budgeting.)

Planning and controlling expenses through budgeting not only impact profitability but also play an important role in controlling cash flow. For instance, every dollar you save by planning to reduce your phone bill accumulates in your checking account. You won't find a better, or easier, way to begin building a healthy, cash-positive business than by controlling expenses (as long as those expenses don't negatively impact your product or service, of course).

Failing to Utilize Your CPA

Make no mistake about it: One of the downsides of a small-business career is that it can be one of the loneliest careers. That loneliness usually leads small-business owners to steer their businesses alone, as opposed to their *Fortune* 500 counterparts, who have their boards of directors and layers of management staffers to help them make decisions.

But you don't have to go at it alone! At least one person in your working environment has the background and knowledge to assist you in directing your business; that person is your CPA, or whoever prepares your business's tax returns. What makes your CPA so important?

- ✔ No one can provide conclusive advice on how to run a business without first understanding and applying the information generated by financial statements.

- ✔ Most CPAs have experience working with other small-business owners and their financial statements.

- ✔ Most CPAs who prepare financial statements for small-business owners are small-business owners themselves.

- ✔ CPAs know how to prepare taxes correctly, which makes both you and the IRS happy.

While CPAs don't exactly give away their time, you don't have to give an arm and a leg to get a little consulting advice. Ask your CPA to tack on an hour to the end of your annual, year-end tax review and another hour in March or April when she's finished your taxes. A few hundred dollars more a year isn't a disproportionate expense for the kind of advice a good CPA can give you.

If your CPA is incapable of giving you the help you need or your CPA wants only to prepare your taxes, not provide any consulting advice, you have the wrong CPA and need to look for a new one. (Turn to Chapter 19 for tips on how to hire the best CPA for your business.)

Failing to Understand How Marketing Applies to Your Business

Every small-business owner confronts a number of marketing myths over the course of her career. These myths tend to confuse and mislead small-business owners, not only in the pre-start-up stage as they set out to develop their marketing plan but also as they graduate into managing the sales and marketing function of their ongoing business. The following are foremost among these marketing myths:

✔ Marketing is all about advertising and promotion. Wrong! Advertising, promotions, and sales are really only three of the many subsets of marketing. According to Barbara Schenck, author of *Small Business Marketing For Dummies* (Wiley), marketing's other elements include market research, product development, pricing, labels and packaging (where applicable), distribution, and customer service.

✔ Sales is a stand-alone function, separate from marketing. From the list in the preceding bullet, you can see that the "sales" activity is but one of the nine functions of marketing. Granted, it may be the most visible of those functions, but it's no more important than any of the others, especially customer service. (Although sales captures customers, customer service keeps them.)

Here's the truth about marketing: Marketing — which includes sales, distribution, pricing, customer service, and so on — is one of the most important parts of your overall business plan (see Chapter 4 for everything you need to know about crafting your business plan). After all, as every small-business owner will eventually find out, the world is full of great products and services, but those products and services won't make a bit of difference if customers aren't motivated to purchase them. Marketing is what drives customers to make that purchasing decision.

Hiring Too Quickly

Why are most small-business owners so quick to hire? What makes this duty so challenging? The primary reason is that hiring new employees falls into the category known as *human resources,* a category that includes tasks related to the management of people in an organization. Although you'd much rather develop a new product or call on a customer or (we hope) review your financial statements, managing people is one of the necessary evils of creating and building a business, and hiring is a key element in the process.

To understand just how important hiring is, try attaching a cost to its failure. If you hire a nonperforming employee, the cost will equal the expense of the mistakes that are sure to follow, plus the cost of the departed employee's wasted training time, plus the time and energy required to start the hiring process all over again.

To improve your hiring skills, follow these two simple rules:

- ✔ Always place hiring at the top of your to-do list, and leave it there until you have successfully accomplished it.
- ✔ Hire slowly. Take your time. After you make the hire, undoing it is expensive.

Taking Too Long to Terminate Nonperforming Employees

If we had a nickel for every time we've heard a small-business owner say something like the following, we'd be rich!

> "Sure, I know Charley is a pain in the neck, but I can't fire the guy. He's been around too long." And then, two weeks later . . ."I finally fired Charley and my business is running so much more smoothly now. I wish I would've fired him five years ago."

Within 30 days after hiring an employee, most small-business owners can determine whether or not they've made a mistake. Yet, they wait another six months, or maybe five years, to do something about it. The underlying reason for this far-too-frequent mistake is that small-business owners prefer to spend their time doing the things that they enjoy and are proficient at doing, so they procrastinate doing unpleasant tasks. Understandably, firing isn't an enjoyable activity for most business owners and most people aren't proficient at it, but it's as important to the success of a business as any of the other three team-building functions — hiring, training, and motivating (see Chapter 16 for details).

Businesses that don't get rid of the bad workers are at greater risk for losing their high-performing employees to businesses that better recognize and reward the best and dismiss the worst. After all, the nonperforming employee who remains on a business's payroll not only takes too much of management's time but also drags down the rest of the team. Those employees who are performing begin to resent the employee who isn't performing; soon after that, the team's performers also begin to resent the business owner for allowing the slacker to continue his employment.

Assuming Your Employees Are Motivated by the Same Things You Are

"Why don't my employees do things the way I would do them?" is the typical small-business owner's lament after another employee has failed to solve a customer's problem, neglected to follow up on an assigned task, or driven out of the parking lot precisely at five o'clock, leaving behind a desk stacked with unfinished work. Ask any veteran small-business owner and she'll quickly tell you that a vast majority of her workplace frustrations evolve from an inability to understand why her employees do what they do and act the way they act. In short, employees drive small-business owners nuts. (And vice versa.)

The primary reason for this owner/employee disconnect is simple: Employees aren't motivated by the same things that small-business owners are. (This difference is usually for the best. After all, can you imagine what your business culture would be like if all your employees were like you?) While the typical entrepreneur is motivated by such things as growth, creativity, and independence, the typical employee is motivated by such things as being part of a team, having problems solved, and feeling secure. The two lists are entirely different.

Given the extreme difference in motivation between the owners of businesses and their employees, is it any surprise that employees react to situations differently than their owners would prefer them to react?

To be a successful small-business owner, you have to understand how your employees are wired and why they do things the way they do. Then you have to make the necessary adjustments in your management techniques to cope with those differences. Like it or not, the burden for change is always on you, the small-business owner, not your employees.

Considering Training to Be an Expense and Not an Investment

Imagine that you own a small business and your revenues are growing at a rate of 25 percent a year. For most people, that kind of growth would be a positive and exciting trend, yet it can mask a number of dangers (such as expenses that grow too rapidly or too many slow-paying customers) to the unwary small-business owner. To avoid those dangers, you and your key employees must be growing at a similar, or faster, rate as your business. If you aren't, your team is in danger of being outgrown by your business, a situation that happens far too frequently with rapidly growing small businesses.

Enter the element of training. In truth, the dollars you spend on relevant and effective training aren't an expense; they're an investment. Although they may appear under the expense category on the profit and loss statement, those dollars could just as well be capitalized (on the balance sheet) and then written off over a period of time. After all, you capitalize investments as the result of such activities as upgrading your technology equipment and adding to your real estate inventory, so why not do the same when it comes to training expenditures? People are assets, too!

Unfortunately, too many small-business owners have relied on trial and error (rather than training) as their primary learning tool. They roll the dice when they make their decisions, and when those decisions work out, they move on. When they don't, they pay for their mistakes and then start over. Yes, training costs money and time, but so does every other investment — and this one is one of the most important of all.

Failing to Take Advantage of Available Resources

Numerous potential resources are available to help you maintain and grow your business. Those resources include

- Professionals, including CPAs, attorneys, and bankers
- Boards of advisors
- Local business organizations
- Consultants
- Mentors and coaches
- Colleges, universities, and Small Business Development Centers (SBDCs)
- Service Corps of Retired Executives (SCORE)
- Industry trade organizations

Given this wide range of resources, why are so many small-business owners reluctant to take advantage of them? Unfortunately, independence is a major factor. While the desire for independence plays a significant role in many of the decisions you make to start a business, it can work against you, too. If you embrace independence too tightly, you may be reluctant to ask for help — even when you really need it. How can you embrace that independence without letting it drag you down? Get out of the office, mix with your peers, seek help from outsiders, and keep your eyes open for educational and training opportunities.

The wheel has already been invented. There's no sense in reinventing it.

Failing to Maintain an Up-to-Date Organization Chart

Every business, large or small, that includes employees is constructed around a team that requires, among other things, a defined chain of command. After all, an organization's chain of command is what determines who is managing the team and judging the performance of its members, who is promoting and demoting team members as a function of their performance, and who should be encouraging and empowering team members to perform and succeed. Sometimes that organization chain is official and published; other times it exists only in the minds of those concerned. In both cases, however, you should be able to identify the different layers of employees within the organization and turn that layering into an organization chart.

A properly constructed organization chart provides the following benefits:

✔ An orderly way to solve problems

✔ An orderly way to make decisions

✔ An orderly way to get jobs done

If you believe, as most successful small-business owners do, that employees are the number one asset of any organization, how can you not insist on creating and publishing a functional organization chart? After all, the organization chart is nothing more than an itemized and organized inventory of your employee assets, just as an inventory listing is an itemized and organized compilation of your inventory assets.

Not only is the organization chart a guide for managing people, but it also serves as a financial tool for managing expenses and, subsequently, cash. Consider this: The largest expense on most businesses' profit and loss statements is the wages and salaries account, and before you can manage that account, you have to structure it.

Chapter 22

Ten Tips for Small-Business Success

As you have no doubt learned, the skills and talents required to create and build a successful small business are many. One of our goals in writing this book is to show you that you have to wear many hats in a variety of shapes and sizes as you and your business grow. In other words, the lessons you need to learn are endless.

The following ten tips are designed to give you a head start on becoming a successful small-business owner. Although these tips won't give you the specific answers you're looking for as you face your everyday problems, after you understand and adopt the logic behind them, they will give you a base for making the best decisions to resolve those problems.

Focus on the Execution

Nolan Bushnell, the founder of the interactive game publisher Atari, once offered the following quote to a magazine writer: "Anyone who can take a shower can have a good idea; what matters is what happens after you towel off." What Mr. Bushnell is saying here is that although good ideas are a dime a dozen, the kind of people who can take those good ideas and turn them into successful action are definitely not a dime a dozen. Within the context of small business, this means that many people have good ideas that, when executed properly, would result in a good business. Unfortunately, history has proven that many of those people are unable to follow those good ideas with equally good execution.

Every banker, venture capitalist, and angel investor is familiar with this axiom. While those people who make their livings assisting and financing small businesses are certainly interested in the validity of the founder's idea, they're more interested in the person who will be implementing that idea (that's you). Hence, when these capital providers open the pages of your business plan, the first place they go is your resume. They want to know whether or not you'll be able to execute your idea. If you can't, they really have no reason to read on.

The successful bankers, venture capitalists, and angel investors have learned this lesson well: Small-business success is always in the execution. A perfect example of this is Sam Walton. His idea was to start a discount retail store (Wal-Mart, of course). The banker he approached must have known that there were plenty of other businesses operating in that space, yet he ultimately approved the loan. In short, he financed the fire in Sam's eyes, a decision that proved to be right.

The bottom line: Your idea probably isn't what's going to make or break your business. You are.

Assemble a Team of Superstars in Game-Breaker Positions

Every successful small-business owner is responsible for performing a host of important duties as she goes about creating and building a successful business. But of all the important duties the owner must perform, the one at the top of the list is assembling a team of superstars in the business's game-breaker positions.

The process of assembling superstars in game-breaker positions includes the following three elements:

- **Identify the game-breaker positions.** These are the make-it-or-break-it positions in any business. Depending on the size of the business, these positions may include the sales manager, marketing manager, operations manager, finance director (bookkeeper, controller, or CFO), office manager, human resources director, and/or product development director. And, of course, don't forget the founder/president/owner. That's you.

- **Identify the characteristics of superstars.** The meaning of the word *superstars* varies from business to business. For coauthor Jim, a superstar is someone who a) subscribes to the owners' ethics and principles, b) welcomes change, c) is capable of synergy with his other superstars, d) is creative, and e) displays a work ethic similar to the owners.

> ✔ **Assemble the team members.** This part of the process includes hiring, training, and motivating the superstars. And, of course, given the variables of human nature, it may also, from time to time, include their firing. (See Chapter 16 for details on finding and keeping superstars.)

Your company can only be as good as the people who make up your team. If it's a winning business you want to grow, you need people on the team who know how to win. Only you are in a position to collect them.

Work Hard, Get Lucky

"The harder you work, the luckier you get." Who knows where this statement originated, but the person who made it popular was Gary Player, the hard-working, focused, Hall of Fame golfer from South Africa. Gary was known for his unmatched work ethic; rarely a day went by when he didn't do at least an hour or two of calisthenics in the morning mixed with hitting hundreds of golf balls in the afternoon.

Curt Carlson, the Minneapolis mega-entrepreneur and founder of such companies as Gold Bond Stamp, Radisson Hotels, and TGI Fridays, puts it another way: "Weekdays are when I keep up with my competition. Weekends are when I get ahead of them." The lesson Gary and Curt are preaching here is one that every small-business owner must learn. There's absolutely no substitute for hard work. While it does pay to be smart, intelligence alone never wins the small-business game. Neither does the uniqueness of your niche — although some are certainly better than others. And who in their right mind would ever go through life depending on luck to carry them through?

No, long hours and hard work have no substitute, especially in the early stages of your business. Those start-up days and months (and sometimes years) are always fraught with long hours. Jim worked six ten-hour days a week in the early days of his business career — and sometimes longer when the going got tough.

Now we're not saying that you can't break up the long hours to fit your family's schedule. When your son's teacher wants to meet the parents, or when the afternoon softball game beckons, or when a family emergency arises, remember, you're the boss. You can leave the office any time you feel like leaving (as long as you make up the lost time later, of course). But prepare to bid farewell to such time-sapping activities as golf (unless you're Gary Player), fishing trips, and opening week of deer season — during business's early, formative years, anyway. Time is finite and the success of your business waits for no one.

Realize the Difference between Profits and Cash

Not so long ago, Jim ran into a business-owner friend of his at a Chamber of Commerce meeting. "How's business?" he asked. "Great! Our sales were up 25 percent," she replied, beaming proudly. Then, noticing Jim's furrowing brow, she added with a smile, "Don't worry, Jim. My profits were up, too. By 15 percent!" After Jim congratulated her, she continued. "I must admit, however, I'm having a harder time paying my bills this year than I did a year ago, when my business wasn't growing so fast."

Several well-placed questions later and Jim determined the problem. As a result of her increased sales, her accounts receivable (customers who owed her money for products or services already provided) had increased appreciably. She had also, in the past year, brought in a slew of new inventory to support her increased sales. Finally, she had recently purchased a new software system to go along with several new computers, monitors, and printers. The cash outflow required to pay for all those increases in assets had more than eaten up any increase in cash that resulted from her increased profits. In short, she had spent her hard-earned cash on those items that show up on the balance sheet but not on the profit and loss statement. Despite (and in part because of factors associated with) increasing her sales, her business had a cash flow problem.

The operative point here is that the word *profits* is nothing more than an accounting term. It refers to a number at the bottom of the profit and loss statement — a number that determines how much in taxes the business is going to owe. Meanwhile, *cash flow* is the operating term that's used to measure the tangible flow of cash in and out of the business. The woman Jim had spoken with had learned the lesson the hard way: Cash, not profitability, pays the bills.

Hire for Attitude, Teach Skills Later

This lesson was espoused by Herb Kelleher, cofounder, Chairman Emeritus, and former CEO of Southwest Airlines. He must have applied it well because Southwest Airlines grew quickly in its early years, hiring thousands of people a year. Not only did Herb's company hire them quickly, but it also hired them well. Southwest is consistently named among the top five Most Admired Corporations in America in *Fortune* magazine's annual poll.

Basically, what the phrase "hire for attitude, teach skills later" means is that you can forget what the person you're hiring knows how to do because you need to focus on who he or she is. After all, assuming your potential hire is of reasonable intelligence, you can teach him the skills he needs to learn the job. What you can't teach him is attitude — that is, how he'll react to adversity, how he'll get along with his peers, and most importantly, where you and many other companies are concerned, how he'll treat your customers.

Hiring for attitude is significantly more difficult than hiring for skills. You can hire for skills by reading the interviewer's resume and asking specific, direct questions and waiting for the yes or no answers. No problem there. The difficulty when hiring for attitude, however, comes in looking for those subtle hints that belie the interviewee's attitude. Check out the potential employee's body language when he answers a tough question and watch for voice inflection variations in his responses. Learn to listen with your eyes and your intuition as much as your ears.

Remember, you're trying to find answers to two primary questions in the interview:

✔ Will your new hire get along with your team members (and you — after all, you're a team member, too)?

✔ Will your new hire treat your customers the way you want them to be treated?

You can't find out the answers to these questions by asking direct, yes or no questions. Ask thoughtful, open-ended, situational questions and then read between the lines for the right answers.

Create an Exit Strategy

Make no mistake about it: One way or another, all business owners are eventually going to exit their business. You may exit your business feet first or head first, but exit it you will. The inevitability of making an exit is an immutable law of the universe — and also of the small-business environment.

The two ways to exit a business are planned and unplanned. In the planned scenario, you pick a date or determine a goal (or both) and then manage your business and your eventual exit around those selections. After the set time has arrived and/or you've achieved the set goal, you wave good-bye and make your scripted exit. In the unplanned exit, you wait for an unfriendly and/or random event to take place. Perhaps an attack of burnout suddenly strikes you, or a severe financial crisis looms, or your favorite banker moves out of town. Whammo, an unfriendly event shakes the foundations of your business and you react by doing whatever your frazzled emotions dictate at the time. Wouldn't you rather make a planned, well-thought-out exit over a frazzled, crisis-spurred one?

Assuming that you're a typical small-business owner, you have the following exit options:

✔ Your partner (if you have one) buys you out.

✔ Your business merges with another business.

✔ Another business acquires your business.

✔ You sell your business to your employees.

✔ You sell your business to an outsider.

✔ You hand down your business to a family member.

✔ You do an *initial public offering* (selling stock in the company to the public).

Your task is to select one of these exit options and then begin to construct a strategy for making it happen. You should start implementing that strategy today, although it may not include anything that impacts the day-to-day operations of your business, other than you recognizing that you do, in fact, have an evolving exit strategy and that you're the one driving the exit strategy (not the other way around).

Grow or Die — There's No In-Between

A magazine article Jim once read talked about the owner of a small printing company whose revenues had been flat for five years. When asked to describe the path of the business, the owner had shrugged and said, "Oh, we're maintaining." Two years later Jim read a follow-up article in the same magazine. The business had subsequently failed, and the owner had learned the grow-or-die lesson the hard way.

A small business (or any organization, for that matter) has only two options: to grow or to die. Anything other than growth is stagnation, and stagnation is the precursor to death. This phenomenon is true in both nature and business. In fact, the grow-or-die phenomenon is the reason why *Fortune* 500 boards of directors terminate those CEOs who don't continue to grow the company even though the corporation is still making boatloads of money. Fortunately for most *Fortune* 500 companies, they have sufficient financial reserves to allow them adequate time to work through the grow-or-die cycle. Unfortunately, most small businesses don't have those reserves. As the owner of the small printing company learned, as soon as the cycle of growth ends, the cycle of dying begins. If the small business doesn't have enough cash in reserve to weather the storm and turn the business around, its meter will surely run out. Don't let this happen to your business. Remember, cash is king, and it's your job to see that you manage it royally.

Transition to Manager As Soon As You Hire Someone Else

To most small-business owners, the word *manager* is not unlike the words *boss, supervisor,* and *superior.* Small-business people typically don't like those words, and they don't like their connotations, either; *bureaucracy, chain-of-command,* and *pecking-order* come to mind. Like it or not, as a small business grows, the owner's role in it must make a slow but sure transition. As soon as you hire your first employee, you have to begin to fulfill the role of manager, and the more employees you hire, the more manager you have to become. So instead of spending your time working with customers and fussing with product development (the kind of things most small-business people like to do), you spend too much of your time performing such tasks as training, motivating, and managing employees.

In short, the small-business owner's role is to "create and foster," while the manager's role is to "maintain and grow." Fulfilling these roles takes two different skill sets. Sometimes the small-business owner is capable of making the transition from small-business owner to manager, but too often he isn't.

To successfully make the transition to manager, you must develop a collection of, well, *managerial* skills — skills that make you dependable, consistent, and logical in the way you manage your employees and run the business. These managerial skills include focus, follow-up, clarity, delegation, and attention to detail. The transition to manager will be the toughest challenge you'll have to make as you guide your business from five employees to fifty and upward. But the only way to really grow your business is by leveraging the skills of your employees, and the only way to do that is to figure out how to manage them.

Develop an Insatiable Appetite to Learn

Successful business owners come in degrees; on a scale of one to ten, some are ones, a few are tens, and most are somewhere in between. Examples of tens include Bill Gates and Steven Jobs. The ones include the small gift store retailer who scrapes out her livelihood by selling t-shirts and trinkets. The in-betweens include the vast majority of the rest of us — people who have survived and hopefully prospered in this competitive but rewarding vocation.

So just what is the number one characteristic that sets the Bill Gates and Steven Jobs apart from the lady who manages the gift store? Is it, say, her educational background, her intelligence, or the niche she has chosen? How about her intuition, her financial backing, or her innate creativity? Which of these separates the ones from the tens?

We found the answer several years ago in Michael Gerber's book *The E-Myth Revisited: Why Most Small Businesses Don't Work and What to Do About It* (HarperCollins). "The number one characteristic of successful entrepreneurs," Mr. Gerber informs his reader, "is an insatiable appetite to learn." Thanks, Mr. Gerber; that statement makes sense to us, too. After all, the same concept was true when we were in school, and when you think about it, not that much has changed since then. Those students who had an insatiable appetite to learn English Lit garnered the As in the class, while the ones who had an insatiable appetite to pursue other nonacademic interests garnered the Bs and Cs. The same is true in business: Motivation begets effort, and effort begets results. So develop an insatiable appetite to learn, and then try to satisfy it.

Do What You Love

As anyone who has followed small businesses over the years knows, there are favorable niches and there are not-so-favorable niches. The favorable niches offer ample opportunity for growth. For instance, as of this writing, a wide variety of technology and Internet-related sectors provide extremely achievable chances to succeed in a big way. Similarly, consumer electronics, bio-engineering, and, of course, software development currently offer excellent opportunities for growth. Meanwhile, a host of other niches, such as the airline, steel, and retail industries, provide more difficult and, thus, less favorable opportunities to succeed.

Neither of your humble authors has any idea what niches are going to be hot 10 or 20 years from now. But we do know that the best niche for you, whether you're a current or wannabe small-business owner, should involve a product or service that you already know something about. And more importantly, your niche should involve a product or service that you can become passionate about. Jim ended up in sports-related niches because that's where he was comfortable and because athletics were what he liked to do. Eric, meanwhile, matriculated into finance-related businesses because he had learned from the classes he took in college that that was where he belonged and that's what made him happy.

We certainly advocate that you select a niche that has a wide, inviting window for growth, but no matter how hot you think the niche is or how hot you may think it promises to be, if you can't develop a passion for the product or service, you'll never develop a passion for the business that follows. And operating a business without passion is a sure path to mediocrity. Small-business ownership is a blessing and a privilege for those of us who have enjoyed success in this risky but rewarding vocation. But small business is at its best when we're doing something we enjoy. Only then is work no longer work; only then does work become fun.

Index

• **C** •

• F •

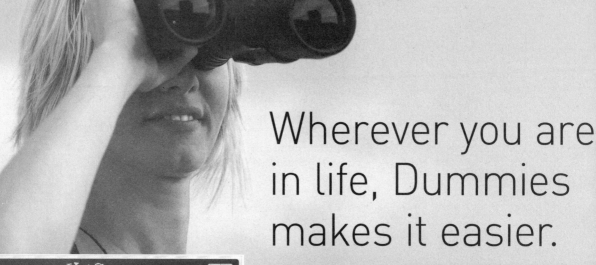